# Alone
# of All Her Sex

# Alone of All Her Sex

## THE MYTH AND THE CULT OF THE VIRGIN MARY

## MARINA WARNER

A WALLABY BOOK
PUBLISHED BY POCKET BOOKS NEW YORK

Grateful acknowledgment is made to the following for permission to reprint copyrighted material:

Joan Daves for sixteen lines from "Eve" by Frank O'Connor. From *Irish Poetry* by Frank O'Connor, published by Macmillan Publishing Co., Inc. Copyright © 1969 by David Greene and Frank O'Connor.

Macmillan Publishing Co., Inc., for ten lines from "The Mother of God" by William Butler Yeats. From *The Collected Poems of William Butler Yeats*. Copyright 1933 by Macmillan Publishing Co., Inc. Renewed 1961 by Bertha Georgie Yeats.

Macmillan Publishing Co., Inc., for four lines from "Two Songs From A Play" by William Butler Yeats. Copyright 1928 by Macmillan Publishing Co., Inc. Renewed 1956 by Bertha Georgie Yeats.

Photographic permissions may be found on pages ix-xiii.

POCKET BOOKS, a Simon & Schuster division of
GULF & WESTERN CORPORATION
1230 Avenue of the Americas, New York, N.Y. 10020

*For my mother and father*

# CONTENTS

## Part Five INTERCESSOR

# Illustrations

*Black-and-white plates—following page 100*

FIGURE 1. A Biblical leaf juxtaposing Luke's account of the Visitation with the Old Testament story of King David's arrival in Jerusalem. Canterbury or St. Albans (?), twelfth century. *Pierpont Morgan Library, New York.*

FIGURE 2. A Biblical illumination that shows the close relationship between the life of Samuel, Luke's narrative of the birth of John the Baptist, and the apocryphal account of the birth of the Virgin. St. Swithin's Priory, Winchester, 1175–1200. *Pierpont Morgan Library, New York.*

FIGURE 3. The earliest extant image of the Virgin. Catacomb of S. Priscilla, Rome, second century. *Scala, Milan.*

FIGURE 4. The flight into Egypt, from the apocryphal *Gospel of Pseudo-Matthew*. From Martin Schongauer's *Life of the Blessed Virgin Mary*, c. 1470–5. *The British Museum, London.*

FIGURE 5. St. Anne and St. Joachim supervise the Virgin's first steps. Mid-fourteenth century orphrey, English. *Victoria and Albert Museum, London.*

FIGURE 6. A *Vierge Ouvrante,* illustrating the view that without the Virgin the redemption would not have taken place. Middle Rhine, c. 1300. *Metropolitan Museum of Art, New York, gift of J. Pierpont Morgan, 1917.*

FIGURE 7. Three miraculous mothers of the New Covenant: the Virgin Mary, St. Anne, and St. Elisabeth. Eighth-century niche, S. Maria Antiqua, Rome. *Scala, Milan.*

FIGURE 8. The identification of Eve, or Woman, with evil became so natural that the serpent acquired female features. Michelangelo, *The Fall,* Sistine Chapel ceiling (detail), 1508–12. *Scala, Milan.*

FIGURE 9. The apostles gather and Christ descends at the Dormition of the Virgin. Tenth-century ivory from Constantinople, placed by the German Emperor Otto III on the cover of his Gospel Book. *Munich State Library.*

FIGURE 10. St. Thomas also doubted the Virgin's Assumption, but she dropped her sash from heaven to convince him. Filippino Lippi (d. 1504), *La Madonna della Cintola. Alinari, Milan.*

FIGURE 11. St. John's vision of "a woman clothed with the sun," pursued by a seven-headed monster, was identified with the Virgin. St. Albans (?), c. 1250. *Pierpont Morgan Library, New York.*

FIGURE 12. Maria Regina is arrayed in the insignia of a Byzantine empress. *Istituto Centrale del Restauro, Rome.*

FIGURE 13. The image of the rod of Jesse shows the Virgin and Child as the descendants of David and of the kings of Israel. Italian, anonymous, sixteenth century. *The National Gallery, London.*

FIGURE 14. Mary embodies the spirit of the new Church and becomes its mother. Botticelli, *Descent of the Holy Ghost*, fifteenth century. *City Art Gallery, Birmingham, England.*

FIGURE 15. Queen Blanche of Castile, enthroned on the right of her son St. Louis IX of France, raises her hands in intercession exactly as the Virgin does in portals of French cathedrals raised before and during Blanche's hegemony. France, *c.* 1235. *Pierpont Morgan Library, New York.*

FIGURE 16. The Virgin becomes Christ's bride and also his mirror image. Agnolo Gaddi, *Coronation of the Virgin. National Gallery of Art, Washington, D.C.*

FIGURE 17. The Mystical Marriage of Christ and his mother. Detail, gable of a fourteenth-century (?) Florentine diptych. *Museum of Fine Arts, Boston.*

FIGURE 18. Mary is crowned Queen of Heaven by the Trinity. Velásquez, *Coronation of the Virgin. Museo del Prado, Madrid, Marnel Collection.*

FIGURES 19, 20, 21, 22. Details from a fourteenth-century French manuscript, showing miracles worked by the Virgin. MS Douce, *Bodleian Library, Oxford, England.*

FIGURE 23. The Virgin as the barefoot model of exemplary humility. *Madonna of Humility*, attributed to Masaccio, *c.* 1425. *National Gallery of Art, Washington, D.C., Andrew Mellon Collection.*

FIGURE 24. The Virgin and Child on a Jesse tree with allegorical figures. Nardon Pénicaud (?), Limoges, *c.* 1470–1542. *Isabella Stewart Gardner Museum, Boston.*

*Black-and-white plates—following page 292*

FIGURE 25. Joseph, a young carpenter, weds Mary the Virgin. Murillo, *Marriage of the Virgin. Wallace Collection, London.*

FIGURE 26. Jesus displays his wounds and Mary bares her breast in order to win the mercy of God the Father towards sinners. Florentine, *c.* 1402. *Metropolitan Museum of Art, New York, The Cloisters Collection, purchase 1953.*

FIGURE 27. Toil and childbirth were both considered consequences of Adam's Fall. Liège, thirteenth century. Detail. *Pierpont Morgan Library, New York.*

FIGURE 28. The mistress of Charles VII of France, Agnès Sorel, portrayed as the enthroned Virgin. Jean Fouquet, the Melun Diptych (detail), *c.* 1450. *Copyright A.C.L., Brussels.*

FIGURE 29. The Mystic Hunt. Christ the unicorn lays his head in the lap of the Virgin. Dutch, sixteenth century. *Copyright of the Fitzwilliam Museum, Cambridge, England.*

# Author's Note

I am very grateful to the staff of the Library of Congress in Washington, D.C., who helped me use their vast resources and allotted me a desk of my own; to Mrs. Southcote Aston, of the Princeton Index of Christian Art at Dumbarton Oaks, Washington, who allowed me to work in its invaluable files; and to the staff of the London Library, who are unfailingly kind. So many friends helped me with advice and encouragement, with debate and dissent, that I could not begin to name every one of them. But in particular I want to express my profound gratitude to John Roberts, who gave me matchless advice before I embarked on the book and illuminating criticisms of the finished manuscript; to Caroline Elam, who also read the manuscript and gave me generously of her knowledge and perception. I also wish to thank Jonathan Sumption, who read several chapters and redressed my woeful ignorance in many areas; and David Esterly, whose far-ranging reading deepened my understanding of many facets of Marian imagery. To all of them I owe many ideas and many escapes from error; the imperfections that now remain are all my own. Peter Brown's wisdom was a great source of inspiration to me, and I am also deeply grateful to Father Eamonn Carroll, O.C., Father Peter Levi, S.J., Sister Benedicta Ward, O.L.G., Dr. Rosemary Radford Ruether, Verity Saifullah Khan, Tony Smith, Peter Jenkins, Polly Toynbee, Nick and Anne Zill, Sebastian Walker, and Christiane Besse, all of whom gave me rich bibliographical references, pressed appropriate books and iconographic material on me, or stimulated my thoughts by their questions. It is impossible to express fully how much I appreciated their interest. I alone am responsible for the use made of the material and I hope it will not give undue offence. I thank also my sister, Laura Warner, who patiently translated Greek material for me. The staffs of many galleries and museums, the sacristans of many churches, and the curators of shrines have often been extremely kind. I would like to express my particular gratitude to Père Valentin of the Abbey of Montserrat and to Ted Amussen of the National Gallery of Art, Washington, D.C. Above all, my thanks are due to Christopher Falkus for his original inspiration and enthusiasm throughout, to Gila Curtis for her invaluable help in the later stages, and to Carol Brown Janeway for her editorial comments and advice.

Although it may seem an act of perversity in a book about a Catholic cult, I have used the King James Authorized Version of the Bible. Its imagery and its cadences are so integral to the English language and its strength and beauty so marked that I could not pass it over. Where a divergence between the Authorized Version and the Catholic interpreta-

tion is material to my theme, I have supplied the Catholic Douay translation. For similar aesthetic reasons, I have generally quoted poetry in the
original language and supplied a translation; but I have quoted prose
passages directly in English, unless they are particularly striking in the
original and lose greatly in translation.

# ALONE OF ALL HER SEX

*She . . . had no peer*

*Either in our first mother or in all women*

*Who were to come. But alone of all her sex*

*She pleased the Lord.*[1]

— CAELIUS SEDULIUS

# PROLOGUE

*We do not know, and never shall know, anything about the first origin of beliefs and customs the roots of which plunge into a distant past; but, as far as the present is concerned, it is certain that social behaviour is not produced spontaneously by each individual, under the influence of emotions of the moment. Men do not act, as members of a group, in accordance with what each feels as an individual; each man feels as a function of the way in which he is permitted or obliged to act. Customs are given as external norms before giving rise to internal sentiments, and these non-sentient norms determine the sentiments of individuals as well as the circumstances in which they may, or must, be displayed.[2]*

—CLAUDE LÉVI-STRAUSS

INVOCATIONS TO THE VIRGIN MARY marked out the days of my childhood in bells; her feastdays gave a rhythm to the year; an eternal ideal of mortal beauty was fixed by the lineaments of her face, which gazed from every wall and niche.

On February 2, the feast of the Purification, we wore starched white veils of tulle that stood out around us like a nimbus. With the medals of the Sodality of Our Lady on blue ribbons round our necks, we processed with lit candles up to the communion rails to be blessed. In another convent school, on the same day, each young girl laid a lily at the feet of the Virgin's statue: "Mary, I give you the lily of my heart, be thou its guardian for ever."[3]

The blue ribbons—blue is the colour of the Virgin, "the sapphire," as Dante wrote, who turns all of heaven blue—signified that the wearer was a child of Mary, and had dedicated herself to the Virgin and promised to emulate her in thought, word, and deed: her chastity, her humility, her gentleness. She was the culmination of womanhood. As my agnostic father maintained, it was a good religion for a girl.

Under the chapel there was a crypt, with a grotto of the Virgin made from chunks of cork oak from the Holy Land and hung all about with rosaries. On special occasions—the death of a pope, for instance—we were allowed to file into this darkened and scented place to kneel before the statue of Our Lady of Lourdes and recite our Hail Marys. The worship bit deep into our imaginations: I was no exception when, secretly and with intense excitement, I made myself my own grotto. Finding a rhododendron bush so old that its dusty dark green foliage framed a hollow chamber, I used to crawl in during breaks and after study hours and kneel to pray. "Holiness," as we called it, was natural, a part of living as simple as drawing breath. "She's so *holy*," we'd say in admiration of a classmate who spent particularly long on her knees before the thirteenth Station of the Cross: "Mary takes her beloved son to her bosom." Only moments before we had been stifling our giggles at that risqué word "bosom."

So our holiness was a shallow affair, although most of us considered with complacent resignation the vocation to the cloister, which might suddenly come upon us. Other Christians are often shocked by Catholic frivolity. Our religion was certainly untroublesome, because it consisted of simple certainties, outlined in the crisp rhetoric of the Catechism we learned by heart. And the Virgin was the chief of these certainties.

In her mercy, her sweetness, her overflowing goodness, she was incapable of withholding her favour if approached with the right courtesies and the correct salutations. The bond of motherhood that attached her to her son and to the whole human race through him presupposed a natural law of inalienable, irreducible, indestructible love. All the antiphons that pealed from the choir beseeching her to save us were, despite their imploring words, so much praise and thanksgiving. She did not really need to be asked.

We were not troubled by questions about the Virgin's personality, about what her life had been, what she had been like. We sometimes chattered about the colour of her skin—swarthy?—or the shape of her nose—Jewish? But we never probed history deeper, and although we did study the New Testament, we never noticed—it was not indeed called to our attention—how the Virgin is passed over almost in silence.

The world of music, flowers, perfumes, and painting that enfolded her was filled with joy. It was only in the last two years at school, when I had been a devout Mariolater all my conscious life, that I felt the first chill wind sigh in this blissful pleasure dome. Doubts about doctrine caused minor tremors compared to the absolute misery that shook me when I was confronted, in puberty, by the Church's moral teaching.

For although the Virgin was steadfast, the human heart was faithless; although she never abandoned a votary, her votary could abandon her, and then, like Orpheus turning to grasp the vanishing shade of Eurydice, the intimate bond that once existed was severed. The price the Virgin demanded was purity, and the way the educators of Catholic children have interpreted this for nearly two thousand years is sexual chastity. Impurity, we were taught, follows from many sins, but all are secondary to the principal impulse of the devil in the soul—lust.

It is wry now to remember, at this distance, the terror this inspired: the children who spent the night cruciform on the dormitory floor after a "dirty thought," the tears of shame and embarrassment in the confessional after teenage gropings at lights-out parties. But even while the terror gripped me, I was already doubtful. Although I could not have articulated it then as I can now, I sensed that the problem of human evil was more complex than concupiscence—at least in its narrow sexual definition.

The Virgin, sublime model of chastity, nevertheless remained for me the most holy being I could ever contemplate, and so potent was her spell that for some years I could not enter a church without pain at all the safety and beauty of the salvation I had forsaken. I remember visiting Notre Dame in Paris and standing in the nave, tears starting in my eyes, furious at that old love's enduring power to move me. But though my heart rebelled, I held fast to my new intimation that in the very celebration of the perfect human woman, both humanity and women were subtly denigrated.

In this book I have tried, by exploring aspects of the Virgin's cult in Europe, to describe this paradox more fully. I started with a simple question: what was it I had worshipped? It is therefore the outcome of a private journey. But there are millions of Catholics who share the same experience. For almost all the 659 million of them in the world, the religious landscape encloses at its very heart the powerful and most beloved figure of the Virgin. Wayside shrines in Italy, with a poor plaster of paris statue, a ring of cracked fairy lights, and a withered bunch of flowers; the Angelus bell in France; even the dedications of village churches in England—once Roman, now Anglican—are fragments of the same myth that inspired Botticelli to paint the Virgin's portrait, that raised the spire and towers of Chartres, and that moved Dante to give voice in Paradise.

I have not pursued the historical Mary, the woman of Nazareth, because theology and belief have only rarely focussed on her. The reader will find nothing about life in Galilee in the first decades of our era. I have concentrated on the different aspects the Virgin assumes at different times and have attempted to uncover the convergence of circumstances that might have made such a symbol satisfying. The Virgin Mary has been formed and animated by different people for different reasons, and is a truly popular creation. That does not mean the "people" as opposed to the ruling classes or to the intelligentsia, for she has been the beloved patroness of saints as brilliant as Bernard of Clairvaux, or a pope as intellectually refined as Pius XII, or a king as gallant as Henry V of England.[4] It is an insular assumption that—as one often hears in England—the cult of the Virgin is the refuge of a poverty-stricken peasantry.

The finer points of Mariology have always been and still are a delight to the subtlest and clearest thinkers in the Church. Four dogmas have been defined and must be believed as articles of faith: her divine motherhood and her virginity, both declared by councils of the early Church and therefore accepted by most of the reformed Christian groups; the immaculate conception, sparing her all stain of original sin, which was proclaimed in 1854; and her assumption, body and soul, into heaven, which Pope Pius XII defined in 1950. The Vatican is still pondering whether the Virgin Mary experienced death at all, and whether the traditional and widespread faith in her perpetual virginity—her unbroken hymen—*post partum* (after birth) as well as *in partu* (during), is necessary. With scholastic nicety, she is entitled to a special worship of her own—*hyperdulia*. God is owed *latria* (adoration) and the saints *dulia* (veneration), but Mary occupies the principal mediating position, as a creature belonging both to earth and heaven. Pope Paul VI has a learned and profound devotion to the Virgin, as his 1974 apostolic exhortation *Marialis Cultus* bears witness. Since medieval times the aristocracy have opened their purses to build churches in her honour, to commission paintings, statues, masses, and votive crowns for her shrines. There are two colleges at Oxford placed under her patronage, although both—Oriel and New College—are known under their sobriquets.[5] But she is also, as is more visible to the Mediterranean tourist, the focus of a vigorous and fertile grassroots piety that knows nothing of Duns Scotus' casuistry or Pius XII's ratiocinations.

A myth of such dimension is not simply a story, or a collection of stories, but a magic mirror like the Lady of Shalott's, reflecting a people and the beliefs they produce, recount, and hold. It presents their history in a certain light and in a way that singles them out. For the Virgin is a protagonist in the drama of the Incarnation and the Redemption of Christ, and consequently in the personal salvation of each individual who feels himself to belong to Christian history and professes Christian beliefs. (Until the Reformation this applied to almost all Christians, but now it is restricted to Catholics, Orthodox, and High Anglicans.) Just as Aeneas provided Roman citizens with historical roots in the noble past of Troy and descent from the goddess Venus, his mother, and at the same time furnished a standard of conduct that they regarded as exemplary—Virgil's "pius Aeneas"—so the Virgin Mary, an ordinary woman who gave birth to Christ, in whom all found new life, becomes the symbolic mother of the Church, gives each of its members a part in God's plan, and also stands as a model of perfect humanity.

Myth, while providing a historical viewpoint and an ethical code for its adherents, also follows certain characteristic but easily overlooked patterns of thought. For instance, the Christian equivalence between spiritual impurity and bodily decay provides the basic argument behind the doctrine of the Assumption, which declares that the all-pure Virgin was spared the dissolution of the grave. In such patterns, the sacred and the profane, as well as human desires and fears, can to some extent be deciphered.

I have not undertaken a history of the cult of the Virgin as such, but in chronological order I have taken aspects of her composite personality at their zenith and then worked backwards and forwards in time showing the ideas that contributed to their genesis and growth and lingered on in the tiredness of old age. The idea of the Virgin's queenship had a value during the emergence of powerful kings in western Europe that it no longer has; but the image, stripped of its original strength, survives as a stock in trade of contemporary prayer and ritual. So although Pope Pius XII proclaimed Mary queen only in 1954, I have discussed the idea of her majesty at the point I consider it had maximum force: during the early middle ages. The most evident function of the Virgin today is intercession: she is prayed to for redress against private and public wrongs and to bestow graces of all kinds. Mediation has been the most constant theme of her cult, so in the later chapters about the different areas in which her help is particularly sought, the reader will find much early as well as contemporary material. Throughout I have used iconography, because it cannot be stressed enough that most believers until modern times were illiterate, and the walls of the churches were their Bible. Although this method tends to present history as a smooth continuum, and to perceive the common culture of different nations and epochs rather than their differences, I feel such a perspective is justified in the case of a figure like the Virgin Mary, because she belongs to a vast community of people and represents a gradual accretion of their ideas, the deposit of popular belief interacting with intellectual inquiry, until, like the result of the coral insects' industry, a doctrine breaks to the surface like a new atoll. It is possible to probe this process only so far, however, and after consideration, I have avoided explanations arising from Freudian psychology. I do not think it is adequate to say that men will always yearn for a pure mother who will never let them down, and that that is why the Virgin Mary flourishes; one has to ask why purity and motherliness have been defined the way they have in the case of the Virgin and accept the fact that the ultimate reasons for her hegemony can never be fully understood. Nor does the Jungian archetype explain the myth of the Virgin Mary, for such figures are not innate, but cultural and historical products. I do accept, however, as the Jungians maintain, that such a symbol exercises a sway over our unconscious lives. The Virgin Mary is a manifestation of the principle the Chinese call *yin* and represents the quintessence of many qualities that east and west have traditionally regarded as feminine: yieldingness, softness, gentleness, receptiveness, mercifulness, tolerance, withdrawal. But whereas the Orient and to some extent Jung realized that both masculine and feminine qualities must be present in the whole individual in balanced measure, it has been the constant tendency of western thought, both when it was dominated by the Church and afterwards, to equate the feminine with the female of the species; and to insist that the female sex was and should be feminine, according to its definition. The Virgin Mary, a polyvalent figure who appears under many guises, is the Church's female paragon, and the ideal of the feminine personified. But, in the Church's attitudes to women, the oscillation between regarding them as equal in God's eyes (endowed with an immortal soul) and yet subject and inferior to the male in the order of creation and society ("And thy desire shall be to thy husband, and he shall rule over thee"—Genesis 3:16) has never ceased, and provides continual background interference to any discussion of the Virgin, the model of the sex, who accurately reflects this perennial ambivalence. Therefore, as when *yin* is defined its complement *yang* takes shape by implication, so much of the matter that follows affects men as well as women, and defines the masculine as well as the feminine.

Whether we regard the Virgin Mary as the most sublime and beautiful image in man's struggle towards the good and the pure, or the most pitiable production of ignorance and superstition, she represents a central theme in the history of western attitudes to women. She is one of the few female figures to have attained the status of myth—a myth that for nearly two thousand years has coursed through our culture, as spirited and often as imperceptible as an underground stream.

# Part One

# VIRGIN

*Chapter One*

# MARY IN THE GOSPELS

*He came all so stille*
*    There his mother was*
*As dew in Aprille*
*    That falleth on the grass.*
*He came all so stille*
*    To his mothers bower*
*As dew in Aprille*
*    That falleth on the flower.*
*He came all so stille*
*    There his mother lay*
*As dew in Aprille*
*    That falleth on the spray.*
*Mother and maiden*
*    Was never none but she;*
*Well may such a lady*
*    Goddes mother be.*[1]

—ENGLISH CAROL
(FIFTEENTH CENTURY?)

IN HIS URGENT MISSIVE to the Galatians, St. Paul stresses that Jesus was fully human and yet the son of God. To drive his point about Jesus' humanity home, he tells his readers that Jesus was "made of a woman" (Galatians 4:4). It is the earliest reference to the mother of Christ that has come down to us; and it is a very quiet entrance for the Virgin Mary.

St. Paul's Epistle to the Galatians was probably written in A.D. 57; his letters as a whole are the earliest work in the New Testament, which is itself the earliest source for Mary, and the only one with any claim to historical validity. Apart from this passing and anonymous mention in Galatians, Paul never refers to Jesus' mother again. Nor is the rest of the New Testament more generous. In Mark, which may be the earliest of the Gospels, she appears once in an unflattering light (Mark 3:31) and is mentioned once as the mother of Jesus (Mark 6:3). In the Fourth Gospel, the last to be composed, she makes two appearances: at the wedding feast at Cana with Jesus, and at the foot of the Cross. In the Acts of the Apostles she prays with them in Jerusalem after the Ascension (Acts 1:14). Marian knowledge is concentrated therefore in the two accounts of Christ's infancy, as found in Matthew and in Luke.[2]

Both infancy narratives are now acknowledged by scholars to be later additions to the Gospels. They were written more than eighty years after the events they describe took place. It is not difficult to imagine what the life of a great man—Napoleon or Mao Tse-tung—would become if an oral tradition alone had conserved the story of his origins for nearly a century and no contemporary written accounts had survived. Like the legend of Roland and Oliver in the pass at Roncevalles, recorded nearly a hundred years after the mysterious events that felled the heroic warrior had occurred, the story of Jesus' birth belongs to the realm of the myth.

The two evangelists who describe Jesus' birth and childhood agree that when he was born heaven was present on earth in sign and prodigy. They also agree that Jesus was of the house of David, his birthplace Bethlehem, his father's name Joseph, and that his mother was called Mary. Otherwise their stories diverge.

In Matthew, Jesus says during the sermon on the mount: "Think not that I am come to destroy the law, or the prophets: I am not come to destroy, but to fulfil" (Matthew 5:17). In his picturesque opening narrative, Matthew bears out the saviour's claim in a sequence of events that despite centuries of dulling familiarity still conserve a strange, Oriental beauty. But they cannot be regarded as historical, and are empty of what any contemporary writer would consider biographical data, for they are openly modelled on the Old Testament in order to demonstrate that Jesus was the Messiah, and the fulfilment of the law.[3]

The Gospel opens with a long genealogy of Jesus. Abruptly and unconditionally, the evangelist states that "Mary was found with child by the Holy Ghost." Then he shifts focus to Joseph, her husband, who doubts her virtue, but does not want to shame her by repudiating her publicly. An angel appears to him and reassures him: "that which is conceived in her is of the Holy Ghost." The angel tells Joseph to call the child Jesus, and reveals that he will be the saviour. When Joseph wakes he does not reject Mary as he had considered doing, but "took unto him

Mary his wife and knew her not till she had brought forth her firstborn son: and he called his name Jesus" (Matthew 1:25).

"The wise men from the east" who have followed the star to Jerusalem appear before Herod and ask to see the King of the Jews. Herod is troubled and consults the priests and scribes, who tell him the Messiah is to be born in Bethlehem. So the wise men follow the star to Bethlehem, "and, lo, the star which they saw in the east went before them, till it came and stood over where the young child was." They worship him and offer gold, frankincense, and myrrh. A dream warns them not to return to see Herod (Matthew 2:1–12).

An angel now appears to Joseph for a second time and tells him: "Arise, and take the child and his mother and flee into Egypt, for Herod will seek the young child to destroy him" (Matthew 2:13). When Herod dies, an angel appears for the third time to Joseph and tells him to return with the child and his mother to Israel; this he does, but when he hears that Herod's son Archelaus reigns in Juda, he is afraid and turns to Galilee and settles in Nazareth.

No less than five times, Matthew links an incident to a prophecy from the Old Testament. The conception of Jesus "before they [Mary and Joseph] came together," fulfils a prophecy of Isaiah: "Behold a virgin shall be with child and shall bring forth a son . . ." (Isaiah 7:14). Although the wise men are following the star, they stop in Jerusalem to hear where the Messiah is to be born from the chief priests, whom Matthew uses as the mouthpiece of another biblical prophecy, in order to underline the authenticity of Jesus' messianic claims: "And thou Bethlehem, in the land of Juda, art not least . . . for out of thee shall come a Governor, to rule my people Israel" (Micah 5:2; Matthew 2:6). Jesus' birthplace thus confirmed and emphasized, the wise men once again follow the faithful star.

The detour to Jerusalem reveals Christ's fulfilment of the Old Law. Again, when Joseph is sent to Egypt by the angel in a dream, Matthew explains that the family's exile fulfils the words of the Lord's prophet, Hosea, who wrote: "Out of Egypt have I called my son" (Hosea 11:1). The massacre of the innocents similarly realizes another prophecy, Jeremiah's, that Rachel would weep for her dead children (Jeremiah 31:15; Matthew 2:18). Finally, Matthew ends his tale of Christ's birth and infancy with Joseph's decision to live in Nazareth, so that "it might be fulfilled which was spoken by the prophets: He shall be called a Nazarene" (Matthew 2:23). The historical Jesus manifestly came from Nazareth in Galilee, but this messianic prophecy Matthew quotes to support Jesus' authority as saviour does not come from the Bible and has not been traced elsewhere.[4] Matthew, in his enthusiasm to demonstrate Jesus' fulfilment of the law, outruns the book itself. As no messianic prophecy concerned Nazareth, Matthew supplied one.

The major episodes Matthew does not explicitly illuminate from the Old Testament are as deeply coloured with its oracles and its imagery. The adoration of the wise men enhances the mythic might of the new-born child and marks him out as divine, as does the miraculous wandering star, a common device in the Greco-Roman world to designate the birth of a hero. But the visit of the men from the east also fulfils Isaiah's prediction: "the Gentiles shall come to thy light . . ." (Isaiah 60:3) and "they shall bring gold and incense" (Isaiah 60:6). The myrrh appears elsewhere, in the Book of Exodus, when the Jews at Moses' order mix a chrism with which they anoint the Ark of the Covenant—an apt symbol that the child who accepts the wise man's myrrh is the anointed one who will inaugurate the New Covenant. The worship of the wise men was recognized early on as the fulfilment of Isaiah's prophecy, for in the writings of the great Greek exegete Origen (d. 254) they have already metamorphosed into kings from Arabia, following the words of Isaiah that complete the prophecy: "And kings shall come to the brightness of thy rising . . ." (Isaiah 60:3) and "from Sheba shall they come" (Isaiah 60:6). Matthew never mentions kings, nor does he say they were three in number. But Christian imagery, in art, music, and poetry, prostrated eastern potentates before the baby in the stable, and as early as Bede gave them the exotic names of Gaspar, Melchior, and Balthasar.

The sequence about Egypt—the flight, the massacre of the innocents and Jesus' miraculous deliverance, the safe return of Mary, Joseph, and the child—forms a harmonious parallel to the adventures of the infant Moses, the founder of the Old Law. The symmetry between Moses' escape from Pharaoh's massacre of all the first-born of the Hebrews and Jesus' safety is no accident in a Gospel saturated with biblical memories.[5] Elsewhere, Matthew emphasizes the diptych of Moses/Jesus, the Old Law and the New, when Jesus, like Moses, is transfigured "on a high mountain" (Matthew 17:1–6). Not only the story of Moses, chief among the heroes of Israel, but also the story of Israel itself are recapitulated by Matthew in the figure of Jesus, Israel's redeemer, who like his country and his people flees into Egypt and is then safely delivered by God's providence.

The figure of Joseph himself is dyed in Old Testament associations. Like the old Joseph of Genesis, who interpreted dreams in Egypt, Joseph the father of Jesus is a dreamer who no less than three times is visited by an angel in his sleep and granted a prophetic vision. The biblical colouring in Matthew's infancy Gospel is indeed so vivid that if Luke did not corroborate Joseph's existence, he might have remained a type of God's merciful plan, fusing the Old and New Covenants, and never have attained the status of a historical character.[6]

Luke was writing after Matthew. If he knew Matthew's account, he rejected it. For in the first two chapters of Luke, Joseph does not dream, the wise men do not come to adore the child, Herod does not massacre the innocents, and the holy family do not flee to Egypt. Luke does not quote openly from the Bible, but he skilfully interweaves biblical memories and images to create a profound and emotive meditation on the coming of the saviour. Matthew unashamedly linked Jesus of Nazareth to the Old Law; Luke's intention was similar, but his strategy was more adroit. Where Matthew is a primitive, Luke is a consummate old master, building up tone, colour, and texture in layer upon layer of glowing oils. In Luke's Gospel, the resurrected Jesus instructs the two disciples on the road from Emmaus: "And beginning at Moses and all the prophets, he expounded unto them in all the scriptures, the things concerning himself" (Luke 24:27). When Luke blends ingredients from the Bible, in particular from the stories of Abraham, Samuel, and David, to create the sumptuous feast that is his infancy Gospel, he may be taking the lead from Jesus himself, reporting his master's thought in a highly truthful but generally unsuspected way.

Luke's infancy Gospel is the scriptural source for all the great mysteries of the Virgin; the only time she is the heart of the drama in the Bible is in Luke's beautiful verses. Luke tells the stories of the Annunciation, the Visitation, the Nativity, and the Purification (or Presentation of Christ in the Temple), and he describes the mysterious scene when Christ is lost and found among the doctors in the temple—the only occasion apart from the wedding feast at Cana when Christ and his mother speak to each other. In Luke's Gospel Mary speaks four times; in Matthew she is silent.

Luke refers in the opening words of his Gospel to "eyewitnesses, and ministers of the word" whose example he is going to follow (Luke 1:2). An early tradition therefore held that Luke received his story of Christ's birth from Mary herself, and made her true portrait not only in words, but in paint also. Icons of the Virgin by St. Luke can be found in several Mediterranean towns, the object of love from the locals and the butt of sceptics (see Chapter 19). Catholic scholars still support the idea of a first-hand source for Luke's infancy Gospel, because when the original Greek of Luke 1:5-12 is translated into Hebrew it is richly alliterative in a manner typical of Hebrew poetry. The passages may have originated in a group of Christians centring on St. John in Ephesus, where the Virgin traditionally lived with him after the Ascension. "Its contemplative personal mood shows it was conceived in a feminine mind," remarks one scholar, when "Mary was sharing the first years of the church in contemplation of the Incarnation with John, before heresies and persecutions overcame them."[7]

But a closer look at Luke's first two chapters is enough to strip almost all narrative realism from the central incandescent mythological core, for Luke is intent on revealing to the reader the divinity of Christ, and not to write his biography, as a contemporary historian might.[8]

Luke begins his infancy Gospel with the story of the birth of John the Baptist. Zacharias, a priest, is married to Elisabeth and they are childless. While he is performing his duties in the temple, an angel appears to him and tells him a son will be born to him, whom he is to call John. Zacharias is astounded, and asks for a sign that the message is true. The angel identifies himself as Gabriel, and strikes Zacharias dumb. When he returns home after his duties in the temple are over, his wife Elisabeth conceives.

Luke then turns to the story of Jesus' conception. In the sixth month of Elisabeth's pregnancy, the same angel Gabriel "was sent from God unto a city of Galilee, named Nazareth, to a virgin espoused to a man whose name was Joseph, of the house of David; and the virgin's name was Mary" (Luke 1:26-7). From then on, the story follows the Baptist's in a beautifully wrought double helix. Gabriel appears to Mary in Nazareth and greets her with the famous words of praise: "Hail, thou that are highly favoured, the Lord is with thee, blessed art thou among women." Mary is "troubled" and does not understand the angel's salutation. (Zacharias, too, was "troubled.") Gabriel reassures her: "Fear not, Mary, for thou hast found favour with God." (Gabriel comforted Zacharias: "Fear not, Zacharias, for thy prayer is heard.") Gabriel prophesies the birth of Jesus, and tells Mary of his great destiny, as he told Zacharias of his son John's high mission. Mary's son is to be called Jesus. Mary answers—her most precious speech in Mariology, for it implies her innocence and virginity: "How shall this be, seeing I know not a man?" (Luke 1:34).

Zacharias had also demurred: "Whereby shall I know this? For I am an old man, and my wife well stricken in years." Gabriel continues, telling Mary: "The Holy Ghost shall come upon thee, and the power of the Highest shall overshadow thee: therefore also that holy thing which shall be born of thee shall be called the Son of God." He then reveals to her, as a sign of God's power, that her "cousin Elisabeth . . . who was called barren," has also conceived a son. (This sign parallels the dumbness of Zacharias.) Mary, hearing this, acquiesces in her destiny with the famous words, her fiat: "Behold the handmaid of the lord, be it unto me according to thy word" (Luke 1:38).

The angel Gabriel leaves Mary, and she "with haste" makes her way through the hill country to the house of Zacharias and her cousin Elisabeth. The double helix converges, and the two stories become intertwined. Mary greets her cousin, and when Elisabeth hears Mary's salutation, the baby in her womb leaps, and she is inspired by the Holy Spirit to praise Mary "in a loud voice": "Blessed art thou among women, and blessed is the fruit of thy womb" (Luke 1:42).

She calls Mary "mother of my Lord," and prophesies the fulfilment of the Lord's promises to Mary. Mary answers her cousin's rejoicing with equal energy and joy, in the words of the great hymn the *Magnificat,* by far her longest speech in the Bible. In some manuscripts, however, it is Elisabeth who recites the *Magnificat,* not Mary.[9] In the hymn, she does not mention the child she has conceived but gives thanks to God for his kindness and his might. Mary stays with Elisabeth for three months, and then returns home.

John the Baptist is born, and eight days later he is circumcised. Zacharias regains his power of speech, and, prophesying, he gives thanks to God in the majestic poetry of the second Lucan canticle, the *Benedictus*. The melodies that had reached a diapason at the Visitation when the two women greeted each other now separate again and answer each other softly, at a distance.

In his second chapter, Luke tells the story of the Nativity of Jesus. Each man was to be taxed in his own city, by decree of the Emperor Augustus. So Joseph leaves Nazareth for Bethlehem, the city of David and his town of origin, with Mary, who was "great with child." She gives birth and lays her son in a manger "because there was no room for them in the inn" (Luke 2:7). That night the shepherds are told by angels of the Messiah's birth, and visit him. They tell everyone what they have heard, but Mary "kept all these things, and pondered them in her heart" (Luke 2:19).

The responding harmonies start up again. Jesus, after eight days, is circumcised, as the Baptist was. Mary goes up to Jerusalem to be purified and to dedicate the first male child to God, according to Mosaic law. After she and Joseph have offered, as the poor are required, two turtle doves to the temple, Simeon, an old man like Zacharias, is inspired to recite the third lovely canticle of Luke's Gospel, the *Nunc dimittis*. In mid-flow, Mary and Joseph marvel at his exalted prophecies, just as

Zacharias' neighbours, before the *Benedictus,* were struck with fear. Simeon then turns to Mary with the sombre words, "Yea, a sword shall pierce through thy own soul also" (Luke 2:35)—a prophecy that has puzzled Christians and that eventually led to the western cult of the Virgin's sorrows, represented by a sword transfixing her breast (see Chapter 14).

After Simeon's canticle, the prophetess Anna joins the holy family and gives thanks to the Lord for granting her this sight of the redeemer. Then Mary and Joseph and the child return to Nazareth, where "the child grew, and waxed strong in spirit, filled with wisdom, and the grace of God was upon him" (Luke 2:40). Of John the Baptist, Luke had written, "And the child grew, and waxed strong in spirit, and was in the deserts till the day of his shewing unto Israel" (Luke 1:80).

As a coda to his account of Jesus' birth, Luke appends the extraordinary incident in the temple at Jerusalem, when Jesus was twelve years old. Mary and Joseph have gone as usual to Jerusalem for the Passover; but they find on their return journey that he is not with them or their friends and relatives in the company as they thought. So they go back to search for him in the city, and "after three days" they find him with the doctors in the temple, asking and answering questions. "And all that heard him were astonished at his understanding and answers." Mary and Joseph are "amazed" to see him thus, and Mary speaks to him: "Son, why hast thou thus dealt with us? Behold thy father and I have sought thee sorrowing." Jesus answers: "How is it that ye sought me? Wist ye not that I must be about my Father's business?"

Then Luke writes: "And they understood not the saying which he spake unto them." This is the first of the two conversations between mother and son reported in the Gospels. Jesus returns with them to Nazareth and "was subject to them." Again, says the evangelist, "his mother kept all these sayings in her heart." The Lucan infancy Gospel then comes to its end: "And Jesus increased in wisdom and stature, and in favour with God and man."

In his next, third, chapter, which originally opened his Gospel, Jesus comes to John and is baptized in the Jordan. Luke follows this with a genealogy of Christ, also traced through Joseph, but quite different from Matthew's. Thus the stories that began with the birth of the two first-born sons and came together at the meeting of the two mothers converge once again with the encounter of the two grown men about thirty years later.

A solid architecture governs the internal structure of Luke's narrative. Carefully constructed as to form, it is also highly sophisticated as to content, and a veritable labyrinth of Old Testament reminiscence. The two annunciations—to Zacharias and to Mary—echo the appearance of Gabriel to Daniel (Daniel 9:21) who prophesies the coming of the Messiah and the destruction of the temple, an event that when Luke was writing had taken place very recently. Gabriel hails Daniel, "thou art greatly beloved" (Daniel 9:23), just as he greeted Mary, "thou that art highly favoured" (in Greek, *kekaritomene*). Daniel later sees an angel, who is not named but who reminds him of Gabriel in his earlier vision. The angel's words, "Fear not, Daniel" (Daniel 10:2), Gabriel echoes to both Zacharias, and Mary at the Annunciation. Daniel is then struck dumb, as Zacharias was.[10]

During another apparition of an angel, Gideon is greeted in the same words as Gabriel used to Mary: "The Lord is with thee" (Judges 6:12). Gideon then asks for a sign, as does Zacharias.[11] The angel Gabriel's opening salutation to Mary disturbs and puzzles her, because, say Catholic exegetes, it departs from conventional words of greeting to echo the rapture of the prophet Zephaniah (Sophonias in the Vulgate) when he invokes fair Sion, the true remnant of Israel, and asks her to sing of her coming triumph (Zephaniah 3:14-17). Mary, say the apologists, was well versed in the Bible, and, recognizing the messianic ring in the angel's words, was alarmed by its weighty significance. The association of Mary with the true remnant of Israel is later deepened by Luke in her triumphant hymn the *Magnificat*.

During the Annunciation to Mary, Luke works a second vein of association, that of Mary with the Ark of the Covenant. The verb he uses to describe the action of "the power of the Highest" on Mary is very particular—"overshadow"—a verb that explicitly picks up the mysterious image that closes the Book of Exodus, when the *shekinah*, the cloud that is the spirit of God, covers the Ark of the Covenant "and the glory of God filled the tabernacle" (Exodus 40:34). Just as God was present at the Ark of the Old Covenant, so he covers the Ark of the New with his overshadowing power.[12] Again, at the Visitation, Luke recalls the Ark. David goes up to a city of Juda and is anointed king (2 Samuel 2:1); Mary goes up to a city of Juda, and is proclaimed by Elisabeth the mother of her Lord, the new heavenly king. Her exclamation, "And whence is this to me, that the mother of my Lord should come to me?" echoes David's cry as he conducts the Ark of the Covenant to Jerusalem: "How shall the ark of the Lord come to me?" (2 Samuel 6:9). Mary stays three months with Elisabeth, just as the Ark "continued in the house of Ob edom the Gittite for three months" before it was brought to "the city of David" (2 Samuel 6:11) (figure 1).[13] Luke's paramount concern with the typology rather than the story gives commentators anguish, for on a psychological and narrative plane, Mary should have stayed with Elisabeth to help with the birth, yet Luke leaves this completely ambiguous.[14]

The double annunciations to Zacharias and to Mary, and the miraculous births of John and Jesus stir myriad memories of other tales of prodigious and unexpected fertility in the Bible. The conception of John the Baptist by Elisabeth in her old age recalls in particular the story of Isaac, born to Abraham and Sarah after she had long been thought barren. Luke also blends in fragments of Samson's birth to Manoah, also announced by an angel (Judges 13:3–4), of the twins' birth to Rebecca (Genesis 25), and, above all, of Samuel's birth to Hannah.[15]

Hannah provides a particular model for both Elisabeth and Mary, and echoes of her story, that of the most faithful and loyal mother in the Bible, reverberate through the Visitation and the *Magnificat,* the Presentation and the finding of Jesus in the temple (figure 2). Samuel, prodigy child and wise adult, is Christ's prototype as mythic hero, and his mother Hannah is Mary's forbear, a relationship so close that by the second century Mary's mother was believed to be called Anna, another form of the name of Hannah, according to the legendary *Book of James* (see Chapter 2).[16]

Hannah calls herself handmaid no less than five times in the first chapter of the first book of Samuel. It is her leit-motif, borrowed by Mary when she answers Gabriel's greeting. This could be coincidence if Luke did not display such consistent art and if he did not sow other references to Hannah's story throughout his infancy Gospel. Hannah gives thanks to God in an exultant hymn of rich psalmodic imagery that is the *Magnificat's* direct ancestor. It is also ten verses long, and phrases and feelings overlap unmistakably. If the *Magnificat* was originally recited in some manuscripts by Elisabeth, as Irenaeus and Nicetas of Remesiana both describe, and not by Mary, then the circumstances are identical; for Hannah sang to give thanks for the conception of Samuel after years of barrenness.

Few Christians now consider the *Magnificat* to be Mary's spontaneous creation at the moment Elisabeth saluted her. The complex allusions to the Old Testament are widely recognized, and although this would not by itself rule out the authorship of Mary, it was well-established practice for an author to ascribe a hymn of praise to his subject: Mary praises God, but she also extolls herself. The tangle of biblical motifs, images, and echoes in the *Magnificat* and Zacharias' *Benedictus* has been unscrambled by M. D. Goulder and M. L. Sanderson in their article on St. Luke's Genesis, and the results reveal Luke's literary method (see Appendix A).

The bellicose and triumphalist character of the *Magnificat* echoes both Hannah's hymn and the paean of Miriam, the sister of Moses, who struck her timbrel and danced for joy with the women of Israel when Pharaoh and his army were swallowed up by the Red Sea. Thus Mary's thanksgiving is not a psychological poem on the mystery of the conception of Christ, or even on the miracle of the virgin birth—which she does not mention at all—but a rousing cry that the Jewish Messiah promised by God has arrived to vanquish his enemies and to rehabilitate the true remnant of Israel who have remained faithful to the law.

Subjected to similar scrutiny, the entire familiar Christmas story, centring on the overcrowded inn, the stable, and the manger, also evaporates. For there is no mention of a stable, but only of a manger, which from the Greek *thaten* could just as well have been translated "crib." In the Septuagint, the Greek Old Testament, which was translated in Alexandria in the third century B.C., the prophecy of Isaiah—"The ox knoweth his owner and the ass his master's crib" (Isaiah 1:3)—used *thaten* for crib in this context, and the connection that later commentators made between the Lucan nativity scene and this passage from Isaiah inspired the reading of "manger" and also the image of the familiar worshippers of the baby—the ox and ass that in many lovely Christmas paintings kneel and warm the infant with their breath. Luke says the baby was laid in a manger because "there was no room for them in the inn" (Luke 2:7). The word he used for "inn" is *katalemna*, a Greek word that in the Septuagint is used of temporary shelters. God also uses it when he tells Nathan that he has wandered without a dwelling place since Israel left Egypt "but have walked in a tent and in a *tabernacle*" (2 Samuel 7:6).[17] Is Luke implying that at the moment of the Incarnation, the son of God had left the temporary accommodation the Jews offered him on their wanderings and come to rest in a crib where he would be recognized as the Messiah?

Whatever the meaning of Luke's brief and pregnant verse, it does not contain the story of the holy family turned away by the innkeeper and then given a corner of his stable for the night. But its very cryptic character means that it will bear, as it has done for nearly two thousand years, the great garland of picturesque anecdote embroidered around the Christmas story. It requires a herculean effort of will to read Luke's infancy Gospel and blot from the imagination all the paintings and sculptures, carols and hymns and stories that add to Luke's spare medita-

tion the hay and the snow and the smell of animals' warm bodies as the
Christ child was born that first Christmas night. Yet none of this circum-
stantial detail—with the exception of the swaddling bands—is present in
the text. It is all the collective inheritance of western fantasy.

The amount of historical information about the Virgin is negligible.
Her birth, her death, her appearance, her age are never mentioned. During Christ's ministry she plays a small part, and when she does appear the
circumstances are perplexing and often slighting. She is never referred to
by any of the titles used in her cult; in fact, she is not even always called
Mary. Twelve times she is called Mariám, which when applied to the
sister of Moses in the Greek Old Testament becomes Miriam. She is
called Maria seven times. The meaning of the name is elusive: doctors of
the Church have derived it from Hebrew words for "myrrh" and "light-
bearer"; Jerome glossed it as *stilla maris* (a drop of the ocean); using
allegorical exegesis, her name connects with Marah, where the waters
were bitter until Moses sweetened them, just as the incarnation in Mary's
womb dissolved the bitterness of the Fall (Exodus 15:23–5).[18] Less suitably, some etymologists have traced the name Mary to words for "stub-
born" and even "corpulent." It is an extremely common name in the
New Testament, where it is used of so many women it is often difficult to
tell which Mary is which (see Chapter 15 and Appendix B). But both its
lack of significance and its frequency strongly suggest that it really was
the name of the historical mother of Jesus. That at least seems certain.

Otherwise the material is scanty. After the account of Christ's birth,
Matthew mentions the mother of Jesus only one more time. Mark de-
scribes the same scene, slightly differently—and it is the only time the
Virgin appears at all in his Gospel.

Mark tells us that after Jesus' preaching had attracted multitudes, his
"friends" decide he has lost his mind, and want to prevent him from
teaching (Mark 3:21). They suggest his charisma is the work of the
Devil, and he naturally rejects them in anger. Then the crowd around him
informs him that his "mother and brethren" are "standing without, sent
unto him, calling him" (Mark 3:31). The sequence of events implies
strongly that Jesus' "friends" have marshalled his mother and relatives
to help their efforts to stop his ministry. For Jesus retorts: " 'Who is my
mother, or my brethren?' And he looked round about on them which sat
about him, and said 'Behold my mother and my brethren! For whosoever
shall do the will of God, the same is my brother, and my sister, and my
mother' " (Mark 3:34–5). Thus Jesus rebuffs his earthly family to embrace the larger family of his spiritual fellowship. His relatives' interven-

tion is in vain, for Mark starts his next chapter: "And he began again to teach." Mary his mother never appears again.

In Matthew and Luke, where the visit of Jesus' "mother and brethren" is also recounted, the conflict between family and child is considerably softened, for whereas in Mark, Mary and Jesus' brothers appear to hang back because they want to draw him away from his audience, in Luke they "could not come at him for the press" (Luke 8:19).

In Luke's Gospel, Jesus' retort is matched in a later episode, when a woman cries out from the crowd: "Blessed is the womb that bare thee, and the paps which thou hast sucked." Jesus answers, again sternly deflecting his followers' thoughts from the earthly family to the spiritual community; "Yea rather, blessed are they that hear the word of God, and keep it" (Luke 11:7–8). Mary is not necessarily excluded from Jesus' reply, but it certainly rings harshly. The Catholic Church has consistently overlooked the apparent hard-heartedness in Jesus' words and stubbornly fastened on this passage as an example of the honour given Mary in the Gospels. Pope Paul VI, in his 1974 statement on the cult of the Virgin, urges all Christians to follow the woman's example in praising Mary as the mother of God, the instrument of the Incarnation.[19] Jesus' reply does not contradict or deny the woman's accolade, but rephrases it in a loftier and more Christian way in order to emphasize the spiritual motherhood of the Church, which is prefigured by his own mother, the Virgin.

In the Fourth Gospel (John), the cooperation and loyalty of the Virgin to her son are marked, and her connection with the Church adumbrated, although Jesus' behaviour towards her remains at a psychological level as troublesome as in the three Synoptic Gospels (Matthew, Mark, Luke). The Gospel According to St. John was written within the first century, but after the other three, and it differs so considerably from them that for a time even its inclusion in the canon was at risk. Its authorship is disputed by scholars, but the Catholic Church attributes this Gospel and the Apocalypse (Revelation) to the apostle John, whom it identifies with the beloved disciple who laid his head in Christ's bosom at the Last Supper (John 13:23).

The Fourth Gospel never mentions the mother of Jesus by name, and does not repeat any of the incidents concerning her in the three Synoptic Gospels. It opens with the numinous description of the coming of the Word, and proclaims his Incarnation: "And the Word was made flesh, and dwelt among us" (John 1:14). John also proclaims the birth of each child of God through faith: "Not of blood, nor of the will of the flesh, nor of the will of man, but of God" (John 1:13), and it is possible that he is suggesting that the Christian's birth through the spirit follows the model of Christ's virginal conception. (The new Jerusalem Bible has even adopted a variant reading of this verse, which gives a clear statement of the virgin birth by altering the verb from the traditional plural to the singular. This translation is not upheld by manuscript evidence but by many references of the Fathers, including Ambrose and Augustine, and it has gained support among many contemporary theologians, Catholic and Protestant. The Jerusalem Bible reads: "But to all who did accept him, he gave power to become children of God, to all who believe in the name of him *who was born not out of human stock or urge of the flesh or will of man but of God himself*" [John 1:12–13; italics added]. The interpretation smooths out some of the knottiness in John's powerfully gnomic text, but the controversy is by no means closed.)

The Virgin Mary is not, however, a central figure in John's opening proclamation, as she is in two later episodes in his Gospel, which are momentous in Mariology: the miracle of Cana and the vigil of Mary at the foot of the cross.

The miracle of Cana records one of the two conversations extant between Jesus and his mother:

Mother: They have no wine.
Jesus: Woman, what have I to do with thee? Mine hour is not yet come.
Mother [to the servants]: Whatsoever he saith unto you, do it (John 2:3–5).

Jesus then orders the servants to fill six pots with water, and to pour them before the governor of the feast, who marvels, for the water has been changed into wine. The sequence of thought skips like a dusty Gramophone needle. Mary, apparently rebuffed quite brutally by her son, understands that he will nevertheless perform a miracle. In Mariological teaching, her intervention illustrates her pity, compassion, and thoughtfulness; but, more importantly, its prompt effect—the inauguration of Christ's messianic mission by a spectacular miracle—radiantly reveals the efficiency of her intercession with Christ, while the actual prodigy itself, the transformation of Jewish purificatory water into wine, prefigures the passing of the Old Covenant before the New, with a miracle that symbolizes the central mystery of eucharistic wine. Thus the association of Mary with the Church, through whom the sacrament of the Eucharist is granted, deepens.

Nevertheless, the rudeness of Christ's reply could not simply be overlooked. Theologians of the Greek Church, like St. John Chrysostom (d.

407), interpreted it as a rebuke to Mary's motherly pride and impatience, which had prompted her to goad her son to working the wonders of which she knew he was capable. But the western Church never accepted the idea that Mary could be at fault in any way, and has tentatively glossed Christ's sharp words as a prophecy of the "hour" of the Church, when salvation will come through the sacraments and particularly the Eucharist, after he has accomplished his "hour" in the sacrifice of the Cross. But the episode is still discussed. The caveat of the eminent Johannine scholar A. Feuillet stands as the breakwater against scepticism:

His detached attitude and his apparent hardness regarding Mary, attested equally in the Fourth Gospel and the Synoptics, should not be interpreted according to the laws governing ordinary human psychology; they are . . . a sign of the absolute transcendence of Jesus.[20]

The defence seems at first glance slender, for the Gospels have been read as narrative and anecdote for so long; but the tissue of literary reminiscence and typological figures and incidents is often so dense as to weaken the argument for the Gospels' historical authority and to provide support for theologians' metaphysical interpretations.

In the Fourth Gospel, Mary encourages the first public act of Christ's ministry, and then she follows him to Capernaum (John 2:12). The impression that she always formed part of his entourage is not sustained, however, for Mary disappears from view throughout Christ's teaching life until the Crucifixion. Then John describes a scene that has proved seminal in Mariology. For as Jesus hangs dying he sees "his mother" and "the disciple standing by, whom he loved" and he says to his mother: "Mother behold thy son!" Then he turns to the beloved disciple and says to him: "Son behold thy mother!" Then, says the evangelist, "from that hour that disciple took her unto his own home," and adds, to underline the major import of his commitment, "After this, Jesus knowing that all things were now accomplished . . ." drank vinegar and hyssop, and said, " 'It is finished': and he bowed his head, and gave up the ghost" (John 19:26–30).

So the last undertaking of his mortal life is to entrust his mother to his beloved follower and him to her, in a scene of stark and enigmatic force. As at the wedding feast, Jesus calls his mother "Woman." Exegetes have been at pains to point out that "woman" is an honorific form of address, and also one that projects Mary beyond the restrictions of her temporal life onto an eternal plane, where she becomes universal motherhood itself, and a type of the mothering Church. John the disciple, into whose keeping she is given, stands for humanity, for all Christians adopted into the fold of Christ's Church.

At the simple historical level, the episode at the Crucifixion lends authority to the Fourth Gospel, for it implies that John cared for Mary as his own mother after the death and resurrection of Jesus and therefore heard about him from her lips; at a theological level, it provides the richest seam for contemporary Catholic ecclesiology, which affirms that the Virgin is the model and perfect type of the Church, and of every faithful soul within the Church, for in her silent vigil at the Cross, Mary consents to the Atonement, as she had to the Incarnation, adapting her will perfectly to harmonize with the divine plan. As the constitution of the Second Vatican Council declared:

She . . . united with Him in suffering as He died on the cross. In an utterly singular way she cooperated by her obedience, faith, hope and burn-ing charity in the Saviour's work of restoring supernatural life to souls. For this reason she is a mother to us in the order of grace.[21]

Mary's association with the Church is deepened by Luke's fleet-ing mention that "Mary, the mother of Jesus" was present in the "upper room" at Jerusalem where the apostles and "women" and "brethren" of Jesus prayed together after he had ascended into heaven (Acts 1:14). Her presence at the Ascension was assumed from this passage, and although she is not mentioned again, the nar-rative flows on without explicit change of locale or interruption in time, so that the descent of the Holy Spirit on the day of Pentecost described in the next chapter of the Acts has always been painted in this same upper room. Often Mary sits among the apostles and receives the cloven tongues of fire upon her head. In iconography of medieval Chris-tendom and later, she often holds the centre stage, both at the Ascension and at the gift of tongues; a towering figure, she becomes the very embodiment of *Mater Ecclesia,* brimming over with the grace and power of the Spirit, and before whom the apostles sometimes kneel in awe (figure 14).

The Virgin's presence among the apostles and other followers of Jesus after the Ascension, even if it remains ambiguous whether she received the Holy Ghost and the gift of tongues herself, mitigates the Markan impression that she resisted Christ's mission. But the sum total of the Virgin's appearances in the New Testament is startlingly small plunder on which to build the great riches of Mariology. Of the four declared dogmas about the Virgin Mary—her divine motherhood, her virginity, her immaculate conception, and her assumption into heaven—only the first can be unequivocally traced to Scripture, where Mary of Nazareth is undoubtedly the mother of Jesus. The Immaculate Conception—which spares the Virgin all taint of original sin—and the Assumption do not come into the Gospels, since neither Mary's birth nor death are described; as for her virginity, the evangelists, far from asserting it, raise a number of doubts.

Matthew is the only evangelist to make a clear statement about the virgin birth: he says unequivocally that Jesus was conceived by the power of the Holy Ghost, *before* Mary and Joseph "came together." He reiterates this assertion in the words of the angel to Joseph, "that which is conceived in her is of the Holy Ghost" (Matthew 7:20). But characteristically, Matthew reinforces his statements with Isaiah's prophecy; and his transparent use of Old Testament messianic messages to give structure and form to his story becomes more problematical when the Isaiah prophecy itself comes under scrutiny. These are the only words from the Old Testament applied to Mary in the New: "Behold a virgin shall be with child, and shall bring forth a son, and they shall call his name Emmanuel, which being interpreted is, God with us" (Isaiah 7:14; Matthew 1:23). They form the lynch pin of the Christian argument for the virgin birth of Christ, which almost all Christians hold, and the virginity of his mother Mary, which Catholics and some reformed Churches believe to have continued all her life. As has been pointed out many times before, Matthew was using the Greek Septuagint translation of the Bible, where the Hebrew word *'almah* had been translated as *parthenos* in Greek. The two words are not synonymous, for *'almah* means a young girl of marriageable age, with a primary connotation of eligibility. It is applied, for instance, to Rebecca before her marriage to Isaac (Genesis 24:43) and even to the girls in the harem of the beloved in the Song of Songs (Song of Solomon 7:3; 6:8).

Naturally, the venerable elders at work in Alexandria around 300 B.C. on the Greek version of the Hebrew Bible would expect a young, eligible woman to be a virgin; but *parthenos* carries a sense of intact virginity, of physical maidenhead far more strongly than *'almah*, which could have been translated by the Greek *neanis* (girl). Furthermore, Matthew has given the prophecy a value it does not possess. At a time of great danger, the prophet Isaiah promises God will give the anxious King Ahaz a sign of his continuing, beneficent presence, symbolized by a child who will bear his name. The accent of the prophecy falls on the symbol of the child, and not at all on the virginity of the mother. As a scholar has written:

The sign of Emmanuel would seem to have had a Messianic significance for the prophet, and to have referred to a future Davidic king. . . . But there is no suggestion of a miraculous birth from a virgin.[22]

It would seem that Matthew was simply using another passage of the Bible to prove that Jesus was the promised saviour. Elsewhere, Matthew is quite unconcerned with providing further evidence or support for the virgin birth: his Gospel opens with Jesus' family tree traced through Joseph: "And Jacob begat Joseph the husband of Mary, of whom was born Jesus . . ." (Matthew 1:16).[23] He sees no inconsistency therefore in showing Jesus' Davidic descent in the paternal line, although he explicitly denies that Joseph was Jesus' biological father. For Matthew the virgin birth was a symbol that gave Jesus legitimacy as a god, and was not inconsistent with his legitimacy as a social being with an official, socially recognized father.[24]

Both Matthew and Luke trace Jesus' descent from David through Joseph, although Luke does add that Joseph was the father of Jesus "by repute." The genealogies of the two evangelists are otherwise inconsistent. Even Joseph's own father is different (Heli in Luke; Jacob in Matthew). The pressure to prove Jesus' Davidic descent and consequent authenticity as the Messiah outweighed the urgency of arguments for the virgin birth at the time Matthew and Luke wrote and for the audience they addressed. Paul too, in his Epistle to the Romans, the earliest writing in the New Testament, expresses the same scale of values, when he asserts that Christ is the son of God on a metaphysical plane, through his resurrection from the dead, but "made of the seed of David according to the flesh" (Romans 1:3–4). Nor does Paul's choice of words in Galatians stand as a bulwark to the doctrine of the virgin birth, since Jesus is "born of a woman" not "of a virgin" (Galatians 4:4).

The Fathers of the Church expeditiously developed a solution to the problem of the patrilineal descent of Jesus. Mary, they declared, was Joseph's cousin, herself of the house of David. Ephrem of Syria (d. 373) in the fourth century, a powerful poet and one of Mary's most eloquent worshippers, explained: "The series of kings is written according to the names of men, instead of women, Joseph, the son of David, betroths the daughter of David, because the child cannot be enrolled in the name of its mother."[25] In other words, in a patriarchal society, even the Messiah can only be legitimate if his mother is properly married.

Luke is unclear about Mary's virginity at the time of the Annunciation, and the virgin birth, which seemed to Matthew the essential precondition of Christ's divinity, is ambiguously treated in the Lucan infancy
Gospel. The evangelist calls Mary a virgin twice at the Annunciation. He
uses the same word, however, to describe Mary's relationship with Joseph
at the time of the Annunciation ("a virgin *espoused* to a man"
[Luke 1:27]) and at the time of the Nativity ("Mary his *espoused* wife"
[Luke 2:5]), which implies that their union was the same on both occasions. Yet Mary says to Gabriel when she is told she is to bear a son, that
she does not "know" a man, which indicates her single, virginal state.

The only way to explain this discrepancy and reconcile it to the doctrine of the virgin birth is sociological, and the tentative answer clears up
ambiguity in Matthew's Gospel as well. The Jews married after a year-
long betrothal period, during which the woman was the man's legal wife
according to a social contract that could not be abrogated except by
divorce or death. The actual union began only after the nuptial rites had
been performed. Both Matthew and Luke, writing from Jewish backgrounds, would therefore take for granted an interval of time during
which a marriage was contracted but not consummated.[26] It could be
that in Matthew, Joseph's doubt and his eventual acceptance of Mary as
his wife fall at the beginning and end of this betrothal period, as do the
Annunciation and the Nativity in Luke. Mary would then be chaste, but
married, in the old-fashioned English sense of "spoken for."

Much more damaging to belief in the virgin birth is Luke's account
of the finding of Jesus in the temple. There are numerous interpretations
of Jesus' brusque rejoinder when his mother, in natural anxiety, reproaches him for causing her and his father worry, and the most convinc-
ing dismisses the story as a literal narrative to elucidate the loftier, typological meaning. Jesus' rejection of his parents then comes to symbolize
his first theophany, when he reveals to Mary and Joseph that he is indeed
divine and has a Father in heaven whose business he must fulfil. By his
abrupt and antithetical rejoinder, Jesus is raising his parents' consciousness and reminding them sharply of his heavenly mission. The "three
days" Joseph and Mary spend searching for him may be intended as a
presage of the three days in the tomb before his triumphant return.[27]

But for Catholics and especially for devotees of Mary, the passage,
however symbolic, remains disturbing. First, Luke refers to Joseph and
Mary as Jesus' parents (Luke 2:41). Above all, during one of the exchanges between mother and son in the Bible, Mary herself refers to
Joseph as Jesus' father: "Behold thy father and I have sought thee sorrowing" (Luke 2:48). And when Jesus counters that he must be about

his Father's business, neither she nor Joseph understands what he means (Luke 2:50). Yet it is obviously psychologically improbable that Mary and Joseph would have forgotten the events that surrounded Christ's conception and birth.

It can be argued that this does not represent a lapse on Luke's part, for he was not setting out a coherent biography. By using Old Testament allusions, his account of Jesus' origins had established that he had entered the world as the messianic hero should.[28] The technical virginity of his mother was never a matter of primary concern to the evangelist, as it was to his later readers.

The virginity of Mary after the birth of Christ is even more difficult to defend from the Gospel texts. Matthew's very endorsements of her virginity at the conception and during the pregnancy jeopardize her virginity afterwards. "Before they came together, she was found with child . . ." (Matthew 1:18) could imply that they did "come together" afterwards. "Then Joseph . . . took unto him his wife: and knew her not till she had brought forth her first born son . . ." (Matthew 1:24–5) also points to a subsequently consummated marriage. To combat these inferences, Christian exegetes, intent on the importance of the absolute physical integrity of the Virgin's body, combed the Bible for passages where clauses introduced by "before" or "till" do not describe an event that later took place. The Fathers managed to sift some examples, but the strain is evident: "And he [Noah] sent forth a raven, which went forth to and fro, until the waters were dried up from off the earth" (Genesis 8:7) was one, because the flood did not recede for the raven, but only afterwards, for the dove. Another example was: "Be not ye therefore like unto them: for your Father knoweth what things ye have need of before ye ask him" (Matthew 6:8), because obviously God knows anyway, without being asked.[29]

Luke's mind does not focus on the issue of Mary's virginity after Christ's birth any more than Matthew's. Both evangelists express themselves in ways that have taken centuries of explanation on the part of the Virgin Mary's devotees. For when Mary goes to the temple after the required days for her purification have elapsed, she presents Jesus because "it is written in the law of the Lord, Every male that openeth the womb shall be called holy to the Lord" (Luke 2:23). Luke characteristically underlines Jesus' obedience to the Old Law, but the verse sends shivers through Catholics, who hold (not as an article of faith, but as a cherished and ancient belief) that Mary was *virgo intacta post partum,* that by a special privilege of God she, who was spared sex, was preserved also through childbirth in her full bodily integrity. The only escape from Luke's passing remark is to maintain he was not describing Mary, but the law which she, as a dutiful member of the Old Covenant, obeyed.

The appearance of Jesus' brethren and sisters with his mother in all three Synoptics (Luke 19:21; Mark 3:31; Matthew 12:46) and the importance of "James, the Lord's brother," in the early Church in Jerusalem, where St. Paul met him (Galatians 1:19), also embarrasses the defence of Mary's lifelong virginity. Origen, Gregory of Nyssa (d. 394), and other leading thinkers of the Greek Church claimed that these "brethren" were Joseph's children by a first marriage. Thus Joseph, the ageless dreamer and husband of Matthew's Gospel, metamorphoses into the hoary-headed old widower leaning on a staff so familiar from Christian paintings. Hilary (d. 368) and Ambrose (d. 397), in the Latin Church, accepted this Greek solution, but St. Jerome (d. 420) sprang to Joseph's defence. How could that "just man," he cried, be so casually struck from the honourable roll of virgins? He declared, "He who was worthy to be called the father of the Lord, remained a virgin." And the "brethren" were "brethren in point of kinship," but "not by nature"— that is, either cousins or adopted.[30] The Jews, it was pointed out, had a limited vocabulary for relationships—brothers, cousins, friends were all brethren—and the vagueness of the Hebrew designations had influenced Mark and Luke, who in the Greek therefore used a word—*adelphoi*— with a stricter meaning of sibling. St. Jerome prevailed, and the Latin Church has honoured Joseph as a virgin since his time.

In the early middle ages *The Golden Legend,* one of the earliest European bestsellers, found marvellously devious loopholes to champion Mary's virginity. Its author, Jacobus de Varagine (d. 1298), declared that James was only called the Lord's "brother" because he looked exactly like him. Jacobus claims that this extraordinary resemblance was the reason for Judas' identifying kiss in the garden (otherwise unnecessary, as Jesus had been preaching openly in Jerusalem). In order to avoid confusion between Jesus and his twin James, Judas kissed his master.[31]

*The Golden Legend* displayed even greater ingenuity about the other mentions of brethren. It describes how St. Anne, the mother of the Virgin Mary, was married twice before she married Joachim, Mary's father, and by each of her former husbands had a daughter called Mary. These other Marys, the sisters of the Virgin, in turn had children, who were Jesus' "brethren."[32] Popular northern paintings of the fifteenth century like Quintin Massys' *The Kinship of the Holy Family* portray these numerous relations assembled together.

It did not matter to the medieval man who read *The Golden Legend* that this triad of Marys, or ennead of kinfolk, was a little far-fetched, any more than all the questions raised by the Gospels regarding Mary have ever caused Catholics much lasting anxiety. The few fragments about her have yielded a rich, luxuriant, and enduring Mariology that tradition has sometimes exuberantly watered and at other times cautiously pruned; but tradition has always affected how the Gospels were read.

The Gospel problems regarding her title to the very name Virgin Mary were and still are as straw before the belief in virgin birth. And my enumeration of the lack of scriptural evidence is not intended to pour an outdated, Protestant pulpit-type scorn on it, but only to show that from the earliest times, the New Testament itself was out of joint with the embattled desires and ideas of Christians for whom the virgin birth was a necessary precondition of Christ's divinity. This stemmed from a mythological tradition that will be examined in Chapter 3. It predated the Gospels and has proved, and still proves, stronger than Scripture itself. Matthew, writing in about A.D. 80, may have already been influenced by it (this point is heatedly debated and difficult to prove either way), but the other evangelists and writers of the New Testament were not affected by it, because they were more profoundly concerned with the reality of the Resurrection and Christ's heavenly kingdom.

This central preoccupation with the *kerygma,* or doctrine of the resurrection, yielded by the fifth century to another set of ideas, which raised the Virgin Mary to a position of critical importance. The Resurrection was still the keystone of the Christian salvation, but in its foundations were embedded two complementary, momentous assumptions: the virgin birth as the essential sign of godhead and virginity itself as the essential sign of goodness. And in the early Church, there circulated many documents—some learned, some popular—that propounded and upheld this view.

## Chapter Two

# MARY
# IN THE APOCRYPHA

*Myth is the history of its authors, not of its subjects;
it records the lives not of superhuman heroes, but of
poetic nations.*[1]

—E. B. TYLOR

ON THE WALLS of the Arena chapel in Padua, Joachim and Anna, the parents of the Virgin, embrace before the Golden Gate of Jerusalem. Anna clasps her husband's head between her hands; he returns her movement, holding her by her shoulders. Their gesture is full of reverence and gravity, but an undeniable sweetness propels them towards each other and gives their massive, scarcely touching bodies that energy of human emotion which Giotto uniquely infused into his characters.

In Giotto's frescoes, this moment marks the conception of the Virgin Mary by Anna, and the event is an integral part of the grand schema of redemption that covers the chapel walls and climaxes with the last reckoning on the day of judgement above the high altar. By 1305, when the Arena chapel was consecrated and its donor Scrovegni felt that its beauty expiated in part his earthly sins, the miracles that attended the birth of Mary and set her apart as holy above all creatures ranked with the Resurrection as a Christian truth. The *Gospel According to the Pseudo-Matthew,* as Giotto's chief source is known, had as its ultimate inspiration the earlier *Book of James.*[2] Both works have always been excluded from the canonical writings of the New Testament, and are thus considered apocryphal, "secret" or "hidden."

The *Book of James,* "the Lord's Brother," is an eastern tale that deeply influenced the cult of the Virgin in the west. For as Christianity itself was originally an Oriental religion, so the worship of the mother of God sprang up and was fostered in the rites and documents of the eastern peoples of Asia Minor, Egypt, and Syria.

In the *Book of James,* Joachim, the father of Mary, is portrayed as a man of exceptional wealth and charity, who every year divides his goods into three parts: one for himself, one for the poor, and a third for the temple. But his wife, Anna, is barren, and when he goes to the temple to make his customary offering, the High Priest chastises him for his childlessness, a stigma of the Lord's displeasure. His offerings rejected, Joachim flees in misery to the desert to do penance for forty days.

Anna, weeping at home for the loss of her husband and her barrenness, puts on her bridal dress and wanders out into the garden. There the sight of a nest full of baby sparrows inspires a yet more bitter threnody. But, as she weeps, an angel appears to her and promises her a child. In the desert, an angel appears also to Joachim, who rushes joyfully back to town and, at the gate of Jerusalem, meets his wife, who "ran and hung upon his neck" (*Book of James* 4:4). It is this moment that Giotto, and many artists before and after him, painted (colour plate I, figure 1).

In gratitude to God, Anna promises to dedicate the child to the temple. Mary is born, and her infancy is attended by prodigies. At six months she walks seven steps (figure 5); at a year, Joachim holds a birthday party with "the priests and the scribes and the assembly of the elders and the whole people of Israel" (*Book of James* 6:2). When she is three years old, her parents fulfil their promise and take her to the temple. The priest sits her down on an altar step, but she is inspired: "And she danced with her feet, and all the house of Israel loved her" (*Book of James* 7:2). Angels bring her heavenly food. But when she reaches puberty, the high priest Zacharias fears "lest she will pollute the sanctuary of the Lord," and after being instructed by God, he assembles in the temple all the widowers of Israel, telling each man to carry a rod in his hand, for God will give a sign of his choice of a husband for Mary. (In the later Latin version, the *Gospel According to the Pseudo-Matthew,* Mary refuses to be married, protesting she has vowed to be a virgin.[3])

Joseph hurries up with the other suitors, and a dove flies from his rod and perches on his head. In some accounts, his staff, left overnight in the temple, bursts into flower (colour plate I, figure 1).[4] The exquisitely illuminated Books of Hours of the Virgin, which became the most coveted treasures of the fifteenth-century nobility of Europe, often show the disappointed widowers dashing their rods against their knees in fury that they have not won Mary's hand. But in the *Book of James,* Joseph himself remonstrates against the honour, pleading his age and his family: "I have sons, I am an old man, but she is a girl: lest I become a laughing stock to the children of Israel" (*Book of James* 9:2). In the English medieval miracle plays, this scene becomes the occasion sometimes for bawdiness, sometimes for poignancy:

> Her warden and her keeper will I ever be . . .
> In bed we shall never meet
> For I wis, maiden sweet
> An old man cannot rage.[5]

The high priest orders Joseph to accept his destiny, which he does, leaving Mary at home with his family while he goes to fulfil a building contract.

The priests of the temple recall Mary to weave the sacred veil of the tabernacle, for she is still "undefiled before God" (*Book of James* 10:1). Seven virgins become her handmaids, and she draws by lot the most august colours to spin and weave: the purple and scarlet. She returns home to start work on the veil (colour plate I, figure 1).

The *Book of James* then tells the story of the Annunciation to Mary in substantially the same words as Luke, although Mary sees the angel twice, once as she is drawing water, and again at home as she is spinning. She learns of Elisabeth's pregnancy and visits her. During her sixth month, Joseph returns and reproaches himself bitterly that his young charge is now having a child; a consecrated virgin of the temple is pregnant because he who was entrusted with her did not keep her safe. Joseph calls Mary to account, and she protests her innocence: "As the Lord my God liveth, I know not whence it come unto me" (13:1). As in Matthew, Joseph still thinks of repudiating her, but he is then reassured of her honesty in a dream. A priest visits them and sees that Mary is pregnant, and accuses Joseph of defiling her. Mary and Joseph are arraigned but again she pleads: "I am pure before him [God] and know not a man" (15:3). They are made to submit publicly to the biblical ordeal of the Book of Numbers (5:26) and drink the bitter waters of conviction, which will kill them if they are lying. But, amid great rejoicing, they emerge unharmed.

When the census is announced, Joseph prepares to take Mary and his sons to Bethlehem, but worries whether he should register her as his wife or daughter: "She is but a child." On the journey, Mary is saddened by a vision of "two peoples," one weeping, the other exulting: allegories of the Jews, who will reject Christ, and the Gentiles, who will accept him. Before they reach Bethlehem, Mary asks to be helped down from the donkey she is riding because she feels labour coming on. They find a cave and Joseph leaves her with his sons to find a midwife. He meets a woman on the road, tells her about Mary—"she has come to be my wife and has not become my wife, but is pregnant by the Holy Spirit"—and takes her to the cave. A cloud of light overshadows the cave "until the young child appeared: and it went and took the breast of its mother Mary" (19:2) (figure 3). The midwife is astounded and proclaims the miracle. But when she meets another woman, Salome, outside the cave, she finds her sceptical, and wanting proof. Salome asks Mary to show herself, and then examines her. Immediately Salome howls in pain, for her blasphemous hand is withered by fire. She begs forgiveness for her unbelief and says that if her hand is restored she will heal in Jesus' name. An angel tells her to pick up the baby, and when she does, she is made whole again (colour plate II, figure 2).

In the later Latin story, Mary finds a stable, and lays Jesus in a manger, where, in fulfilment of Isaiah's prophecy, the ox and ass worship him. As in Matthew and Luke, the wise men and the shepherds come to adore the child, and Joseph is warned about the massacre of the innocents and told to flee into Egypt.

Some versions of the *Book of James* interpolate an episode about John the Baptist before the flight into Egypt, in order to explain the problems raised in Matthew: how did John, a baby at the time, escape Herod's slaughter? In these apocrypha, Elisabeth runs away and a mountain miraculously opens to give her shelter. But Herod's soldiers discover Zacharias, John's father, in the temple, and when he refuses to talk, they butcher him by the altar, as his earlier namesake in the Bible.[6] Christ mentions this Zacharias who was also killed, in his lament on Jerusalem (2 Chronicles 24:20–1; Matthew 23:35; Luke 11:50–1). The author of the *Book of James* appears to have read the passage erroneously as a prophecy of the death of John the Baptist's father.

The story of the flight into Egypt is like a Grimm fairytale, though not as magical or sinister; dragons and lions and leopards adore the child Jesus, fulfilling Isaiah's prophecy; the two thieves who will hang beside Christ at the Crucifixion rob the holy family, but one of them repents and Jesus promises him salvation. When they are thirsty, a spring gushes forth at their feet; when they are hungry, a palm tree bends its lofty branches to offer them its fruit (figure 4). In Egypt, the idols of the gods of Hermopolis fall off their pedestals and are shattered, again in fulfilment of a prophecy of Isaiah (Isaiah 19:1), and the governor is converted.

Back in Nazareth, the story becomes alarming, and its popularity in Christian belief and art proportionately declines. The child Jesus performs wonder after wonder: when the son of a scribe destroys a series of pools and dikes Jesus is building in the mud, Jesus strikes him down dead; when another boy hits Jesus, he also is struck down. "All his words become facts," writes the author. Jesus angrily rejects Joseph, saying he is not his father and has no authority over him. At school he knows everything and leaves his teachers dumbfounded. He works more miracles: he raises a boy from the dead, picks up water he has spilled, and stretches the planks Joseph has sawn too short.[7] (In a later version it is the apprentice who saws them—to save Joseph's face.) The earliest source of these tales—the *Gospel According to Thomas*—then closes with the story of Jesus among the doctors, as it appears in Luke. The document is Gnostic in origin, for it proclaims Jesus' godhead at the expense of his full humanity and stresses arcane knowledge, not moral goodness. But, in this context, Jesus' rejection of his parents in the temple of Jerusalem becomes intelligible, along completely heterodox lines.

The walls and retables, the manuscripts and liturgical objects, the embroidery on medieval vestments, the misericords of choir stalls and even the bosses in chapel vaults are incomprehensible without a knowledge of these myths woven around the central protagonists of the central Christian mystery of God's Incarnation. In order to show that the Word was made flesh, early Christians fleshed out the bare paragraphs of the canonical Gospels. But the process was not a slow evolution and accretion; for some scholars date the *Book of James* at the end of the first century—just after the last of the writings in the New Testament. Clement of Alexandria (d. 215), and the greatest of early Christian exegetes, Origen, both cite the *Book of James* in support of the virgin birth. It was therefore in circulation among the learned and accepted by the second century, if not before. But in spite of its antiquity, it was never a serious contender for inclusion in the canon, and it was condemned in the Gelasian decree. The decree, long attributed to the vigorous Pope Gelasius I (492–6), has now been ascribed to an independent cleric of a century later, in southern Gaul or northern Italy, who did not have the authority of a pope to proscribe books.

The condemnation nevertheless sowed confusion all over western Christendom. The east received the *Book of James* as authentic (it is extant in Greek, Ethiopic, and the oldest manuscript is in Syriac) but, surprisingly, it was not translated into Latin until the sixteenth century. In the west the *Book of James* and the *Gospel According to Thomas* were combined to form two apocryphal books: the *Gospel According to the Pseudo-Matthew* and the *Story of the Birth of Mary*. They were both written in Latin, probably as early as the eighth or ninth century, with prefaces purporting to be by St. Jerome. This stratagem—invoking the name of the great biblical scholar and translator of the inspired Latin Bible, the Vulgate—only added to the confusion. For in these spurious prefaces, "Jerome" admits the contents of the books are dubious, but backtracks to say he is publishing them to "unmask the deceit of heresy." In the preface to the *Story of the Birth of Mary* (now attributed to the Carolingian scholar Paschasius Radbertus in the ninth century), "Jerome" excuses the tales on the grounds that great miracles must indeed have preceded Mary's birth.[8]

When the gifted nun Hroswitha of Gandersheim, playwright and poet (d. before 1002), composed the first Latin verse narrative of Joachim and Anna and the birth of Mary, she noted in her preface: "When I started, timidly enough, on the work of composition, I did not know that the authenticity of my material had been questioned." But she was not deflected by her discovery; she continued to draw on the condemned apocrypha, and finished her skilled poem "Maria."[9] For she was a learned and widely read woman, and she knew from the Fathers of the Church whom she had studied that the material in the *Pseudo-Matthew* had the stamp of orthodoxy and the weight of tradition to support it. Nor was Hroswitha disobedient to the tenets of her Church when she believed the stories of Mary's and Jesus' births.

Until the Reformation, the embrace of Joachim and Anna and all its miraculous consequences scarcely provoked a query. One of the most widely disseminated books after the invention of printing, Jacobus de Varagine's *Golden Legend,* included the cycle in its entirety; and although the Council of Trent in the sixteenth century forbade, for the first time, the depiction of such apocryphal events as Joachim and Anna's embrace in Christian art, the Catholic imagination is steeped too deeply in the stories ever to wash out their high colouring.

St. Anne is a beloved saint, a real person who really mothered Mary. In the ruins of S. Maria Antiqua in Rome, the ancient church in the Forum, St. Anne carries Mary in her arms (it is the earliest devotional image [*c.* 649] of Mary as a baby) and although time has disfigured the baby, one earlobe can still be seen, with a jewel hanging from it in the Oriental fashion. St. Anne has become a historical woman with a historical life, and an official cult. As recently as 1954, Pope Pius XII recommended pilgrimage to her famous shrine in Brittany. Her relics were once scattered throughout Europe: her right hand in Vienna, her head in Cologne, and a fragment of her wrist, with the flesh still miraculously adhering, in the church of St. Anne at Beaupré. In Jerusalem, visitors attend mass in the church of St. Anne, described in the guidebooks as "the birthplace of the Blessed Virgin." Joachim, though less popular, has inspired his own cult, which still endures; and the feastday of Mary's parents is kept in the new calendar on July 26, St. Anne's old feast. (Joachim's was held separately on August 16.)

Yet the most casual reading of the *Book of James* reveals translucently its mosaic-like structure and derivativeness. The author drew heavily on the Pentateuch, but he blends Jewish material with Greco-Roman customs in a very unrabbinical manner, which indicates to some scholars that he was a Greek Jew of the diaspora. Abraham and Sarah, cursed with barrenness, provide the model for Joachim and Anna, as they did for Zacharias and Elisabeth in Luke. Picking up the evangelist's associations with Hannah, the mother of Samuel, the author of the *Book of James* names Mary's mother after her, puts Hannah's lament for her childlessness on Anna's lips, and after her prayer has been heard, makes her vow her child to the temple just as Hannah vowed Samuel (1 Samuel: 11). The dove that lights on Joseph recalls the story of Noah and God's indication that his vengeance was at an end. When Joseph's staff blossoms, as it does in some versions, the analogy with the Old Testament is closer, for Aaron's rod flowered with an almond blossom when it was left overnight in the tabernacle (Numbers 17:1–8). The image of Mary as the holy Ark, suggested in Luke, is wilfully underlined in the *Book of James.* The author uses the word "overshadow" for God's presence in a cloud of light over the cave (Exodus 42:34) and then describes how the midwife Salome is struck down for her presumption in touching Mary, just as Uzzah "put forth his hand to the Ark of God . . . and the anger of the Lord was kindled against Uzzah; and God smote him there for his error . . . " Uzzah dies for his trespass (2 Samuel 6:7–8).

The description of the scenes in the temple relies completely on Exodus' concatenation of ritual requirements as ordered by Moses for Aaron and the priests. The author describes the costume of the high priest and the gleaming plate on his forehead, into which Joachim gazes to see his sins (Exodus 39:30). Mary weaves a veil of purple and scarlet for the tabernacle just as Moses did, "with cherubims made he it of cunning work" (Exodus 36:35). The ordeal derives from the Book of Numbers, where it is prescribed as the test of a wife by a jealous husband. The author of the *Book of James,* taking characteristic license with

Jewish law, extends the test to include the husband Joseph as well. He then adapts the trial by ordeal of Numbers to fit the context of Mary's consecrated virginity rather than her infidelity (the priests try her and Joseph because they might have sinned *together*). Throughout, he is influenced by this concern with Mary's virginity; and he directs all his material to prove the virgin birth, a theme quite alien to Judaism.

Women were not even allowed in the inner court of the temple at Jerusalem, but only into the outer. The idea that a young girl, or a woman, could be dedicated to God's service and live in contact with the Holy of Holies in the care of the high priest would have been utterly abhorrent and sacrilegious to the Jews. Also, virginity itself was an unknown and unholy course. The author of the *Book of James* does show himself sensitive, however, to some Jewish ideas, for he echoes a Jewish taboo when he describes the high priest's fears that Mary at puberty will defile the sanctuary.

The custom of virgin priestesses was not Jewish, but pagan, being widespread throughout Syria, where the earliest manuscript of the *Book of James* originates. And there were examples of temple hierodules, dedicated to serve the deity as his brides throughout the empire. In the temple of Zeus Ammon at Thebes, according to Strabo and confirmed by Juvenal at the time the *Book of James* was probably being composed, young girls of perfect beauty and good family served the god until the onset of puberty, and were then married off, after a period of mourning their first, divine bridegroom.[10] The author of the *Book of James* could have attended services in the temple of Diana at Ephesus, where mysteries were performed by hierodules whom Plutarch likened to the vestals of Rome; or he could have known of the temples at Corinth and on Mount Eryx in Sicily, where Aphrodite was similarly served, though lifelong chastity was not required; he would certainly have heard of the powerful vestals themselves, whose virginity was jealously guarded. In pagan worship the virginity of the priestesses was, however, a ritual requirement, not an ascetic statement about morality and the corruption of the flesh.

Christian commentators were often troubled by the widespread belief in Mary's vow of virginity, which originates in the apocrypha. For they knew, if only from the laments of the women of the Bible, how terrible a stigma barrenness and indeed spinsterhood was for a Jewish woman, and they therefore felt, with untypical historical awareness, that it was very unlikely that a young Jewish girl like Mary would make such a vow. Also Mary's reply—"How shall this be, since I know not a man?"—taken by Augustine as evidence of her vowed commitment to a life of virginity, hardly supports such a weighty meaning. But Mary's childhood under-taking remained a widespread Catholic belief, which inspired hymns and poems and much moral exhortation, until the Second Vatican Council in its constitution of 1964 permitted Catholics an open mind on the subject.

The *Book of James* was responsible for other assertions of Mary's virginity, for it builds on the Gospels in order to buttress belief in the virgin birth: Joseph becomes a widower to explain away "the brethren of Jesus"; Mary, in some versions, has vowed to remain a virgin, which solves the problem of her marriage to Joseph in another way; Joseph is away when she becomes pregnant; above all, the expert witnesses are produced, with a flourish, from the defending counsel—the midwife who believes, and the midwife who doubts and is then convinced. Salome provides the material, literal proof of the doctrine that Jesus was born from a *virgo intacta.*

It was this aspect of the *Book of James* that made it acceptable to the Fathers. Clement of Alexandria quoted it as authority: "For after she had brought forth, some say she was attended by a midwife, and was found to be a virgin."[11] Origen drew on it for his theory that Joseph had been married before, in order to solve the brethren question. Epiphanius (d. 403), Eusebius (d. 340), Athanasius (d. 373), and John Chrysostom (d. 407), fervent upholders one and all of the virtue of sexual asceticism, believed it genuine testimony. The real St. Jerome, who shuddered in horror from the *deliramenta apocryphorum,* refused to accept that a mid-wife was present at the birth, not because he doubted her witness, but because he maintained that Christ's virgin birth was so serene and pain-less that a midwife would have been superfluous and Mary would never have sent Joseph to fetch one.

The *Book of James,* and all the apocryphal books that derive from it, tilted the emphasis of the Gospels from the divinity of the adult Christ to the prodigy of his arrival on earth. The issues of the virgin birth and the miraculous virginity of Mary were taken up in other commentaries and other writings, but no other document was more crucial to the very idea of the Virgin Mary.

## Chapter Three

# VIRGIN BIRTH

*The threefold terror of love; a fallen flare*
*Through the hollow of an ear;*
*Wings beating about the room;*
*The terror of all terrors that I bore*
*The Heavens in my womb . . .*
*What is this flesh I purchased with my pains,*
*This fallen star my milk sustains,*
*This love that makes my heart's blood stop*
*Or strikes a sudden chill into my bones*
*And bids my hair stand up?*[1]

—W. B. Yeats: "The Mother of God"

I N THE PRE-CHRISTIAN Roman empire virgin birth was a shorthand symbol, commonly used to designate a man's divinity. It is impossible to establish for certain whether Matthew or Luke were influenced by the external tradition of virgin birth when they wrote their accounts of the Christian saviour's origins, but it is evident that the author of the *Book of James* was aware of it when he expanded on the theme. The Christian religion was unusual in using the idea to set an enduring seal of approval on asceticism, but its use of virgin birth as the key to the argument that Jesus was the son of God was classical in spirit, and dependent on long-lasting and erroneous ideas about human generation that were also inherited from classical philosophy.

In his *Metamorphoses,* Ovid wickedly tells the story of the conception of Bacchus, who was born of a mortal, Semele, after a visit of the god Jupiter. Juno is jealous and, disguised as Semele's nanny, she calls on the girl, and shakes her head and sighs at her story, saying: "I pray that it might be Jupiter! But the whole business disturbs me: many a man has made his way into an honest girl's bedroom by calling himself a god."[2] Juno is not the only one to entertain doubts about such claims: the earliest Christians had to leap to the Virgin's defence on account of similar slanders. Origen refuted a story current among Jews and pagans that Jesus was the son of a Roman centurion càlled Pantherus;[3] in Alexandria it was also alleged Mary had conceived incestuously with her brother.[4] These rumours enjoyed brief lives, and the doctrine of the virgin birth was attacked far more frequently because it was common in pagan belief than because it was unlikely in nature. Its resemblance to the metamorphoses of the gods of antiquity exposed a Christian nerve.

Christians, aware of the antique pantheon, are still worried by the parallel between Christ's story and the dozens of virgin births of classical mythology. The most sophisticated counterattack, developed first by Origen in his *Contra Celsum* and continued in modern times in the writings of Cardinal John Henry Newman (d. 1890) and the contemporary Jesuit Hugo Rahner, is that God prepared the world for the greatest mystery of all, the Incarnation of his son, with a sequence of beliefs and creeds and symbols that foreshadowed it and thus made its acceptance easier.[5] But this smooth argument, which so ingeniously draws the sting from the pagan aspects of Christian mythology, has not been universally used by the Christian Church.

It is just as possible to defend the Gospels and the early Fathers against accusations of pagan influence as to prosecute them, and an exact point of interchange and the extent of interpenetration is hard to establish. The historical fact remains that the virgin birth of heroes and sages was a widespread formula in the hellenistic world: Pythagoras, Plato, Alexander were all believed to be born of woman by the power of a holy spirit. It became the commonplace claim of a spiritual leader: Simon Magus, the prophet, with whom St. Peter successfully contended in the Forum in Rome, claimed his mother was a virgin.[6] (The church of S. Maria Nova preserves the slab with the giant footprints made by Simon when, after boasting he could fly, he crashed to the ground in front of Peter.)

The attitude of early Christian writers to their religion's cultural inheritance was very varied. Justin Martyr (d. *c.* 165) maintained that Jesus' birth differed from the birth, say, of Apollo or Bacchus because God did not woo and overcome the Virgin Mary, nor was he united with her in a voluptuous theogamy, as was Jove with Leto, or with Semele, or with any of the innumerable mortal beauties who caught the Olympian's eye. Justin scorned the parallel with Danae, who conceived the hero Perseus when Jupiter visited her in a shower of gold, as a travesty, a black mass, the work of the Devil mocking truth. Mary remained a virgin after the Annunciation, declared Justin in the *Dialogue with Trypho,* and therefore differed completely from the objects of Jupiter's escapades.[7] But when one looks at Correggio's languorous painting of Danae in the Borghese Museum in Rome, in which an angel lifts the sheet above her sleeping form so that the shower of gold descends to cover her, Justin's indignation seems justified: the maid, the angel, and the streaming light—Correggio's profane Annunciation.

Origen failed to make Justin's distinction betweeen parthenogenesis and divine impregnation. He interpreted the classical myths as presages of the virgin birth of Christ, and cited the legend that Plato was born to Perictione after Apollo appeared to Ariston, Plato's father, and told him not to consummate his marriage.[8] At the same time, however, Origen argued the possibility of parthenogenesis from natural phenomena, as understood in his day, and was forced into the strange position of likening the birth of his God to the generation of snakes from corpses, bees from oxen, wasps from horses, beetles from donkeys, or worms from almost anything,[9] as described by Pythagoras at the end of Ovid's *Metamorphoses.* In the same tradition, the popular *Physiologus,* or *Bestiary,* compares the Virgin to the vulture, a bird it says brings forth spontaneously.[10]

Lactantius (d. 320) went further than Origen, and actually compared the conception of Jesus to the fertilization of the twelve mares of Erichthonius by Boreas, the North Wind.[11] But other Christians rejected pagan parallels in anger. St. Epiphanius complained that in Alexandria, in the temple of Kore-Persephone, a hideous mockery was enacted on the Christian Epiphany: "And if anyone asks them what manner of mysteries these might be, they reply, saying: 'Today at this hour Kore, that is the virgin, has given birth to Aion.' "[12]

The sober-minded Diodore, bishop of Tarsus (d. before 394), also found the closeness of pagan myth abhorrent and argued against the oversimple and literal view that Jesus could have been the son of God only if he had no human father. Diodore's views influenced the Antiochene school and the unfortunate Patriarch Nestorius (d. *c.* 457), who was disgraced at Ephesus (see the next chapter). His glimpse of the idea that the spiritual and material worlds can overlap without necessarily cancelling each other out—that Jesus could be both the son of God and of human parents—had no permanent influence.[13]

The concept that divine paternity was the precondition of virgin birth and of Christ's divinity overcame all others in Christian orthodoxy. The question was therefore raised: how did Mary conceive Jesus? Origen, as we have seen, did not establish the difference between spontaneous generation and quickening by the deity. By mining the multi-layered meanings of the word *logos,* he suggested that Mary had conceived Jesus the Word at the words of the angel. He intended perhaps to make a characteristic Alexandrian point, about the conception of wisdom in the soul by the power of the spirit, as expounded by Philo Judaeus' (d. *c.* 45) school of mystical philosophy. But Origen's idea quickly acquired a literal stamp, celebrated by Ephrem of Syria and many medieval poets after him. A sixth-century hymn tentatively attributed to the vigorous Venantius Fortunatus (d. 609?), and still sung today is explicit:

> *Mirentur ergo saecula*
> *quod angelus fert semina*
> *quod aure virgo concepit*
> *et corde credens parturit.*[14]

(The centuries marvel therefore that the angel bore the seed, the virgin conceived through her ear, and, believing in her heart, became fruitful.) Much prettier is the thirteenth-century English dancing song:

> Glad us maiden, mother mild
> Through thine ear thou were with child
> Gabriel he said it thee  . . .[15]

It brings a smile to one's lips: yet Plutarch quoted in all seriousness the Egyptian belief that cats conceived through the ear and brought forth through the mouth,[16] while the *Physiologus,* again, says that weasels conceive through their ears.[17]

Iconography, however, has generally concentrated on the action of the Holy Spirit in the conception of Christ, as expressed by St. Ambrose:

> *Non ex virili semine*
> *Sed mystico spiramine*
> *Verbum Dei factum est caro*
> *Fructusque ventris floruit.*

(Not from human seed but by the mystical breath of the Spirit was the Word of God made flesh and the fruit of the womb brought to maturity.)[18]

Ever since the Holy Spirit descended on the head of Christ at his baptism in the form of a dove, the Third Person of the Trinity had been most commonly depicted as this bird. The Holy Ghost presents such a pitfall for theologians and has tumbled so many into heresy that the visual imagery has been remarkably static and uninventive, Christian artists preferring to play it safe with the traditional white bird poised in flight, like a hawk or a lark, but quite unlike a dove, which in reality does not hover. Birds are an ancient symbol of spirit: in Egyptian friezes the dove hieroglyph stands for the soul of the departed and, much later, in medieval miracle plays, a bird, representing the soul soaring to heaven, was pulled upwards on a string when an actor lay down and died.[19]

In the topography of classical myth, the categories of above and below were sharply defined and birds were in consequence associated with the life of the heavens. Zeus transformed himself into a variety of species to visit his earthly paramours: a swan for Leda, an eagle for Aegina. When he wooed Hera, he was changed into a cuckoo, the bird whose cry heralds the spring—an interesting correspondence, since the Annunciation, when the bird of the Holy Spirit descends on Mary, is celebrated at the vernal equinox, March 25. Zeus even transformed himself into a pigeon, kin to the dove, when he seduced the Achaian nymph Phthia.

The influence of pagan bird metamorphoses on ideas about Christ's birth appears to have been stronger in the western, Latin world, where it endures into the late Renaissance, than in eastern Christianity, where the Holy Spirit's gender was unclear. The Apostles' Creed, developed at the end of the fourth century and finally drawn up in the eighth, expresses the idea that the Holy Spirit carried the whole child into Mary's womb to be nourished there, rather than quickening it to life. Jesus Christ, it affirms, was "conceived by the Holy Ghost, born of the Virgin Mary" (*conceptus est de Spirito Sancto, ex Maria Virgine*). The Holy Ghost, like a mother, conceived the child and then took possession of Mary until the day of the child's birth.[20]

Origen and Jerome quote, without criticism, passages from the apocryphal *Gospel According to the Hebrews* in which Jesus calls the Holy Ghost his mother. In the long romance *The Acts of Thomas,* the apostle invokes the Holy Spirit: "Come, O communion of the male . . . come . . . the holy dove that beareth the twin young, come, the hidden mother . . ."[21] The dove itself, sacred in the Greco-Roman world to the goddess of love, appears in the Bible in the Song of Solomon when the lover calls his beloved. In the *Book of James,* the dove flies from Joseph's staff as a sign that he has been chosen as Mary's bridegroom.[22] The bird's amorous and gentle nature has made it Venus' immemorial symbol.

Later in the west, the dove's feminine aspect receded and its action at the Annunciation came to be seen as more and more virile, while in iconography the scene of the Annunciation resembles more and more a restrained theogamy. The Virgin's first systematic theologian, Francisco Suarez (d. 1617), even felt bound to deny that the encounter was sexual:

The Blessed Virgin in conceiving a son neither lost her virginity nor experienced any venereal pleasure . . . it did not befit the Holy Spirit without any cause or utility to produce such an effect, or to excite any unbecoming movement of passion . . . On the contrary the effect of his overshadowing is to quench the fire of original sin . . .[23]

The creed in the new liturgy has adjusted the passage on the virgin birth to read, "by the power of the Holy Spirit he was born of the Virgin Mary and became man." The shift from "she" to "he" in the case of the Third Person may have occurred in the west for linguistic reasons. The spirit of God, the *shekinah,* was feminine in Hebrew, neuter in the Greek *pneuma,* feminine as *sophia* (wisdom), invariably feminine in Syriac, but in Latin it became incontrovertibly masculine: *spiritus sanctus.*[24]

Ideas about the virgin birth have always been to some extent dependent on knowledge about human reproduction. After the spread of Aristotelian biological ideas in the thirteenth century, the overshadowing power of the Holy Spirit was closely identified with the operation of the male in human generation. But while Origen and later Aquinas could find natural phenomena to uphold them, the men of the contemporary empirical world cannot. The result of this has been that with the march of scientific discovery, the doctrine of the virgin birth has become more and more curious.

The continuing need to explain miracles like the virgin birth arose because two traditions were combined in Christianity: the Jewish belief that all is possible with God, and the Greek view that some things are impossible in nature and that "God does not even attempt such things at all, but that he chooses the best out of the possibilities of becoming. . . ."[25] The outcome of this contradiction was the typical Christian miracle: the resuscitation of the dead, the virgin birth, and other "unnatural" phenomena, manifesting the presence and power of God.[26]

The marriage of these two divergent attitudes in Christian thought created the paradoxical position of theologians who struggle to comprehend the virgin birth, indeed to explain a miracle, without damaging its miraculousness. This spirit of inquiry led them to rely on available biological data and beliefs, which until this century in the west were confused in such a way that the virgin birth was much more acceptable as a "possibility in nature" that at the same time, however, was a supreme intervention of God.

In the hellenistic world, the Stoics maintained that man's seed, divided into body and soul, joined with a part of the woman's *pneuma,* or soul, to form the embryo. In their view, the whole child entered the woman's womb, and she provided none of the matter, only a little of the spirit. Tertullian (d. 230?), one of the most eloquent of the Christian writers, echoes this when he says that "the whole fruit is already present in the semen."[27] In Christian art, the concept is sometimes depicted: the original and richly coloured *Book of Hours* of the Chevalier de Rohan shows Gabriel kneeling to Mary while the child Jesus wings his way towards her down a beam of light. The Virgin holds a baker's tray in her hand, for she is the oven in which the bread of life—the baby Jesus himself—is to be baked.[28]

The Stoic view, which gave the woman such a negligible role in reproduction, was not widely held. Indeed, in the fifteenth century, St. Antoninus, archbishop of Florence (d. 1459), pronounced the idea heterodox and proscribed it from Christian art: "Painters are to be blamed when they paint things contrary to our faith . . . when in the Annunciation, they represent a small infant Jesus in the Virgin's womb, as if the body he took on were not of her substance. . . ."[29] It was instead Aristotle's view that from the thirteenth century onwards shaped and conditioned western thinking on human generation and became the authorized teaching of the Church, principally because the Church's greatest theologian, St. Thomas Aquinas (d. 1274), gave it his authority.

In *On the Generation of Animals,* Aristotle declared that woman provided the matter for the embryo, while the man gave the matter form and motion. He used a vivid image: "Compare the coagulation of milk. Here, the milk is the body and the fig juice or the rennet contains the principle which causes it to set. . . ."[30] Menstrual blood was "the prime matter" while semen contributed no material substance but in fact evaporated after quickening and forming the blood. This view of human reproduction gives woman an all-important role; but slanted through the glass of Greek contempt for matter, that role was considered animal and therefore inferior, while the male performed the spiritual, noble, and infinitely superior function of imparting life. Aristotle himself went so far as to say that women were "a deformity, though one which occurs in the ordinary course of nature." Aeschylus, in the terrifying trial that closes the *Oresteia,* dramatizes conclusively the Greek view of paternity. Orestes stands charged with the murder of his mother Clytemnestra, but he cries out in protest to the Furies: "And dost thou call *me* a blood-relation of my mother?" His scorn for his mother's womb is total. When Apollo comes to arbitrate, he gives judgement for Orestes: "The so-called offspring is not produced by the mother. She is no more than the nurse, as it were, of the newly conceived foetus. It is the male who is the author of its being . . ."[31]

Aquinas undertook to interpret the whole of patristic theology in the light of Aristotelian philosophy, previously regarded as a grave threat to Christianity. The Angelic Doctor also accepted Aristotelian biology, with far-reaching consequences on the attitude to women's role in European society. He saw man as the vital source of life, and woman solely as the incubator, the blood-transfusion unit. The highest soul was infused by God, he declared, forty days after conception in the case of a boy, eighty in the case of a girl. But in Jesus' case, body and soul entered Mary's womb together, whole and perfect and sanctified. Dante, describing and expanding Aquinas, summed it up: woman is passive, man *la virtute attiva* (the active virtue).[32]

The *De secretis mulieribus,* a popular medieval work long attributed to Albertus Magnus, Aquinas' teacher, maintains that man is the craftsman, woman the stuff of his creation, and stoutly declares: "And it must be said that the menstrual flow of a woman is nothing but a super-fluous food."[33] If the material substance of a child is wholly provided by the woman (such was the prevalent view) and given form and move-ment by the operation of the male, then it is indeed easy to see how simple seemed the virgin birth—the overshadowing action of the Holy Spirit on Mary's womb. The paradigm was the creation, when the spirit of God, brooding over the waters, pulled that passive and amorphous mass into shape and divided and classified it, giving form to substance; or the creation of Adam, "who was made of the dust of the ground," inanimate matter until the Lord God "breathed into his nostrils the breath of life; and man became a living soul" (Genesis 2:7).

The stamp of mythological figures of speech is so strong that such figures continued to be mistaken for facts by men who knew a great deal more about biology than St. Thomas. As late as the seventeenth century, William Harvey (d. 1657), an empiricist of genius who discovered the circulation of the blood, still clung to Aristotelian ideas. In 1651 he wrote that the conception of a child in the womb was like the conception of thought in the brain. Furthermore:

The woman after contact with the spermatic fluid in coitu, seems to receive influence, and *to become fecundated without the cooperation of any sensible corporeal agent,* in the same way as iron touched by the magnet is endowed with its powers and can attract other iron to itself. When this virtue is received the woman exercises a plastic power of generation, and produces a being after her own image [Italics added].

Harvey then explains the resemblance of children to their fathers in Platonic terms: the man, "being the more perfect animal," impresses his "form" on the offspring. Significantly Harvey describes this "form" as "immaterial."[34]

The microscope eventually revealed the importance and function of the ovum in human generation. From the investigations of Von Baer in 1827 women's role in reproduction was rehabilitated, and the mother emerged as a vital procreative, not merely a nutritive, force in the genesis of a human life. The revelation of the behaviour of sperm and egg made the virgin birth more of a mystery, for, as Plutarch had pointed out long before, it was difficult to accept that a spirit could unite with matter to produce physical offspring: such a metamorphosis offended his sense of distinctions, as it does the perceptions of a twentieth-century man.[35] Aquinas declared that Jesus' "flesh was perfectly formed, of moderate quantity, and taken from the most pure blood of the virgin."[36] Contemporary theologians still wonder what Jesus and Mary looked like, and maintain that they must have resembled each other closely, as his body's substance came entirely from her.[37] In the light of modern genetics, this is much more improbable than it would be according to Aristotelian ideas. Belief therefore requires a greater act of faith.

Rationalists still pursue an explanation for the virgin birth of Jesus. In the Russell divorce case, which titillated high society in London in the twenties, Christabel Russell was sued for divorce by her husband on the grounds of her adultery. She was pregnant at the opening of the case, and had long since had the child by the time it was settled. Her husband stated that the marriage had not been consummated; his wife agreed, but contended that she was innocent of adultery because she had been and indeed still was a virgin. On examination by reputable gynaecologists who gave testimony on oath, her declaration was upheld. The case of this virgin birth went to the House of Lords, which cleared Christabel Russell and gave the child she had borne the Russell name. She never claimed the conception or birth was a miracle, but that she had conceived by her husband without full coitus. No one said the Russell birth was parthenogenetic.[38] Nevertheless, Christians—practising or lapsed—become excited at such stories and have permitted themselves speculation along these lines.

Spontaneous generation still provides another avenue of exploration. Although Pasteur's discovery that bacteria are necessary to the germination of worms in meat seemed to have foreclosed this possibility for good, the research of certain modern biologists has opened it. Poultry scientists at Pennsylvania State University hatched one thousand unfertilized eggs during a twelve-year-long study. They conjectured that these virgin-born, fatherless turkeys resulted from the stimulating action of a virus: "In parthenogenesis, an outside agent—possibly a virus—apparently triggers duplication of the mother's set of chromosomes. This, in turn, touches off embryonic development."[39] Even more suggestive is the genetical work of other contemporary scientists who, finding evidence of spontaneous division of the ovum in human beings, estimated that "virgin births" occur as often as twins and twice as often as identical twins among white Americans, or that in one case in ten thousand births the eggs might have divided of their own accord, without any contact with spermatozoa. These findings have overjoyed the more extreme wing of the women's movement who wish to declare men redundant. They should obviously be treated with a great deal of caution.[40]

Such revelations have soothed Christians, however; the possibility of a rational explanation dispels the disquiet that the Church may have lied about Mary and Jesus all these centuries. But a reaction like this, however natural, warps the fundamentals of Christian doctrine. For the virgin birth of Jesus, like his Resurrection, is the luminous sign of his divinity precisely because it suspends the natural order. To argue, as Christians have done since Origen, that it is possible in nature is to miss the religious, or mythological, point.

Many devout Catholics display the same inconsistency with regard to Mary's virginity *in partu* and *post partum,* the belief that her physical integrity was not damaged during or after the birth of Jesus, as the midwife Salome's withered hand bore witness in the *Book of James* (colour plate II, figure 2), and that she did not suffer labour or any of the pains or problems of childbirth. As Francisco Suarez declared: "That troublesome weariness with which all pregnant women are burdened, she alone did not experience who alone conceived without pleasure."[41]

Origen in Alexandria and Tertullian in Africa had both found virginity *in partu* hard to accept. They were affected by the struggle against Gnosticism, for a painless birth jeopardized the full human condition of the incarnate God, and came perilously close to the heterodox position that Jesus passed through Mary as water through a channel. When the heresy's danger had passed, this type of imagery inspired some of the loveliest Christmas poetry, like the triumphant sequence long wrongly attributed to St. Bernard of Clairvaux (d. 1153), where the birth of Jesus is compared to the light of the heavens that never diminishes the stars:

> *Angelus consilii*
> *Natus est de virgine*
> *Sol de stella;*
>
> *Sol occasum nesciens,*
> *Stella semper rutilans,*
> *Semper clara.*
>
> *Sicut sidus radium,*
> *Profert virgo filium,*
> *Pari forma.*
>
> *Neque sidus radio,*
> *Neque mater filio*
> *Fit corrupta.*

(The angel of counsel is born of a virgin, the sun from a star; A sun that knows no setting, a star that is always shining, always bright. As a star puts forth its ray, so the virgin put forth her son, in like manner. The star does not lose virtue by giving forth its ray, or the mother by bearing a son.)[42]

The image passed rapidly into the vernacular, and was expanded to become one of medieval Christendom's most attractive figures. The jongleur Rutebeuf hymned the miracle in the thirteenth century:

> *Si com en la verriere*
> *Entre et reva arriere*
> *Li solaus que n'entame*
> *Ainsi fus verge entiere*
> *Quant Diex, qui es ciex iere*
> *Fist de toi mere et dame.*

(Just as the sun enters and passes back through a windowpane without piercing it, so were you *virgo intacta* when God, who came down from the heavens, made you his mother and lady.)[43]

*The Meditations on the Life of Our Lord,* also an extremely influential medieval work, written around 1300 and long attributed to St. Bonaventure, described the birth in terms that both reflected and affected iconography:

The Virgin rose and stood erect against a column that was there. But Joseph remained seated . . . taking some hay from the manger, placed it at the Lady's feet and turned away. Then the Son of the eternal God came out of the womb of the mother without a murmur or lesion, in a moment . . .[44]

The visions of St. Bridget of Sweden (d. 1373), which gripped four-teenth- and fifteenth-century Europe, stressed the sudden, dramatic, and painless appearance of the baby in the stable with celestial light and sound effects that recall the *Book of James* (colour plate II, figure 2).[45]

The succinct summation of Catholic orthodoxy—the catechism of the Council of Trent—continued to uphold the virginity of Mary during and after Jesus' birth. But Christians are finding this increasingly difficult to accept, and the dogmatic constitution of the Second Vatican Council of 1964 refrained from proclaiming it an article of faith.

At one level, the grounds for doubt are Christological, as they were for Origen and Tertullian. But at another level, virginity *in partu* simply stretches credulity too far. Here the mechanism of Christian belief once again reveals itself: the virgin birth is a possible miracle, the corporeal intactness of the virgin after birth is impossible. Contemporary doubt focuses on the unlikelihood of Mary's integrity *post partum*, but the actual conception of a child by a virgin does not present an equal prob-lem, because God or the power above is still felt, even by sceptics, to be the origin of all things, who holds life itself in his gift and is therefore ultimately responsible for all birth, not only Christ's.

Belief in the activity of the divine in human genesis lies at the heart of the Christian myth of the Incarnation. Edmund Leach, the anthropolo-gist, has compared belief in the virgin birth of Jesus to the opinions of several primitive tribes, that men play no part in the generation of a child. The Trobriand Islanders and the Tully River Blacks of Australia denied all knowledge of physiological paternity. Women, they asserted, conceived when the spirit of a dead ancestor entered them: "virgin birth" was normal.

The most startling feature of such societies is that sex was a wide-spread and carefree pleasure before marriage and yet babies were not born to single girls. When questioned as to how this could be, the people appeared nonplussed, and indicated further examples to support their view: ugly or disfigured women with whom, they said, no one would consider sex, but to whom the gods in their kindness had given several children. They also assured the curious anthropologists that they did not practise contraception, and did not need to, for children came from heaven at the right time in the right circumstances, that is after, and not before, marriage.

For these tribes, virgin birth, conception by the gods, was the essential symbol of their closeness to heaven. In societies where the people feel themselves continually in contact with the spiritual world, where they have, in one sense, a high opinion of themselves and their relations with the omnipotent and the immortal, the idea of virgin birth appears, for it binds deity to creature in a unique and indissoluble way.[46]

Among the tribes Leach cites it was the rule; in pagan mythology, it was frequent; and in Christianity an exception, but one that nevertheless proved the intimacy of God with man and gave the latter a special, elevated place in the natural order.

The tribesmen who believed that all children came from the gods did not therefore experience any alienation. Their compact with divinity was solid. Christians, on the other hand, demonstrate their intimacy with the divine through their belief that God became one of them, but establish the virgin birth as a unique occurrence, a special propitiation, because they also believe that they are participants in the continuing tragedy of the Fall, which alienates man from God through man's corrupted nature. Leach points out that the tribesmen knew perfectly well that children resulted from human intercourse, because, for instance, they understood that the breeding of animals required prior copulation.[47] But they suppressed the empirical data and denied that they took any precautions, in order to sustain their religious beliefs, which required them to place the demarcation lines between matter and spirit in such a way that mankind was superior because it belonged to the latter.

Similarly, in Christian civilization, men and women do not believe reproduction is unadulteratedly animal, but maintain the special higher character of the species by a muddled but profound belief that all children come from God, who creates in each individual a unique soul. So that although the virgin birth of Christ is a single miracle that reveals his divinity, all births are considered to some extent the work of the Spirit. There are elements of this type of absurd thinking in the Catholic ban on contraception: although sex undertaken without a view to conceive is sinful, the rhythm method is allowed, but any man-made method is forbidden because it places human intercourse on the practical level of animal reproduction, and so God no longer appears to determine and intervene in the origin of every human life.

The Christian idea of the virgin birth gives rise to a further, interesting puzzle. There is no more matriarchal image than the Christian mother of God who bore a child without male assistance. The liturgy invokes her as the *radix sancta,* the holy root of salvation, because through her the Incarnation was possible. A niche in S. Maria Antiqua in Rome, painted in the eighth or ninth century, captures the impressive mother-worship of the doctrine, for it places St. Anne with the child Mary in her arms and St. Elisabeth with John the Baptist on either side of the Madonna and Child: a triple goddess with her miraculous offspring (figure 7). The popular medieval image of the Rod of Jesse, based on Isaiah's prophecy (Isaiah 11:1), shows Mary and the child as the apex of God's historical purpose (figures 1, 13). In fourteenth- and fifteenth-century Europe, the statues of the *Vierge Ouvrante,* a fetish-like Madonna whose belly opened to reveal the Trinity concealed within, became objects of devotion (figure 6).

It is highly paradoxical that this parthenogenetic goddess fitted into the Aristotelian biological scheme, and that it was a deeply misogynist and contemptuous view of women's role in reproduction that made the idea of conception by the power of the Spirit more acceptable. For many matrifocal societies also entertain erroneously exaggerated ideas about the material contribution of women in parturition and belittle the biological role of the man. But in their case the imbalance leaves mothers in the ascendant, while in Christianity identification of the womb with the lower, carnal order gives fathers precedence. Thus the self-same ideogram of the mother and child can be worshipped by both societies that respect and despise women for their maternity.

Christianity also parted company with paganism and the cultures of most tribes who believe in parthenogenesis in its use of the symbol of virginity. By insisting on the chastity of the mother goddess, the matriarchal image could be utterly transformed as to content, although to all outward appearances it remained unchanged.

For in the case of pagan goddesses, the sign of the virgin rarely endorses chastity as a virtue. Venus, Ishtar, Astarte, and Anat, the love goddesses of the near east and classical mythology, are entitled virgin despite their lovers, who die and rise again for them each year. Diana, the virgin huntress, goddess of the moon, who imposed a vow of chastity on her nymphs, appears at first glance to be an exception. To our eyes, however, her very prominence is a cultural distortion: her cult in Roman times was negligible. Christianity fastened on her and added such typical feminine Christian virtues as modesty and shame to her personality so that the chthonic myth of Diana and Actaeon, in which a goddess sacrifices a man to the underworld, has become a feeble story of a prude's

moral indignation.⁴⁸ In the case of Artemis (whom the Romans assimilated to Diana, formerly a minor woodland spirit) and of Hippolyte, the
Amazon queen, and of Athene Parthenos, the Maid, their sacred virginity
symbolized their autonomy, and had little or no moral connotation. They
spurned men because they were preeminent, independent, and alone,
which is why the title virgin could be used of a goddess who entertained
lovers. Her virginity signified she had retained freedom of choice: to take
lovers or to reject them. Temple virgins like the vestals were forbidden
intercourse during their period of office largely because their exalted
position gave them political power that might be abused by a lover. The
vestals themselves could marry when they left the temple. (Among married women in Rome, chastity was a virtue—but that is a different
matter.)

The use of the image survives in some cases: Elizabeth I was hardly
entitled the Virgin Queen because she refused lovers—a succession of
favourites characterizes her reign. For although she may have been technically chaste, her virginity principally indicated she could not be subjugated or possessed. In Christian times, however, virginity only rarely
preserved the notion of female independence (see Chapter 5).

There was one particular attitude toward virginity that the Christian
religion did inherit from the classical world: that virginity was powerful
magic and conferred strength and ritual purity. Thus Hera, wife of Zeus
and mother of many, renewed her maidenhead annually when she was
dipped by nymphs in the spring at Canathus, as the famous antique
stone relief called the Ludovisi throne represents.⁴⁹ By extension, celebrants of sacred mysteries in the ancient world often prepared themselves
by abstaining from food and drink as well as from sexual intercourse in
order to acquire the condition of strength and purity appropriate to serving the gods. Vestal virgins and the eunuchs, or *galli,* who served Oriental deities like Cybele (her cult was fashionable in Rome in the second
century A.D.), originate from this idea that continence is a magic state of
power, rather than from ethical considerations about the immorality of
sex itself.⁵⁰ (An analogy would be African tribesmen who abjure their
wives on the night before a hunt.) Elements of this survive in Christian
asceticism (see Chapter 5), and the idea probably had some influence on
the prescribed celibacy of the priesthood.

But the Christian religion broadened the concept of virginity to embrace a fully developed ascetic philosophy. The interpretation of the
virgin birth as the moral sanction of the goodness of sexual chastity was
the overwhelming and distinctive contribution of the Christian religion
to the ancient mythological formula.

Different cultures have used virgin birth to assert man's natural distinction and closeness to the higher orders. For instance, some Yap tribesmen, from the Caroline islands in the Pacific, who also maintained that children came from the gods, were castrating a pig one day in order to prevent it breeding. The anthropologist observing them was surprised, and asked if in this case they did recognize that copulation led to pregnancy. They were baffled, until one of them exclaimed: "But people are not pigs!"[51] It is characteristic of Christianity in particular, however, that the restraint of the lower "animal" passions was a further necessary sign of man's superiority to the beasts. And it was this shift, from virgin birth to virginity, from religious sign to moral doctrine, that transformed a mother goddess like the Virgin Mary into an effective instrument of asceticism and female subjection. As Henry Adams wrote: "The study of Our Lady . . . leads directly back to Eve, and lays bare the whole subject of sex."[52]

## Chapter Four

# SECOND EVE

*I am Eve, the wife of noble Adam; it was I who violated Jesus in the past; it was I who robbed my children of heaven; it is I by right who should have been crucified.*

*I had heaven at my command; evil the bad choice that shamed me; evil the punishment for my crime that has aged me; alas, my hand is not pure.*

*It was I who plucked the apple; it went past the narrow of my gullet; as long as they live in daylight women will not cease from folly on account of that.*

*There would be no ice in any place; there would be no bright windy winter; there would be no hell, there would be no grief, there would be no terror but for me.*[1]

—ANONYMOUS, OLD IRISH

THAT THE MOTHER OF GOD should be a virgin was a matter of such importance to the men of the early Church that it overrode all other considerations, including the evidence of revelation itself. Classical metaphysics contributed to the development of the belief, but the root of it was the Fathers' definition of evil. Sexuality represented to them the gravest danger and the fatal flaw; they viewed virginity as its opposite and its conqueror, sadly failing to appreciate that renunciation does not banish or overcome desire. It is almost impossible to overestimate the effect that the characteristic Christian association of sex and sin and death has had on the attitudes of our civilization. Since the learned Saints Jerome and Augustine (d. 430) tackled the problem of man's tendency to evil, the three separate concepts have been bound together tightly in a web that traps every Christian. For if desire, as natural as breath or as sleep itself, is sinful, then the Christian, like a man in the grip of a usurer, must always run back to the Church, the only source of that grace which can give him reprieve.

Examples of this nexus of ideas can be culled from almost any Christian work, but one of the most naïve and striking occurs in the early thirteenth-century collection of cautionary and other tales of Cardinal Jacques de Vitry (d. before 1240), a most successful preacher. A monk, he said, once loved a woman so much that even when she had died he could not drive the longing for her from his mind. And so he visited her grave and, opening it, gathered up her remains in his arms and buried his face in the breast that he had never embraced in life. "He filled his nostrils with that putrefying flesh," concluded the cardinal, "and the stench of it henceforth cured him of all concupiscence."[2]

Christian theologians have drawn subtle distinctions about sin and desire for centuries; and since the Reformation, the Catholics' position on the inevitability of sin has been less pessimistic than that of the Lutherans or the Calvinists or the Jansenists. Contemporary Catholic theology now fervently denies that concupiscence is sinful in itself, and is at pains to point out that concupiscence does not mean only sex, and that sex is certainly not sinful in itself. Concupiscence is "the tendency to sin," a weakening of the will that makes resistance difficult, that is the permanent legacy of the Fall, the part of original sin not remitted in baptism. The symptoms of original sin itself, the primal lack of grace, are defined as the state of alienation of man from God, that cosmic despair, or *angst,* which is experienced by all creatures when they contemplate the wreck they are making of their lives and that humanity in general is making of its world.[3]

But although the updated formulas are an improvement, they cannot camouflage the still unchallenged structure of original sin: the rebellion of Adam and Eve against God in the Garden of Eden lost mankind the paradise where pain and toil did not exist. When they sinned, death and sex as we know them entered the world. The association of sex, sin, and death is ancient and still endures in Christian symbolism: the soul dies in lust as the body rots in death. Spiritual corruption mirrors bodily dissolution. The monk breathes the corrupt flesh of his desire: the stench is his own sin.

In the fourth century, St. John Chrysostom, patriarch of Constantinople, railed: "Scarcely had they [Adam and Eve] turned from obedience to God than they became earth and ashes, and all at once, they lost the happy life, beauty and honour of virginity . . . they were made serfs, stripped of the royal robe . . . made subject to death and every other form of curse and imperfection; then did marriage make its appearance . . . Do you see where marriage took its origin? . . . For where there is death, there too is sexual coupling; and where there is no death, there is no sexual coupling either."[4]

John, "the Golden Mouth," was a fiery extremist, and other theologians, including Augustine and Aquinas, have held that Adam and Eve did have intercourse in Eden, for otherwise why would God have bothered to create a woman and not a man to be Adam's companion? But the sex that Adam and Eve enjoyed was different in kind, untainted by concupiscence, not flawed by the sufferings of possible pregnancy.[5]

Through the virgin birth Mary conquered the post-Eden natural law that man and woman couple in lust to produce children. Chaste, she escaped the debt of Adam and Eve. Thus the seeds of the dogma of the Immaculate Conception, which was declared in 1854 and spares Mary all stain of original sin, were implanted during the ascetic movement of the fourth century. But from what was the Virgin exempt? What was the original sin?

Adam, the first man, is the first to heap reproach on woman; Yahweh himself comes a close second. When Adam and Eve have eaten of the fruit of the tree of knowledge, their "eyes are opened" and they hide from Yahweh, who is strolling in the garden. But when he calls them, he realizes they have eaten the forbidden fruit because they are aware of their nakedness. He challenges them, and Adam blames the woman, "whom thou gavest to me to be with me, she gave me of the tree and I did eat" (Genesis 3:12). Yahweh turns to the woman, and she blames the serpent. Then Yahweh pronounces three solemn curses. He condemns the serpent to crawl on his belly, and promises him the eternal enmity of the woman's offspring; he later tells Adam he shall work "in the sweat of his face" and that he will decompose after death "for dust thou art and unto dust thou shalt return"; to the woman he says: "I will greatly multiply thy sorrow and thy conception . . . and thy desire shall be to thy husband, and he shall rule over thee" (Genesis 3:19, 16).

For mankind, these curses were the struggle against nature, of which hitherto Adam had been master; mortality of the flesh; and for woman in particular, the pains of childbearing—the whole gamut from menstruation to suckling—and subjection of heart and head to the authority of the male. After this, Adam then names his wife Eve, "the mother of all the living" (Genesis 3:20). God, having instituted the division of labour and the rudiments of social order, makes clothes for Adam and Eve to wear, and throws them out of paradise.

The story of the Fall was not understood, as it is today by everyone except bigots, to be an ancient myth reinterpreted by priestly writers in the fifth or fourth century before Christ in order to account for the condition of humanity in the world—for the great gap between man's intimations of his immortality, his power and his knowledge, and the transience and futility of his brief span on earth. To the Christians of the New Covenant, who believed in a God who was all love, the story of the Fall provided a rich explanation for the painful discrepancy between the benevolent and omnipotent deity and the misery, disorder, and pain visible everywhere in his creation. It was man, through the precious gift of free will, who unceasingly turned against his maker from the beginning and caused evil and suffering.[6]

The disobedience of Adam and Eve was a catastrophe—paradise lost—but through Christ's coming, his death and Resurrection, paradise was regained. St. Paul expressed the antithesis in his letters—the only place where original sin is discussed in the New Testament: "As in Adam all die, even so in Christ shall all be made alive" (1 Corinthians 15:22; see Romans 5:12–21). Augustine, in the last years of the fourth century, defined the doctrine that each individual is born in original sin, a member of the *massa peccati* that is the human race, who has to be cleansed of his stain by baptism. But even after the sacrament, a man would still suffer the penalty of Adam's sin on earth, though redeemed from it in heaven. That penalty Augustine called concupiscence, and its only antidote was the grace of God.

Up to and during the fourth century, there was much debate, east and west, on the consequences of Adam's fall. But it was the opinions of Pelagius, St. Augustine's contemporary, that particularly spurred St. Augustine towards the definition of original sin accepted until modern times. Pelagius interpreted the Fall as the result of God's gift of free will to mankind. This was orthodox enough; but he added that Adam and Eve's sin was personal, and was not transmitted through them to the whole of mankind. He denied St. Paul's statement to the Romans: "as by one man sin entered into the world, and death by sin, and so death passed upon all men, for that all have sinned" (Romans 5:12). "Original" sin did not exist. Man is, according to Pelagius' strikingly modern view, free to do either good or evil as he chooses, and the grace of God is a helpful but unnecessary crutch. Christ's crucifixion did not redeem mankind, because mankind did not need redemption. Adam's sin was his personal sin, and no one else's. Jesus' life and teachings simply held up a supreme example of goodness for men to emulate.

Pelagius' reliance on human willpower and independence of God drove Augustine to tackle the fundamental Christian questions about the inheritance of Adam's sin, its very nature, and the operation of God's grace in the soul.

In the *City of God,* written 413–26, Augustine noted that Adam and Eve, after they had eaten the forbidden fruit, covered their genitals, not their hands or mouths, which had done the deed. From this he reasoned that the knowledge they had acquired was of an inner force, which he called *epithymia* (concupiscence). It affects all areas of life, he wrote, but particularly the sexual act, which cannot be performed without passion. In the involuntary impulse of desire, which cannot be quelled by the will, Augustine perceived the penalty of Adam's sin. The passion aroused by making love was sinful; not the act itself, for the perpetuation of God's creation must be good.[7] Elsewhere, Augustine drew the graphic analogy of the man with a limp who is doing a good deed. The limp does not detract from the good of his deed; nor does the good of the deed improve his limp. "We ought not to condemn marriage because of the evil of lust, nor must we praise lust because of the good of marriage."[8]

Augustine suggested that either the hereditary taint was transmitted through the male genitals themselves during intercourse, and that the body itself, not the soul, was genetically flawed by the Fall, or that because a child cannot be conceived outside the sexual embrace, which necessarily involves the sin of passion, the child is stained from that moment. The premise for this literal connection of intercourse and original sin was the virgin birth of Christ. The son of God chose to be born from a virgin mother because this was the only way a child could enter the world without sin. "Let us love chastity above all things," Augustine wrote, "for it was to show that this was pleasing to Him that Christ chose the modesty of a virgin womb."[9] Augustine thus bound up three ideas in a causal chain: the sinfulness of sex, the virgin birth, and the good of virginity.

Augustine was not alone among men of his day to hold such ideas; but he developed the theory more fully. Ambrose had declared that Jesus would have been sullied by an ordinary birth, and Jerome after him also saw the virgin birth as the supreme seal of approval on the celibate life. "Now that a virgin has conceived in the womb and borne to us a child . . . now the chain of the curse is broken. Death came through Eve, but life has come through Mary. And thus the gift of virginity has been bestowed most richly upon women, seeing that it has had its beginning from a woman."[10] Ambrose, Augustine, and Jerome: the colossi of the Christian Church. Their cumulative impact on the development of the Christian ethic cannot be overemphasized.

Yet why did the Fathers agree that the way of sexual abstinence was holier than another? The Bible does not proclaim the ascetic life; for although the Judaic concern with pollution, codified in the ritual laws of Leviticus, lent some authority to purificatory practices, the Book's heroes, sages, and prophets are married, sometimes polygamous, and unashamedly prolific, almost to a man. Yet Jerome saw Daniel as a virgin, although no evidence exists; St. John Damascene (d. *c.* 749) apostrophized the prophet's body: "So hardened by virginity that the teeth of the beasts were unable to tear it apart."[11] In an Old Testament figure like Susannah, demure before the aged voyeurs, the Fathers saw a forerunner of the Christian virgin. Joseph, refusing the embrace of Potiphar's wife, and Judith, luring Holofernes to his gory death yet preserving her virtue the while, both prefigured the conquest of lust by chastity. Because no mention is made of Miriam's husband, commentators seized on her as the prototype of her namesake, the Virgin Mary. In medieval times, a parallel between Judith and Mary was developed: the widely read *Speculum Humanae Salvationis,* which unveiled the inner typological meaning in Old and New Testament scenes by setting them side by side, shows Judith's triumph over Holofernes beside an all-conquering Virgin Mary, who transfixes Satan with the vexillum thrust deep into his gullet.[12]

The Gospels were not much more forthcoming than the Old Testament on the perils of the flesh: Jesus applies to himself the very word Augustine uses for concupiscence in a positive context: "With desire [*epithymia*] I have desired to eat this passover with you before I suffer" (Luke 22:15). He does not single out carnal sins for particular opprobrium, but reminds the Pharisees who bring him the adulteress that they too are sinners. And then he sends her from him with gentle words.

But in the Epistles of St. Paul the stress falls differently. His severity is notorious. Caught up in his pressing vision of the world's end, Paul urged the Corinthians to remain wed or unwed, whatever their condition, and advocates celibacy in particular as "good for the present distress." A married man or woman has ties and responsibilities, worries and duties that prevent total dedication to God's work. So although Paul concedes that "concerning virgins, I have no commandment of the Lord . . .," he tells the community, "It is good for a man not to touch a woman" (1 Corinthians 7:1). He, Paul, can concentrate all upon the imminent salvation of Christ and the Second Coming: "For I would that all men were even as myself . . . I say therefore to the unmarried and widows, it is good for them to abide even as I. But if they cannot abstain, let them marry; for it is better to marry than to burn" (1 Corinthians 7:7-9).

Throughout these famous ringing passages, the conflict between the things of God and the things of man, between heaven and the world, is perceived in sexual terms, and a hellenistic fear of reason's overthrow by passion—the same fear so vivid in Augustine later—colours Paul's warnings. He tells the Thessalonians: "For this is the will of God . . . that ye should abstain from fornication . . ." (1 Thessalonians 4:3). To the Galatians he lists "the works of the flesh," of which "adultery, fornication, uncleanness and lasciviousness" lead the catalogue of sins (Galatians 5:19)—an accurate reflection of Greco-Jewish morality and taboo. The Apocalypse of John strengthened the eschatological urgency of the ascetic life, for the first fruits of the Redemption, the faithful standing nearest to the throne of the lamb with the twenty-four elders, are the hundred and forty-four thousand virgins: "They which were not defiled with women" (Revelation 14:4).

Like Paul and John, the brilliant men of the ascetic movement of the fourth century were writing within a specific intellectual tradition in which various dualistic ideas about the importance of spiritual detachment from the world played a significant part. Augustine's theology of original sin can be understood only in the context of the long intellectual journey he made before he became a Christian in 387. In pursuit of the central problem—the origin and nature of evil—Augustine had tasted and sometimes accepted many of the philosophical systems abroad in the turmoil of Rome's decline. For nine years he had embraced the Manichaean religion, which held that evil was a separate and independent force, eternally in conflict with goodness. But he had abandoned this dualism, passed through a brief Sceptic phase, and had then become deeply impressed by the writings of Plotinus (d. 270) and the neoplatonism of Alexandria, which considered that evil was the absence of good, rather than a power on its own.

Common to the teachings of Mani (d. 277) and Plotinus, however, and to many of the creeds current in the years of paganism's last stand was a distaste for the world, a profound sense of a breach between things of the flesh and things of the spirit, and a restless quest for spiritual fulfilment through detachment from earthly concerns and pleasures. Plotinus himself, for all his sense of the beauty of the universe, wrote: "The soul has become ugly, by being immersed in what is not itself, by its descent into the body."[13] The sense that flesh itself was vitiated affected deeply Augustine's later analysis of the Fall.[14]

Other currents from different sources also converged in the near east, Egypt, and Asia Minor, where Christianity was nurtured, and however novel and radical the new religion was, it represented a syncretism of many otherworldly quests of the time. Gnosticism had scarred Christian orthodoxy with its contempt for the material universe. The Stoics, who cultivated the bliss of apathy through control of the passions, exercised an influence over Alexandrian thought that persisted until the fifth century and moulded the development of Christianity.

In the deserts of the middle east, in Egypt and Palestine, both Jewish and pagan ascetics had traditionally led lives of harsh self-discipline among a motley crowd of outlaws and runaway prisoners. The Essene sect, who won the ungrudging admiration of the Christian Epiphanius, lived in a completely secluded community, practised chastity, and performed unceasing ritual ablutions to purify their despised and contaminated flesh. Around 270, the first Christians retired up the Nile Valley to pursue lives of equal solitude and rigour, and the great persecution of Diocletian in 303 drove many others to join them. St. Antony (d. 356), wrestling with demons as he inflicted yet more severe austerities upon himself, was among the first desert hermits. His biography, written around 357 by St. Athanasius, vividly described his ordeals, and instantly became the most seminal manual on the ascetic life, with far-reaching effects on western idealism.[15] It was already being read in Gaul within some twenty years of its composition, and its influence has endured for centuries, inspiring Martin Schongauer's extraordinary engraving in the fifteenth, and Flaubert's vituperative fantasy, *La Tentation de Saint Antoine,* in the nineteenth century.[16]

When Augustine, Ambrose, and Jerome endorsed virginity for its special holiness, they were the heirs and representatives of much current thought in the Roman empire of their day. And in this battle between the flesh and the spirit, the female sex was firmly placed on the side of the flesh. For as childbirth was woman's special function, and its pangs the special penalty decreed by God after the Fall, and as the child she bore in her womb was stained by sin from the moment of its conception, the evils of sex were particularly identified with the female. Woman was womb and womb was evil: this cluster of ideas endemic to Christianity is but the extension of Augustine's argument about original sin. St. Jean Eudes in the seventeenth century sympathized with women's plight: "It is a subject of humiliation of all the mothers of the children of Adam to know that while they are with child, they carry within them an infant . . . who is the enemy of God, the object of his hatred and malediction, and the shrine of the demon."[17]

For the Fathers of the Church after Augustine, woman is the cause of the Fall, the wicked temptress, the accomplice of Satan, and the destroyer of mankind. The fury unleashed against Eve and all her kind is almost flattering, so exaggerated is the picture of women's fatal and all-powerful charms and men's incapacity to resist. Tertullian gave his rancour against women the bite of the most accomplished and deadly Latin since Tacitus: "Do you not realize that Eve is you? The curse God pronounced on your sex weighs still on the world. Guilty, you must bear its hardships. You are the devil's gateway, you desecrated the fatal tree, you first betrayed the law of God, you who softened up with your cajoling words the man against whom the devil could not prevail by force. The image of God, the man Adam, you broke him, it was child's play to you. You deserved death, and it was the son of God who had to die!"[18]

Eve, cursed to bear children rather than blessed with motherhood, was identified with nature, a form of low matter that drags man's soul down the spiritual ladder. In the faeces and urine—Augustine's phrase—of childbirth, the closeness of woman to all that is vile, lowly, corruptible, and material was epitomized; in the "curse" of menstruation, she lay closer to the beasts; the lure of her beauty was nothing but an aspect of the death brought about by her seduction of Adam in the garden. St. John Chrysostom warned: "The whole of her bodily beauty is nothing less than phlegm, blood, bile, rheum, and the fluid of digested food. . . . If you consider what is stored up behind those lovely eyes, the angle of the nose, the mouth and cheeks you will agree that the well-proportioned body is merely a whitened sepulchre."[19] It would be mistaken to take such a speech as the ravings of an individual, for it finds many echoes in later writings about priestly celibacy. By the time of Aquinas, the undertow of misogyny in patristic thought was so strong that he had difficulty in reconciling the creation—"male and female"—in God's image with woman's inferiority, propounded by Aristotle and by St. Paul.[20] Paul said: "For the man indeed ought not to cover his head, for as much as he is the image and glory of God: but the woman is the glory of man. . . . Neither was the man created for the woman; but the woman for the man" (I Corinthians 11:7, 9).

Because of the curse of Eve in Eden, the idea of woman's subjection was bound up in Christian thought with her role as mother and as temptress. In iconography, Satan is often female, and not only in minor Books of Hours, but also in masterworks with a permanent influence on the imagination: Michelangelo's Eve on the Sistine ceiling takes the fruit from a strenuous and muscular seductress (figure 8). Ignatius of Loyola

(d. 1556) even saw typical female guile in the devil: "The enemy conducts himself as a woman. He is a weakling before a show of strength, and a tyrant if he has his will."[21]

But it was the eloquent John Chrysostom who resolved the contradiction between the accepted passivity of women and their marked evil hegemony: "Tell me, what kind of people inspire the most horror? Whom do judges and magistrates strike down? Those who drink the fatal poisons, or those who prepare the draught and concoct the envenomed potions?"[22] It was therefore essential that the son of the Highest should not be contaminated by any of this sinfulness, inherent in the whole human species but more pronounced in the female. Thus during the ascetic revolt of Christianity's first centuries, the need to exempt the mother of Christ from tainted sexuality and to proclaim her virgin purity exerted an overwhelming pressure on definitions of doctrine and on scriptural commentaries.

The inauguration of the new era of Christ found in virginity a most satisfying image: a new, incorrupt, untainted world had been created by the Incarnation and the Redemption; just as God moulded Adam from new clay, so he had fashioned his son anew. Because Jesus did not descend to earth but was born of a woman, it was crucial that her clay too should be pristine and unspotted. This symbolism of a new world also influenced the ideas of early Christian theologians far more than the equivocal stories of Jesus' birth in the Gospels.

The fundamental idea that the Incarnation of the godhead had overturned the Old Covenant of sin and death found one of its loveliest images in the concept of the Virgin who gives birth to the redeemer. She is the second Eve, mother of all the living in a new, spiritual sense. St. Paul had triumphantly declared that Christ was the second Adam, the sum of all that had passed since the Creation, the new creature of God in whom all was reborn pure and incorrupt—indeed virgin (1 Corinthians 15:22; 2 Corinthians 5:17; Romans 5:14). Irenaeus (d. *c.* 202) and Justin Martyr, in different milieux and seemingly independently, picked up and extended the Pauline idea to include the Virgin Mary. Justin wrote that Christ was born of the Virgin

in order that by the same way in which the disobedience caused by the serpent took its beginning; by this way should it also take its destruction. For Eve, being a virgin and uncorrupt, conceived the word spoken of the serpent, and brought forth disobedience and death. But Mary the Virgin, receiving faith and grace . . . [gave birth to him] . . . by whom God destroys both the serpent and those angels and men that became like it. . . .[23]

Irenaeus embroidered the same theme a few years later: "as the human race was sentenced to death by means of a virgin . . . the guile of the serpent was overcome by the simplicity of the dove and we are set free from those chains by which we had been bound to death."[24]

The economy and proportion of this Pauline idea gave it great power and appeal. To this day it is a specially graceful analogue, architectural in its harmoniousness, a great vault thrown over the history of western attitudes to women, the whole mighty span resting on Eve the temptress on one side, and Mary the paragon on the other. The imagery of paradise regained through Mary inspired the luxuriant praises of one of the Virgin's earliest and most eloquent poets, Ephrem of Syria, who catches the sudden splendour of his native country's spring when he sings of the Creation clothed once more "in a robe of flowers/ and a tunic of blossoms" at the moment of the Annunciation. Eve, he writes, had covered Adam in a shameful coat of skins, but Mary has woven a new garment of salvation. Mary is the bright eye that illuminates the world, Eve the other eye, "blind and dark." The wine Eve pressed for mankind poisoned them; the vine that grew in Mary nourishes and saves the world.[25]

The idea of the second Eve, through whom the sin of the first was ransomed, was imported to the west, where it inspired the ingenious imagination of the medieval Christian to pun and riddle with a characteristic sense of delight and love of symmetry. For the greeting of the angel—Ave—neatly reversed the curse of Eve: the exquisite antiphon, the *Ave maris stella,* written for the feast of the Annunciation in the seventh or eighth century, plays on the anagram very prettily:

> *Sumens illud Ave*
> *Gabrielis ore,*
> *Funda nos in pace*
> *Mutans nomen Evae.*

(Receiving that Ave from the lips of Gabriel, establish us in peace, changing Eva's name.)[26]

The Fall even came to be seen as a source of joy, for it had made possible the Incarnation through Mary. "*O felix culpa*" (Oh happy fault), wrote St. Ambrose.[27] In the fifteenth century, an anonymous poet of genius thanked God for the Fall, because it had brought about the Virgin Mary:

Ne had the apple taken been,
　　The apple taken been,
Ne hadde never our Lady
　　A been heaven's queen.
Blessed be the time
　　That apple taken was!
Therefore we may singen
　　"Deo Gratias!"[28]

Christian art seized on this suggestive strain, the *gaudium* in the midst of *tristia*. For example, the Sienese master Giovanni di Paolo's gemlike predella panel painted around 1445 (now in the National Gallery, Washington) shows Adam and Eve hounded from paradise by an angel, while Mary seated in a pavilion in the same garden of paradise receives the news of the Incarnation from another angelic messenger (colour plate III, figure 3). Time is telescoped, the cycle brought full circle, and the events, one initiating the Old Covenant, the other bringing in the New, form a diptych. In a Salzburg miniature of around 1481, now in Munich, time is even more compressed, for on one side of the Tree of Life from which the crucified Christ hangs, Eve leads a troop of death and sin, while on the other Mary stands at the head of a group of pious communicants.

The symbolism of the new Eve marked that break with the past, that inauguration of a new era at the heart of the Christian message. But in order to make it plain that God in his wisdom had prepared the world for this greatest and most ineffable of mysteries since the beginning, thinkers of the Church like Origen and his inspired school of exegetes in Alexandria in the third century quarried the Scriptures for symbols that elucidated God's plan to make all things new in Christ virgin born of a virgin mother. The Alexandrian method was to unveil the hidden, typological meaning beneath the written word of the Bible and the superficial narrative. But its great rival, the school of Antioch, adopted a more historical and literal approach that the Greek Christian Methodius (d. *c.* 300) scorned for its limitations: "The Jews who hover about the bare letter of the Scriptures like so-called butterflies about the leaves or vegetables instead of the flowers and fruit as the bee does. . . . "[29]

It was the fruit and the flowers that Origen and his followers were after; and the rationale behind the bee's suck was simple: what was "suitable for God" would be extracted, and all else discarded as incongruous. This was metaphysical speculation at its most inspired, and in the sermons of later medieval mystics like Bernard, the Origenist influence is still vividly apparent. The argument from appropriateness had been the axiom of the Alexandrian school of philosophy since the days of the Jewish mystic Philo, and its effects on theology and Mariology are still immense.[30] Origen was a dazzling polemicist who later in life landed himself in trouble for preaching that even the Devil could be saved.[31] In Origen's view, it was fitting that God's only son be born of the Virgin, and the Old Testament was one unbroken chain of prophecy that foretold it.

The burning bush that Moses saw was, like Mary, inflamed with the spirit of God and yet not consumed by the flames, as she was filled with the fires of the Holy Ghost and yet never felt the heat of lust.[32] When Isaiah prophesied, "For he shall grow up before him as a tender plant, and as a root out of dry ground . . ." (Isaiah 53:20), he was pointing out that the Messiah would rise from a virgin womb, unfertilized, therefore "dry."[33]

In this manner the Fathers of the Church, after Origen, and the medieval lyricists inspired by them, expounded different images and passages of the Old Testament to surround Mary with the myriad trophies and attributes with which she is still invoked in such prayers as the litany of Loreto. She is the tower of ivory, the house of gold, the Ark of the Covenant made of incorruptible timber, the lily among thorns, the rose in Jericho, the rose of Sharon, the tower of David, the holy root, the rod of Jesse.[34]

The operation of God on the virginal womb of Mary was prefigured in Scripture in a score of different ways: she was fecundated, like the fleece of Gideon drenched with dew while all around it remained dry (Judges 6:36–40); the rod of Aaron, like the womb of the Virgin, flowered of its own accord (Numbers 17:8); the stone in the dream of Nebuchadnezzar "was cut out of the mountain with no hands" (Daniel 2:34); the staff of Moses turned spontaneously into a serpent (Exodus 7:9); the manna fell like rain, a free gift from heaven (Exodus 16:14); the unaccompanied finger of God wrote the tablets of the law (Deuteronomy 9:10).

Mary's virginal womb was prefigured in the sensual praises of the Song of Songs: "A garden enclosed is my sister, my spouse; a spring shut up, a fountain sealed" (Song of Solomon 4:12). The same intact maidenhead is concealed behind the words of the Lord to Ezekiel: "This gate shall be shut, it shall not be opened, and no man shall enter in by it, therefore it shall be shut" (Ezekiel 44:2). The pot of gold that preserves manna from rottenness (Ezekiel 16:33) reflects her pure and uncorrupted womb.

On similar lines, the Virgin is the book Isaiah was shown by God, which was "sealed and could not be read" (Isaiah 29:12). The three young men who stood in the fiery furnace and were not burned pre-figured her unimpaired virginity, as did Daniel's invulnerability in the lions' den. In all these events, which suspended the ordinary course of nature, the Fathers saw presages of the miracle of Christ's conception and birth. The magnificent, enraptured sixth-century Greek paean, the *Akathistos,* hymns the Virgin as the destroyer of demons and the slaker of burning desires. The writer of this long and impassioned lexicon of Marian attributes, who may have been Romanos Melodos, also calls her "the ladder in the firmament" by which God came down, the bridge leading men from earth to heaven, and, mining the typology of the Old Testament, the "sea which drowned the spiritual Pharaoh," the rock that gushed with water and quenched the spiritual thirst of the faithful, the pillar of fire leading those lost in the darkness, as the Israelites were led across the wilderness, and the promised land that flows with milk and honey.[35]

Sheer exultation in the prodigy by which God became man marks in particular the hymns and homilies of the Greeks whose devotion to the Virgin inspired the later exhilaration of the medieval Church in the west. But the patristic imagery of the virgin birth, underneath its joyous fertil-ity, betrays lines of thought that should be considered more seriously: first, the equation of the supernatural and the unnatural, the reasoning that the divine can be glimpsed only in phenomena that, like the virgin birth, and Aaron's rod and Gideon's fleece, suspend the normal course of nature; second, the literal interpretation of purity as technical, physical virginity, as the closed womb, the "spring shut up," the "fountain sealed," an unbroken body, and not as a spiritual state of purity.

Both these assumptions are still dynamic in the cult of the Virgin, with lasting consequences, as we shall see.

The principal catalyst, however, to the definition of Mary's role and character and to her veneration as the mother of God in patristic times was heresy—the prolonged and acrimonious controversy surrounding the question of Christ's nature for the first five hundred years of Christianity.

The greatest threat to orthodoxy in the second century was Gnosti-cism, a mystery-cult version of Christianity that held the material uni-verse to be irredeemably corrupt, and therefore denied that the Word was made flesh. The Docetists, one branch of the Gnostics, maintained that Jesus was a divine phantom (from the Greek *dokeo,* I appear), a pure spirit, wholly free of the bondage of matter. In order to combat this heresy, the earliest Christian theologians had to stress the full humanity of Christ, which was best maintained by the human manner of his birth and death. Ignatius of Antioch (d. *c.* 110), addressing the fledgling communities of Asia Minor, emphasized forcibly that Mary truly gave birth to Jesus: "Jesus Christ our God was conceived by Mary of the seed of David and of the spirit of God . . ." (Ephesians 18). To the people of Tralles, he was more urgent: "Close your ears, then, if anyone preaches to you speaking of Jesus Christ. Christ was of David's line. He was the son of Mary; he was verily and indeed, born, and ate and drank . . ." (*Trallians* 9).[36] To Smyrna, he was as insistent: "You hold the firmest convictions about our Lord; believing him to be truly of David's line in his manhood, yet Son of God by the divine will and power; truly born of a Virgin; baptized by John . . . and in the days of Pontius Pilate and Herod the Tetrarch, truly pierced by nails in his human flesh . . ." (*Smyrnaeans* 1).[37] Ignatius' impassioned phrases still echo in the affirmations of the Christian creed.

Asserting Christ's full humanity could, however, tip the scales against his full divinity. Two hundred years later, the greatest menace to the Church was no longer Gnosticism, but Arianism, which did indeed proclaim that Jesus Christ was an ordinary human creature, whom God had only adopted at the baptism in the Jordan when he said: "Thou art my beloved son" (Luke 3:22). In order to confound this heresy, and yet avoid the equal fault of denying Christ's humanity, the birth of Christ from a woman by the operation of the Holy Ghost, and his consequent dual nature as man and God had to be satisfactorily defined.

The struggle was by no means over when the Emperor Constantine, presiding at the Council of Nicaea in 325, pronounced the teachings of Arius to be anathema. The agonized and complex theological debate on the nature of Christ continued for hundreds of years afterwards, arousing intense passions almost impossible for simple modern minds to credit. But as the arguments raged over the empire, the mother of Christ was forced into a more and more prominent position. Her unbroken virginity suspended the law of nature, and thus manifested the presence of the divine, but her full parturition of Christ served to prove his manhood. The virgin birth was the key to orthodox Christology.

In the fourth century, under the impact of Arianism, Mary's virginity was stressed. At the First Council of Constantinople in 381, her virgin motherhood was proclaimed. In Milan, the Christian writer Jovinian, who had dared to deny Mary's virginity during and after the birth of Christ (he never said she was not a virgin when she conceived), was excommunicated at a synod under St. Ambrose and again in Rome, where Jerome fulminated against his heresy. In 390, Pope Siricius proclaimed

Mary an inviolate virgin during the pregnancy and the birth of Christ. But the climax of the controversy came at the beginning of the fifth century, in a bitter power struggle between the rival sees of Constantinople and Antioch, which effectively inaugurated official veneration for the Virgin Mary.

The patriarch of Constantinople, Nestorius, heard the golden-tongued preacher Proclus give a sermon in praise of Mary in about 428, in which Proclus embroidered many a lavish simile of Mary's role in the Incarnation, and gave her the title *Theotokos* (the God-bearer, the mother of God). It was not the first time the title had been used. But Nestorius had been trained in the pragmatic and restrained tradition of Antioch, where the separation of Christ's two natures as God and man was firmly held, and he balked at this excessive—and in his eyes heterodox—term of praise. It implied, he preached in reply, that the Word of God, who had existed from all eternity, was born in the stable at Bethlehem that first Christmas night. God was not a baby two or three months old, he declared, and Mary was either the mother of the man—*Anthropotokos*—or at most, the mother of Christ—*Christotokos*—but she could not be the mother of God, because God had always been. Besides, the use of such an extravagant title dangerously exaggerated her standing and raised her to the rank of a goddess, as worshipped by the heathen.

The issue raised by Nestorius and Proclus' disagreement soon engaged the ancient and inflammatory rivalry between Constantinople and Alexandria, where the zealot Patriarch Cyril leaped to the defence of Proclus. The resulting feud entangled the imperial court in Constantinople as well as the pope in Rome. It is interesting that even at the height of the battle no one suggested Mary was not a virgin—that at least had been established. But they quarrelled about her divine motherhood. Finally, Cyril of Alexandria presided at a heated council held at Ephesus in June 431, and excommunicated his enemy Nestorius. His authority to do so was questionable. Nevertheless, Mary was proclaimed *Theotokos* (mother of God) and in torchlit processions through the city the Ephesians demonstrated their jubilation that the man who had slighted the Virgin Mary had been deposed. "Praise be to the Theotokos! Long live Cyril!" they cheered.

The political and religious wrangling was not ended by Ephesus, however, and in 451, at the Council of Chalcedon, the Fourth Ecumenical Council of the Church, the two natures of Christ were formally reasserted, in an attempt to heal divisions still rankling. The Virgin was officially given the title *Aeiparthenos* (ever-virgin) and her virginity at the conception, *in partu,* and *post partum* thereby affirmed. Two hundred years later, in 649, at the First Lateran Council, Pope Martin I (d. 655) declared Mary's perpetual virginity a dogma of the Church.

The crowd's testimony to the Virgin's popularity in 431 was indeed eloquent, and the decision of Ephesus stands as the first landmark in the cult of Mary as mother of God. Both after Ephesus and Chalcedon, the government asked the approval of Symeon the Stylite (d. 459), who lived on top of a column in a Syrian monastery. Symeon, simple, unlettered, and holy, had won enormous popularity and prestige, and the need for his acceptance suggests that although the conciliar decisions that proclaimed Mary *Theotokos* and *Aeiparthenos* sprang from quarrels in the upper echelons of Church and state and settled complex Christological questions, they did undoubtedly have a base in the faith of ordinary Christians. It must also be remembered, however, as always with regard to spontaneous popular movements, that Cyril of Alexandria's agents had been active at Ephesus before the Council opened and the people's will, so impressively displayed, may have been well oiled.[38]

After the turbulence of the fifth century, the cult of the Virgin grew more smoothly, focussing its attentions on her miraculous virginity and her divine motherhood. The earliest feasts of the Virgin were instituted in the fifth century in Byzantium: the Annunciation (first kept on Ember Wednesday during Advent and then at the vernal equinox, March 25); and a commemoration in honour of her virginity, which was held either before or after Christmas all over the empire (probably on the Sunday before in Byzantium, December 18 in Spain, January 18 in Gaul, January 1 in Rome. It has now been revived in the new liturgy as the Solemnity of the Mother of God on the Christmas octave). Both these early feasts celebrate Mary's vital role in the Incarnation. Around the year 600, the feast of the Dormition, or Falling Asleep of the Virgin, was introduced on August 15; and fifty years later her Nativity and Presentation in the temple, based on the *Book of James,* began to be commemorated on September 8 and November 21, respectively.

Another feast was instituted in Jerusalem as early as the middle of the fourth century: the feast of the Presentation of Jesus in the temple. It was first kept forty days after the Epiphany, on February 14. By the early sixth century in Byzantium, the feast, now called the *Hypapante* (the Meeting), focussed less on the exemplary obedience of Jesus and Mary to Mosaic law than on Simeon and Anna's inspired recognition of the saviour.

Monks fleeing the Moslem invasion of the Holy Land in the seventh century brought the Byzantine quartet of Marian feastdays westwards: the

Annunciation, the Nativity, the Dormition, and the Presentation; the last, when it reached Rome, became the celebration of Mary's purification. The new character the feast acquired is highly indicative of the development of the Virgin's cult in Europe. For in the west, the accent of the feast of the Purification fell strongly on Mary's holiness and came to celebrate the mystery of her purity. Also, it was moved to February 2, where it coincided with the ancient pagan feast of lights, when torches and candles were carried in nighttime processions to exorcize the spirits of plague and famine, of earthquake and all natural disasters emanating from the darkness of the underworld.[39] Under Pope Sergius I, in 701, the Virgin's feast assimilated the symbol; and to this day, on February 2, young Catholic girls walk in procession in white veils and lighted candles to pierce through night's shadows with new light. Mary's holiness, her incandescent purity, is the source of this power over darkness.

The Gospel story had seemed to imply that Mary, like all mothers, was defiled by childbirth and in need of purification, but the feast that commemorated it twisted the Judaic rite into a thoroughly Christian encomium to the power of purity over evil. A Byzantine historian of the second half of the ninth century had chronicled the introduction of the Purification in Byzantium: "In the fifteenth year of the reign of Justinian in the month of October, there was a plague in Byzantium; and in the same year the Purification began to be celebrated on the second day of February."[40] Not surprisingly, later Christians like William of Malmesbury in the twelfth century understood there to be a causal connection: the Virgin lifted the plague because the feast was instituted in her honour. Mary's purificatory fire had supreme prophylactic powers: purity prevailed against impurity.

Thus the invincible association of holiness with physical virginity, of the power of chastity over evil, dyed the entire fabric of the Marian cult from its official beginnings in Byzantium. Her miraculous virginity, the sign of her supremacy, is the strongest theme in the whole symphony of patristic writings, apocryphal tales, and early ritual. Christian asceticism is fundamental to the veneration of the *Theotokos;* it is not surprising that the very first prayer to the Virgin, recorded by St. Gregory Nazianzen (d. 390), is the imploration of Justina to come to the help of a virgin in danger.[41] The cult of Mary is inextricably interwoven with Christian ideas about the dangers of the flesh and their special connection with women.

*Chapter Five*

# VIRGINS AND MARTYRS

*For take my word for it, there is no libel*
*On woman that the clergy will not paint,*
*Except when writing of a woman saint*
*But never good of other women, though.*[1]

—GEOFFREY CHAUCER, "The Wife of Bath"

MARY HAS ALWAYS BEEN the paragon of virginity. In 325, the Council of Nicaea exhorted all women to follow her example: "The Lord looked upon the whole of creation, and he saw no-one to equal Mary. Therefore he chose her for his mother. If therefore a girl wants to be called a virgin, she should resemble Mary."[2] It is in the homilies on the ascetic life, in the exhortations to chastity penned by the Christian Fathers from the second century onwards that the Virgin chiefly appears: in Cyprian's *On the Dress of Virgins,* in Ambrose's *Instructions of a Virgin,* in Tertullian's *On the Veiling of Virgins,* in Jerome's disciplinary letters to his circle of pupils.[3] There has been little deviation from this theme over the centuries. A prayerbook based on the directives of the Second Vatican Council of 1964 includes a section called "We promise to imitate her" and recommends a modern prayer: "Most blessed Virgin Mary . . . your life of faith and love and perfect unity with Christ was planned by God to show us clearly what our lives should be . . . you are the outstanding model of motherhood and virginity."[4]

Through the ascetic renunciation of the flesh, a woman could relieve a part of her nature's particular viciousness as the Virgin Mary had done through her complete purity. The life of self-denial was seen as a form of martyrdom, and the virgin was encouraged to suffer physically. For in

68

times of persecution, martyrdom made amends for nature's wrongs, and proved the faith of the victim; and in untroubled times the equivalent of the arena was the cell, and the equivalent of the wild beast was the renunciation of worldly happiness and the practices of the hair shirt, the waterbowl, and the scourge. Through virginity and self-inflicted hardship, the faults of female nature could be corrected.

Until the peace of the Church in 313, their enemies inflicted sufferings on Christians and won them the martyr's crown; but afterwards Christians inflicted the sufferings on themselves in order to obtain the glory of self-martyrdom, and to prove their love of God by lives of torment and self-denial on earth.

The shift from the rabid violence of the circus to the world of the hermitage or nunnery is a most important one to recognize in moral attitudes towards women, for it created one of Christianity's most important and enduring mythological types: the virgin martyr.

In the light of recent massacres, the toll of martyrs—about one hundred thousand over a period of about two hundred and fifty years (A.D. 64 to A.D. 313)—seems light. But for the young Church, the crisis was galvanizing—the single most important catalyst to unity and strength. The roll of honour from St. Stephen the proto-martyr through the apostles bound Christian to Christian in a struggle against outside circumstances, honing loyalty and belief and equality and brotherhood. The conflict was external; the enemy without. Tacitus, in his celebrated passage about Nero's excesses of A.D. 64, noted the backlash effect:

Their deaths were made farcical. Dressed in wild animals' skins, they were torn to pieces by dogs, or crucified, or made into torches to be ignited after dark as substitutes for daylight. Nero provided his Gardens for the spectacle, and exhibited displays in the Circus, at which he mingled with the crowd—or stood in a chariot dressed as a charioteer. Despite their guilt as Christians, and the ruthless punishment it deserved, the victims were pitied. For it was felt that they were being sacrificed to one man's brutality rather than to the national interest.[5]

Christians were aware of the strengthening results of persecution. But they also sought the martyr's crown to open the gates of heaven, and the ardour of their longing takes the breath away. Ignatius, bishop of Antioch, writing to Rome as he was on his way to execution in about 110, cries out in ecstasy: "I am the wheat of God; and I must be ground by the teeth of wild beasts to become the pure bread of Christ."[6] The eulogies of saints like Perpetua and Felicity, who faced the wild beasts unflinchingly, inspired equal heroism in others. Their martyrdom, under Septimus Severus in 202 or 203 at Carthage, was immortalized in one of early Christianity's most extraordinary documents, told partly in the first person by St. Perpetua herself. Perpetua, recently married, has a small child; but nothing deters her. Her slave Felicity is pregnant, but is delighted when she gives birth prematurely in prison, for even the Romans drew the line at throwing expectant mothers to the beasts, and Felicity yearned for martyrdom.[7]

In A.D. 313 the Emperor Constantine issued the edict of toleration, and from then on, with the exception of the brief and bloody career of Julian the Apostate, the era of persecution was over. There would be no more martyrs to the faith under Roman law—it was a realization that had a profound effect on the ascetic ideal and the cult of virginity.

For, once memories of persecution faded, the reasons for the martyrdom of Christians changed in emphasis. One of the most significant early martyrologies was compiled by Hroswitha in Germany, in the tenth century. She wrote many plays for the convent in which she lived, dramatizing the fortitude of women under the most imaginative and horrific tortures. In her prefaces to a volume of the plays she reveals vividly the difference of motive as it changed from the defence of the faith to the defence of virginity: "My object being to glorify the laudable chastity of Christian virgins. . . . One thing has all the same embarrassed me and often brought a blush to my cheek. It is that I have been compelled through the nature of this work to apply my mind and my pen to depicting the dreadful frenzy of those possessed by unlawful love, and the insidious sweetness of passion—things which should not even be named among us."[8]

For by the tenth century and Hroswitha's day, the Christian struggle for perfection was no longer intelligible as a struggle against the authorities without. The Church had long ago triumphed throughout the known world. Christian struggle now concentrated on the enemy within. And concupiscence, as Augustine had defined it, was the root of sin, and one of its principal manifestations was lust. Virginity and martyrdom became complementary ideas, and the physical subjection of the body to the pains and ordeals of ascetic discipline was an integral part of sanctity.

As the spectre of the era of persecution receded, legends of virgin martyrs altered, and although they still persisted in their refusal to burn offerings to the pagan gods, they died in order to defend their chastity as well. Almost all the female martyrs commemorated in the liturgy were also virgins. In compendia like the *Golden Legend*, they are presented as universally beautiful, graceful, irresistible, accomplished, and virtuous.

Tempted by well-placed youths who often offer their lives in return for their love, they refuse, and are butchered for it.

In Christian hagiography, the sadomasochistic content of the paeans to male and female martyrs is startling, from the early documents like the *Passion of Saints Perpetua and Felicity* into the high middle ages. But the particular focus on women's torn and broken flesh reveals the psychological obsession of the religion with sexual sin, and the tortures that pile up one upon the other with pornographic repetitiousness underline the identification of the female with the perils of sexual contact. For, as they defend their virtue, the female martyrs of the Christian calendar are assaulted in any number of ingenious and often sexual ways: in the *Golden Legend,* Agatha's breasts are cut off; Apollonia's teeth are torn out and she is then burned to death; Juliana is shattered on a wheel "until the marrow spurted out," then plunged into a lead bath; Euphemia is tormented with all sorts of refinements and then beheaded; Catherine of Alexandria is also broken on a wheel.[9]

The theme did not draw to a close in the middle ages, for one of the saints most recently canonized by the Vatican fits into this pattern exactly: Maria Goretti, born in 1890, was murdered at the age of eleven by a young man from her village, whom she knew. He tried to rape her, and when she resisted, stabbed her many times with a stiletto. She was taken to hospital, where she freely forgave him from her heart and was made a Child of Mary by her local priest. She died the next day, July 6, 1902. In 1947, in the presence of her aged mother, Pope Pius XII beatified her by public decree:

Italian girls especially, in the fair flower of their youth should raise their eyes to Heaven and gaze upon this shining example of maidenly virtue which rose from the midst of wickedness as a light shines in the darkness. . . . God is wonderful in His saints. . . . Now he has given to the young girls of our cruel and degraded world a model and protector, the little maid Maria who sanctified the opening of our century with her innocent blood.[10]

In 1950 the pope canonized her a saint. One Catholic woman recalled in a book of memoirs that at her convent school the nuns played their charges a dramatized tape of this exemplary scene, which consisted of much heaving and sighing punctuated by the bloodcurdling cries of the victim.[11] Of all the ways different societies define sexual crime and deal with it, of all the ways sexual mores are instilled into that society's youth, this must rank as the strangest.

Maria Goretti's resistance was, it is stressed, protracted. In the legends of the martyrs before her, every art in the torturer's handbook cannot kill them. This is not because Catholics have peculiarly sadistic tastes, but because they wish to emphasize that virginity confers extraordinary strength, that spiritual virtue is mirrored by physical powers. Jacques de Vitry's collection of exempla includes the story of a young boy who has been brought up in a monastery all his life and has never seen a woman. The abbot takes him on a journey, and when they stop at a smithy on the way to reshoe the horses, the boy picks up the red-hot iron fresh from the anvil and passes it to the blacksmith without a cry, without a burn. That night the abbot and his page stop at an inn, where the keeper's wife seduces the boy. The following day, at another forge, the boy picks up a shoe as he did the day before, and drops it with a yell of pain and horror.[12]

Jacques de Vitry, a sophisticated cardinal and crusader, told such a story in all seriousness, for the relationship of moral virtue to strength of all kinds is central to Christian ascetic thought. The element of magic in Jacques's story is present in all the appalling martyrologies of Christian literature. This understanding helps to illuminate why virginity became such a very important symbol for early Christians and why it was especially prescribed for women.

The idea that virginity confers power operates on two different planes. First, the Fathers of the Church taught that the virginal life reduced the special penalties of the Fall in women and was therefore holy. Second, the image of the virgin body was the supreme image of wholeness, and wholeness was equated with holiness.[13] For both these reasons, the defence of the virginal state was worth all the savagery to which saints like Catherine of Alexandria (d. *c.* 310) and Maria Goretti submitted, and won for them the eternal accolades of the Church.

It is crucial to remember that, in spite of the misogyny that underpins the Christian religion, it offered women a revolution, as long as they subscribed to its precepts. St. Paul wrote: "There is neither Jew nor Greek, there is neither bond nor free, there is neither male nor female; for ye are all one in Christ Jesus" (Galatians 3:28). The early Church offered brotherhood to all men and women, in a manner unknown in the world of late antiquity. Although it considered women socially subject to the male, it granted them an identical immortal soul. Women were therefore equal in religion as long as the Christian code was accepted, and that entailed accepting its view of sex and childbirth.

The paradox central to Christian attitudes towards women is that it attempted to reinstate women by removing the conditions that stamped them as inferior and kept them in servitude: marriage and motherhood. Theologians like Cyprian (d. 258) and Tertullian and Jerome appeal to women to adopt the virginal life because then they will not have to suffer the consequences of the Fall; they constantly harp on the joys of the single life, without a husband to obey or pregnancies to endure. A virgin escaped the multiplied sorrows of conception to which her sex had been condemned at the Fall and she had no desire to her husband and was not ruled by him, for she was spared the marital condition. To some extent, virginity thus reversed the Fall. Jerome wrote: "As long as a woman is for birth and children, she is different from man as body is from soul. But when she wishes to serve Christ more than the world, then she will cease to be a woman, and will be called man."[14]

Such a stand, while it admitted potential virtue to women, failed completely to attack the problem of inequality. Rather, such a conditional offering exacerbated Christian opinions of the sex's inferiority, for the fallen state of the unchaste was stressed in contrast to their virgin sisters.

The importance of virginity for women also hinged on the mental image the Fathers of the Church had of the female body. Virginity was created by God, and was therefore holy: Ambrose wrote that for a girl to lose her maidenhead was "to deface the work of the creator."[15] Jerome wrote: "To show that virginity is natural while wedlock only follows guilt, what is born of wedlock is virgin flesh." He added that marriage was tolerable at all only because more virgins were born as a result.[16] The ascetic homilies of the fourth century, like the sermons of headmistresses today, ring with fury at the use of cosmetics, because they disguise the pristine natural state.[17]

The virgin body was not only pristine, however; it was also whole. The biblical images the Fathers applied to the birth of Christ reveal that they conceived of a virgin's body as seamless, unbroken, a literal epiphany of integrity. The Virgin Mary is a "closed gate," a "spring shut up," a "fountain sealed." Her physical virginity *post partum* was as important a part of orthodoxy in the early Church as her virginal conception by the power of the Holy Ghost.

St. Methodius of Olympus, a Christian neoplatonist philosopher, gives graphic evidence of this train of thought, associating the physical state with the spiritual, in his *Symposium of Ten Virgins*. His leading speaker, the lady Arete, declares: "It is imperative that anyone who intends to avoid sin in the practice of chastity must keep all his members and senses pure and sealed—just as pilots caulk a ship's timbers—to prevent sin from getting an opening and pouring in."[18]

The virgin body was natural and integral, and as such the foremost image of purity. The symbolism was, of course, dependent on inexact medical knowledge, which has proved remarkably tenacious. Until modern times, the hymen was thought to seal off the womb completely, and in many parts of the world, cruel ceremonies of defloration are performed on young girls in order to "open" them so they can become fertile—that is, menstruate. The confusion perhaps arose and persisted in Europe because girls were married off at a nubile age, so that penetration might have seemed the cause of menstruation. But the notion lasted long after child marriage had disappeared. Convent schoolgirls now are still taught that their maidenhead is absolute, that the hymen closes the vagina, and in defiance of all empirical evidence, they are warned not to wear tampons because they will pierce it and irreparably damage their virginity.

It is precisely because of this erroneous mental image that virginity became so much more important a state for women. Men's bodies were not perceived to be integral in the same way: the absence of the unperforated hymen, caulking the body like tar on a ship's timbers, made a man's body an incomplete and imperfect symbol of wholeness.

In the light of this symbolism, some of the ascetic practices enjoined on young women by their confessors, like St. Jerome, become intelligible, and the connection between virginity as an escape from the Fall and as a holy state of wholeness is thereby revealed. Jerome, like many other spiritual directors, but more forcibly, commanded Eustochium, one of the young Roman girls in his charge, to fast unceasingly, to avoid wine, and to seek as companions "women pale and thin with fasting." He waxes eloquent on the virtues of Eustochium's mother, Paula, who, while lying ill of a fever brought about by starvation, refused obdurately the wine her doctors begged her to take. Jerome sent a messenger to persuade her, but her resolution was such that from her sickbed she managed to convert the messenger to abstinence himself.[19] Blesilla, Paula's other daughter, died, and Jerome was angrily accused by the Roman clergy of precipitating her death by the excesses he encouraged.

Fasting, like chastity, was prescribed for both sexes; but like virginity, fasting has a particular character in women that enhances the symbolism of wholeness and purity. Amenorrhea, the absence of menstruation, develops rapidly. Even young girls on a minor diet can miss a period, while starvation (as in the case of the illness anorexia nervosa) can cause permanent damage: menstruation might never begin again.[20]

Jerome represents the radical wing of Christian asceticism; nevertheless, his injunctions to Paula and her daughters are repeated down the centuries by spiritual counsellors to their charges. All-night vigils, fasts, physical discipline—the hair shirt, the scourge, the stone St. Jerome beats against his breast in painting after painting, including Leonardo's unfinished masterpiece in the Vatican—silence, and tears are the means of attaining sanctity. (Although modern psychology has given the Church some doubts about the wisdom of the scourge, the other practices are still encouraged—in moderation. In the 1950s the novices at Woodstock College, the former Jesuit training centre in Maryland, were still given a spiked band to wear on their thighs as a penance.)

The effect on young women of the regime Jerome encouraged would undoubtedly be amenorrhea: the elimination of the curse of Eve. A Christian virgin already avoided the apparent terror of childbirth: as Venantius Fortunatus wrote in the sixth century: "Happy virgin . . . she does not weigh down sluggish limbs with an imprisoned embryo; she is not depressed and worn out by its awkward weight."[21] With the holy life as taught by St. Jerome, she could purify herself of the stain of menstruation, too.

It must be said, in fairness, that of all the major religions, Christianity has displayed the least prejudice towards menstruation. The taboo against women, during both pregnancy and their monthly period, exists all over the world, but has a different and not always negative significance in each society that obeys it, a question far too complex to enter into here. In Christianity the strict Judaic tradition was softened. For instance, the ritual purification of women required by Mosaic law after the birth of a child, and obeyed by the Virgin Mary in the New Testament, changed its emphasis: women were not required to be cleansed after childbirth, but a visit to church was encouraged, to give thanks to God for the child. This euphemistic ceremony, the churching of women, still continues, in Anglican and other Protestant communities as well.

In 601, Pope Gregory the Great wrote to St. Augustine of Canterbury, answering many questions on the impurity of women. The letter is a model of Christ-like contempt for pharisaical attachment to externals. Of course, replies the Pope, pregnant women can be baptized and receive communion; of course women after childbirth should be allowed into church; of course no restrictions apply to a menstruating woman. Hunger is the result of the Fall, but eating is not sinful; likewise with the menstrual flow. Gregory's enlightenment was not entirely characteristic of the Church, which continued here and there at various times until the seventeenth century to discourage menstruating or pregnant women from attending church or the sacraments. The eastern, Russian, and Ethiopian Churches still enforce the old Jewish taboo. While the Gregorian view prevailed in the west, Joan Morris, in her interesting book on women's place in the Church, argues that the ban on female ordination stems from the ancient fear of menstruation's power to pollute, a fear certainly lively in medieval and Renaissance books of lore, like the popular sixteenth-century *Natural Magick* by Giovanni Battista della Porta, and in the *De Secretis Mulieribus,* attributed to Albertus Magnus.

Whether this is the case is difficult to prove, as the silence of true taboo generally reigns over the topic in ecclesiastical writings. But it is empirically true that in the Catholic world little girls and old women are now allowed to help in church at various minor duties, while women in their prime are not. Jerome himself, commenting on Zechariah, wrote: "Nothing is so unclean as a woman in her periods, what she touches she causes to become unclean." It is therefore legitimate to speculate that the way of life Jerome recommended may have appeared holy because it incidentally arrested the flow that constituted part of the penalty of the Fall.[22]

But because it could secure a degree of independence and equality, the ascetic life exercised a tremendous attraction over women from its earliest days, and the history of the Church is illuminated by saints of genius, who were able, once they had capitulated to the conditions the Church demanded, to assert their ideas and their authority as independent and active women. Some of the most notable advances in the worlds of teaching, nursing, and social work of different kinds were achieved by women like Teresa of Ávila (d. 1582), who reformed the Carmelite order, Angela Merici (d. 1540), who founded the Ursulines, Jeanne de Chantal (d. 1641), who set up the Sisters of the Visitation, another teaching and nursing order, and in England Mary Ward (d. 1645), who conceived the revolutionary purpose of educating women and fought the pope tooth and nail to open and maintain her schools. It would be impossible to list the innumerable foundations and orders started by purposeful women who understood that the virginal state gave them a special claim on Christian society, and therefore exploited it to raise the condition of their sex.

As an answer to the problem of female equality, the nun's vocation is similar to the lesbianism some members of the contemporary women's movement in America have chosen.[23] By cutting themselves off from the traditional role of women, and by abjuring all relations with men, consecrated virgins established a certain freedom and autonomy that permitted them to lead lives of greater distinction than their married sisters. Satisfaction at such a state obviously varies from individual to individual, but at a general level, the solution is completely inadequate. For the foundations of the ethic of sexual chastity are laid in fear and loathing of the female body's functions, in identification of evil with the flesh and flesh with woman.

This hatred and contempt continue to influence decision-making in the Church, for even its most honoured saints, like Catherine of Siena and Teresa of Avila, who are the only female Doctors, would not have been admitted to the priesthood. Paradoxically, the veil, and the surrender to a certain system of values that the veil implies, could procure a woman an education, a certain freedom of manoeuvre, and a certain exercise of influence unattainable for other women, with the exception of princesses, queens, and heiresses.

Thus the nun's state is a typical Christian conundrum, oppressive and liberating at once, founded in contempt of, yet inspiring respect for, the female sex. It is, in this regard, a mirror image of the Virgin Mary herself, the sublime model of the virginal life, the *inventrix virginitatis*, according to Hroswitha, and the patroness of countless orders of monks and nuns. She is a preeminent and sublime example of woman, who excites love and awe.

But the very conditions that make the Virgin sublime are beyond the powers of women to fulfil unless they deny their sex. Accepting the Virgin as the ideal of purity implicitly demands rejecting the ordinary female condition as impure. Accepting virginity as an ideal entails contempt for sex and motherhood, with the result that far from remaining a privileged state undertaken by a few women of vocation, virginity and sexual chastity become a general condition of sinlessness applicable to both the married and the unmarried.

According to St. Augustine, the marriage of Joseph and Mary, in which there was no sexual intercourse, was the ideal, and continence was the best expression of love between a husband and wife. A mutual vow of abstinence from sex was the highest good in marriage.[24] In the middle ages, preachers recommended many different days of abstinence from sex: for instance, on Thursday in memory of Christ's arrest, Friday in memory of his death, Saturday in honour of the Virgin Mary, Sunday in honour of the Resurrection, and Monday in remembrance of the faithful departed. In the fourteenth century, Margery Kempe wrote an extraordinary account of her celibate marriage, undertaken after a profound realization of the sinfulness of sex.[25]

The concept of Christian virtue as sexual abstinence permeated the entire community, together with the misogynist premises on which the ethic was founded. Thus the little hard-won independence of nuns was gained at other women's cost, for belief in the inferiority of their state underpinned it.

The arguments operating on the idea of virginity control the entire structure of the myth of the Virgin Mary. For after the Fall, God did not only curse womankind to suffer childbirth in sorrow; he also sentenced all mankind to corruption in the grave. Since Adam and Eve's sin, sex is tainted by concupiscence, and death disfigured by mortal decay. As a symptom of sin, putrefaction is concupiscence's twin; and a woman who conquered one penalty of the Fall could overcome the other.[26]

*Part Two*

# QUEEN

# Chapter Six

# THE ASSUMPTION

*Where, alack,*
*Shall Time's best jewel from Time's chest lie hid?*

—WILLIAM SHAKESPEARE, Sonnet LXV

THE GEM-STUDDED COVER OF THE GOSPEL BOOK that used to belong to the German Emperor Otto III contains at its centre a small, exceptionally fine ivory. The Virgin lies, hands folded, on a bed that is adorned with a richly ruffled valance; she is surrounded by the apostles, and attended by angels, whose hands are respectfully draped like Byzantine courtiers. Standing beside Mary's reclining form, Christ holds up her papoose-like soul as if he had plucked it from her very heart (figure 9).

The ivory panel was carved in Constantinople at the end of the tenth century, and it depicts the *Koimesis,* Dormition, or Falling Asleep of the Blessed Virgin Mary. The irony is that Otto placed the treasure on the cover of his copy of the Gospels, for nowhere in the Bible is the death of the Virgin mentioned.

But that same Gospel silence invited story-telling. From the second century onwards, the manner of the Virgin's death was described all over the near east, in Syria, Palestine, Egypt, Ethiopia. Gregory of Tours, at the end of the sixth century, had heard the tales in Gaul. The feastday of August 15 commemorating her passing was proclaimed throughout the Roman empire by the Emperor Maurice around the year 600 in the east; and about fifty years later the feastday is recorded in the west. The stories of the miracles that shook the world at the death of Mary often originated in heretical circles; but from them a single, coherent tale emerged that won general acceptance in the medieval Church and, though treated with scepticism now, it nevertheless influenced profoundly the dogma of the Assumption, which was proclaimed an article of faith by Pope Pius XII in 1950.

The cult of the saints in the early Christian Church concentrated on their martyrdom, its site, and their relics. But in Mary's case there were no contemporary records at all of her death, and though one Greek writer, Epiphanius, suggested that the sword of which Simeon had spoken at the Purification might have been the instrument of her death, no tradition of her martyrdom existed. Most perplexing of all, there was no knowledge of her grave—no body to venerate, no relics to touch. The disappearance of Mary's body delayed her cult, for there was no shrine, where she, in person, could be venerated. But it inspired the most fertile imaginings, for with the absence of historical data, free rein could be given to speculation along lines engraved in the symbolic fabric of Christianity. For the symbol of purity itself could not be given to the worms for pasture; the image of eternal spring could not rot in the grave. As the historian G. G. Coulton wrote: "If the world knew more about the Virgin Mary, the middle ages would have known far less."

The medieval tradition of the Assumption of the Virgin derives from many ancient eastern stories, of which the earliest extant is probably a fragmentary vision of the afterlife called the *Obsequies of the Holy Virgin,* written in Syriac at the beginning of the third century (according to the Catholic scholar E. Cothenet) or a hundred and fifty years later (according to the document's discoverer and editor, W. Wright).[1]

The *Obsequies of the Holy Virgin* opens with a discussion between Andrew, Peter, and John during which each of them vehemently proclaims total renunciation: of food, of sex, of family and friends. Paul interposes a gentle note, to restrain the others. The author casually tells us that the discussion is taking place "before the entrance of the tomb of Mary." Jesus appears with the archangel Michael and endorses Paul's viewpoint. He then orders Michael to carry the Virgin's body to heaven, and the apostles to mount upon clouds and follow them. "And when they entered Paradise, the body of Mary went to the tree of life; and they brought her soul and made it enter her body." The apostles are then revealed atrocities in the pit of hell. After some stirring apocalyptic passages and other matter, the fragment ends.

The document belongs to the corpus of apocalyptic and hermetic literature that flourished in the second and third centuries, and its prime concern is to establish Paul's authority over the other apostles and the need for God's mercy in the afterlife. The resurrection of the mother of God almost appears as an aside. The probable reason for this is that there was some confusion in the early Christian world about voyages into the afterlife. When St. Paul described how he was "caught up to the third heaven," he added, "whether in the body, I cannot tell; or whether out of the body, I cannot tell, God knoweth" (2 Corinthians 12:2). All mankind would be resurrected in the body on the last day, which raised the question of the real material existence of the eternal places—an insoluble problem, still being discussed. In the light of this enduring dilemma, Cothenet suggests that the author of the *Obsequies of the Virgin* resuscitated her in order to transport her to the pit of hell, not to proclaim the peculiar glory of her immortality.

In other Syriac versions of the story of Mary's death, dated from 350–400 (by Wright), the emphasis has shifted from issues of the nether regions to the Virgin herself. After Jesus has risen from the dead and left this world, Mary "in great sorrow" prays daily by his sepulchre for death, which will reunite her with her son. The Jews, portrayed as deeply embittered against Christ and his followers, are plotting to stone her to death. As she is praying, an angel appears to her and promises her the death she desires. The governor of Jerusalem, Sabinus, gives the Jews carte blanche to proceed against her, but the Holy Ghost wraps Mary in a miraculous cloud of invisibility and she escapes them. Back in Bethlehem in her own house, where she lives with three virgin companions, Mary prays to see Jesus, the apostles, and his disciples once more before her death.

One by one the apostles are called from the corners of the world. John, in Ephesus, is told the news by the Holy Spirit, caught up in a cloud of light, and transported to Bethlehem. He arrives, embraces Mary's knees, and promises her a death of great glory. She confides that she is terrified the Jews will try to burn her body. John reassures her in the words of the Psalm: "Neither wilt thou suffer thine Holy One to see corruption" (Psalms 16:10). "On steeds and clouds of light," the other apostles join Mary and John. The ones who have already died rise from their graves. They talk and perform miracles, then return to Jerusalem with Mary. The Holy Spirit tells them to take her to a valley near the Mount of Olives where they will find three caves, one inside the other. They are to place Mary in the innermost recess. As the procession travels towards this tomb, a Jew tries to shake Mary off her litter, but an angel of fire severs his hands from his body and they remain, stuck to her bed. Mary hears his prayer, restores them to him, and he is converted. Peter gives him a miraculous staff, which cures all whom it touches.

When Mary has been laid down in the innermost cave, angels appear and chariots descend bearing Moses and Enoch and Elias and Christ.

"And they carried the blessed one to Paradise with this glory, and her holy body was placed there. And then she was carried up and reached the gate of Paradise, the sword that surrounds Paradise was taken away, and the holy one went in with glory that is unspeakable into Paradise. . . . And they placed her in boundless light amid the delicious trees of the Paradise of Eden; and they exalted her with glory on which the eyes of the flesh is not able to gaze. . . ." The apostles then beseech Jesus that all who commemorate his virgin mother shall have an answer to their prayers.

This early story of the Virgin's last days on earth never mentions her death: she is translated to heaven, and the moment of her *Transitus*, her passover, is attended by the four men of the Bible who also conquered the mortal fate of every man. Enoch was believed to have gone directly to heaven (see Genesis 5:24; Hebrews 11:5); Moses' death was wrapped in mystery, for at the close of Deuteronomy, it says, "No man knoweth of his sepulchre to this day"; Elijah was swept up to heaven in a whirlwind on a chariot of fire. When Christ is transfigured on the mountain, two men appear in radiant glory beside him—Moses and Elijah, the fore-shadowings of his Resurrection. Like them, and her son, Mary is taken up to heaven, to live there in her glorified body, as a promise of the resurrection of the flesh that will come to every creature.

The Greek account, which claimed the eyewitness authority of the apostle John himself, formed the basis of numerous sermons and hom-ilies in the east from the seventh century onwards. When Jesus arrives in the Virgin's chamber, she asks for mercy for all sinners who call on her, and then, her wish granted, she dies: "and the Lord spread forth his unstained hands and received her holy and spotless soul." This is the scene that Otto's ivory depicts, and the central iconographical theme of all Byzantine pictures of the Dormition of the Virgin (colour plate IV, figure 5). In the Greek story, three days elapse, and then the Virgin's tomb is found empty.

All the eastern accounts—although they differ on the moment and manner of her death and translation to paradise—agree that the Virgin is passive, that her flesh at the moment of her glory is inert, if not inani-mate. But on the journey east to west, the Virgin becomes more vigorous and active. In the great Benedictine abbey of Reichenau, nine fulsome Greek sermons for the feast of the Dormition were translated in the tenth century. They all contained the apocryphal stories of her death. The version that gained the most complete popularity in the western half of Christendom was a Latin translation of a Greek document attributed to Melito, the renowned second-century bishop of Sardis. It is the most concentrated and coherent of all the tales, and it tells substantially the same sequence of events that appear in woodcarvings, stained glass, embroidery, and painting all over the cathedrals and churches of the middle ages, particularly in England and France.

The *Pseudo-Melito,* as it is called, does make a significant addition to the eastern tale, however. Christ tells Mary she must die: "Thou . . . shalt see him [the prince of darkness] indeed according to the law of mankind whereby the end, even death is allotted thee." But the Devil, he adds, cannot hurt her. Peter tells Jesus that, as Mary was his "immaculate chamber," "thou shouldst raise up the body of thy mother and take her with thee rejoicing into heaven." Jesus assents, and commands Michael to bring Mary's soul down again from heaven. The angel rolls away the stone from the sepulchre and Jesus invokes Mary: "Rise up my love and my kinswoman: thou that didst not suffer corruption by union of the flesh, shalt not suffer dissolution of the body. . . ." Mary rises from the dead and falls at Jesus' feet to thank him. "And the Lord kissed her and departed, and delivered her to the angels to bear her into paradise."

This is an assumption; not a falling asleep. She is reanimated immediately after death, by the return of her soul to the body; and she is then carried to heaven by angels. Her body is not taken up to rest in one place until the last day, while her soul enjoys the beatific presence in a higher heaven, as some of the Greek versions suggest. Death cannot prevail against her, Jesus explicitly promises, because she who was not corrupt in conception and childbirth shall not suffer corruption in the grave. The direction of the story is firm; the author is not deflected by visions of hell, or compacts of mercy. He subjects Mary to physical death and thus circumvents any Gnostic-type denial of her full humanity; but he raises her up in the flesh, which also affirms the doctrine of the resurrection of the body, which Gnostic influence on Christianity helped make equally distasteful. Her dignity, as the *immaculatus thalamus* of the son of God, is given by Peter as the warrant for her conquest of death. As she lived pure, she shall not be submitted to the impurity of death, or, like sinful Adam, dissolve into dust.

When Dante, several hundred years later, wrote that the Virgin was "she who most resembles Christ," he hardly meant such a simple mechanism of imitation as governs the stories of Mary's death: her death, burial, and resurrection, and, in some of the tales, an ascension as well. An annunciation (of Mary's death) by an angel; an agony in the garden (Mary weeping and begging to die by Christ's sepulchre); hostile Jews (as in Christ's passion); a sepulchre closed by a stone; and in some of the Greek versions a three-day burial before the tomb is found empty—the framework is openly modelled on the Gospels. The Old Testament also plays its part, as it did in the apocrypha of the infancy. The Jew who attacks Mary on the bier again recalls Uzzah, who was struck down for touching the Ark of the Covenant (2 Samuel 6:6–7). Passages from the Psalms recur, including the chariots of fire, vehicles of the Lord (Psalms 104:3); and the characters address each other in fragments of the biblical books. "Rise up my love," comes from the Song of Solomon, when the lover addresses his bride. "Rise up my love, my fair one, and come away. For lo, the winter is past, the rain is over and gone . . ." (Song of Solomon 2:10–11).

Apart from the occasional scene of grandeur such as this moment of resurrection, the *Transitus* stories are poor literary specimens. Long-winded, puffed up, stuck in a morass of stock images and metaphysical formulas, the episodes are barren of spiritual content. The endless discourses of the apostles on their journey to Mary's bed, the disorganized and repetitive examples of the Jews' enmity: a sour mixture of credulity and prejudice characterizes the whole sequence. The Holy Ghost's magic itself is hardly awe-inspiring, but rather the cheap trickery of a child's conjuring kit, while the stratagems of the *Pseudo-Melito* require the ludicrous clumsiness of Mary's soul going up, coming down, and going up again.

The discrepancies between the stories would alone reflect the absence of a solid historical tradition. Yet theologians wistfully hope that the *Transitus* stories might contain some nugget of fact. For instance, because all the apocrypha agree that the burial took place near Jerusalem, the learned contemporary scholar Jean Galot suggests this might reflect a memory of early Christians. But no other source corroborates this hope. The Empress Helena (d. 330), Constantine's mother, a resourceful archaeologist and an inveterate builder of churches, hallowed the Christian places throughout Jerusalem—but none of her foundations commemorate Mary or her grave. None of the early travellers to the Holy Land mention it either. Etheria, who travelled as a pilgrim around the year 400 and kept an invaluably detailed chronicle, passes over the subject of Mary's tomb in silence.[2] Jerome and his train of pious ladies reveal nothing. Yet how eloquently moved the ascetic Jerome would have been at the sight of that empty sepulchre, at the sight of death overcome by the power of purity.

It is only in the seventh century, when the apocryphal tales were accepted in some quarters and were already old enough to be traditional, that other stories support Jerusalem as the location of Mary's tomb. One legend says that the Empress Pulcheria, just before the important Council of Chalcedon in 451, asked the patriarch of Jerusalem to send her in Constantinople the body of the Virgin Mary, for veneration in the imperial chapel at Blachernae. The patriarch replied that it was impossible, for Mary's body had vanished. Instead he sent the empress the long veil, or *maphorion*, and the sash worn by the Virgin. In a later version, of St. John Damascene, the patriarch sent the empress the Virgin's abandoned graveclothes and shroud—a much stronger argument for her assumption. During the seventh century, pilgrims first begin to mention the empty tomb in the valley of Jehosaphat outside Jerusalem that the Christians revered as the Virgin's.[3] The Venerable Bede records its existence. Pilgrims today are still directed by travel agents to "the Benedictine abbey of the Dormition where our Blessed Mother lived after the Ascension...and the Garden of Gethsemane, Tomb of the Virgin Mary. . . ."

This new Marian fervour, focussing on her death in Jerusalem, coincides with the Moslem invasions of the Holy Land. In 638, Jerusalem, the most holy city of Christendom, where the greatest shrines and most sacred relics were to be found, fell into the hands of the infidel. The Byzantine Church and empire suffered a shock as profound as if its heart had been cut out of its body: God's empire on earth had lost God's own city. The consequences were traumatic; and one of them was the proliferation of legends and stories in which the pious deeds of saints and rulers were connected with the holy places and situated in the past, in order that Christians might be reassured the empire had not lost its heavenly mandate through past omissions or lack of zeal.

The saints most concerned with promoting devotion to the Virgin's Dormition, in passionate and flowery sermons for her feastdays, were men of the unquiet and troubled time that followed the Moslem victories and lasted throughout the era of iconoclasm at Byzantium: Germanus (d. 732), patriarch of Constantinople; Andrew of Crete (d. 740), who was born in Damascus under Moslem rule, and became a monk at the Holy Sepulchre in Jerusalem; and John Damascene, who succeeded his own father as vizier to the caliph of Damascus until his retirement to a monastery at Jerusalem. These three saints of the Greek Church are the foremost reputable authorities, not only for Mary's death at Jerusalem, but also for the authenticity of the apocryphal stories of her passing, for they base their sermons on the testimony of St. John, the evangelist, whom they supposed had been present at the occasion.

Jerusalem's claim to Mary's grave was disputed. Other scholars assert that the Virgin died at Ephesus, where the Council of 431 proclaimed her *Theotokos*, and where she lived in John's care after the Crucifixion. The tradition of John's stay in Ephesus is very strong, and Jesus' recommendation of Mary to his keeping offers weighty support for the argument that she lived with him. This Ephesian claim acquired late, but invaluable, warranty from a German mystic and stigmatic, Catherine Emmerich (d. 1824), who had visions of the house and the tomb of the Virgin at Ephesus, a place she had never visited. Her revelations, published in 1876, sent eager archaeologists to the sites described, where they did indeed find some very ancient foundations—including a tiny first-century house, believed to be the Virgin's. Lazarist missionaries followed the professionals to dig some more and decided that they had discovered the actual tomb.[4] In 1896, the Vatican authorized the pilgrimage, but the same travel agency that promises the Virgin's tomb in Jerusalem is cautious enough to leave it out in Ephesus, restricting itself to "the house where the Blessed Virgin, Mother of Christ, lived during part of her time on earth. . . ."

Such rivalry shows only that the trail to Mary's grave has expired. Saints and writers of the early Church were well aware of the hollowness of the stories and of their low calibre as hagiography. Warnings against them are scattered throughout Christian literature, from Epiphanius, who counselled that Mary's death should not be the subject of speculation, to St. Bernard of Clairvaux, who during the most passionate sermons for the feastday of the Assumption, never commits himself to her mortal death or her corporeal ascent into heaven.

The words of restraint and the clever ambiguities of the saints express regret rather than condemnation. And their caution has not deterred the faithful east and west who have celebrated the feast of August 15 since the seventh century, and have gazed on the rich plating of imagery in stone and paint that has disguised the *Transitus* story's poverty. The feast of the Dormition arrived from the east in the early seventh century in Gaul, and its name changes to "assumption" in some ninth-century liturgical calendars. Pope Leo IV (847–55), possibly in reaction against the Iconoclast heretics in Constantinople, gave the feast a vigil and an octave to solemnize it above all others. Pope Nicholas I (858–67) placed the Assumption on a par with Christmas and Easter— tantamount to declaring Mary's translation to heaven as important as the Incarnation and the Resurrection.

One of the most beautiful examples of a Dormition picture in the west appears in glorious, softly gleaming gold mosaic in the twelfth-century church of La Martorana in Palermo, a precious jewelbox of a shrine that was built in 1143 to the Virgin by George of Antioch, Admiral of the Fleet to Roger II, king of Sicily. George, a Greek from Syria, fought most of his life in the western Mediterranean for a Norman king, and in his church the spiciness of that cosmopolitan time is very pleasant, for he employed Italian craftsmen to adorn the walls with mosaics in the Byzantine style. Round the cupola the four great Byzantine feasts are represented—and the Nativity of Jesus faces the Dormition of the Virgin with harmonious symmetry, for in both Mary reclines. In one she gives birth to the saviour on earth; in the other the saviour gives new life to her soul, which resembles a baby in his arms (colour plate IV, figure 5).

On the great French cathedrals of the twelfth and thirteenth centuries, Mary does not yet rise like pillars of smoke towards heaven. The *Pseudo-Melito* is the source for the sculpture programmes of the portals to the Virgin of Senlis, Angers, Chartres, and, later, Strasbourg, Notre Dame in Paris, and Bourges, but none of them show Mary ascending to heaven. Instead, she sleeps on her bed in the lintel and reappears above in the tympanum in glory, animated and radiant beside her son in heaven. The western iconography departs a little from the Byzantine model, because the body of the Virgin is sometimes gently raised up by angels like nurses helping a convalescent. The scene makes one of its earliest appearances on the tympanum of Senlis cathedral, carved around 1150.[5]

But at the same time, in another part of Christendom, a German nun, Elisabeth of Schonau (d. 1164), was granted colloquies with the Virgin and her son that were to have a profound influence on the imagery of the Assumption, and on the western idea that Mary ascended body and soul into heaven. For in the west the parallel between the Virgin and Christ inspired a more active inconography of the Assumption. A sumptuous embroidery of the sixth or seventh century now preserved in the Treasury of Sens cathedral shows Mary moving towards heaven; and as early as 900 a richly adorned ivory plaque was carved in the monastery of St. Gall, now in Switzerland, showing the Virgin rising towards heaven, and inscribed *Ascensio Sce Maria*—the ascension of the Blessed Mary. This image diverges completely from the Byzantine Dormition scene, and in the early middle ages it was submerged by the Greek tradition of the supine Dormition. But Elisabeth had seen the Virgin rising bodily to heaven, and her visions, taken down by nuns and colleagues in a mixture of German and Latin and then rendered elegantly by her brother, the abbot of Schonau, after her death, quickly achieved a wide circulation.[6] Manuscripts exist in France, Germany, and England, and although the French cathedral sculptures preserved the more tranquil and austere idea of Mary's sleep, the stronger image of her physical, wakeful ascension, body and soul, had taken a firm hold in Europe by the fourteenth century. This inspired some of Christianity's masterpieces, including that ringing fanfare of the Renaissance, Titian's *Assumption,* painted in

1518, in which the apostles reach out in awe and ecstasy towards Mary's soaring form (colour plate V, figure 7).

This dynamic version of the Assumption did not suppress the apocrypha altogether: the Renaissance cycles of woodcuts by Albrecht Dürer, as well as numerous paintings, incorporate her flight heavenwards into a sequence that includes the miraculous gathering of the apostles, the attacks of the Jews, the deathbed scene, and the funeral procession in the same way as the medieval stonecarvers.[7] For although the apocrypha were looked upon askance, they were the only source. Jacobus de Varagine, who included the entire cycle, with embellishments, in the *Golden Legend,* sums up the official position of the Church when he apologizes, saying that the story was apocryphal and did not take place, but that just the same it was true. In fourteenth-century Europe, another legend, that doubting Thomas had been given Mary's sash as proof of her physical presence in heaven, became popular in art (figure 10; see Chapter 18). As Alice shrugged and said to herself when the jury took down the evidence all wrong: "But it doesn't matter a bit."

For although the Virgin's escape from the grave was a special tribute to her purity, the medieval man and woman did not believe that her fate was exceptional in quite the way the modern dogma of the Assumption has made it. Eternal life was the reward of other saints and holy men, as it was the ultimate destiny of every faithful soul. The Assumption of the Virgin reflects a deeply ingrained attitude to the afterlife that is an essential feature of the Christian philosophy.

The resurrection of the body is an article of faith. Each human being will rise in his own body on the last day. It will be individual and recognizable, but, for those who enjoy eternal bliss, transfigured by the sight of God; and for those in eternal fire, disfigured by the loss of that joy. However, all Christian eschatology is highly mysterious, and Matthew confused the issue when he wrote that at the moment of the Crucifixion the bonds of death were broken: "And the graves were opened; and many bodies of the saints which slept arose" (Matthew 27:52). An exquisite ivory panel, carved at Rheims and later set into the Emperor Henry II's *Book of Pericopes,* shows the cracked sarcophagi yielding up the bodies of the saints. White and childlike in their nakedness, they ascend weightlessly, as if exhaled. Matthew is the only evangelist to describe this, and he adds that the risen dead "went into the holy city, and appeared unto many" (Matthew 27:53). It seems, therefore, that a resurrection of the dead took place at the atonement.

The Fourth Gospel added another enigma to ideas about the resurrection of the saints. The closing passages record an early rumour that John was not destined to die. Jesus says: "If I will that he [the disciple whom Jesus loved] tarry till I come, what is that to thee?" (John 21:22). The Gospel then continues: "Then went this saying abroad among the brethren, that that disciple should not die . . ." (John, 21:23). The evangelist himself makes the reservation that "Jesus said not unto him, He shall not die. . . ." But legends about John's immortality flowered, and an apocryphal *Acts of St. John,* written by the mid-second century (not long after the Fourth Gospel) tells the story of John's ascension to heaven.

In the *Acts of Paul,* written around 160, the saint appears to the Emperor Nero after his martyrdom as he had promised, and then rises into heaven. Another later tale in the same genre of apostolic romances that flourished in the first centuries of the Christian era describes the heroic martyrdom of St. Matthew. When the wicked king in the story tries to burn the saint, the fire has different ideas, and instead melts all the king's gold idols, swallows up his soldiers, and eventually takes "the form of a dragon and chased the king to the palace." Matthew calls off the flames, and then dies. The king, most impressed, has the saint's body brought in state to the palace and there "Matthew was seen to rise from the bier and ascend into heaven, led by a beautiful child, and twelve men in crowns, and we saw the child crown him. . . ."[8]

The deaths and resurrections of these saints presage the future glory of each Christian soul, which will also live eternally in the Lord Jesus Christ. The gift of eternal life to the body reflects the more important gift of eternal life to the soul. The resurrection is not necessarily postponed till the last trumpet, but can happen for special saints at the moment of earthly death. The Assumption of John was, for instance, believed widely in Europe in the middle ages: a crowded and exciting French ivory altarpiece in the Metropolitan Museum in New York depicts the whole sequence of events, including the grave empty but for John's shift and sandals.

The idea of an ascension into heaven also derives from the classical tradition of the apotheosis of a hero, which in turn had borrowed the visual imagery of the Roman triumphs to celebrate emperors who, like the unconquered sun, rode the heavens beyond death's long reach. Even Constantine, the emperor who brought the Christian religion peace, continued to identify himself with the sun and had coins struck which showed him streaking up to heaven in a triumphal chariot. The classical idea of apotheosis contains an unmistakably clear message about an individual's greatness. It suspends a man above the ordinary rung of mortality, but does not quite raise him to the topmost ranks of the gods.

In the Greek topography of gods and men, apotheosis marked out the hero: superhuman, but not divine. When Herakles is dying in agony from the poisoned tunic his wife Dejanira had unwittingly sent him, he hurls himself onto a funeral pyre. A flash of lightning, a clap of thunder, and the gods, wrapped in clouds, snatch him from death. In a four-horse chariot the hero rides up to Olympus, where, exactly like the mother of God after him, he is enthroned among the immortals.

The endurance and continuity of ideas in our culture are often startling, and the triumph of the individual, expressed as a physical ascent into the afterlife, still provides, it seems, an adequate metaphor. The Catholic dogma of the Assumption of the Virgin was defined in 1950 in the Papal Bull *Munificentissimus Deus*. Pope Pius XII cited many ancient texts in support of the belief, but none of them came from the apocryphal stories of the passing of the Virgin. He referred the faithful to the eighth-century homilies of Germanus of Constantinople, Modestus of Jerusalem, Andrew of Crete, and John Damascene, who had themselves used the apocrypha as sources; but he omitted all mention of this or of the legend. The dogmatic definition was the fruit of prelates' thinking for generations, and in particular of twentieth-century Mariology. Between 1849 and 1940, 3,387 cardinals, patriarchs, archbishops, and bishops petitioned for its proclamation, and dozens of international Marian congresses were held to debate the question. All came out in favour. When Pope Pius XII appeared on the balcony of St. Peter's on November 1, 1950, to address a crowd nearly a million strong, his announcement that "Mary . . . was taken up body and soul into the glory of heaven" was greeted with thunderous clapping, with tears of joy and resonant prayers. It was the climax of centuries of tradition, and the delay had been caused only by the absence of scriptural sources. But the Vatican scholars invoking the Holy Spirit had returned to their books, and the problem had been overcome. The Assumption dogma depended on the Christian equivalence between sex and death, and consequently between the Virgin's purity and her freedom from the dissolution of the grave.

The fundamental connections between the mysteries of the virgin birth and the Assumption, between the conquest of lust and putrefaction, emerge from the jubilant liturgy for the feast of the Assumption on August 15, which unfolds the structure of the dogma more clearly than the destitute ramblings of the apocryphal *Transitus* stories.

The priest reads Paul's letter on Christ's victory over death and on the promised resurrection of all the saints: "The sting of death is sin; and the strength of sin is the law. But thanks be to God, which giveth us the victory . . ." (1 Corinthians 15:56–7). The passage does not imply Mary's fate is unique, but that it awaits all the faithful. The liturgy also uses biblical passages on the Ark of the Covenant, the figure of Mary's womb that bore the New Covenant. Made of "incorruptible timber," inlaid with gold, the Ark was led by David into Jerusalem, where the priests sang and danced and clashed cymbals and played on harps and lyres to greet its coming, just as, the reading implies, Mary's uncorrupted body is conducted into heaven among a throng of exulting angels. From the Psalms come the voluptuous lines: "Upon thy right hand did stand the Queen in gold of Ophir. Hearken, O daughter . . . and incline thine ear . . . So shall the king greatly desire thy beauty: for he is thy Lord; and worship thou him. . . . The king's daughter is glorious within: her clothing is of wrought gold" (Psalms 45:9–11, 13). The text was a favourite among the Fathers of the Church, like Jerome, who used it to entice young girls into a bridal union with their Lord Jesus Christ, but in the liturgy of the Assumption it expresses Mary's glorious apotheosis at Christ's side in heaven.

But the key Mariological text in the mass for the Assumption is the vision of the Apocalypse, of "a great wonder in heaven; a woman clothed with the sun, and the moon under her feet, and upon her head a crown of twelve stars" (Revelation 12:1). She cries out in labour, and when her son is born, a huge red dragon appears to devour him. But the child is snatched up to safety, "caught up" to God's throne, while the mother flees into the wilderness for safety. Michael the archangel and his battalions then fight the dragon, who still pursues the woman and persecutes her: "And the dragon . . . went to make war with the remnant of her seed, which keep the commandments of God, and have the testimony of Jesus Christ" (Revelation 12:17) (figure 11).

The strata of ideas in this vision are complex, for the "great wonder" recalls the nation Israel crying out to God as a woman cries in birth pangs (Isaiah 26:17–18); she is a type of the Church, persecuted by the devil's agents, and protected by the love and mercy of God; above all, the birth of the child "who was to rule all nations with a rod of iron" (Revelation 12:5) is a clear messianic reference, and identifies the "great wonder" with another mother of salvation, whose coming was promised by Yahweh in the Garden of Eden (Genesis 3:15). Later in the Apocalypse, at the wedding feast of the lamb, John sees "the New Jerusalem" in bridal splendour: the two female visions dovetailed as a symbol both of the glorious eschatological Church and the glorified mother of God. As early as the fifth century, the "woman clothed with the sun" was understood to be the Virgin. Epiphanius in the east (in a doubtful passage), Quodvultdeus, a disciple of St. Augustine, and Oecumenius (d. 550) are the first to apply the vision to Mary, but patristic testimonies later accumulate, and when Pius XII defined the dogma of the Assumption, he quoted a long tradition in support. However strained the interpretation might seem—and there has been bitter controversy over it—the symbolism is solid. The assumed Virgin is clothed with the undying and golden sun, which in paintings envelops her as if in a gilded shell, and the New Jerusalem with which she is associated is built on foundations of imperishable stone: jasper, sapphire, chalcedony, emerald, sardonyx, sardius, chrysolyte, beryl, topaz, chrysosprasus, jacinth, amethyst. The gates are of pearl, the streets paved with gold. All these gems and metals are incorruptible, immune to time. Like the Babylonian garden of the gods, which the hero Gilgamesh discovers on his way to seek the secret of immortal life, the New Jerusalem, a type of the Virgin, is adorned in the eternity of gold and precious stones.

Belief in the Assumption extends an idea fundamental to the virgin birth: that time itself belongs to the material world and is alien from the spiritual, from the supernatural. Death, like birth, belongs to time; freedom from death, like freedom from sex, overcomes it. The unchanged womb of the Virgin, that "closed gate," that "enclosed garden," which experiencing alteration is yet unaltered, is the mirror image of the unchanged body of the Virgin, which experiences death and does not decay. In the words of John Damascene, as quoted by Pope Pius XII in *Munificentissimus Deus:* "There was need that the body of her who in childbirth had preserved her virginity intact, be preserved incorrupt after death. . . ."[9]

Just as the metaphor of the sunrise has survived Copernican astronomy, so Mary's Assumption continues for millions of people to provide a completely satisfying image of holiness' ultimate reward. In inadequate but impassioned sensory language, her flight upwards on ribbons of cirrus cloud among multitudes of carolling angels simply signifies her passage out of time into eternity. Decay marks the passage of the years, freedom from corruption frees her from time. She is lifted out from the plane of humanity, onto what Christians imagine is the time plane of God. The Assumption combines vividly the Catholic affirmation of God's transcendence—the conditions of earth do not obtain in heaven—and simultaneously, the materialism of the Christian doctrine of the incarnate God, which peoples heaven with transfigured bodies.

Mary acquires ubiquitousness—she can appear on earth to visionaries in any place at any time. Other divine attributes like omniscience and omnipotence are not granted her; but agelessness and immortality are hers. (They are not synonymous, as was bitterly discovered by Tithonus, who was going to live forever, growing older each day until Arethusa had him changed into a grasshopper.)

All the Virgin's supernatural qualities coexist with a human body that is real, not phantom. She is a living person, not a spirit, and her physical reality is of extreme importance to her devotees, as was the body of the resurrected Christ to doubting Thomas. Bernadette Soubirous, after her visions of the Virgin in 1858, was anxiously questioned by eminent churchmen about the Virgin's looks. They showed the young girl many of the world's most revered paintings of the Virgin—by Leonardo, Raphael, Botticelli, Dürer—and asked her which was the most accurate. Bernadette was horrified. "My dear mother, how they slander you!" she exclaimed. She instead insisted that the local statue of the Virgin was a perfect likeness.[10]

At 140 Rue du Bac, Paris, the chair the Virgin sat on in 1830 when she talked with St. Catherine Labouré (d. 1875) is still shown to pilgrims. But even more eloquent of this crucial image of mediation between earth and heaven is the bold golden inscription that runs around the dome of the cathedral of Saragossa. On that site, in the year A.D. 40, the Virgin appeared standing on a pillar to St. James (Santiago), patron saint and apostle of Spain. After Compostella, where Santiago himself lies buried, *La Virgen del Pilar* has become Spain's greatest pilgrimage. On the dome the visitor can read that the Virgin blessed Saragossa with her presence *en carne mortal* (in human mortal flesh). It is a curious choice of words, for even if one believes that in A.D. 40 the Virgin was still alive, she can hardly have travelled bodily to Spain to appear to St. James. Spaniards, anyway, do not take this view of the vision. It was the assumed Mary who appeared in glory, arrayed in the sun, transfigured by the beatific vision, as is overwhelmingly clear from the gorgeous chapel, sparkling and blazing with gold, candles, and precious stones, that houses the pillar on which she stood.

Christ and Mary, the only beings Catholics now believe to be in heaven in their bodies (Enoch, Moses, and Elijah's physical presence is doubted), have contravened natural law and thus made manifest the almightiness of God. The reformed Churches dispute the Assumption because they dislike glory paid equally to the mother and son, and the dogma is an obstacle in the ecumenical movement. Luther himself, as an heir of medieval piety, probably would have heard untroubled such joyful carols as the thirteenth-century hymn:

*Cantet omnis creatura*
*(Sua refert nobis jura)*
*(Sua refert nobis jura)*
*Virginis assumptio . . .*

*Dedit suum jus natura*
*(Sua refert nobis jura)*
*Rerum factor fit factura*
*Virginis in gremio*
*O, O*
*Domino*
*Concinat haec contio.*

(Let every creature sing [she hands her privileges to us] of the Virgin's Assumption . . . Nature gives up her law [she hands her privileges to us] the creator of all becomes a creature in a virgin's womb. O, O, let his company sing to the Lord.) [11]

Luther held to the virgin birth and the virginity of Mary; and he did not quarrel with the widespread belief in the Assumption until the later years, when he struck the feast of August 15 from the calendar.

The important question raised by the Assumption is not whether Mary should be held in such honour (Catholics simply answer that they do not consider her Christ's equal, and protest his supremacy as sole mediator), but why the resurrection of the body should be considered an honour at all. The idea was quite alien to Alexandrian neoplatonism, which influenced early Christianity's view of the body, that at best it was a poor tattered obstacle, at worst the gaoler of the divine spark.

But in the Old Testament the idea begins to develop after the exile in Babylon, under the influence of Zoroastrian concepts of the physical resurrection.[12] And the core of the Kerygma was the Resurrection of Christ in the body. Through the teachings of St. Paul in his letters to the Thessalonians, the resurrected body became the vital ideogram of the Christian salvation, of the participation of each creature in the eternal life of Christ. The completeness of this eschatological body reflected in microcosm the mystical, unassailable body of the Church, and simultaneously, differentiated man from matter. At one and the same time, it affirmed the goodness of the created world and the flesh, and the difference between the matter of a human creature, made in God's image and likeness, from the rest of the material universe, subject to the law of inevitable decay. St. Ambrose had said that virginity is the one thing that separates us from the beasts; in the Virgin's case, the Assumption was another sign of her superiority, and a promise that each creature too could attain such rank.

The deep reverberating fears that a Christian feels about the dissolution of the flesh do not belong to "a collective unconscious." A Hindu cremation in Bali, where the relatives bring the bones and dust of their dead to burn in a mass fiesta accompanied by much singing, laughing, shouting, and eating, or the idea that obtained in imperial China that the most filial gift a child could give a parent was a richly decorated coffin or a grave plot chosen according to the specifications of a leading geomancer, reveal that different religions codify and organize feelings about death in extremely varying ways.

For very complicated reasons—which can only be hazarded with hesitation—Christianity has not assuaged the horror of the grave by promises of eternal life. One reason is certainly the idea of the day of reckoning, when the sentence to heaven or hell (or purgatory) is passed on each soul by Christ the Judge at the Last Judgement, and in Catholic belief at least, the Virgin plays a crucial mediating role (see Chapter 21).

But at a psychological level, Christians are also anguished at the prospect of death because they fear obliteration: Aquinas discussed at length the problem of identity, affirmed the uniqueness of each individual soul created by God at the moment of conception, but also demonstrated that the soul's personality is expressed by and through the body. The implication of this teaching—that spirit could not exist without matter—was condemned after Aquinas' death; but the essential point—that the body and soul *together* form the individual—is fundamental to Christian doctrine. (Which is why ideas about the migration of souls or reincarnation could never be absorbed by Christianity.) The pivotal theme of many a horror story or film, like Mary Shelley's *Frankenstein,* in which a doctor uses a man's body to create someone else; or the common nightmare in which friends and lovers pass by with blank stares of nonrecognition while one cries out that underneath the altered features beats the same heart; and even the shudder the transplantation of vital organs sometimes inspires—all stem from a Christian heritage that accords the body a very high place in the definition of human personality. It is precisely this stress on the body that makes the separation from it in death such a prospect of terror, and makes reunion with it on the last day such a consolation.

The Catholic accolade to the Virgin that she alone of all created beings was holy enough to be assumed bodily into heaven is also grounded in the metaphysical relationship of sin and death, both results of the Fall of Adam and Eve. In death, the body slowly dissolves into oblivion—its boundaries are broken down and the substance of man fuses once more with the clay from which he was made. Any attempt to circumvent this process is anathema. Cremation was forbidden by the Catholic Church until recently, and in the middle ages, when the bodies of princes, warriors, and bishops—including King Henry V of England— who died in foreign lands were boiled so that their dry bones could be transported for burial at home, the Church roundly condemned the custom, Pope Boniface VIII (1294–1303) calling it "an abuse of abominable savagery, practised by some of the faithful in a horrible way and inconsiderately."[13]

of the Fall, and therefore the destiny of each sinful man, is recalled by the priest on Ash Wednesday, who mutters as he thumbs a smoky cross on each penitent's forehead: "Remember, man, dust thou art, and to dust thou shalt return." Sexual union, too, destroys the virgin body in a particular way, as we have seen, and it also blurs contours, for it unites two beings and lessens their sentiment of themselves as individual units. This is what Augustine may have feared when he inveighed on the vileness of lust: the loss of control of self, the *petite mort,* as the French call orgasm. The operations of lust and of death on the body are kinsmen in Christian symbolism; and the puns it works on are almost cutely witty. Corruption and integrity have all at once a literal and a metaphorical meaning.

There could be a historical link between the pagan world and this Christian set of ideas. For in Egypt, the embalmer's craft was exquisite. With the greatest ingenuity, the flesh of the pharaohs was preserved from mortal decay in spices and unguents, and from their shuffled coil a semblance of eternal life was created. The myth relates that Isis and Nepthys, with the help of Thoth, the scribe of the gods, invented the recipes of mummification when they reassembled the dismembered body of Osiris; certainly their formulae were potent. For when the tomb of Queen Thuya, Tutankhamen's great-grandmother, was opened, her hair tumbled out of the mummy bands as blonde as it had been four thousand years ago; and the scientists who unwrapped the Pharaoh Amenhotep I could still smell the delphiniums that had been used in his preservation.

Some scholars believe that the apocryphal tales of the Virgin's death, in which she is spared mortal decay, sometimes even given "a garment of incorruptibility" by Jesus, originated among the Christian community in Egypt. A long tradition existed there that viewed incorruption as a privilege of true greatness. The whiff of those delphiniums, that lingering fragrance, speaks most eloquently of Amenhotep's enduring dignity.

The stench of death, its most terrifying signal, is constantly used in Christian writing to describe evil; and, by contrast, the odour of sanctity is an equal commonplace. In one medieval miracle, the Devil impersonates a man but is unmasked by the good offices of the versatile Virgin. In a rage, he vanishes, leaving behind a reeking stench. In the chronicles of the abbey of Saint-Denis, one monk is continually assailed by the Devil, but whatever his disguise, he can recognize him from his putrid smell. After the Devil's visits, says the chronicler, "we must needs strip that lay brother of the frock he had worn [so pestilent was the stench thereof] and clothe him with one of the other brethren's frocks."[14]

An exemplum from Jacques de Vitry's collection describes a man and an angel walking together. They come to a putrefying corpse and the man holds his nose, while the angel appears unaware. Then they pass a beautiful youth, and it is the angel's turn to hold his nose in disgust. The rankness of the youth's sins, the angel tells his companion, is enough to make him retch.[15] In the ceremony of exorcism, the priest invokes the *odor suavissimus* of the Holy Ghost to descend, once the demons have been expelled.[16] In an early legend by St. Ephrem, Mary the Harlot embraces her holy uncle Abraham, and by contrast to the stinking Devils, "as she was kissing him, she smelt the fragrance of austerity that his lean body breathed."[17]

The Virgin Mary, as the conqueror of sin, smells ambrosial. She is addressed as the "lily of the field," the "rose of Sharon," the "bundle of myrrh." In pictures of the Annunciation, Gabriel greets her with a lily staff, and its heady perfume, filling her chamber, symbolizes her incorruptibility. Pots of lilies often decorate her room; lilies or roses spring up in her empty tomb in paintings of the Assumption, like Pinturicchio's mille-fleurs evocation in the Borgia Apartments of the Vatican; sometimes multicoloured petals tumble down her flight path. In the liturgy of the Virgin as the "seat of wisdom," she is given the richly aromatic text from *Ecclesiasticus:* "I gave a sweet smell like cinnamon and aspalathus, and I yielded a pleasant odour like the best myrrh, as galbanum, and onyx, and sweet storax, and as the fume of frankincense in the tabernacle . . ." (*Ecclesiasticus* 24:15).

Doctors of the Church expounded the Song of Songs (Song of Solomon) in Marian terms (see Chapter 8) and particularly saw a presage of the Assumption in the beautiful verse: "Who is this that cometh out of the wilderness like pillars of smoke, perfumed with myrrh and frankincense, with all powders of the merchant?" (Song of Solomon 3:6). For St. Bernard, who used this text in his sermons for the Assumption, the costly ointments Mary Magdalene used to anoint Jesus' feet, and the oils and perfumes mentioned in the Song of Songs are all images of the virtues Mary possesses, which the Church should emulate. "Steep yourself in odours such as these," exhorts the saint, "that by them the foul stench of your sins may be dispelled and your own heart be rendered redolent of these same fragrances which are as strong to save as they are sweet."[18]

When Mary, during the middle ages, became the subject of love poetry, the monk Gautier de Coincy (d. 1236), who had a pretty turn of phrase and a sweet, light touch with a song, wrote a ditty to the Virgin in the style of a pastourelle. He tells her that she is his *amie,* and surpasses all other sweethearts because she is so beautiful, and never gives him any trouble. Her fragrance in particular enchants him:

> *C'est la fleur, la violete,*
> *La rose espanie*
> *Qui tele odour done et gete*
> *Tous nos rasasie*
> *Haute odour seur tote fleur*
> *A la mere du haut seignour.*

(She is the flower, the violet, the full-blown rose, who gives out such a scent that she satisfies us all. The mother of the lord most high is scented beyond any flower.)[19]

At the shrine of Montserrat in the Catalonian plain, a roundelay has been sung to the Virgin since the thirteenth century. Translated now into Catalan, it sings her praise as the rose, the sun, the stars, the jewel, the "chaste topaz," the fiery diamond, the ruby, and sweeter smelling than any flower.[20]

Gems share in the idea of eternity, for they are unchanging; flowers for the sweetness of their scent. As early as the tenth century, the intimate association between the aromas of herbs and flowers and the victory of Mary over death was celebrated in the ritual of the feast of the Assumption. Medicinal herbs and plants were brought to church on that day. Periwinkle, verbena, thyme, and many other ingredients of the herbalist's art were laid on the altar, to be incensed and blessed. Then they were bound into a sheaf and kept all year to ward off illness and disaster and death. But the ceremony was abolished in England at the Reformation, and is extinct everywhere now except in some towns of northern Italy.[21]

Although the Virgin is unique in that her incorrupt body was taken up into heaven, the idea of preservation pervades Christian hagiography.

Just as the intact bodies of holy virgins gave them powers over their assailants, so holiness defied the law of the grave (*Dedit suum jus natura*), and a saint's body could resist decomposition, and survive fresh and fragrant as the dew. The Venerable Bede had remained noncommittal about the Virgin when he had visited her tomb in the valley of Jehosaphat near Jerusalem where "Saint Mary, the mother of God is said to have reposed for a time; but by whom or when the body was taken away, nobody knows."

He is more definite, however, about Etheldreda, wife of King Egfrid of Northumbria, daughter of the king of the East Angles, who refused to consummate her marriage but instead became a nun at the convent of Ely and eventually its illustrious abbess. As Bede remarks: "Although she lived with him [Egfrid] for twelve years, she preserved the glory of perpetual virginity. This fact is absolutely vouched for by Bishop Wilfrid of blessed memory, of whom I made inquiry when some people doubted it. He said that Egfrid promised to give estates and much wealth to him if he could persuade the queen to consummate the marriage . . ."

Etheldreda died around 660, of a tumour on the neck. Bede quotes the doctor who operated unsuccessfully on her and was present when they opened the grave years later to move the body: " 'Then I saw the body of the holy virgin . . . as though asleep . . . when they uncovered her face, they showed me that the incision which I had made had healed. This astounded me; for in place of the open gaping wound with which she was buried, there remained only the faint mark of a scar. All the linen cloths in which the body had been enfolded appeared so fresh and new that they looked as if they had been wrapped that very day around her pure body.' " Bede himself comments: "And there is no reason to doubt that such a thing could happen in our own day, since reliable histories record it as having happened on several occasions in the past. . . . For the miraculous preservation of her body from corruption in the tomb is evidence that she had remained untainted by bodily intercourse."[22]

In much more recent times, an equal prodigy; and, as Bede says, reliable histories record it. In the church of S. Cecilia in Trastevere in Rome, the saint carved in white marble lies in an awkwardly twisted position—her knees bent, her head collapsed on one side. On approaching the altar, one realizes why: her white throat is slit. Stefano Maderna, the great architect of many Roman churches, sculpted the saint in 1599. When the catacombs were first opened and explored, the cypresswood coffin where St. Cecilia's remains had lain ever since Pope Paschal I had transferred her in 821 was moved to her basilica in Trastevere. The coffin was opened and, inside, wrapped in a green silk veil, Cecilia lay intact, a young Roman patrician dressed in a garment shot with gold thread. Her dress was stained with blood, shed nearly thirteen hundred years before when she was martyred. Pope Clement VIII rushed to the catacombs to see the marvel, and before the extraordinary relic crumbled into dust, sketches were made from which Maderna carved the twisted form of the young woman.[23]

In the middle ages, hundreds of believers claimed similar miracles at the graves of their favourite patrons. The body of St. Rose of Viterbo (d. 1252) inspired a similar cult. In the reliquary caskets of many saints in French, Italian, Spanish, and Belgian churches, their bodies can be seen. The black and wizened countenance of St. Clare (d. 1253) is termed pure and incorrupt by the guardians of her tomb in Assisi. St. Catherine Labouré, who conversed with the Virgin several times, is preserved in Paris and is the object of pilgrimage. At Nevers, where she died, Bernadette lies in a glass case. She is dressed in her nun's habit, and reclines on sumptuous lace pillows, with a rosary threaded through her clasped hands. Her expression is very serene. Her fingernails are painted and her face powdered and rouged. Yet it would have been far greater tribute to that brief, pain-wracked life to have been buried beyond the embalmer's reach or inquisitive eyes.

The art of the taxidermist, tricks of the atmosphere, expensive and hermetic cypresswood coffins—these are pragmatic solutions to the bodies of Saints Etheldreda, Cecilia, and others. But if one's interest lies in asking why people believe such things rather than how they came about, then the preserved body of a saint provides another image in the Christian repertory of wholeness.

In a precise and literal way, the Virgin embodies the Christian ideals of homogeneity and independence. Through her virginity and Assumption, she expresses the particular interpretation of wholeness of the Catholic Church, and reflects two of its most characteristic aspects: its historical fear of contamination by outside influence, and its repugnance to change. In Buddhism created things at their highest point of fulfilment merge and flow back into nothingness, where all form is obliterated. This is one view of wholeness. The Catholic world's view could not be more opposite. It longs for the formal, immutable, invincible, constant, unchanging perfection of each resurrected individual. For its most sublime example, it looks to the assumed Virgin.

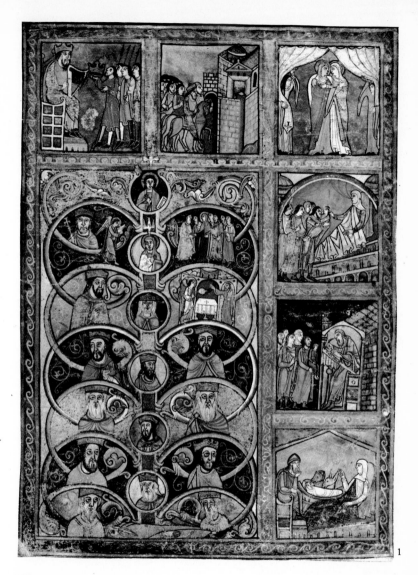

1

The verbal correspondences between Luke's account of the Visitation and the Old Testament story of King David's arrival at Jerusalem with the Ark of the Covenant are fully recognized by the illuminator of this biblical leaf, who juxtaposed the two scenes, *top center and right,* above a tree of Jesse, which emphasizes the unbroken descent of Christ from the kings of the Old Testament through Joseph of the house of David, who married the Virgin. Canterbury or St. Albans (?), twelfth century. (Chapter 1)

The close relationships between the life of Samuel, Luke's narrative of the birth of John the Baptist, and the apocryphal account of the birth of the Virgin inspired the illuminator of this English Bible to draw on traditional iconography: Hannah prays for a child, *bottom left,* like St. Anne in early Byzantine art, and Samuel is presented to the temple, *top right,* by his mother, as was the infant Jesus. St. Swithin's Priory, Winchester, 1175–1200. (Chapter 1)

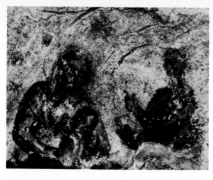

3

The earliest extant image of the Virgin shows her with the child at her breast while an angel or prophet points upwards to a star. Catacomb of S. Priscilla, Rome, second century. (Chapters 2 and 8)

During the flight into Egypt, in the apocryphal Gospel of pseudo-Matthew, Mary tells Joseph she would like some dates, and he is worried that they are running short of water. Whereupon "Jesus sitting in Mary's lap with a joyful countenance bade the palm give his mother of its fruit. The tree bent as low as her feet and . . . he bade it rise again and give them of the water concealed below its roots." The picture below is from Martin Schongauer's *Life of the Blessed Virgin Mary*, c. 1470–5. (Chapter 2)

4

5

At right: St. Anne and St. Joachim supervise the Virgin's first steps. Mid-fourteenth-century orphrey, English. (Chapter 2)

6

A *Vierge Ouvrante,* illustrating the popular but heterodox view that without the Virgin the redemption would not have taken place. On the wings, the mysteries of the incarnation of Christ. In the centre, enclosed in the Virgin's womb, is the figure of Christ the redeemer, holding his cross. Middle Rhine, *c.* 1300. (Chapter 3)

7

Three miraculous mothers of the New Covenant: the Virgin Mary, *centre;* her mother, St. Anne, *left,* who bitterly lamented her barrenness until she conceived Mary; and St. Elisabeth, *right,* the Virgin's cousin, who was "well stricken in years" when she bore the infant John the Baptist, the Precursor. Eighth-century niche, S. Maria Antiqua, Rome. (Chapter 3)

8

9

Opposite, above: the identification of Eve with evil became so natural in Christian thought that the serpent acquired female features. Michelangelo, *The Fall*, Sistine Chapel ceiling, 1508–12. Detail. (Chapter 4)

Opposite, below: the apostles gather at the Dormition, or Falling Asleep of the Virgin, and Christ descends to gather up her soul and take it to heaven, in the traditional Byzantine iconography of Mary's death. Tenth-century ivory from Constantinople, placed by the German Emperor Otto III on the cover of his Gospel Book. (Chapter 6)

St. Thomas also doubted the Virgin's Assumption, but she dropped her girdle, or sash, from heaven to convince him. Filippino Lippi (d. 1504), *La Madonna della Cintola*. (Chapter 6)

St. John saw "a great wonder in heaven; a woman clothed with the sun . . ." who is pursued by a seven-headed monster but escapes. Fifth-century commentators identified the vision with the Virgin, but their interpretation was first depicted in the remarkable and novel imagery of English medieval monastic artists. St. Albans (?), *c.* 1250. (Chapter 6)

The huge eighth-century icon of Maria Regina portrays her as a Byzantine empress, with Pope John VII prostrated before her. The mutilated Latin inscription reads, "As God himself made himself from thy womb, the princes among the angels stand by and marvel at thee, who carried in thy womb the child who is born." S. Maria in Trastevere, Rome. (Chapter 7)

13

"And there shall come forth a rod out of the root of Jesse, and a flower shall rise up out of his root," prophesied Isaiah, and the messianic ring of his words inspired the image of the rod of Jesse, with the Virgin and Child as the descendants of David, Jesse's son, and of the kings of Israel. Italian, anonymous, sixteenth century. (Chapters 4 and 7)

Although the Acts of the Apostles are unclear about the Virgin's presence at Pentecost, she embodies the spirit of the new Church and becomes its mother, *Mater Ecclesiae,* in images like Botticelli's *Descent of the Holy Ghost,* fifteenth century. (Chapter 4)

14

15

In a moralized Bible written and illuminated for Queen Blanche of Castile, she sits enthroned on the right of her son St. Louis IX of France, and raises her hands in the *orans* gesture of intercession exactly as the Virgin does on the Last Judgement portals of French cathedrals raised before and during Blanche's hegemony. France, *c.* 1235. (Chapter 7)

Left: in Agnolo Gaddi's *Coronation of the Virgin*, the Virgin becomes both Christ's bride and also his mirror image. (Chapter 8)

Below: the Mystical Marriage: Christ clasps the right hand of his mother with the formal and legal gesture of nuptial union, *dextrarum iunctio,* in the gable of a fourteenth-century (?) Florentine diptych. Detail. (Chapter 8)

16

17

During the Counter-Reformation, artists like Velásquez stressed that the Virgin was united with the totality of the godhead and that the Trinity crowned her Queen of Heaven. *Coronation of the Virgin.* (Chapters 7 and 8)

19

The Virgin's unfailing attention to her devotees: above, she reclaims a bridegroom who had dedicated himself to her, and he leaves his bride and his wedding feast; below left, she rescues a woman who had been promised to the devil by her husband by riding to the rendezvous instead of her; below right, a pilgrim to Mont St. Michel who has been shipwrecked is safely delivered of a child; and at bottom, the Virgin holds up Michael's scales at the Last Judgement in order to spare a sinner. Details from a fourteenth-century French manuscript. (Chapters 10, 18, 21)

20

21

22

23

On the ground, with bare feet like a peasant, the Virgin became the principal model of exemplary humility in Christian circles inspired by the new mendicant orders' simple ideals. *Madonna of Humility,* attributed to Masaccio, *c.* 1425. (Chapter 12)

The Virgin and Child on a Jesse tree graced by allegorical figures. *Clockwise, from top right:* Obedience, Poverty, Patience, Charity, Compassion, Praise (Adulation), Truth, Humility, Prudence, and Purity—the bouquet of perfect feminine virtues. Nardon Pénicaud (?), Limoges, *c.* 1470–1542. (Chapter 12)

*Chapter Seven*

# MARIA REGINA

*Lady, flower of alle thing,*
*Rosa sine spina,*
*Thou bore Jesu, heavenes king,*
*Gratia divina.*
*Of alle thou bear'st the prize,*
*Lady, queen of Paradise*
*Electa.*[1]

—ANONYMOUS (*c.* 1250)

A T THE ASSUMPTION, Mary becomes Queen of Heaven, and the crown she wears on her head is the token of her triumph. Her crown seems the simplest symbol to express her supremacy, an accessory so natural and so commonplace that it is almost invisible. Yet its appearance subtly underlines many arguments and tenets of the Catholic Church, not only about the glory of Mary the individual, but also about the power of the Church itself, for which the Virgin often stands. Contemporary Mariology focusses on the ancient patristic theme of Mary's identity with the Church, and as the Bride of Christ and the Queen of Heaven she reveals the Church's most profound ambitions for itself, both in the afterlife, when it hopes to be reunited like the New Jerusalem with Christ the Bridegroom, and on earth, where it hopes to hold sway in plenitude of spiritual power.[2] It is noteworthy that the image of the *Regina Caeli* holds up a mirror to the fluctuations of the Church's self-image: in times of stasis and entrenchment, as under the popes Pius XII and to some extent Paul VI, veneration of the Virgin is encouraged, and in times of strong ecumenicalism and change, when the Church is less self-righteous and assured, devotion to the Virgin, especially under her triumphant aspect, is restrained and declines.

This oscillation has ancient precedents, for the first image of *Maria Regina* on a wall of the church of S. Maria Antiqua,[3] the oldest Christian building in the Roman Forum, was painted in the first half of the sixth century. Seated in majesty on a throne, the Virgin Queen contains a multi-layered message: she belongs to a classical tradition of personifying cities and institutions as goddesses, and as such, in the heart of Rome, she embodies the new Rome which is the Church just as the *Dea Roma* now on the Capitol represented the pagan city. And because she is arrayed in all the pearl-laden, jewel-encrusted regalia of a contemporary secular monarch, she also proclaims, in a brilliantly condensed piece of visual propaganda, the concept that the Church is a theocracy of which the agent and representative is the pope, the ruler of Rome.

So although a crown now seems such a normal part of Mary's appearance that it hardly seems worthy of comment, the symbol—like all symbols—is not quite so innocent. For by projecting the hierarchy of the world onto heaven, that hierarchy—be it ecclesiastical or lay—appears to be ratified by divinely reflected approval; and the lessons of the Gospel about the poor inheriting the earth are wholly ignored. Also, from the point of view of the Virgin's relationship to the role of women in the west, it is crucial that she was cast in an exceptional role—that of a queen. The honour paid Mary as queen redounded to the honour of queens, to the exclusion of other women; and the fact that the Virgin was female was mitigated by her regal precedence over all other women. Of course, it is only natural for men to attempt to convey the idea of excellence according to the lights of their society. Nevertheless, the cult of Mary as queen served for centuries to uphold the status quo to the advantage of the highest echelons of power.

The Fathers had identified Mary with the Church, foreshadowed by such scriptural figures as the New Jerusalem and the "great wonder" of the Apocalypse. Early Christian art, by borrowing one image in particular from the vocabulary of official imperial art, had increased support for the idea that the Church was an authority mightier than all earthly kings. For the adoration of the magi was modelled by Christian artists on the offering of tribute by the vanquished at a Roman triumph, in order to underline the supreme power of the king whom the wise men worship[4] (colour plate III, figure 4). On Christian sarcophagi and artefacts from the second century onwards the three wise men wear outlandish dress, peaked caps, short cloaks, and leggings. Such garb signals clearly that these men are foreigners, paying the customary tribute, the *aurum coronarium* of barbarians acknowledging the mastery of the Roman empire. On the obelisk of Theodosius I in Constantinople, contemporary with many sarcophagus carvings of the three wise men, the scene still depicts prisoners-of-war paying homage to their conquerors.[5]

The eastern barbarians laying the symbols of sovereignty at the feet of the infant Christ and his mother helped to define Mary's majesty because, as we have seen, the magi were understood to be kings. Although in the visual arts they only exchanged their foreign caps for crowns in the tenth century, the Fathers, from Origen onwards, had interpreted their submission as an epiphany of the greater majesty of the "son of the Highest," which eclipsed all temporal power.

This counterpoint of victory and subjection governs the growth of the cult of Mary as queen. Although on the walls and sarcophagi of the third and fourth centuries she remains an inconsequential figure, in the mid-fifth-century mosaics on the glittering triumphal arch of S. Maria Maggiore, built by Pope Sixtus III (432–40) at the time of the Council of Ephesus, her dim figure acquires sudden, splendid definition as an Augusta arrayed in all the paraphernalia of imperial rank. Band upon band, the scenes from the Bible rise up the huge wall, as in the victory columns of the emperors, until they culminate with the throne of God. Throughout, the triumph of Christ is proclaimed in the imagery of Roman art, and Mary, her black hair dressed under a narrow diadem, robed in pearl-sewn cloth of gold, with a huge collar of gems, takes her seat on her son's right hand as he receives the three magi in imperial audience.

Scholars argue whether the mosaic sequence was influenced by the proclamation of the *Theotokos* at the Council of Ephesus. If it had been, it would seem likely that Mary would occupy an even more prominent place in the scheme, and receive the magi herself, as she does for instance in the later basilica S. Apollinare Nuovo of the Ostrogothic King Theodoric (474–526) at Ravenna. There, the Virgin, not the Christ child, extends a welcoming hand to the barbarians, who, in gorgeous costume, present her with gifts.

The regal role of Mary as the mother of the God-Emperor became a central and forceful symbol of power, which could be and was used to reinforce the authority of the Church on earth.[6] From the sixth century onwards, when the popes in Rome were struggling to assert their wishes and their outlook against the influence of the Byzantine emperor in Constantinople and his representative in Italy, and against the Lombard kings in northern Italy, the image of the triumphant Virgin, as a figure of the triumphant Church, was an important medium of propaganda for their argument. Politics and piety interacted, and the nexus of circumstances that fostered the cult of Mary in the west can be deciphered vividly from the archaeological palimpsests of early Christian Rome. The more the papacy gained control of the city, the more veneration of the mother of the emperor in heaven, by whose right the Church ruled, increased.

For instance, the church of S. Maria Antiqua had connections with imperial authority, for it had been fashioned out of the lofty vestibule of the Emperor Domitian's palace and then, after its consecration in the fifth or sixth century, it had served as the private chapel of the Greek emperors and their representative in Rome. But it became the first church in Rome where the Church usurped the functions of the civil authorities, where an ecclesiastical diaconate took over such civil duties as the care of the sick and the old, hospitality to wayfarers, and the distribution of bread to the poor.

After the barbarian invasions, particularly under Pope Gregory the Great (590–604), the papacy assumed administrative powers in the city, and this responsibility, coupled with the Church's natural claim to spiritual authority, created varying tensions with the nominal ruler of Rome, the emperor in Constantinople. Pope Martin I (642–9), for instance, used the walls of S. Maria Antiqua to denounce the emperors' Monothelite heresy, in bold visual statements of orthodoxy over the triumphal arch. (The Monothelites held that Jesus' divine and human wills were one.) Martin I was captured by the Byzantines, imprisoned, and brutally maltreated until he died in exile in 655. Pope Sergius I (687–701) defied the Lombard king in the north and central Italy, and the Byzantine exarchs in Ravenna; he was also the pope who, following the time-proven custom of the Roman authorities, put on a grand display for the populace to stir their faith and their allegiance. He instituted candlelit all-night processions through the city on the feastdays of the Annunciation, the Purification, the Nativity of the Virgin, and the Dormition. On the vigil of August 15 he himself led the crowds barefoot from the Lateran to vespers in S. Maria Maggiore and back again, through the Forum to S. Maria Antiqua before mass in the morning. (These night-long revels were only abolished, for various abuses, by the austere Pope Pius V in 1566.)

Sergius' successor, John VII (705–7), united in himself qualities and circumstances that made his brief reign exceptional in the developments of the cult of the Virgin in the west. John was a Greek whose father, Plato (d. 686), was the curator and restorer of the Byzantine emperor's palace in Rome, which included the chapel, S. Maria Antiqua. John was *eruditissimus,* educated in Constantinople, and had imbibed such a lively love of the Virgin that the *Liber Pontificalis* actually finds it worthy of comment. An inscription found on a marble ambo John gave S. Maria Antiqua describes him in Latin and Greek as John, "servant of the mother of God," in imitation of the emperor in Byzantium, who styled himself "servant of God."

Just as the Virgin was the protective deity of the Byzantine ruling house in their chapel of Blachernae in Constantinople, so John emphasized her patronage in the palace chapel of the emperors in Rome, where once the pagan rulers had implored the goddess Minerva to watch over their safety. The greetings of the angel Gabriel and of Elisabeth to the Virgin—later to become the beloved prayer the Hail Mary—were inscribed on the walls of S. Maria Antiqua at this time; and frescoes, votive images, and a magnificent pulpit were commissioned to adorn it. For Old St. Peter's, John VII ordered mosaics that depicted the mysteries of her life and Christ's, and the fragments that survive, in the crypt of St. Peter's and in S. Maria in Cosmedin, show the depths of his attachment to the Virgin. Above all, John VII was the first pope to have himself painted during his lifetime in the Greek ceremonial attitude of prostration, the *proskynesis,* at the feet of the Virgin in majesty, for a painting in the basilica of S. Maria in Trastevere.[7]

This magnificent icon, over six feet high, sumptuously framed and inscribed with votive words of praise, amplifies the image of *Maria Regina* as it appears in the sixth-century fresco of S. Maria Antiqua (figure 12). To all the pearly and glittering insignia that adorned the latter is added the cross-surmounted staff—another symbol of imperial power. Angels stand at her side, carrying spears like the *protospathari,* the imperial guard. Mary is seated on an imperial purple cushion, stiff with jewels, with her feet resting above the ground, on a *subpedaneum;* a great arcaded diadem crowns her head and a huge nimbus irradiates about her. But the most important aspect of the icon is the presence of the reigning pope at the Virgin's feet. For this mingling of the living and the dead plucks the Virgin out of an inaccessible heaven and brings her within reach of the one appointed emissary on earth who, like an emperor's minister in Constantinople, can grasp his master's foot and be assured his wishes will be granted. In consequence, the legitimacy of the pope as the channel and interpreter of the divine will on earth is affirmed.

Sergius I and John VII, though both Greeks, withstood the ambitions of the emperor in Constantinople over the Church, by refusing to sign the reform decrees of Justinian II's synod of 691, and thus attempting to assert Rome's sole right to legislate on Church affairs. In Rome itself, rivalry with the other claimants to temporal power in Italy continued to fashion the imagery with which the papal entourage reverenced the Virgin. In a side chapel of S. Maria Antiqua, Pope Zachary I (741–52) flanks the Madonna in majesty holding a cross staff, but his portrait probably substituted an earlier one of John VII. In the same chapel, the papal minister Theodatus, a layman and the *primicerius* (first minister) of the papal court, commissioned frescoes which though badly mutilated still represent him, his wife, his small son and daughter, all wearing the square haloes of the living, in courtly attitudes of reverence before the Virgin and child. In another fresco, Theodatus kneels, holding up lighted tapers as was the custom in the imperial court. As the pope's chief administrator, Theodatus felt that he and his family were in touch with the highest mysteries. The paintings, faded and fragmentary, vividly communicate the confidence of the Church's men over a thousand years ago.

The chief catalyst to the cult of the Virgin in the west at this time was the Iconoclast heresy. Under the gifted and forceful Emperor Leo III, the Isaurian (reigned 717–40), the first blows against the use of images and relics in Christian worship were struck by the Byzantine imperial court. Around the year 727, a crowd composed mainly of women rioted when a revered icon of Christ over the bronze gate of the Sacred Palace at Constantinople was removed at the emperor's command.[8] Leo III's son, Constantine V, an equally imposing but even fiercer leader (reigned 740–75), called a council in 753 or 754 that officially denounced all icons in Christian cult and declared all who continued to use them outlaws. The heretics thereafter were fanatical, and for nearly a hundred years imposed their views, claiming savagely the lives of many Christians who refused to break with the iconodule traditions of their church. There was a respite from persecution from 780 to 815 under the Empress Irene, but after her the Emperor Leo V the Armenian (reigned 813–20) reinstated the ferocious puritanism of his predecessors, which lasted until the Triumph of Orthodoxy in 843 under the Empress Theodora (reigned 842–56) and the Emperor Michael III (reigned 842–67).

During the Iconoclast trauma, numerous fugitives, ecclesiastical and lay, made for the west, where Greek culture was not entirely alien and they could practice their cherished customs. Sicily and Rome in particular received an influx of iconodule Byzantines and were infused with the fervent, excitable strain of piety that had until Iconoclasm been the unrestrained character of Greek worship of the Virgin and the saints. At a more political level, the Iconoclast emperors' usurpation of the pope's authority in spiritual matters and their continued heretical defiance also galvanized the west. Iconoclasm marks the tragic beginning of the schism between the Greek and Latin worlds. It was at this time also that the papacy emerged as a western power: Pope Stephen III (752–7) crossed the Alps to ask the aid of Pepin, the Frankish king, against the ambitions of the Lombards in central Italy. Pepin complied, defeated the Lombards twice, and in 756 the pope was given the papal state.

The image of the Virgin in triumph therefore served a twofold purpose: it asserted the orthodoxy of images themselves, and its content indicated the powers of the pope as the ruler of Christian hearts and minds at a secular as well as spiritual level. During the Iconoclast heresy in Byzantium, a current of energy electrified Rome, the city of the papal rulers. Churches were built, and adorned with golden mosaics, with bright frescoes and magnificent icons. And all over the city, the new blend of defiance and pride inspired the takeover of pagan buildings, hitherto shunned, and their conversion to Christian worship. And through all these undertakings pounds an excited dithyramb in praise of the Virgin, instrument of the Incarnation, and personification of the Church.

The popes of the period showed her their love: Gregory III (731–41) built a monument at the tomb of St. Peter's that depicted the Virgin on one side, Christ on the other, and he placed an icon of the Virgin near the relic of the crib in S. Maria Maggiore; Stephen III had a golden effigy of the Virgin cast for the same basilica; Paul I (757–67) dedicated two chapels in Old St. Peter's to her, and decorated them with mosaics. Paschal I (817–24), who welcomed refugees from the second wave of persecutions under the Emperor Leo IV, commissioned some of the most memorable mosaic apses in Rome—S. Prassede, S. Cecilia in Trastevere—but above all S. Maria in Domnica, where, flanked by throngs of angels whose azure haloes recede like the waves of the ocean, Pope Paschal, wearing, like Theodatus before him, the square halo of the living, humbly clasps the red slippered foot of the Virgin in triumph.[9]

All the circumstances present in the upsurge of Marian worship in Rome converge in the wondrously beautiful and holy church of S. Maria in Cosmedin,[10] which stands in the former cattle market of ancient Rome, the Forum Boarium, across a curving space from two toy-like pagan temples, once dedicated to Vesta and to Portunus, god of harbours. This chaste but opulently marbled church has now been restored again to the Greek monks who were first given it to embellish and tend in the eighth century after they had fled to safety in the west. Nostalgically, the Greek fugitives called their church after a quarter of Constantinople famous for its beauty, the *Kosmidion,* "from the Greek word for decoration, and for the world, which is God's most beautiful work of art."[11] In winter, when the church is cold, the melodious Greek Orthodox services are held in a side chamber, built above a sixth-century B.C. temple to Ceres, which was only deconsecrated at the end of the fourth century, when the Emperor Theodosius finally ordered the closure of all pagan temples. It was then converted into a food distribution centre for the city, which, along the lines of S. Maria Antiqua, was taken over either in the later sixth or the seventh century by the ecclesiastical authorities and administered as a diaconate for the care of the old, the poor, the sick, and pilgrims. The massive *opus quadratum* blocks of stone of this ancient building are still embedded in the side wall of the chamber where mass is sung in winter, and still visible in the crypt below the church, now a special votive shrine of the Virgin.

In the gallery above the nave, looking towards the main altar, imposing fluted columns with Corinthian capitals and stucco reliefs of grain baskets form the visible skeleton of the church. They are the pillars of a *statio annonae,* a market inspector's imperial office and granary, which stood adjacent to the temple of Ceres, the corn goddess. Like new vegetation clothing an ancient rock face, the Christian church grew up between the granary and the temple, at once cancelling the former pagan places and yet avoiding the false magic of their exact position. Later, under Pope Adrian I (772–95), nephew of the Theodatus of S. Maria Antiqua, the church was enlarged until it absorbed the ancient substructure into the Christian fabric. But the functions of the sacred spot survived: there the church distributed bread, and sang the praises of a goddess whose cult has continued uninterrupted in S. Maria in Cosmedin until today.

It was in the twelfth century, however, that the church was richly embellished with the many-hued *opus sectile* marbled pavements and walls that make it such a work of art. Pope Calixtus II (1119–24), who identified strongly with his predecessor Calixtus I (217–22), the reputed founder of the great basilica of S. Maria in Trastevere, commissioned the decorations. And it was, significantly, Calixtus II who scored the chief papal triumph of the middle ages when he signed the Concordat of Worms in 1122 with the Emperor Henry V, settling the long bitter dispute about investitures and reserving for the Holy See the prerogative of appointing bishops. He commemorated this signal victory of Church over state in the monumental chapel of St. Nicholas in St. John Lateran, where he installed a fresco of Mary enthroned above two popes, and he transformed S. Maria in Cosmedin into a monument to the rights of the papacy by using the imagery of *Maria Regina,* the living embodiment of the Church triumphant, by inscribing her praises on the walls and by raising a splendid marbled bishop's cathedra in the central apse.

Secular imagery was used to depict the Virgin Mary in Rome by the popes in order to advance the hegemony of the Holy See; and her cult was encouraged because she was in a profound manner identified with the figure of the Church itself. But this triumphalism fostered by the Church was turned on its head in the later middle ages, when temporal kings and queens took back the borrowed symbolism of earthly power to enhance their own prestige and give themselves a sacred character. The use of the emblems of earthly power for the Mother of God did not empty them of their temporal content: rather, when kings and queens wore the sceptre and the crown they acquired an aura of divinity.

To Byzantine eyes after the traumatic era of Iconoclasm, such mingling of the material and spiritual realms constituted an appalling solecism. The Lady of Heaven and her son could not ape the fashion of mortals, however special the relationship between them. Thus the Santa Sophia mosaic that celebrates the Triumph of Orthodoxy in 843 shows the Virgin Mary, simply clothed and in the long dark blue veil, the *maphorion,* with the Christ child on her knees. The archangels Michael and Gabriel, in huge sweeping rainbow-coloured wings, stand on either side of them, and the inscription proclaims: "The images which the impostors had cast down, the pious emperors have again set up."[12]

The restraint and caution of the iconography was to remain the unchanging hallmark of Byzantine art. The coins of the post-iconoclast empire also highlight the contrast between the austere Virgin and the luxury-loving rulers. On the coins of the sister empresses Zoe (d. 1050) and Theodora (d. 1057), the Virgin confers power on heaven's delegates on earth, sometimes by holding a crown over their heads, sometimes by grasping their cross-staff. But their dress proclaims their difference.[13] The flexible approach of the west, which allowed the Virgin to wear the egg-sized pearls of temporal queens, was to remain foreign and repugnant to Byzantine eyes.

But because western imagery obscured the demarcation lines between the spiritual and material spheres, and fortified the special relation between the court of heaven and the court on earth, the kings of Christendom laid claim to higher, spiritual authority by extending the sacred meaning of royal attributes and rituals. Thus although the splendid coronation of Charlemagne in St. Peter's Rome in 800 implied that the pope had the sovereign power of creating kings, it also elevated the king to a holy state: he was consecrated in the sight of God. Otto III, the

German emperor, was crowned no less than three times: king of the Germans in 983; king of the Lombards in 995; and holy Roman emperor in Rome in 996, when he was sixteen years old. Around the year 1000, he was painted in a *Gospel Book,* crowned by the hand of God emerging from a large nimbus above, surrounded by the symbols of the evangelists and seated on a raised throne supported by a naked personification of earth—in short, as Christ in his aspect of the ruler of the world.

Although the emperor in Constantinople (whose elegant culture the Ottonians were so anxious to emulate) saw himself as the vicar of Christ on earth, he would never have impersonated his redeemer, as Otto III does in this illumination. As John Beckwith has written: "The Byzantine court would have thought such a representation outré and bizarre. Such telescoping of the natural with the supernatural order was to them deplorable."[14] But as the lines of communication from Byzantium become stretched, these distinctions become blurred, and aggressive claims to total authority on the part of Christian kings continue to find expression in brave propaganda images. One of the most striking is a golden mosaic in the beautiful Martorana church in Palermo, where Roger II, king of Sicily, another king who longed to match the splendour and sophistication of the Byzantine court, appears before Christ, who crowns him. Richly dressed in the *loros,* the jewelled stole of the emperors, Roger inclines his head. The image copies the Byzantine model precisely, except that Roger's face is startling, for he resembles Christ. The mosaic asserts not only that the king is divinely appointed, but that kingship itself has a God-like character.

The Virgin Mary was the special patron both of the Ottonians and of the Norman kings of Sicily. It is interesting that both Otto III and Roger II lost their fathers as children and were brought up by their mothers. Otto's father died in 983 when he was three; Roger's in 1101, when he was five and a half. In both cases, their mothers ruled as regent in their stead. Theophano, mother of Otto III, was a Greek princess, who brought her religious civilization to the north with her; and Adelaide of Montserrat, Roger's mother, was a Ligurian, who, faced with the task of ruling an island only very recently pacified, spurned the Norman soldiers of her late husband in favour of Greeks (and Arabs) who knew Sicily well. This Oriental and exotic upbringing had a marked effect on Roger: a taste for Arabian-night pleasure gardens and for Byzantine customs in his worship were both formed by his childhood experiences. Thus the resemblance of the Madonna and child to the imperial regent and her son cannot have missed anyone in either the German or the Sicilian courts, conscious as they were of the Greek concept that the emperor was Christ's vicar on earth.

At the same time as Adelaide reigned in Palermo, the Norman dominions of southern Italy were in the hands of other widows: Adela of Flanders held court in Naples during her son's minority; Constance of France in Taranto ruled as regent for her son. And at the end of the twelfth century, a formidable woman held the throne of France for her son, the future saint, Louis IX. The devotion of Blanche of Castile and her crusader son to the Virgin has no more eloquent testimonial than the cathedrals of Chartres and Paris, which they lavishly endowed.

By the reign of King Louis, another transformation of a Byzantine imperial image had entered the stream of western art: the coronation of the Virgin, one of western Christendom's favourite themes, first appears in the twelfth century, in the unforgettable apse mosaic of S. Maria in Trastevere, and on the powerful tympana of French cathedrals. The image was based on the Greek emperor's coronation by Christ or the Virgin, familiar from Byzantine mosaics and coins. But in the west the terrestrial sphere once again imposed its pattern on the heavens, and Christ was shown crowning his mother queen. It switched the moment of Mary's triumph from the Incarnation to the Assumption: she is crowned queen of heaven after death, as Andrew of Crete and John Damascene had described in their homilies on the feast of the Dormition when they applied Psalm 45 to the Virgin's royal progress into paradise. Although Maria Regina the Theotokos, as she appeared in S. Maria Antiqua or on John VII's icon, was eclipsed by this new scene, the metaphor of Mary's queenship still served to project authority's claims.

Émile Mâle, the great art historian, has attributed the invention of the image to Suger, abbot of St. Denis, the first masterwork of the Gothic style. A true iconodule, Suger believed in the stimulation of piety through pictures, pageants, and pleasure. *"Mens hebes,"* he wrote, *"ad rerum per materialia surgit"* (The dull mind rises up through material things).[15] Suger married images to theology with remarkable flair for innovation and energy in execution. About ten years after the consecration of his sumptuously redecorated abbey church of St. Denis in 1140, Suger presented the old church of Notre Dame in Paris with a stained-glass window commemorating the triumph of the Virgin. The window survived the destruction of the old church and was incorporated into the thirteenth-century cathedral that still dominates Paris today; but it did not survive the iconoclasm of the Age of Reason. In the eighteenth century the art historian Le Vieil found it crude and smashed it. He noted beforehand, however, that it depicted the triumph of the Virgin, and remarked on "the brilliance of the colours, especially the blue."[16]

The blue glass is irretrievable, and St. Denis stands defaced by a mob of the French Revolution. But Mâle believes the glass showed the Virgin crowned on Christ's right hand. Suger's novel iconography inspired the portals of other cathedrals of France: Senlis (c. 1170), Mantes (1180), Chartres (c. 1205–10), or the *Portail de la Vierge* at Notre Dame (*c.* 1210–20) and later at Strasbourg, Lyons, Longport. The theme appears in the twelfth-century glass of Canterbury cathedral, and the altarpieces of medieval Italy, where the Virgin takes her son's right hand like the queen of Ophir and receives her crown of glory—from him, or from an angel. In the west, the idea of apotheosis, at the heart of the Assumption, crystallized in the medieval centuries in the image of the Virgin's coronation.

Suger is the foremost example of the social mobility of the twelfth century: an obscure clerk of peasant stock, he rose rapidly to power, the beneficiary of the Capetian kings' policy of rejecting the hereditary barons in favour of servants who would repay their advancement with undivided loyalty. Suger was above all a royal minister, not a papal servant, and the gravitational tug of this prior commitment, evident in the art he influenced, made him affirm again and again the special sacredness of the kingly state. As Suger's king was Louis VII, who left his kingdom to take the Cross, his task was thereby made a little easier.[17]

It was Suger who, in his flamboyant visual imagination, crystallized the iconography of the rod of Jesse, which shows Mary and the child springing from a line of kings (see figures 1, 13). It was under Suger's influence over French art and architecture that Queen Blanche of Castile, Louis's overpowering mother, gave the glorious rose window of the north transept to Chartres cathedral—the sparkling colours proclaim the Virgin Queen of Heaven.[18] In a moralized Bible written and illuminated for the queen mother and her son around 1235, the royal mother and child appear side by side. Blanche is veiled and crowned, wrapped in an ermine-lined blue mantle over a simple belted russet tunic, and she holds up both hands as if in supplication to her son, who holds the orb and sceptre of kingship (figure 15).

Blanche's appearance reproduces exactly the appearance of the Virgin on the triumphant tympana of French cathedrals of her time. To the medieval French churchgoer, heaven resembled the court of his monarch, a palace inhabited by noble men and women. And the Virgin, in particular, looked like their suzerain's mother. Blanche herself identified so strongly with the religious ideal that she was buried in a nun's habit.

The image of the Virgin as queen is scored so deep in western imagination that many Catholics still think of her as a medieval monarch. When she appeared in visions at Knock in Ireland in 1879, and at Pontmain in France in 1871, she wore the long dress, sash, veil, and crown of the thirteenth-century feudal lady. The massed accumulation of images has frozen her into a costume plate.[19]

This was a rapid result of the extraordinary wave of adulation that raised eighty cathedrals in France within a century. In 1460, Jean Fouquet, illuminating a *Book of Hours* for Étienne Chevalier, painted his patron praying before a statue of the Madonna and child. Etienne, with his patron saint Stephen beside him, kneels in a Renaissance hall, with ornamental swags on the ceiling, a richly marbled floor, Corinthian columns, and frolicking putti. The Queen of Heaven opposite him sits on a high Gothic throne under an ogival arch, with angels and saints sculptured in the archivolts, as on the portals of Chartres or Notre Dame. Jean Fouquet and Étienne Chevalier had moved on with time, and their surroundings were "modern," but the Virgin and child had come to a standstill in Gothic. In the twelfth century, the Virgin was remote in rank; two hundred years later, she was remote in time as well.

The Virgin Queen had a spiritual dimension in the middle ages that was expressed more eloquently in the hymns than in the pictures that began circulating widely in the twelfth century.[20] The antiphons of the Virgin invoke her as the lady of heaven (Dante's *donna del cielo:* Paradise 32:29), mistress of angels, queen of paradise, whose mercy can save the most abject sinner. The *Salve Regina* first appears in a Cistercian *antiphonarium* compiled in 1140, and five years later Peter, abbot of Cluny, prescribed it for the procession on the feast of the Assumption. It has been attributed to Adhemar, bishop of Le Puy, who led the first crusade and died in Antioch in 1098. Deeply melancholic, this cry from the depths paints all life on earth as exile from God. It pleads for the Queen of Heaven's mercy:

> *Ad te clamamus, exules filii evae*
> *Ad te suspiramus, gementes et flentes*
> *In hac lacrimarum valle.*

> To thee we cry, banished children of Eve.
> To thee do we sigh, groaning and weeping
> In this vale of tears.

The crusaders may have sung it in the field—its delicate sadness would have made it one of history's strangest battle cries.

The *Regina Caeli,* attributed to Pope Gregory V (d. 999), and the *Ave Regina Caelorum* (not earlier than the tenth century), also became popular hymns from the end of the twelfth century. The new orders of monks promoted their recitation enthusiastically: the Franciscans included them in their breviary from 1249 onwards. In the circle of the Church Triumphant in Dante's *Paradise,* the souls sweetly sing the *Salve Regina,* as the Virgin rises to the higher spheres. Pope Clement VI introduced the four antiphons into the office of the Curia in 1350, and Pius V (1566–72), the reformer of the liturgy, prescribed the *Alma Redemptoris Mater,* as well as the three others, to be sung each canonical hour. The *Salve Regina* is still the Catholic world's best-loved hymn. At the shrine of Montserrat near Barcelona, the choir boys who are dedicated to the Virgin by their parents and live secluded in the monastery sing it at compline every evening. The old Benedictine plainsong has been discarded in favour of a more rousing nineteenth-century tune, but the power of the brief antiphon, with its haunting envoi, is overwhelming in the darkened monastery church, where the sanctuary lamps glow softly and the Black Madonna above glints in her gold and silver shrine:

> *O clemens, o pia*
> *O dulcis Maria*

> O merciful, kind, sweet Mary

The queenship of Mary expresses her signal triumph, through her virginity and her Assumption, over human weakness and evil; second, the modern theology of Maria Regina is grounded in her supremely efficient powers of intercession with Christ (see Chapter 19); furthermore, the association of Mary with the allegorical figure of the Church makes her regal authority an assertion of the Church's power. All these strata were present in the thought of Pope Pius XII when he officially proclaimed Mary as Queen of Heaven in 1954, four years after the proclamation of the Assumption.[21] He could hardly have intended any medieval mimesis of earthly monarchs—Elizabeth II in England and Juliana in the Netherlands were the two unlikely exemplars holding their thrones. Rather, at a time of crisis in the faith and the Church, he was attempting to reassert Rome's influence.

But the symbol retains its temporal associations if only because it justifies the kind of economic tribute fit for a queen. At Saragossa, for instance, one of the few treasuries of the Virgin that has survived despoliation by bankrupt governments is hoarded behind heavy oaken doors in the sacristy. The Virgin of the Pillar has been given crown after crown for her small and pretty head, necklaces and bracelets and brooches to adorn her, capes and robes barnacled in gems to wear on her feastdays. Huge sunburst nimbi of thousands of diamonds, emeralds, and rubies frame her crowned head. The largest crown in her possession, containing over a million diamonds, was given by public subscription in 1905. Although Saragossa is uniquely rich, the phenomenon is widespread in the Catholic world: school children save their pennies or give away their wristwatches to shrines like Walsingham in England or Czestochowa in Poland so that the Queen of Heaven's statue or icon can wear a fitting crown.

It would be difficult to concoct a greater perversion of the Sermon on the Mount than the sovereignty of Mary and its cult, which has been used over the centuries by different princes to stake out their spheres of influence in the temporal realm, to fly a flag for their ambitions like any Maoist poster or party political broadcast; and equally difficult to imagine a greater distortion of Christ's idealism than this identification of the rich and powerful with the good.

# Part Three
# BRIDE

## Chapter Eight

# THE SONG OF SONGS

*Vox tua to me was full sweet*
*When thou me bade, "babe be still"*
*Full goodly gone our lips meet*
*With bright branches, as blossom on hill.*
*Favus distillans that went with will*
*Out of thy lips when we did kiss*
*Therefore, mother, this is my skill*
*Veni coronaberis.*[1]

—ANONYMOUS, FIFTEENTH CENTURY

IN THE CONCH of S. Maria in Trastevere's central apse, the Virgin and Christ are seated side by side on a lyre-shaped double throne against a golden field. The Virgin Queen has the long oval face, the straight nose, curving brows, and tiny mouth of Byzantine icons, and under her pearl-hung diadem her grave eyes brim with inner fire. In the dim light of the basilica, the gems and gold of her elaborate and encrusted costume gleam faintly, while beside her, Christ gazes into the distance with enormous, steadfast black eyes. The two figures loom over the church, an awesome and wondrously beautiful theophany (colour plate IV, figure 6).

The mosaic, created in 1140, was the first in Rome for three hundred years; and the pope who commissioned it, Innocent II (1130–43), appears on Mary's right, next to a model of the church he embellished nearly a thousand years after its foundation. Eighteen months before the mosaic was made, St. Bernard, Cistercian abbot of Clairvaux, and a man who overshadows the whole century and far beyond, had visited Rome, and it was largely through the saint's cunning manoeuvres and prestigious influence that Innocent II had defeated his rivals, the anti-popes Anacletus II and Victor IV. The apse mosaic of S. Maria in Trastevere uses the triumph of the Virgin as Queen of Heaven to commemorate that victory; and it simultaneously enshrines the passionate imagination of the saint who engineered it.

Unlike the coronation of the Virgin on the tympana of medieval French cathedrals, or the icon of *Maria Regina* of John VII, the inspiration for the golden queen of S. Maria in Trastevere comes from the Song of Songs, which since 1135 St. Bernard had been expounding in an extraordinary sequence of sermons to the monks of Clairvaux.

In the mosaic Mary holds up a phylactery that reads: *Leva eius sub capite meo et dextera illius amplexabit me* (His left hand should be under my head; and his right hand should embrace me) (Song of Solomon 8:3). Christ's right arm does indeed encircle her, and the book on his knee reads: *Veni electa mea, ponam in te tronam meam* (Come my chosen one I shall place thee on my throne). Mary's scroll quotes from the Song of Songs, Christ's is inspired by it and by Psalm 45, but it is in fact a direct quotation from an antiphon for the feast of the Assumption, found in the eighth-century *Liber Pontificalis* attributed to Pope Gregory the Great.[2]

Christ's embrace recalls the gesture Roman emperors used in imperial iconography to designate their trusted ministers and companions. In Christian Roman art, this expression of intimacy and confidence is translated into the celestial sphere. The sixth-century mosaic apse of the church of SS. Cosmas and Damian above the Forum shows Peter and Paul putting their arms around the saints' shoulders to lead them into the presence of the Redeemer. Paschal I (817–24) resumed the image in S. Prassede, where the conch mosaic depicts the saints placing an avuncular arm around Saints Prassede and Pudenziana, as they are ushered towards Christ. The young girls are dressed in cloth of gold, like Byzantine princesses, but the splendour of their robes is bridal, thus elucidating their relationship to the saviour. And in the twelfth-century mosaic of S. Maria in Trastevere, this imagery becomes explicit: Mary, triumphantly assumed into heaven and embraced by Christ, prefigures the Church's future glory and the soul's promised union with Christ in terms of the mystical love song, the Cantica Canticarum, or Song of Songs. Her youthful beauty, unquestioningly accepted from this date on, has a theological purpose: the Virgin is no dowager queen mother, but the beloved Shulamite, bride of Christ.

Such a transition from Virgin Mother to bride was possible because, as we have seen, a virgin in the Bible was not a young girl who had renounced marriage but one who was ripe for picking. However contradictory, Christian asceticism absorbed the Jewish virgin bride as a primary symbol.[3]

There was a long biblical tradition of nuptial imagery. The prophet Hosea, writing before 721 B.C., came into contact with the Canaanites' fertility cult and its central drama of the annual marriage of the god Baal to his sister Anat, consummated in order to unleash the forces of nature. Hosea, while remaining faithful to the monotheistic and patriarchal nature of the Hebrew God, boldly adapted this rich nuptial imagery of the rites of Baal to describe the relations of Yahweh and his faithless bride, Israel. Like Hosea's own wife, Israel is a harlot who deserts her lord and master. He, in his just jealousy, punishes her fickleness, but he promises to reward her in the future if she learns to return his love with loyalty and faith. The antithesis between this lovely bride of the future and the wanton of the present, between the loving god who promises peace and the thundering lord of vengeance who reigns over his wife through terror, colours much of the prophetic writings of the Bible after Hosea: for Jeremiah, Juda is Yahweh's new bride and as treacherous and irresponsible as Israel; for Ezekiel, the Babylonian captivity is the revenge of an infuriated spouse on his chosen people's adultery with other gods, the idols of Egypt and Assyria and Chaldaea; Isaiah rings with promises of the nuptial bliss that will follow the consummation of Israel and Yahweh's love and the fulfilment of the pact between them (Isaiah 62:4–5).

God and his earthly bride dance around each other, sometimes clashing violently, sometimes uniting in loving harmony. The conflict corresponds not only to the Canaanite cult of Baal, but also to other mystery religions of the near east: the Syrian rites of the shepherd Tammuz, lover of the sky goddess Ishtar; the Phrygian cult of Cybele and Attis, who died castrated under a tree; of Isis and Osiris in Egypt. The nuptials of these divinities mirrored the greater nuptials of the sky and the earth, from which comes forth plenty: the rites of regeneration each year imitated the original union of sky and earth at the beginning of the world.

Thus marriage was the pivotal symbol on which turned the cosmology of most of the religions that pressed on Jewish society, jeopardizing its unique monotheism. It is a symptom of their struggle to maintain their distinctiveness that the Jews, while absorbing this pagan symbol, reversed the ranks of the celestial pair to make the bride God's servant and possession, from whom he ferociously exacts absolute submission.

When St. Paul uses the symbol of a bride for the first time in the

New Testament, he instantly recalls the fury of this relationship. Speaking as an anxious matchmaker, he admonishes his flock to behave well. In Paul's perspective, today is the testing time, tomorrow the marriage feast. In his letter to the Ephesians, Paul elaborates the image: the Church is Christ's bride, "a glorious Church not having spot, or wrinkle, or any such thing" (Ephesians 5:27)—a Jewish girl inspected before her wedding for disfigurement or disease.

The evangelists add substance to the figure of Christ the bridegroom: in the Synoptics, some of John the Baptist's disciples approach Jesus and ask him why his followers do not fast as they do. Jesus cryptically replies: "Can the children of the bridegroom mourn, as long as the bridegroom is still with them?" (Matthew 9:15; see also Mark 2:18–20; Luke 5:33–5). In the Fourth Gospel, John the Baptist describes himself, as Paul had done in the letter to the Corinthians, as the go-between and best man, who works for the bridegroom's interests. "I am not the Christ," he says. "He that hath the bride is the bridegroom: but the friend of the bridegroom . . . rejoiceth greatly because of the bridegroom's voice" (John 3:28–99). The identity of the bride is ambiguous in both passages, and in two nuptial parables that Matthew recounts—the king's wedding feast that the invited guests will not attend (Matthew 22:1–14) and the wise and foolish virgins (Matthew 25:1–13)—the bride also remains a mystery, anonymous and even absent. Both stories stress the urgency of readiness for the last day, and are not primarily concerned with the bridal pair. The marriage feast had become a conventional setting for eschatological writings, as the Apocalypse confirms: after the cataracts of fire and the bloodcurdling monsters, after the devastating plagues and the fury of the avenging angels, the final peace of the Church is celebrated as a wedding—the nuptial banquet of the lamb, at which Christ is united with all his followers in the Church.

It is at this point that the symbol of the bride enters Mariology. For, at the Apocalyptic wedding feast, John sees "the New Jerusalem, coming down from God out of heaven, prepared as a bride adorned for her husband" (Revelation 21:2). She stands for the new era of the Church, the break with the past, the pure, beautiful, spotless creation of God, free of all the taint and strife of all that has gone before. In patristic thought, Mary was a figure of the Church and vice versa; and in the Apocalypse, the radiant bridal appearance of the Church is preceded by and associated with the "great wonder in heaven," already established as a figure of the Virgin.

Because first Yahweh and then Christ appear as bridegrooms, and because the Virgin was identified with the Church, the bride of Christ, it was possible for rabbinical fathers to read the passionate poetry of the Song of Songs as an allegory of God's love, and for later Christian exegetes to identify the lover of the Song with Christ and his beloved with the Church, each Christian soul, and the Virgin Mary. From the point of view of western literature, this was a fateful and fortunate decision; but it still remains astonishing that an ascetic religion should ever have included in its sacred canon a text so remarkable for its undisguised sexuality.

The Song of Songs was attributed to King Solomon, who is mentioned as the lover of the poem (Song of Solomon 3:7, 9), and it was therefore placed among the Wisdom books of the Bible, also ascribed to the great sage. Debate over its date and its authorship continues. Scholars, who believe the poem describes the relationship of Yahweh and Israel, date it to the second half of the fifth century B.C. but not earlier; but if, as seems more likely, the book is composed of several love lyrics, the folk songs of a poetic pastoral people, then it could have been written and compiled at different, earlier times.

"Let him kiss me with the kisses of his mouth . . ." opens the poem, and from then on the luxuriant images of desire and longing, of exultation and the peculiar anguish of love palpitate ever more potently. "A bundle of myrrh is my wellbeloved unto me," says the Shulamite. "He shall lie all night betwixt my breasts" (Song of Solomon 1:13). When he calls her, wooing her in the springtime, she says: "For, lo, the winter is past, the rain is over and gone; the flowers appear on the earth, the time of the singing of birds is come, and the voice of the turtle is heard in our land . . ." (Song of Solomon 2:11). Further on, when she has lost him, she searches the streets, thinking of the glory and splendour of his bed: "He made the pillars thereof of silver, the bottom thereof of gold, the covering of it of purple, the midst thereof being paved with love . . ." (Song of Solomon 3:10). Then he invokes her beauty: "Thy two breasts are like two young roes that are twins, which feed among the lilies" (Song of Solomon 4:5). In increasing excitement, he cries out: "Thy lips, o my spouse, drop as the honeycomb; honey and milk are under thy tongue . . ." (Song of Solomon 4:11).

Later, he calls on her in the night, his head drenched with dew. She opens to him: "My beloved put in his hand by the hole of the door, and my bowels were moved for him. I rose up to open to my beloved; and my hands dropped with myrrh, and my fingers with sweet smelling myrrh . . ." (Song of Solomon 5:4–5). But her lover has vanished, and so, weak with longing, she goes out to search for him once more, for she is "sick of love" (Song of Solomon 5:8). It is her turn to describe his beauty, "white and ruddy, the chiefest among ten thousand" (Song of Solomon 5:10). In similar strain he sings: "Thy navel is like a round goblet, which wanteth not liquor: thy belly is like an heap of wheat set about with lilies" (Song of Solomon 7:2).

There has never been a more intense communication of the experience of desire. The scent of apples, the laden vines, the flowing milk, the brimming honey and wine; young animals leaping with new life, roe, deer, singing birds, bursting pomegranates, swelling figs, mandrake, animals calving and sheep bearing twins—the imagery of fertility accumulates until the reader is himself spellbound by its sensuality and becomes drowsy with voluptuousness. The theme is plain: "Love is strong as death" and "many waters cannot quench love, neither can the floods drown it . . ." (Song of Solomon 8:6–7). When the sequence closes, with an envoi of genius, the emotions still hang in the air, pregnant with promised joy: "Make haste, my beloved, and be thou like to a roe or to a young hart upon the mountains of spices" (Song of Solomon 8:14).

The sequence met some opposition among Jewish scholars in the first century A.D., but on appeal to the prophetic tradition of nuptial imagery, it remained part of the canon and continued to be attributed to King Solomon. Early Christian mystics developed the allegorical tradition of interpreting the Song of Solomon: Methodius of Olympus, Origen, and Gregory of Nyssa in the east and Ambrose in the west expounded the canticle as the love of Christ for his Church. It was Ambrose who first coalesced the Virgin, the Church, and each Christian soul as the smitten Shulamite of the Song of Songs. "From that womb of Mary was brought into the world the heap of wheat surrounded by lilies [the faithful]: while the kiss the beloved receives is the kiss of the Holy Spirit at the Annunciation"[4]

But in the early Church the love songs of Solomon and the Shulamite were predominantly applied to the love of Christ and the consecrated virgin or nun. In the second century, Methodius of Olympus in his *Symposium* or *Banquet of Ten Virgins* describes the studious and pleasant conversations of ten young women in a garden under a symbolic *agnus castus* tree. They expound on the Song of Songs, and for the first time in an extant commentary, liken the beloved to a virgin dedicated to Christ. Methodius' speaker picks her way fastidiously through the erotic imagery, stressing its spiritual content. "For the Word is in love with none of the things of the flesh—such as, for example, hands or face or feet. . . ." At the end of the book, the virgins process with lighted candles, intoning a stately *epithalamium* to Christ their bridegroom.

Keeping a slow measure, they describe the Bible's prototypes of purity, chanting the refrain:

> Chastely I live for Thee
> And holding my lighted lamps,
> My Spouse I go forth to meet Thee.[5]

In the third century, Cyprian of Carthage accused the wayward virgins in his flock of committing adultery against their true husband Christ when they flirted with other men.[6] Jerome, in his letter to Eustochium, insists on her sacred nuptials, drawing his imagery from the Canticle:

Ever let the privacy of your chamber guard you; ever let the Bridegroom sport with you within. Do you pray? You speak to the Bridegroom. Do you read? He speaks to you. When sleep overtakes you He will come behind and put His hand through the hole of the door, and your heart shall be moved for him; and you will awake and rise up and say: I am sick of love.

Later he warns her: "Jesus is jealous," and he tells the mothers of girls who have taken the veil to rejoice proudly for they have become the mothers-in-law of God.[7]

The theme became second nature in Christian writing, leading to instances of unconscious hilarity, like the story of Thaïs the reformed courtesan, as told in the tenth century by Hroswitha of Gandersheim. In a vision, one of the characters in her play *Paphnutius* sees "a splendid bed. It was adorned with white hangings and coverings, and a crown was laid on it and round it were fair radiant virgins. They stood there as if they were guarding the crown. There was a great brightness round the bed, and a multitude of angels. . . ." Then comes a voice from heaven: "This glory is prepared . . . for the harlot Thaïs."[8]

The middle ages saw no decline in the metaphor's popularity as propaganda for the virginal state. The lively thirteenth-century alliterative homily *Holy Maidenhead* expatiates at great length on the pleasures of marriage with Christ and the horrors of marriage with men.[9] St. Catherine of Alexandria, who, according to legend, was martyred in 307, and her namesake St. Catherine of Siena (d. 1380) were both reputed to have contracted a mystic marriage with Christ. The first known account of the Alexandrian's wedding occurs in 1337, but earlier paintings exist showing her accepting a ring from the infant Christ in the arms of his mother. In the *Golden Legend,* she spurns her suitors, saying she would never exchange an immortal spouse for a mortal husband. As Millard Meiss has so brilliantly illustrated in his *Painting in Florence and Siena after the Black Death:* "At this time [first half of the Trecento] painters as well as poets tended to transform the metaphors by which the Middle Ages expressed spiritual qualities or relations into more concrete, though still symbolic, scenes of familiar human circumstances and events—birth, marriage, motherhood, death."[10]

The wedding of Catherine of Alexandria is the subject of hundreds of Christian paintings from the fourteenth century onwards; with one exception, the Virgin always assists her son in placing the ring on the martyr's finger. In the English *Hymn of the Pearl* of the same period—it was written between 1350 and 1380—the father sees his dead two-year-old daughter as Christ's bride among the 144,000 virgins at the altar of the lamb.[11]

The ceremony of a nun's consecration keeps the symbolism fresh today. "My beloved spake and said unto me," reads the priest. "Rise up, my love, my fair one and come away. . . ." As the woman, holding a lighted candle, takes the veil, and accepts the ring that designates her the bride of Christ, the lover's urgent call to his beloved is read out. In one ancient form of the ritual, the nun was crowned with a garland: *"Accipe signum Christi in capite,"* said the celebrant, *"ut uxor eius efficiaris, et si in eo permanseris, in perpetuum coroneris."* (Receive this sign of Christ on your head, that you may be his wife, and if you remain in that state, be crowned for all eternity.) Three days' retreat followed, like a honeymoon, and then the newlywed's veil was lifted and her face revealed, and with her companions she sat down to a wedding feast.[12]

Nuns are not the only brides of Christ, for the sacrament of the first Holy Communion is treated with great solemnity in Catholic countries. In Belgium, France, and Spain photographers' shops display pictures of little girls in their white communion dresses, posed as brides, carrying bouquets and wearing tulle veils under small garlands of flowers. In 1945 the Marquesa de Llanzol of Madrid commissioned the great couturier Balenciaga to design her daughter Sonsoles' first communion dress. These first nuptials were echoed later, when Sonsoles married—again in a dress by Balenciaga.[13]

Although Mary, as the supreme model of virginity in the eyes of the fourth-century Fathers and afterwards, and as a figure of the Church, was associated with the bride of the Song of Songs, the flower of Mariological mysticism lay in bud until the twelfth century, when it opened to full glory in the impassioned love and language of St. Bernard.

During the year 1135, and from then on at intervals until 1153,

Bernard of Clairvaux gave eighty-six sermons on the Song of Songs that together form one of Christian mysticism's most astonishing masterpieces,[14] in which the saint's sheer joy climaxes in an irrepressible diapason. From the root that God is love—*Deus caritas est* (1 John 4:8)—to the kiss of consummation Christ bestows on the soul that leaps towards him, Bernard uncovers a mystical system by which the Christian is transfigured by love.[15]

Christ is the lover of the Canticle, his bride sometimes the Church, sometimes the individual soul, sometimes the monks of Clairvaux, his audience, and sometimes the Virgin. But the object for all is attainment of that divine likeness in which man was created and from which he has fallen through concupiscence and sin. Since God is love, through love alone can man reflect his maker once more. At the moment she becomes inebriated with love, the soul can obtain the kiss of her spouse. This love must be an utterly spontaneous motion of the heart, utterly disinterested: "I love because I love, I love that I may love. A great thing is love, provided only that it return to its principle, look to its origin, and flowing back towards its source draw thence the pure waters wherewith it may flow unendingly."[16]

The antinomy at the crux of Christian thinking lies nakedly exposed in Bernard's use of erotic imagery. For, in his mysticism, one expression of love—carnal desire—disfigures the pristine soul, but another expression of love—the leap of the soul towards God—restores the primal resemblance. But both loves are expressed in the same language, which is principally drawn from that most languorous and amorous of poems, the Song of Songs. On this tragic tension, Christian discipline flourishes. As the soul reaches for the embrace of her spouse, the mortal coil reasserts itself as her gaoler. Humanity can never quite be joined to God, be dissolved into his essence, because although he made man in his own image, God always transcends his creature. But, preaches Bernard, the practice of humility, or physical mortification and self-denial, the contemplation of mankind's wickedness and pride compared to the supreme self-sacrifice of the Cross, and the suppression of fleshly appetites can assist the soul on its upward climb. Through austerity, the Greek *askesis,* the soul can be emptied of self-interest and filled with love.

The "kisses of his mouth" become, in Bernard's sermon, the special symbol of the moment of ecstatic union. But such moments cannot be sustained, and remain mere promises of future bliss in heaven. Only one creature ever attained this perfection: the Virgin Mary. Assumed into heaven, seated at Christ's right hand, she becomes the example for every Christian of his future joy. She was, according to Bernard, filled with love because she bore love itself in her womb. In one of his sermons on the Assumption he says that, just as John the Baptist leaped in Elisabeth's womb at the mere sound of her voice, so the hearts of the angelic throng and the company of saints leaped for joy when they saw her coming.[17] He quotes from the Canticle: "Who is this that cometh up from the wilderness, leaning upon her beloved?" (Song of Solomon 8:5).[18] And if such is the joy of heaven, the rejoicing of Christ himself can hardly be described:

With what a tranquil face, with what an unclouded expression, with what joyous embraces was she taken up by her son! . . . Happy indeed were the kisses he pressed on her lips when she was nursing and as a mother delighted in the child in her virgin's lap. But surely will we not deem much happier those kisses which in blessed greeting she receives today from the mouth of him who sits on the right hand of the Father, when she ascends to the throne of glory, singing a nuptial hymn and saying: "Let him kiss me with the kisses of his mouth."?[19]

Mary is, exults Bernard, "as the morning, fair as the moon, clear as the sun" (Song of Solomon 6:10), and she rises into paradise like "pillars of smoke, perfumed with myrrh and frankincense" (Song of Solomon 3:6). He is so carried away with his theme that at the end of one of these sermons on the Assumption he actually apologizes to his listeners, saying, "There is nothing that delights me more than to speak on the glory of the Virgin Mother." But, he adds thoughtfully, everything loses in the telling, for nothing can ever express the full extent of her excellence.[20]

This intensely personal love of the Virgin that welled in St. Bernard's heart infused her cult after him with the same highly wrought and intimate sweetness. His eloquence on the Canticle, the Annunciation, and the Assumption mark the fulcrum of devotion to the Virgin in the west. Till now she had remained a remote majestic figure, used to define the complexities of Christological doctrine, or to symbolize the authority of the Church. There had been little personal devotion to her in the west at a popular level and her cult—in terms of prayers, processions, and feastdays—only formed a quiet accompaniment to the greater mysteries of the Christian year.

In the tenth century began the first stirrings of the adoration that transformed the Virgin from a distant queen into a gentle, merciful mother, "Our Lady," the inspirer of love and joy, the private sweetheart of monks and sinners, and the most prominent figure in the Christian hierarchy. St. Ulrich of Augsburg (d. 973) recited daily the Little Office of the Blessed Virgin Mary, a sequence of meditations, psalms, and prayers. This reveals a fundamental change—from organized communal chanting of the congregation to private prayers made in a spirit of interior contemplation. Peter Damian (d. 1072) also promoted the Virgin's cult when he prescribed the Little Office as an antidote to the laxity of monks, which he so deplored. At first the Office was recited on Saturdays, specially dedicated to Our Lady; but it was soon in daily use among monks.[21]

By the mid-twelfth century, the experiences of pilgrims, crusaders, and merchants in Byzantium, where the Virgin had long been the object of ardent faith and love, had passed into the common store of western Christendom; and men like St. Bernard, in his unfettered delight, reflected the upsurge of popular emotion. Bernard also profoundly influenced the development of devotion to the Virgin, for his order, the Cistercians, after the original foundation of Cîteaux in 1098, established hundreds of abbeys all over Europe and took the Gospel beyond the Pyrenees into Aragon and Castile and Portugal on the edge of Moslem territory, and into Hungary, Poland, Sweden, Austria, Wales, and the borders of Scotland, thus extending hugely the empire of the Church.[22] The passion of its most illustrious saint was typical of the Cistercian order: it was dedicated to the Virgin, her image appeared on the seals of its abbeys, its members wore white in honour of her purity, sang the antiphon the *Salve Regina* at vespers, and began the custom of building a special lady chapel in their churches. This marked love of the Virgin, with its character of personal intensity, was thus carried all over Europe, where during the next hundred and fifty years cathedrals rose in her honour, lay confraternities were founded, and altarpieces commissioned to sing her praise.

It would be tedious to quote the numerous echoes of Bernard's commentary on the Song of Songs in writers after him, the many imitations of his rapturous praises of the Virgin as queen and bride that were carried over Europe by a network of monasteries. Godfrey of Admont (d. 1165) suggested all three persons of the Trinity were Mary's lovers. The *Golden Legend* uses the *Pseudo-Melito* story of Mary's Dormition as its source for her Assumption, but quotes Christ calling to his mother: "Come from Libanus, my spouse, come from Libanus, come: thou shalt be crowned"—a quotation from the antiphons of the feast, but based on the Song of Songs.

The sculptured portals of France's medieval churches and the paintings of Italy mirror the monks' enslavement. Mary accepts her queenship in the full radiance of youth. No medieval king crowned his mother queen, but many a sovereign bequeathed his station on his bride. Throughout the middle ages, artists and poets worked this theme in their images of paradise (figure 16). In the gable of a Florentine fourteenth-century painting of the Crucifixion, a unique scene in iconography is depicted: Christ does not crown the Virgin queen, but seated beside her among angels, takes her right hand in his, the ancient nuptial gesture of *dextrarum iunctio* (figure 17).

Although the Virgin continued to be the focus of many Catholics' sublimated desires until the present day, the Counter-Reformation made the Church acutely sensitive to the potential abuse and ribaldry of such a literal use of the ancient symbol of the marriage of God and his bride. Alphonsus of Liguori (d. 1787) tries to blunt its erotic edge by introducing Joseph. When he describes Mary's triumphant entry into heaven, it is her husband who is, quite properly, overwhelmed with joy. She is then crowned Queen of Heaven by the Trinity: "The Father . . . by imparting his power to her, the Son, his wisdom, the Holy Ghost, his love. . . ."[23] The theogamy of mother and son was thereby avoided, as the great spiritual painters of the seventeenth century, Velásquez and El Greco, convey in their interpretations of Mary's apotheosis. In El Greco's painting in the Prado, the Father and Son sit high above, dramatically foreshortened, braced against metallic sheets of cloud, and the Holy Ghost with wings outspread hovers over Mary's veiled head, bathing her in golden light, as she drifts upwards on a huge slice of the moon, her eyes revolving in rapture towards heaven.

In Velásquez's slighter later treatment, also in the Prado, the Virgin is crowned in roses by the Holy Trinity. As in El Greco, the Father and the Son are distinguished by age—but neither is designated the Virgin's bridegroom (figure 18). Carl Jung viewed this painting and the doctrine it expresses as a transcendental quaternity that resolved the oppositions between mortal and immortal, flesh and spirit. He despised Protestants for rejecting the mystery it depicted: the Assumption was, he wrote, "the most important event since the Reformation." And further: "The equality of women . . . requires to be metaphysically anchored in the figure of a 'divine' woman, the bride of Christ. Just as the person of Christ cannot be replaced by the Church, the feminine, like the masculine, demands an equally personal representation."[24] There is wormwood here, however, even in the pinnacle of Mary's glory, for Jung chose to overlook the kind of woman who had been permitted this equality. George Bernard Shaw, Jung's contemporary, was more perceptive. He said: "A woman is not considered womanly unless she is of use to a man." Mary was principally extolled for her virginity, her motherhood, and her submission—qualities that modify her apparent equality beside Christ's throne. Furthermore, the image of union was riven down the centre, with violent seismic effects on the whole Christian edifice. For the union of Christ and Mary was consummated in heaven, and was thus a love deferred; furthermore, the metaphor of love, the imagery of the Song of Songs remained a mere metaphor and inaccurate at that, for the love deferred was also love denied.

Plato in the *Symposium* retells the myth that each creature at the beginning was cloven in two, to spend the rest of life searching for his or her lost other half: "Thus anciently is mutual love ingrained in mankind, reassembling our early state and endeavouring to combine two in one and heal the human sore. . . ."[25] Bernard, in his commentary on the Canticle, had cried out the joys of union with God in these same terms: metaphors of merging, dissolving, fusing, absorbing swim in his stream of consciousness:

As a small drop of water mingled in much wine seems to be wholly lost and to take on the colour and taste of the wine; as a kindled and glowing iron becomes most like to fire, having put off its former and natural form; and as air, when flooded with the light of the sun is transformed into the very brightness of light, so that it seems not to be so much illumined as to be the light itself, so it must needs be that all human affection in the saints will then, in some ineffable way, melt from itself, and be entirely poured over into the will of God. . . .[26]

But the most immediate act of fusion, the one experience every human being has of combining two in one, is forbidden. The icon of Mary and Christ side by side is one of the Christian Church's most polished deceptions: it is the very image and hope of earthly consummated love used to give that kind of love the lie. Its undeniable power and beauty do not heal: rather, the human sore is chafed and exposed.

## Chapter Nine

# TROUBADOURS

*Heaven knows! in all my love it was you, and you
only I sought for. I looked for no dowry, no al-
liances of marriage. I was even insensible to my own
pleasures; nor had I a will to gratify. All was
absorbed in you. I call Abelard to witness. In the
name of a wife there may be something more holy,
more imposing; but the name of mistress was ever
to me a more charming sound . . .*[1]

—HELOÏSE TO ABELARD, TWELFTH CENTURY

A T THE SAME TIME St. Bernard was preaching on the Song of
Songs, and the cult of the Virgin was moving towards its zenith, a revolution in secular literature was taking place. This new phenomenon is
usually called courtly love, and under that title shelters a broad-ranging
conception of civilized behaviour as well as a literary mode. Because the
idealization of woman in the lay poetry of the period coincides with ac-
celerated devotion to Our Lady, these two strands of medieval thought
have been confused and the cult of the Virgin is traditionally seen as
both a cause and an effect of courtly love. Such thinking is a crude amal-
gamation of two independent and disparate social currents. The two currents were reconciled only in the thirteenth century by one of the Church's
most successful intellectual operations, whereby the pagan joy of the
troubadours and their heirs was transmuted into the typical Christian
quest for the other world through denial of the pleasures in this. However, because the figure of the Virgin and of the beloved lady of romantic
sonnets and epics are meshed in the popular mind as twin types of the

virtuous and untouchable maiden, it is well to examine more closely the curious and complex relationship between courtly love and Marian cult.

The two phenomena were not united in their reverence for women: the adulation of the Virgin excludes other women, and it is nonsense to imagine that the elaborate code of manners fundamental to courtly literature and its accent on the artistic and interior pleasures of music, poetry, dance, dress, and conversation were followed outside a coterie of feudal aristocrats. The love that courtly poetry encourages and celebrates is altogether different in spirit from the love of the Virgin. But one striking resemblance does emerge, and it is the bond of unity, the means through which the Church was able to achieve a remarkable syncretism. Courtly love, as its name describes, took place in courts: it is steeped in social distinctions of rank and class. As we have seen, in the early and medieval Christian view, heaven or the other world was also a court, where Christ ruled with his mother as Queen of Heaven beside him. Surprisingly, it is through this active and vigorous metaphor that the Virgin was able to assume so much of the character and functions of the original beloved of Languedoc poetry and to rob it and its many descendants of its dangerous hedonism and permissiveness. Courtly poets addressed ladies of higher rank and posed as their vassals, because that was a common social situation of the times; prayerful Christians followed the model but subverted its content.

In a dawn song written in Provençal by the troubadour Guiraut de Bornelh (active 1172–1220), a man prays for his friend, who is spending the night with his beloved:

> *Beau compagnon, j'ai veillé loin de vous*
> *Toute la nuit, et j'ai fait à genoux*
> *A Jésus-Christ une prière ardente*
> *Pour vous revoir à l'aube renaissante.*

(All right, my handsome companion, I have watched far from you, and on my knees, I have prayed ardently to Jesus Christ that I might see you again with the new dawn.)

Later, the lover himself takes up the theme:

> *Le plus beau corps qui soit né d'une mère*
> *Est dans mes bras et je ne m'émeus guère*
> *Du jaloux ni de l'aube.*[2]

(The most beautiful form born of a woman lies in my arms and I don't care about her jealous husband or the dawn.)

The friend implores Jesus himself to help the lover steal away undiscovered before the full light of day, for adultery is an infraction of the social code but does not stir divine discontent; the lover, equally innocent of shame, defies his mistress's husband as well, the ubiquitous "jealous one" of troubadour poetry. As can be seen in these simple verses of Guiraut de Bornelh's *aube,* and could be duplicated from dozens of early troubadour lyrics, the love songs championed adultery's cause and saw no conflict or sin in sexual joy. This is not the usual sense in which people have traditionally understood respect for women. Nor does it bear any relation whatsoever to Christian teaching or worship at any time. Between this poem and the troubadour lady of popular imagination, between this defiant pair of lovers and the cult of the Virgin there lies a chasm.

From the end of the eleventh century until the beginning of the thirteenth, the literature of southern France celebrated human love for its powers to ennoble man and elevate his soul. Passion and reason were not bitter enemies, but could be reconciled in the camp of civilization, by directing desire and love at an object of sublime moral and physical beauty; the body and soul were not locked in mortal combat, for the ability to love in this way at all was the distinguishing human mark, defining man's superiority to the animal, which cannot shape its instincts and desires in an ideal mould. A man or woman in love was not a brute in prey to lusts, or a creature of God invaded, like saints Antony and Jerome, by demons in enticing human form. By disciplining their overflowing emotions into the mould of *courtoisie,* lovers asserted humanity's claim to precedence in nature. As C. S. Lewis wrote in *Allegory of Love,* this constituted a complete revolution in feeling: "The new thing itself, I do not pretend to explain. Real changes in human sentiment are very rare—there are perhaps three or four on record—but I believe that they occur and that this is one of them."[3]

Because the prevailing accent of the troubadour lyric is suffering and because the bliss of union that the poet seeks is yearned for and not enjoyed, it has been widely assumed that the love the Provençaux celebrated was chaste. This is partly a historical confusion of the early period of the poetry with the later European lyric it inspired, and partly a psychological misapprehension. For it did become axiomatic in later literature that love was noble when denied, and that chastity was the highest dynamic of the struggling heart; because of this, frustration became the keynote of love poetry, an existential pleasure sought after for its own elevating sake, while fulfilment was considered *ipso facto* a debasement of the emotional coinage.

But the early poetry of the Languedoc does not celebrate chastity for its own sake and it needs only the first-hand experience of a love affair for anyone to understand that yearning, pain, and frustration do not necessarily cease with the attainment of the beloved object, but that indeed possession itself can exacerbate the fear of loss, the sensitivity to pain, and set the pendulum of the human heart in an anguished and erratic motion, and that in the very midst of union and delight the loved one can seem even more remote than before—all of which the early troubadours chronicled with extreme melancholy awareness.

By the early thirteenth century, lyric poets no longer sang of the joy or agony of physical love, but accepted without demur the premise that their lady was worthy of their love precisely because she was too pure to reciprocate it. Thus the quarrel between the body and the soul was reestablished. And on that division, Christianity flourished. The introduction of the Christian ascetic ideal into Provençal poetry created a particular sentiment that was a travesty of the original wanton temper of the troubadours but was to prevail as the very fibre of lyric verse. Six hundred years afterwards Shelley was still writing in this vein:

> I can give not what men call love
> But wilt thou accept not
> The worship the heart lifts above
> And the heavens reject not—
> The desire of the moth for the star,
> Of the night for the morrow,
> The devotion to something afar
> From the sphere of our sorrow?[4]

Because heaven and earth, soul and body, reason and passion were once again severed and set against each other, the Virgin Mary could become a symbol of the ideal to the poets, artists, and practitioners of courtly love.

Before the Albigensian crusade, when Provençal poetry was changed by the theory of love's sinfulness, the troubadours were lusty, rumbustious, and explicit. Bernard de Ventadour would like to kiss his lady's mouth: *Si que d'un mes i paregra lo sens* (So that the marks would linger a month).[5] Elsewhere he berates his mistress—perhaps the formidable Ermengarde, ruler of Narbonne and patroness of many poets—for her flightiness and inconstancy. "Hanging around waiting for a woman's whim," he writes, "turns a lord into a stable boy."[6]

Bernard's contemporary Raimbaut, Count of Orange, loved Beatrice, Countess of Die, who reciprocated his feelings. Boldly, she writes that a woman who desires to have a good reputation should give her love to *un preux et vaillant chevalier,* and she should not conceal it, for honest passion only inspires sympathy in noble hearts.[7] Arnaut de Mareuil described his ideal beauty: white forehead, straight nose, gray eyes full of laughter, small mouth, rosy complexion, teeth whiter than polished silver, chin, throat, and breast as white as snow or as hawthorn blossom, white hands, slender, smooth long fingers, pleasant jokes and agreeable conversation, and open answers to his questions. As he thinks of her— she may have been his patroness, the Viscountess of Béziers—he swoons by day and tosses by night, longing to take her in his arms and kiss her eyes and mouth so gently a hundred kisses might seem like one.[8] Guiraut de Bornelh instructs his lady that if her husband notices anything, they should increase their guile because such happiness as theirs is very elusive.[9]

The troubadours often project the fulfilment of their happiness into the future—but this does not stem from any concern with chastity. Dante recognized this when on the terrace of lust in Purgatory he found Arnaut Daniel, *il miglior fabbro,* and Guido Guinizelli, *il padre mio,* both undeniably amorous poets—Arnaut had promised to offer one thousand masses and light one thousand candles if he obtained his lady's love.[10] Nor does a man always woo a woman: Beatrice de Die was one of many Provençal poetesses who spoke out openly of their love for a man.

Whatever the origins of courtly love, the first troubadour was Guilhem IX, Count of Poitiers and Duke of Aquitaine (d. 1127), and it was his granddaughter, Eleanor of Aquitaine (*c.* 1122–1204), who carried the sunniness and sophistication, the songs and *courtoisie* of her native land first to the blunt court of King Louis VII of France and then to the even grimmer court of Henry II of England. Her move northwards through Europe, with her retinue of courtiers and musicians and poets, spread the erotic and exotic mores of the southern French and taught the Anglo-Norman poets the conventions of the troubadours. Her daughter Marie de Champagne (d. 1198) inspired Chrétien de Troyes—or so he tells us—to compose *Lancelot,* in which Celtic legend and the principles of courtly love were spliced in a revolutionary way: the poem contains the notorious scene when Lancelot kneels to pray as at a shrine beside Queen Guinevere's bed before he steps into it to join her.

Chrétien was Marie's court poet; her chaplain was Andreas, who drafted the rules in *De Arte Honeste Amandi,* where the dislocation between Christian ethics and courtly love is just as evident. "Love," runs his celebrated (and timeless) definition, "is a certain inborn suffering derived from the sight of and excessive meditation upon the beauty of the opposite sex, which causes one to wish above all things the embraces of the other and by common desire to carry out all love's precepts in the other's embrace." Above all, love must be freely given, by mutual consent on both sides, through the free exercise of free will.[11] Because it is thus freely chosen, it is an act of humanity and civilization, neither a daemonic possession such as hurled Dido upon her funeral pyre or Medea upon her children, nor the base stirrings of concupiscence.

Andreas' book outlines the chemistry of the human heart: the pallor and palpitations, fears and ready suspicions, and jealousy, the hallmark—"He who is not jealous cannot love"—the fluctuation of passion, the singlemindedness of a lover, who acts only with the beloved in mind and finds joy only in what gives joy to him or to her.

Andreas' other rules focus on the social condition of love and lovers. The first rule is: "Marriage is no real excuse for not loving." Indeed, as lyric poetry of the time makes plain, the beloved is almost invariably married. Rule eleven declares: "It is not proper to love any woman whom one would be ashamed to seek to marry." The beloved must therefore be equal, or higher in rank. The feudal stamp of their relationship, in which the lover acts as vassal to his lady, even addressing her sometimes as *midons* (my lord), does not simply express the slavery of a lover to his lady but perhaps reflects their actual social position. Furthermore, Andreas restricts the etiquette of *courtoisie* to the equal in rank: he advises a knight to use "a little force"—*modica coactio*—to make a peasant girl yield.[12]

One further rule casts a sombre complexion over Andreas' proud argument: love must be kept hidden. The identity of the lady must not be revealed, and discretion, an integral part of courtesy, must be maintained. Such subterfuge indicates shame, wholly absent in Andreas' other principles. For although, within the laws of courtly love, each married man and woman might equally love another, the laws of the "outside" world preserve their force and each could be punished by their lawful spouse. Bernard de Ventadour tells his lady that if her husband beats her she must not let him beat love from her heart. The lines reverberate unpleasantly: in this world of song and courtesy, tournaments and gallantry, did men beat their wives?

The rules of courtly love describe the alchemy of human emotion; they did not alter the structure of society. A woman might be the lord of her troubadour, but she remained the vassal of her husband. The need for secrecy reveals the unacceptability of courtly love—the cult of adultery

—at one level; but it does not shake the troubadours' belief in the active goodness and justice of their passions. They might transgress society's rules, but they do not sin.

This contradiction can only be explained by looking at the specific social setting in which courtly love flourished. The chief psychological spur must have been the absence of love in arranged marriages, often contracted when both partners were still children. But a less personal catalyst was the feudal law of inheritance, which permitted a woman to hold rank and property in her own right. The main reason for wifely fidelity—the preservation of the purity of the male line—was weakened by this law. Andreas' rule, that a man must never love a woman whom he would be ashamed to marry, is crucial, for it indicates the exclusively aristocratic context of courtly love, and secondly implies the importance of the woman's social position in marriage transactions of his class and time. (In rigidly patriarchal societies, like contemporary WASP U.S.A. or Victorian England, a gentleman can marry a chorus girl because women, having little independent status, possess great social mobility according to their husband's position.)

In the society in which the troubadours wrote, an heiress could become the lynch pin of a dynasty's destiny. Obscure and landless knights could inherit powerful fiefs, or even, in the crusader lands of Outremer, principalities and kingdoms by marriage to the right woman. For in the matter of wills, Roman law still applied in the Mediterranean, and a woman could inherit her father's wealth and titles, either exclusively, in default of a son, or shared with her brothers. The courts that listened to the poetry of courtly love were used to rich, influential daughters of feudal barons. A glance at the family trees of the great houses of England, France, Italy, and Outremer of the twelfth and thirteenth centuries reveals the extent of noble-born women's unique position.

The conditions that so often resulted in the absence of a direct male heir are various—male mortality in battle and disease, particularly in Outremer, contributed—but their frequency is indisputable. By the eleventh century, it was a common occurrence for a woman, on her father's death and in the absence of a son, to swear his vassals to her fealty and pay homage to his overlord. Both vassals and overlord recognized her right to title and lands. A delicate balance thus resulted, between acknowledgement of her status on the one hand and, on the other, reluctance, in a military society, to take orders from a woman. Hence her overlord's overriding concern was that she should marry someone on whose allegiance he could count. Therefore women often became the playthings of political puppet-masters, who plucked them from one marriage to install them in another when the first proved unsuitable. Depending on her character, however, a woman could retain her independence and consolidate a legitimate position of authority.

The troubadours, when they pledged themselves to a lady and abased themselves before her, were using the language of feudal relations for a novel, psychological purpose, but they were not transposing it from an altogether alien male world. It was not, as some critics have suggested, an inexplicable inversion of the state of affairs obtaining in the society they knew. For the acquisition of land was the constant most pressing need of feudal society, and one of the most efficient and bloodless ways of meeting it was marriage. However unimportant women may have been in other respects in the warrior world of the middle ages, they wielded enormous power as heiresses.

The political tension this system's intricacy created in Europe is remarkable. Eleanor of Aquitaine is the most celebrated example. She inherited the fabulous dowry of the duchy of Aquitaine, embracing Poitou and Gascony, from her father, Guilhem X of Poitiers, which gave her control over the greater part of France and made her the greatest heiress in Europe. She proceeded to take her inheritance first to the French crown, on her marriage to Louis VII in 1137, and then fifteen years later to the English crown, on her marriage to Henry II, extending English territory in France from Normandy right down to Aquitaine.

Joanna, Eleanor s daughter by Henry II, married William II of Sicily. Because they had no children, Henry VI Hohenstaufen, the German emperor, claimed the crown of Sicily through his marriage to Constance, William II's aunt. Henry VI had a son, Frederick II, *Stupor Mundi,* Holy Roman Emperor, and in 1225 he married a child who became Queen Isabella II of Jerusalem by birthright. This child queen, who died before Frederick could claim the throne of Jerusalem through her, was herself one of five women who since the foundation of the crusader kingdom, had been acknowledged queen in their own right.[13] Her grandmother, Isabella I, had been ruthlessly apportioned in one marriage after another, the puppet of dizzy-making political machinations and, unlike Eleanor of Aquitaine, had not asserted her own wishes. But women in this position could decide for themselves. In 1150 Constance, heiress to the principality of Antioch, rejected the three suitors proposed by her overlord the king of Jerusalem and married Reynald of Châtillon, a petty knight of appalling character who had taken her fancy.[14]

Such examples of women's powers in the higher ranks of society could be multiplied, and the purpose of this genealogical labyrinth is not to daze the reader, but to illustrate the intricate way women's rights of inheritance played on feudal society. And it was in this milieu that the songs of the troubadours found approval and fortune: in the court of Queen Eleanor, in the Sicilian pleasure domes of Frederick II, in the crusader castles of Outremer. Because a sovereign female was a familiar figure in medieval society, the Virgin was able to slip on the mantle of the poets' love object.

Ironically, it was the prominence of woman that allowed troubadour literature to countenance, if not praise, adultery—something songs to the Virgin could never do. For it is only in a society where inheritance passes exclusively in the male line that the adultery of a married woman poses a real danger. If a woman can inherit her rank and possessions and preserve them inviolate after marriage, so that even when she is separated from her husband by divorce (as was Eleanor of Aquitaine) she can still keep them to bestow on someone else, then the father of her children becomes comparatively unimportant. Matriliny greatly diminishes the social disruptiveness of a wife's adultery, while patriliny requires first and foremost the chastity of a wife, for otherwise she could deceive her spouse with heirs that are not his flesh and blood. The latitude of the great Frankish ladies of Outremer was in consequence so marked that it amazed the eminent Moslem prince of Sharzar when he visited the crusaders' cities.[15]

The eleventh and twelfth centuries were, however, in a state of flux over the question of rightful inheritance. Primogeniture was becoming established in northern France—one of the reasons why there were so many young Normans seeking their fortunes in the crusades. Guilhem IX of Poitiers, the troubadour who led the French army on the crusade of 1101, was the bitter enemy of another crusader leader, Raymond of Toulouse, because Guilhem considered the County of Toulouse to be his by right through his marriage to Philippa, the daughter of Raymond's elder brother.[16]

Thibault IV of Champagne, another troubadour, was born in 1201, the posthumous son of the Count of Champagne and Brie. His right to the title was disputed by a knight, Erart of Brienne, who was married to Philippa of Champagne, Thibault's first cousin. Such a claim, which seems very distant to twentieth-century eyes, shows the potential authority of the female line in questions of inheritance.[17]

Erart did not succeed in his suit for the title and it would only be accurate to insist that throughout the period there was a constant bias towards patriliny. Nor was adultery ever openly acceptable, no matter how rich and powerful a woman might be in her own right. The secrecy required of the courtly lover, the scandals that surrounded Eleanor and eventually led to the collapse of her marriage with Louis, and the taint of unchastity that could lead to repudiation—Agnes de Courtenay was divorced by Amalric of Jerusalem on the grounds of kinship, but her morals may have had more to do with it[18]—are evidence that neither the celebration of carnal love nor the frequent occurrence of heiresses had eroded patriarchal principles. It was over this issue that during the twelfth and thirteenth centuries Church and state were bound in a common interest.

In the temporal sphere, the general concept of the state and the centralized reign was gaining muscle. In France the rules of Philip Augustus (b. 1164; king 1179–1223), or Louis IX (b. 1215; king 1226–70) saw the gradual success of the Capetian dynasty's policy of curbing the feudal barons' powers. The territories of the Angevin kings of England in France were largely recovered; the Albigensian crusade, waged in Languedoc and Toulouse from 1209–13 against the widespread Cathar heretics with all the cruel excess of men who believe God to be on their side, broke the princes and nobles' hold on the area. With the erosion of the southern aristocracy's influence and independence, the bargaining position of heiresses declined; and with centralized power there evolved a natural dislike for the centrifugal tendencies of feudal inheritance patterns. This dislike eventually culminated in 1328 in the application of Salic law to the crown of France and the exclusion of women from the succession.[19]

The Church shared the interest of the state in subduing the south of France. For at the end of the twelfth century, Provence and Languedoc and northern Italy were in the grip of the Cathar heresy, a fierce and ascetic form of Manichaeism, which held that an evil god had created the material world and that the pure spirit of man was imprisoned in the flesh. At a time when the priesthood was notorious for its laziness and corruption the heresy's success was stupendous: when Raymond VI, who inherited Toulouse in 1195, vacillated in his allegiance, the Catholics were left without a single powerful defender of the faith among the southern nobility. The preaching of St. Bernard, sent in to convert the fallen, was of no avail. Indeed, the saint commented unhappily on the favourable comparison between the Cathar renegades and the loyal men of the Church: "No sermons are more Christian than theirs, and their morals are pure."[20] St. Dominic, who took up the cause, also achieved nothing. At the beginning of the thirteenth century, Pope Innocent III decided to call a crusade, and with alacrity the lords of northern France sprang to the faith's defence in order to press their own political advantage.

The Albigensian crusade devastated the farmlands of the south with unparalleled terror and butchery, which the poets of the Languedoc bitterly chronicled in their songs. When Carcassonne was sacked in 1209, the south's political independence was at an end.

The Cathar heresy itself proved more difficult to eradicate, and the Inquisition was set up to interrogate its adherents. The records of its proceedings reveal two aspects of the heresy that made it especially heinous in Catholic eyes: first, the movement gave genuine equality to women, who could become priests of its highest order of "Perfects." Steven Runciman, the historian of the heresy's origins and development, comments on the tremendous popularity it consequently enjoyed among the great ladies of the south, who, like the Roman matrons of early Christianity, gave their property and their houses to their heterodox church.[21] Secondly, the Dominicans, who staffed the Inquisition, were horrified to discover that the Cathars, in spite of the rigorous asceticism of their ideals, believed that casual fornication and buggery were less reprehensible than organized or institutionalized sex, as in marriage, because procreation perpetuated the material universe. Each child was another prisoner of loathsome matter, and therefore to beget children was to continue the Devil's work and the bondage of the flesh.

This position was in direct contradiction to the position that the Church was then consolidating on matters of sex, marriage, and procreation. For, in the Catholic view, chastity was the principal disinfectant of evil; and monogamy the only, inadequate, compromise with human sexuality, supported by Christ's unequivocal statement on the indissolubility of marriage and the pope's exclusive power to grant divorce.[22]

Therefore, the political outcome of the Albigensian crusade—the subjugation of the south by the central power—had a concomitant effect on the moral and social principles of the southern peoples—troubadour and heretic alike—who from very different vantage points had held equally casual attitudes to the sanctity of marriage and procreation. Both were anathema to the Church, which was placing the full weight of ecclesiastical authority behind matrimonial reform.

Church courts dealt with questions of marriage and divorce, so that ultimately questions of legitimacy depended on canon law. The twelfth century found a new interest in the legal complexities of matrimony: Gratian's *Decretum,* one of the most influential law books of all time, was compiled in the first half of the twelfth century. It deploys hypothetical marriage situations and contingencies with some relish. The difficulty for the Church was that marriage did not require the blessing of a priest in church to be legally valid. *Sponsalia,* a secular contract, took place in the church porch, as the wife of Bath reminds us:

> My lords, since when I was but twelve years old,
> Thanks be to God Eternal for evermore,
> Five husbands have I had at the church door.[23]

Matrimony was the sacrament, which was not always performed. The medieval man and woman's attitude to marriage was often free and easy, influenced by the Church's repugnance in dealing with the question of holy sexual relations. However, Paul had called marriage a *mysterion* (Ephesians 5:32), translated in the Vulgate as *sacramentum,* and early patristic witness (notably St. Ignatius) revealed that bishops had blessed the union of Christians in the early Church.

In the twelfth century, the debate concerning marriage that had begun under the papacy of the great reformer Gregory VII (Hildebrand: 1073–86) became more acute. Was it the remedy of human weakness or a holy sacrament? The Church tried to prevent casual union and equally casual separation. Popes like Alexander III (1159–81) would have liked to enforce Church ceremony in the presence of a priest as the only way to contract a valid marriage. But to do so would have rendered null and void (and therefore sinful) most contemporary unions. Alexander had to be content with the idea of free and mutual consent, sealed by sexual consummation. In 1215, at the Fourth Lateran Council, the Church tried to strengthen its hold by ordering the reading of banns and the public performance of the wedding, measures that would abolish, it was hoped, hasty marriages or elopements and make reversal or dissolution afterwards far more difficult. Benediction, however, was still unnecessary.

Given the Catholic Church's contemporary view on the sanctity of marriage, it comes as a surprise that matrimony was only definitively proclaimed a sacrament and the Church ceremony decreed an indispensable condition of validity as late as 1563 at the Council of Trent.[24]

But the roots of the Tridentine decision run back deep in time. The seriousness with which the medieval popes viewed the cynical treatment of marriage is illustrated in an extraordinary story recorded by John of Salisbury, who was an eyewitness when Pope Eugenius III (1145–53) was hearing divorce proceedings brought by a Norman of the south, Count Hugh, against his wife. The pope dismissed the case, "and then, his face covered with tears, he leapt down from his throne, in the sight of all, great man though he was, and lay at the feet of the count, so that his mitre rolled in the dust and was found between the feet of the astounded count after the bishops and cardinals had lifted the Pope up." He begged the Norman not to cast his wife aside and, taking his ring off his finger, presented it to him as if he were plighting the husband to the lady once more.[25]

It was therefore at this early date that the seeds of the western idea of love-in-marriage-till-death-us-do-part were sown—an idea that collided violently with the casual commerce of the feudal match at one level and that at another weakened the psychological impetus to enjoy passion elsewhere. Thus Eugenius' despair rang an early knell on the troubadour world, committed to marriages of convenience and adulterous dalliance.

The budding sentiments of the Church regarding matrimony coincided with the new ecstatic strain of piety, as expressed by St. Bernard, which was transforming the devotions of Christendom by stressing the love of God for mankind, the humanity of Jesus himself, and the supreme act of self-sacrifice he made on behalf of his creatures on the Cross.

New orders of monks, like the Praemonstratensian Canons founded by St. Norbert in 1120, as well as the remarkable Cistercians, were infusing western religion with a new sweet rapture, which was often close in terminology to *le gay saber* of the troubadours, though as distant in meaning as the fables of China. Chivalry and asceticism were also related in their cult of suffering and self-sacrifice—the lover's discipline on behalf of his lady was easily transmuted into the ancient Christian ideal of self-martyrdom, although the psychological aims of both are distinct.

After Simon de Montfort's armies had left the fields and castles of Provence and Languedoc in smoking ruins, the Church stepped into the breach to reassert its lost authority. A young Castilian, Dominic de Guzman (1170–1221), burning with the zeal characteristic of his age, had preached unsuccessfully to the heretics of the Languedoc before the crusade. The year before he died he founded the Dominican order (*Domini canes*—the hounds of God) to fight heresy and teach. The Inquisition was established in the twelfth century and staffed with Dominic's Black Friars, who, as we have seen, went to work to exterminate the last vestige of Catharism in southern France. Forty-four convents were established in the area in a few years. One by-product of this renewed ecclesiastical activity was the indoctrination of local poets in the Christian sexual ethic. Another was the rapid growth of the cult of the Virgin in the south.

For it was after the Albigensian crusade that the Mariolatry of the twelfth century became intertwined with the secular love lyric. One had been the product of intense introspective meditation on the mysteries of the faith by high-minded celibates breathing the pure air of the Christian ascetic tradition; the other the diversion of gay and carefree courtiers indulging a sweet tooth for voluptuousness laced with melancholy. But each was too strong to be destroyed by the other; and, amazingly, they were combined.

The symbol of the Virgin Mary helped to fuse them. Yet she seems an unlikely instrument of propaganda for a Church committed to female subordination. A *magna mater* holding preeminent sway over the heavenly throng, a mother unassisted by man, she towers over the infant son in her lap. It would be natural to deduce—as archaeologists have done from similar images, as in the throne room of Knossos, for example —that it would be a society with matriarchal tendencies that worshipped her, as a fitting symbol of woman's supremacy. But the feudal courts of the great queens of the twelfth and early thirteenth centuries did not sing of the mother of God as the beloved muse. She was an all-powerful intercessor but she was not the mistress of their hearts.

There is very little evidence of the cult of the Virgin in the literature of courtly love in its first troubadour phase in the south of France, or in its second *trouvère* phase at the court of Marie de Champagne. It was the next generation, of Eleanor's granddaughter, Blanche of Castile (d. 1252), mother of King Louis IX (d. 1270), that focussed its ardour on the Virgin Mary. And it was encouraged to do so by both Church and state. Rarely has a religious movement of such fervour received such approval in official circles. The Virgin Mary became an establishment prop, acceptable because, as we have seen in the symbol of her queenship, she could be used to affirm the legitimacy of the *status quo*. In her traditional aspect of queen, she blended in easily with the aristocratic lady of the lyricists' passion; and as a woman who won her position through her son she did not confirm the feudal authority of an heiress who enjoyed her rank and property in her own right. Instead, she lent symbolic support to the figure of a mother, and as the model of virginity she challenged all justification of carnal love.

By interfusing the ethic sung by the poets of courtly love with the ancient adherence of the Church to sexual chastity and female submission (see Chapter 12), the danger of the *haulte déesse,* as the poet Villon later called her, could be undone and she could be deftly woven into the fabric of patriarchal politics. By continuing the traditional cult of Mary's virginity and purity, by coupling it with a constant emphasis on the feminine virtues of humility, obedience, modesty, and self-effacement, the menace contained in the idea of the *regina angelorum* could be wiped out. Above all, by contrasting human women with the sublime perfection of the Virgin, earthly love could be discredited and men's eyes turned once again heavenwards.

## Chapter Ten

# MADONNA

*All other loue is lych the mone*
*that wext and wanet as flour in plein . . .*[1]

—ANONYMOUS, MID-FOURTEENTH CENTURY

THE TRAGIC *Song of the Crusade*, lamenting the rapine and pillage of Provence by the armies of Simon de Montfort, identified Folquet of Marseilles, bishop of Toulouse, as the Anti-Christ, the "fire no waters could extinguish." The poem mourns half a million adults and children whom he destroyed body and soul.[2]

Before Folquet joined the crusade, he was a troubadour, and had found fortune with several noble ladies in Provence and Toulouse, married, and had two children. Suddenly converted, he retired to a Cistercian abbey and gave his poems to the flames. Dante, in *Paradise*, recognizing his intemperateness, placed him in the sphere of love marred by wantonness.[3] The Church later canonized him for his crusading enthusiasm.

As a poet, Folquet composed an *aube*, one of the first religious troubadour poems, which reveals the effortless legerdemain needed to transform the meaning of courtly love's favourite metaphors. For the dawn that once parted the lovers now symbolizes the coming redemption through Christ:

> *Vers Dieus, el vostre nom et de Sancta Maria*
> *M'esvelherai heymais, pus l'estela del dia*
> *Ven daus Jerusalem, que m'ensenha qu'ieu dia:*
> > *Estatz sus e levatz,*
> > *Senhor que Dieu amatz,*

*Que.l jorns es aprosmatz*
*E la nuech ten sa via . . .*

(True God, I shall wake up today invoking your name and Holy Mary's, for the morning star has risen over Jerusalem, and teaches me to say: "On your feet, all who love God, the day has come and the night has gone its way . . .")[4]

Folquet's *aube,* chastened of all erotic overtones, purified in the flames of the crusade and the fires of the Inquisition, is a powerful symptom of the changing stuff of troubadour poetry, which was gradually to win approval from the Church. Fifty years after Folquet's death, Pope Clement IV (1265–8), himself a Provençal and an ex-troubadour, granted one hundred days' indulgence for the recital of one of Folquet's poems to the Virgin. The love lyric was becoming edifying: after the crusade, the poet Guilhem Montanhagol introduced the word chastity into Provençal poetry for the first time, in a neat passage on the Christian ethic:

> *Ben devon li amador*
> *de bon cor servir amor*
> *quar amor non es peccatz*
> *anz es vertuts que .ls malvatz*
> *fai bos, e.lh bon son melhor,*
> *et met om'en via*
> *de ben far tot dia;*
> *e d'amor mou castitaz,*
> *quar qui.n amor ben s'enten*
> *no pot far que pueis mal renh.*

(Lovers must continue to love, for love is not a sin, but a virtue that makes the wicked good, and the good better, and puts men in the way of doing good each day. Chastity itself comes from love, for whosoever truly understands love cannot be evil-minded.)[5]

The essential claim of the early troubadours had been that human love and longing for fulfilment in the embrace of the beloved ennobled the spirit; the idea that chastity comes from love, that true love denies its own goal, would have been nonsense to them. The courtly lovers of the twelfth century—Chrétien's Lancelot and Guinevere, Gottfried of Strasbourg's Tristan and Yseult, and the real Heloïse and Abelard, whose passion had ignited Europe—had not been chaste, nor had they been stained by their lack of chastity. The notion that true courtliness and true nobility demand that a man—like the "bold lover" on Keats' Grecian urn—pursue his lady for a kiss forever, and that a virtuous woman always refuse is a perversion of the troubadour ideal, and an accurate reflection of the returned authority of the Church and of the ascetic tradition of the Fathers.

While the Albigensian crusade was being fought, the bitter troubadour Peire Cardenal wrote one of the first Provençal hymns to the Virgin, the Fathers' ideal of chastity. Punning and alliterating with delight, he begs her for her intercession with her son:

> *Vera maire, ver'amia*
> *Ver'amors, vera merces,*
> *Per la vera merce sia*
> *Qu'estend' en me tos heres.*

(True mother, true friend, true love, true mercy, may your son grant me by your true mercy his protection.)[6]

The Italian troubadour Lanfranc Cigala revealingly wrote a little later that the Virgin was the only woman he could praise "without fear of contradiction." In 1289, Giraut Riquier recanted the "folly" of his predecessors and his own youth and the matter of their poetry, to address the Virgin. It is no surprise that he was the last troubadour of Provence:

> *Ieu cujava soven d'amor chantar*
> *El temps passat e non la conoyssia*
> *Qu'ieu nomnava per amor ma folia;*
> *Mas era.m fai Amors tal Don' amar,*
> *Que non la puesc honrar pro ni temer*
> *Ni tener car endreg de sieu dever;*
> *Ainz ai dezir que s'amors me destrenha,*
> *Tant que l'esper qu'ieu ai en lieys n'atenha.*

(Often in the past, I thought I sang of love, but I did not know what love is, for it was my madness I called by that name. Now Love makes me love such a Lady that I cannot pay her enough honour, nor fear her nor cherish her as she deserves; but I long for her love to hold me so tight that I might obtain the boons I hope from her.)[7]

It is almost sacrilegious, this neat transferral of the courtly conventions from the here-and-now into the other world. The polarization of earth and heaven also affected the meaning of the melancholy typical of troubadour song. For where the lovers had complained that their service was not rewarded as it should be, they now lamented, in much the same tone, that earthly love was in itself a sorrow and an illusion. The counterpoint between the fulfilment of the love of God, and the disappointment of the god of love is fundamental to medieval lyricism. By the fourteenth century the Dominican grip on southern France was so firm that only religious lyrics were allowed at the *jeux floraux* in Toulouse, and poets of hymns to the Virgin were crowned. And, in England, after the handful of love poems in the Harley collection (written down around 1235) until Chaucer (*c.* 1340–1400), who was the first secular poet writing for a secular audience for over a hundred years, lyric poetry was devotional in character.[8] The finest of it praised the Virgin, like the enchanting song:

> A love-liking is come to me
> To serve that lady, queen of bliss  . . .[9]

Ideas then travelled rapidly, carried along the routes of the crusaders and of the pilgrimages to Rome, Compostella, and the Holy Land, by the comings and goings of students between the great universities, and encouraged by a civilization that was comparatively settled and cosmopolitan. The transference of yearning and desire to the figure of the Virgin was but a single stitch in the huge tapestry of the Church's increasing control of the world of learning in the late twelfth and thirteenth centuries. It had previously tried to obliterate, but now it compromised, following a policy of syncretism that was to turn out a supreme success. The heroes of romances were transformed: so many Sir Lancelots into Sir Galahads. As Kenneth Sisam has written: "Her (the Church's) real power to suppress books was ineffective to bind busy tongues and minds . . . [so] it seemed good to mould the *chansons de geste* to pious uses, and to purify the court of King Arthur."[10]

All over Europe, alongside the chaste consuming fires of the Knights of the Grail are found elegies of this life's disillusion in love. Adultery is purged from poetry. In the Harley lyrics, that rich collection of early English poetry, the transience of human love is contrasted with the Virgin's constancy. The poet sees the roses of summer fade and turns for hope to his "secret love" and begs her in terror to free him from hell:

> My heart was shuddering with dread
> For fleshly sins on which I fed,
> Of which my life was made.[11]

Priest and layman alike, passing beneath the tympana of their cathedrals where Christ the Judge loomed over the furnaces and torments of hell, shivered before the penalties of concupiscence. Of course, the Church could not stamp out sexual desire or carnal love—indeed that was the source of its strength. As long as men and women continued to sin, they continued to need the grace of the sacraments available only through the Church. But if chastity was a prerequisite of a pure heart, women, considered the occasions of sin, were once again to blame. "Satan," wrote the Provençal Matfré Ermengaud, around 1288–92 in the *Breviari d'Amor,* "in order to make men suffer bitterly, makes them adore women; for instead of loving, as they should, the creator with fervent love, with all their heart, with all their mind and their understanding, they sinfully love women."[12]

In a celebrated English tenson, or discussion, written in the thirteenth century, a misogynist thrush attacks the regiment of women. The nightingale in reply cites the Virgin Mary, the supreme example of feminine perfection. Its defence is spirited and generous:

> Man's highest bliss in earthly state
> Is when a woman takes her mate
> And twines him in her arms.
> To slander ladies is a shame!

The thrush admits defeat and flutters off disgraced.[13]

But the nightingale's argument—that all women resemble the Virgin Mary—is very rare, for every facet of the Virgin had been systematically developed to diminish, not increase, her likeness to the female condition. Her freedom from sex, painful delivery, age, death, and all sin exalted her *ipso facto* above ordinary women and showed them up as inferior.

The *Roman de la Rose,* the most popular and influential romance of the high middle ages, concludes with a speech by Genius in which he describes how the Garden of Love in which the Dreamer has wandered until he plucked the Rose is only the ephemeral and flawed imitation of the Garden of Love above. In this paradise, this perfect platonic world of ideas, the medieval Christian visualized one lady alone who could fulfil his love and bestow a rose on him.

It was during the twelfth century that the Virgin was first given her feudal title Notre Dame, Our Lady. The name was not entirely new. Jerome had glossed the name as Lady in Syriac; the sixth-century *Akathistos* hymn had also addressed her as "lady," and Pope Gregory II (715–31) had spoken of her *omnium domina,* a title officially adopted at the Second Council of Nicaea in 787.[14] But the universal popularity of the title Notre Dame belongs to the thirteenth and fourteenth centuries, as the most concise expression of the personal nature of Christian veneration of the Virgin.

One of Notre Dame's earliest and most enchanting *trouvères* was Gautier de Coincy (d. 1236), the Benedictine prior of St. Médard at Soissons, who collected miracles wrought by her intercession and wrote songs to the Virgin in a light, intricately verbal style that borrows as much from folk music as from courtly love. His *Chansons de la Vierge* delighted his generation and influenced the *trouvère* Rutebeuf ("rough ox"), who was the attraction of all Paris, and later still King Alfonso X, *El Sabio,* who turned Gautier's miracles into Spanish songs.

Gautier's natural gift of lyricism sometimes suffocates under his equal gift of ingenuity, and he loves a pun:

> *Marions nous a la Virge Marie:*
> *Nus ne se puet en lui mas marier.*
> *Sachiez de voir, qui a lui se marie*
> *Plus hautement ne se puet marier.*

(Let us marry the Virgin Mary; no one can make a bad marriage with her. Believe you me, he who marries her could not make a better match.)[15]

In another song, he tells us that the love of women is chaff; that of Mary is true wheat.[16] He can communicate an intense sweetness that, mingled with the pleasant attitudinizing of the stricken swain, brings vividly to mind the gentle countenances of so many thirteenth- and fourteenth-century Madonnas:

> *Laissons tuit le fol usage*
> *D'amour qui foloie . . .*
> *Amons la bele et la sage,*
> *La douce, la quoie.*

(Let us leave off the mad practice of love which drives men mad. . . . Let us love the one who is beautiful and good, sweet and quiet.)[17]

Rutebeuf, more mischievous than Gautier, later resumed the monk's play on words:

> *Quar qui se marie*
> *En tele Marie*
> *Bon mariage a:*
> *Marions nos la.*

(For he who marries such a Mary makes a good marriage. Let us marry her then.)[18]

Thibault de Champagne, champion of Queen Blanche of Castile, managed to boast of his amorous conquests by comparing them to love of the Virgin. At a gathering of knights and their ladies a jongleur sang, at Thibault's orders, of the sinful green fruit that filled Thibault's orchards but which he spurned for the new fruit of repentance. One can almost see him winking at his friends:

> *Que de l'aultre ai je senti plus*
> *C'onques, ce croi, se senti nus.*

(For of the other [fruit] I've tasted more than anyone ever—believe me—has done!) [19]

The relationship with the Virgin, however, was intensely felt by others at a very personal level: the medieval Madonna is the intimate of painters and writers, passionate in her affections and fiery in her loyalties. An enormous corpus of miracles, often dramatized as plays, proclaimed her the unfailing champion of sinners before the judgement throne of God (see Chapter 21) and her language when she banished a devil was as forthright and colloquial as a volley over the garden fence from the next door neighbour's wife. The special dramatic genius of the middle ages, which could transform arid theology into vivid pictures and lively theatre, created the Virgin in the image of a human, approachable, supremely adorable woman who stood by humanity like a mother but loved it like a mistress. [20]

In a beautiful lament of the Virgin written in the fourteenth century, a knight rides up to a maiden weeping and overhears her piteous song, with its aching refrain from the Song of Songs: *Quia amore langueo* (For I am sick of love). The poem also exists in another version, in which Christ himself is the speaker, complaining of mankind's cruelty to him. He addresses the human soul as his sister and his spouse, his "fair love" for whom he has prepared a bed in heaven, and tells her: "Wax not weary, mine own dear wife." Similarly, the Virgin in her version ends with a promise of love:

> Now man, have mind on me forever
> Look on thy love thus languishing;
> Let us never from other dissever . . .
> Take me for thy wife and learn to sing,
> *Quia amore langueo*. [21]

Scholars disagree about which is the original poem. But that the idea of the divine bride should develop alongside the idea of the divine bridegroom is hardly surprising. The principle of analogy holds fast in much of Mariology; and if consecrated virgins believed themselves the brides of Christ, then celibate priests and clerics might well imagine themselves the grooms of Mary. Nevertheless, the Virgin's proposition, "Take me for thy wife," struck clerical ears as overbold—the last stanza is left out in later copies of the poem.

Marriages of the Virgin with her votaries take place frequently in the legends of the middle ages. The tendency to organize the realm of heaven according to the customs of earth, as in the mystic marriage of St. Catherine, was highly developed in the fourteenth century. Religious dramas followed the *Book of James'* account of the betrothal and marriage of Joseph and Mary, but transformed it into a medieval village romp. The sphere of the divine was not remote and fearsome: the Virgin often swears in miracle plays.

But this very nearness of the divine order made it impinge more drastically on the world, and the Virgin's claims on her lovers were exacting and even fatal. In one of the fourteenth-century *Miracles de Notre Dame par Personnages,* a young canon who had promised to serve the Virgin forever is told by his uncle that he has inherited a great fortune and must marry a girl his uncle has chosen. He remonstrates that he wants to take orders and serve *Dieu et nostre dame* but the girl turns out to be a paragon of wealth, connections, and beauty. He gives in. On his wedding night the Virgin summons John the evangelist and several angels, and in the haughty tone of a severely vexed suzerain announces she has some business on earth with *un mien sergent.* She descends into the young man's bedroom and swoops down on him:

> *Comment est ce, si je suis telle,*
> *Que pour autre femme me laisses?*
> *Malement, ce semble, m'abaisses*
> *Et ma valeur et ma biauté . . .*
>                         *Es tu yvres*
> *Qui tout ton cuer et t'amour livres*
> *A une terrienne femme?*
> *Et tu me laisses, qui sui dame*
> *Du ciel? Dy me voir, ou est celle*
> *Qui plus est de moy bonne et belle?*

(How can this be, since I am who I am, that you are leaving me for another woman? It seems you're badly underrating my worth and my beauty. . . . You must be drunk to give your whole heart and all your love to a woman of this earth? And to leave me, the lady of heaven?

Tell me true, where is the woman with greater goodness and beauty than I?)[22]

But she does not leave her vengeance at that. She tells the cleric that since he has been unfaithful, he shall burn for it in hell.

The play then turns into high comedy: the wretched bridegroom tears his hair, and begs his mother to spend the wedding night with him and his bride in their room. She is amazed. Then he pleads for help from the Virgin against the charms of his young wife—*la belle que je voy nue*.[23] Finally he runs away. The next morning, when the family call on the newlyweds, and find the girl alone, they think he must have passed out drunkenly somewhere. Then they find a letter, in which he tells them that the Virgin was:

> *si jalouse*
> *De lui qu'en paradis son lit*
> *Lui avoir fait pour grant delit*
> *Qui lui sera du tout defait.*

(so jealous of him because she had made him a bed in heaven, and he had unmade it by his great crime).[24] The young wife follows her husband's example and becomes a nun; the Virgin appears and takes the hero with her to heaven.

In other versions the protagonist marries the Virgin by placing a ring on the hand of a statue of her. Gautier de Coincy describes how her hand closed on this pledge: *si fermement que nus ne l'en peust retraire* (so firmly that none could draw it off). He also gives the Virgin a splendid speech when her lover forgets her for another. First crackling with indignation, it then fades to a melancholy reproach: *Me laisses qui par amors t'amoie?* (Are you leaving me when I loved you with love?) (figure 19).[25]

Sometimes the disloyal bridegroom is a Roman nobleman (as in a work attributed to Bede), sometimes the brother of the king of Hungary, sometimes a gentleman from Pisa.[26] St. Edmund Rich, Archbishop of Canterbury (d. 1242), plighted his troth with the Virgin when he became a priest, according to his legend.[27] In the collection of *Miracles* compiled by the Dominican priest Johannes Hérolt in the fifteenth century the same story takes on a sinister aspect: a German youth who has always, in spite of a taste for gambling and drink, professed the greatest love of the Virgin and kept himself chaste in her honour, decides to get married. On his wedding day, as he is reciting his daily sequence of *Ave Marias,* the Virgin suddenly appears "shining more brightly than the sun." She tells him: "because, trifler and erring as you were, you did for all that keep your body in clean chastity, soon a deadly fever shall seize you and on the third (day), you shall come to me without any stain on your flesh."[28]

Jesus would come, warned Matthew, as a thief in the night. Mary here again resembles her son. Hérolt also tells the story of a dying Cistercian who feels the Virgin "throwing her arms round my neck, she gave me a kiss." Then she tells him he will die.[29] It is an ancient folk tale, Celtic in origin, that a phantom lover makes her victims fey, and once bewitched, carries them off into the realm of death. It inspired Keats' *La Belle Dame sans merci,* and it may be one of the few Marian legends that is northern, not eastern, in origin. However, as William of Malmesbury set in Rome a similar story about a young man who gave himself over to the power of Venus by placing a ring on her statue in the Forum, the legend may have a Latin source.

The concreteness of the Virgin's physical and emotional personality in these medieval stories betrays the extraordinary certitude with which contemporaries confronted the spiritual sphere. Such a faculty of belief was never recovered by Catholics, even at the height of the fervour of the Counter-Reformation. The Virgin of thirteenth- and fourteenth-century miracles was hearty and real and lovable—even though her claims included death. Later she was always more remote, and bad language or amorous phrases never passed her lips again.

An attempt was made in the late sixteenth and seventeenth centuries to renew the love affair. St. Stanislaus Kostka (d. 1568), a young Polish nobleman who became a Jesuit, lies in effigy in Rome in an upper room of Bernini's gem Sant' Andrea al Quirinale. With gentle, wasted features the young novice gazes on a locket in his hand as he lies dying. The face of his beloved in the locket is that of the Virgin Mary. In another Counter-Reformation product in Rome, a painting in San Bernardo alle Terme, Mary and the child appear in a vision to St. Robert Abbot, the founder of the Cistercian order, and while Mary slips a wedding ring on his finger, he falls back in rapture. For the clergy of the Counter-Reformation had none of the scruples that made one early Greek monk attempt "to rid himself of the 'spirit of fornication' that tormented [him] by trampling on the beautiful idealized portrait of the Virgin with which he lived."[30]

The Greek was sensitive to the falsehood, the cheat in the celibate's love of Mary; but his action stirs no response now. The Virgin is still considered the special patroness of priests and the guardian of their celibacy. Stephen Dedalus, confessing to his impurity, is told, "Pray to our Blessed Lady when that sin comes to mind."[31] A contemporary seminarian was instructed that whenever "bad thoughts" troubled him, he should "think about Mary."[32] Such sublimation is more perverse than pathetic. For the love of the Virgin was counterposed to earthly love, and the latter—the *terrienne femme*—was light in the balance. The scales were held and watched by ecclesiastics, and in the fourteenth century and after, the vast literature of love for the Virgin, the soaring cathedrals, the paintings that portray her as the most beautiful of all women bear witness that their verdict was not disregarded. The Queen of Heaven became the staple antidote to love on earth. She was feminine perfection personified, and no other woman was in her league.

## Chapter Eleven

# DANTE, BEATRICE,
# AND THE VIRGIN MARY

*Amor, ch'a nullo amato amar perdona* . . .

(*Love, which absolves no one beloved*
*from loving* . . .)

—INFERNO 5:103

AFTER THE MILLENNIUM, the chronicler Ralph Glaber wrote that Christendom was clothing herself in a white garment of churches. By the year 1350, this robe was already a splendid and opulent cope: the great cathedrals of France with their spires and many-figured portals were for the most part completed. In Chartres, Paris, Coutances, Amiens, the Virgin was paid majestic tribute; in Sicily, Florence, Rome, and Siena (where the *Maestà* altarpiece, Duccio's great achievement and the harbinger of the Renaissance, was carried in triumphal procession to the main altar of the Duomo in 1311), in Germany, the Netherlands, all over Europe, the Virgin was the chief recipient of men's prayers and adoration.

The architecture and painting of the middle ages reflect popular feeling, if that is expressed by the purses of patrons, by the taste of nobles, merchants, chapter houses, and town councils that financed the building of churches and their adornment. There was at the time no comparable passion for the Virgin in the doctrinal writings of the Fathers and schoolmen of the medieval church—indeed for a compendium of Mariology corresponding to Aquinas' *Summa*, the Church awaited the Counter-Reformation and the Marian analyses of the great Jesuit Francisco Suarez. But the voice of the vernacular lyric, singing its fresh free music in twelfth-century Europe, picked up the harmonies of the mass emotion expressed by the great cathedrals and, as we have seen, hymned the Virgin's beauty and goodness.

There was no necessity, however, for this mystical figure of the Mother of God to have been confused with the love object of lyric poetry and the human heart. The intellectual and emotional distinction between them could have been maintained, as it was in the masterpiece of medieval literature, Dante's *Divine Comedy.* The *Divine Comedy* succeeded where other lesser Christian poets had signally failed: it synthesized the highest Christian ideal of fulfilment through love with the celebration of a living human creature, Beatrice. And the Virgin Mary emerges from the poem as the cornerstone of the architecture of the Christian salvation, the instrument of the Incarnation and the merciful intercessor for sinners, including Dante himself. But she does not substitute for human love. In this respect as in so many others, the *Divine Comedy* is a unique document; but its very uniqueness in this respect points to the tragic failure in other love literature of its day and afterwards, in which palinodes became the rule.

Dante wrote of Beatrice in the *Divine Comedy* that she was *quella che 'mparadisa la mia mente* (she who imparadises my mind) (*Paradiso* 28:3). In the *Vita Nuova,* written probably in 1295, some twenty years beforehand, he tells us that his beloved was called Beatrice "by many who did not know what it meant to call her this."[1] Beatrice: she who beatifies. He saw her, he writes, for the first time when she was nine years old. She was wearing a crimson dress—the colour of the seraphim, spirits of love, and of the virtue of love in heaven and the earthly paradise. His most wretched moments in the *Vita Nuova* follow the refusal of Beatrice to greet him when they pass each other in Florence. Her greeting is her *salute,* but it is also his, for *salute* means salvation. The famous sonnet

> *Tanto gentil e tanto onesta pare*
> *La donna mia quand' ella altrui saluta . . .*

(So deeply to be reverenced, so fair, my lady is when she her smile bestows . . .)[2] conceals the deeper meaning that when Beatrice greets someone with a smile, she heals and saves him. For she is, from the moment Dante experiences that love for her, *quella gentilissima, la quale fue distruggitrice di tutti li vizi e regina de le virtudi . . .* (that most gracious being, the queen of virtue in whose presence all evil was de-

stroyed . . . ).[3] Her goodness, reflected in her surpassing beauty, makes
heaven itself long for her presence: *che non have altro difetto / che
d'aver lei* . . . (One imperfection only heaven has / the lack of her . . . ).[4]
For she is *quanto de ben po far natura; / per esempio di lei bieltà si prova*
(The sum of nature's universe / To her perfection all of beauty tends).[5]

The crescendo of light that explodes ever brighter in paradise finds
its loveliest radiance in her laughter and her eyes: for a time Dante
cannot look at the wheeling heavens except in their reflection in her face
(see *Paradiso* 1:64–9; 5:4–6; 23:46–8).

The Provençal poets had developed the concept of love's ennobling
powers; and the Italians of the *dolce stil novo* had later expanded it,
defying the palinodes of the last troubadours. Dante's idea that Beatrice
was a creature from heaven was not new: it appears in the lyrics of
Guido Cavalcanti (d. 1300) and Guido Guinizelli (d. 1276), to whom
Dante paid loving tribute in *Purgatorio XXVI* as *il padre / mio e delli
altri miei miglior che mai / rime d'amore usar dolci e leggiadre* (the
father of me and of others my betters, whoever have used sweet and
graceful rhymes of love). In one poem, Guinizelli stands before God
on the last day and refuses to recant. God rebukes him:

> *Ch'a me convien la laude
> E a la reina del reame degno,
> Per cui cessa ogni fraude.*

(Praise should be paid to me and to the queen of the noble realm,
through whom all evil comes to an end.) But Guinizelli retorts:

> *Tenea d'angel sembianza
> che fosse del tuo regno:
> Non mi tu fallo s'eo le posi amanza.*

(She looked like an angel, as if she came from your kingdom. It was no
wrong on my part when I made love to her.)[6]

The divine order, which denies moral beauty to human love, stands
challenged. It was Dante's unique genius that he was able to achieve a
reconciliation of this eternal quarrel between the body and the soul in the
sublime synthesis of divinity and humanity that is Beatrice. Devoted as
Dante shows himself to be to the Virgin, living as he did during the rise
of her cult, he focussed his love on a mortal woman whom he had
known, whose appearance, dress, and manner were important to him, to
whom he had spoken and who had, in life, exchanged smiles and conver-

sation with him as she walked in the narrow streets of Florence. Beatrice affirms the grandeur and nobility of the created world, of the human attempt to reach, know, and love goodness. She is not the tool of defiance against a God who forbids earthly attachments, but the special instrument of mediation between earth and heaven. A woman who had been a child in a crimson dress at a party, and then a married lady of Florence doing the ordinary social round of weddings and funerals—as Dante gives us glimpses of in *La Vita Nuova*—Beatrice even in paradise does not reject her mortality like a foul carapace, but in the midst of delight at her present beatitude, recalls with pride her former beauty:

> *Mai non t'appresentò natura o arte*
> *piacer quanto le belle membra in ch'io*
> *rinchiusa fui, e sono in terra sparte . . .*

(Never did nature or art set before thee beauty so great as the fair members in which I was enclosed, and they are crumbled to dust . . .) (*Purgatorio* 31:49–51).

The *Divine Comedy* is the drama of Dante's personal salvation, wrought by Beatrice. When she appears on the triumphal chariot of Revelation on the summit of the mountain of Purgatory, in the earthly paradise, she is dressed in the colour of living flame, under a white veil and a green mantle, and her head is garlanded with olive. Dante, remembering, writes:

> *d'antico amor sentì la gran potenza*

(I felt old love's great power) (*Purgatorio* 30:39).

When she first speaks to Dante, she is as sharp with him as a magistrate with a recidivist delinquent. Dante cowers with shame and, weeping, confesses that *le presenti cose / col falso lor piacer* (present things with their false pleasure) turned him from the right path after Beatrice's death (*Purgatorio* 31:34–5).

His flight upwards through the succeeding spheres of Paradise at Beatrice's side crowns his own spiritual struggle. In the empyrean, Dante makes a calm but intense prayer:

> *sì che l'anima mia, che fatt' hai sana,*
> *piacente a te dal corpo si disnodi.*

(So that my spirit, which thou hast made whole, may be loosed from the body well-pleasing to thee) (*Paradiso* 31:89–90). Silently, Beatrice vanishes from his side to take her place among the ranks of the saints in the Mystic Rose, and Bernard of Clairvaux, at her injunction, petitions the Virgin for Dante's salvation. The stately and poignant paean Dante placed on the lips of the Virgin's greatest lover closes with a prayer that Dante's human impulses be controlled:

> *Ancor ti priego, Regina, che puoi*
> *ciò che tu vuoli, che conservi sani,*
> *dopo tanto veder, li affetti suoi.*
> *Vinca tua guardia i movimenti umani . . .*

(This too, I pray of thee, Queen, who canst what thou wilt, that thou keep his affections pure after so great a vision. Let thy guardianship control his human impulses . . . ) (*Paradiso* 33:33–7).

Dante's moral theology stemmed from the thought of Thomas Aquinas, his compatriot, born only forty years before Dante himself. God is love itself; First Principle, Pure Act, Prime Motion is all love, that love that moves the sun and the other stars, as Dante writes in the closing line of the *Comedy*. Love is the fountainhead of all moral thoughts and deeds. Nature is created good, and only errs because God has, in his munificence, given man the greatest gift of all, free will, which he misuses to pursue love that is not good, that blots out the original likeness of creature and creator. When Virgil, Dante's guide, described the terraced plan of Purgatory to Dante, he made it clear that every fault is rooted in the perversion, the lack, or the excess of love. Pithily, he summed up this essential Christian paradox:

> *altro ben è che no fa l'uom felice;*
> *Non è felicità, non è la bona*
> *essenza, d'ogni ben frutto e radice.*

(Other good there is which does not make men happy; it is not happiness, it is not the good essence, the fruit and root of every good) (*Purgatorio* 17:133–6).

The appetites deflect the *anima semplicetta che sa nulla* (the simple little soul that knows nothing) (*Purgatorio* 16:98), once it flutters newborn from the hands of the creator. But among all the vices and corruption to which the appetites lead, Dante has, throughout the *Divine Comedy,* a gentle, lyrical approach to those who have sinned through sensuality.

To tell Dante her story, Francesca is released a moment from the unceasing gyre of her private hell where she whirls forever with her lover Paolo in punishment for their lust. He, Dante, has no word of censure for her, but only tacit understanding of her sad reproach of the author of the Lancelot story—Chrétien de Troyes?—which aroused their mutual desire. And when she finishes her tale, Dante, in a crisis of pity, swoons and falls: *e caddi come corpo morto cade* (And I dropped as a dead body falls) (*Inferno* 5:142).

In Purgatory, those who sinned in voluptuousness are purified by fire on the seventh and topmost terrace, at the very edge of the earthly paradise. There Dante sees the throng of souls churning restlessly past, exchanging swift kisses and crying out aloud of the sexual outrages of history. And among the shades Dante finds Guido Guinizelli, the poet he once imitated in the *Vita Nuova*. (*Amore e'l cor gentil sono una cosa* resembles Guinizelli's famous *Amor al cor gentil sempre ripara*.) Dante here acknowledges his debt as they talk of the *dolce stil novo*—Guinizelli uses the phrase. The canto ends with the troubadour Arnaut Daniel, the *miglior fabbro,* who materializes from the chastening fire, weeping of his *passada folor*. Both poets' unabashed and outspoken rejection of the Church's morality forced Dante's hand, and he could not entirely absolve them of sinfulness. Their philosophy rather than their actions made expiation necessary. But in the third sphere of Paradise, the sphere of Venus, where souls who loved overmuch are kindled to a blaze in the breath of God, Dante finds an extraordinary motley gathering of people whose wanton lives and loves he must have known well but who he considered had repented. Cunizza, the wife of the Count of St. Bonifazio, eloped with the troubadour Sordello, a protegé of her husband, had many love affairs afterwards, and acquired two more husbands. She confesses to Dante serenely:

*mi vinse il lume d'esta stella*

(the light of this star [Venus] overcame me) (*Paradiso* 9:33).

Folquet of Marseilles, the troubadour turned bishop, notorious for his cruelty in the Albigensian crusade, keeps Cunizza company in this piece of Paradise. He compares his many passions to the dementia of Dido and others, and tells Dante with equanimity:

*Non però qui si pente, ma si ride*
*Non della colpa, ch'a mente non torna*
*ma del valor ch'ordinò e provide.*

(Yet here we do not repent; nay, we smile, not for our fault, which does not come back to mind, but for the power which ordained and foresaw) (*Paradiso* 9:103–6). Folquet points out to Dante a spirit, sparkling clear as a sunbeam in clear water; it is Rahab the harlot, who of all the souls of the Old Covenant in limbo was caught up to heaven first (*Paradiso* 9: 119–20).

In this same sphere of Venus, Dante is reminded of the power the star exercises over his own heart, when Charles Martel, one of his heroes, recites the opening line of a song Dante himself wrote, in which he repented of his fickleness, when another love distracted him from Beatrice, the *angiola ch'n cielo è coronata* (the angel who is crowned in heaven). Thus in Paradise's circle of penitent lovers, Dante remembers the weakness he describes in *La Vita Nuova,* when a beautiful girl gazed on him after Beatrice's death with such pity for his grief that his heart was moved. Then, he rejected this new love as *vilissimo,* but his anguish when he first meets Beatrice in the earthly paradise and she so scorchingly upbraids him for his infidelity proves how seriously he viewed this brief lapse in his total dedication to Beatrice.

Lust—*altro ben è che non è la bona essenza*—was the sin to which Dante felt prey. As the Dantist John Sinclair has pointed out, Dante shares the penance of the shades only on the terraces of pride, anger, and lust. The fires in which Arnaut Daniel and Guinizelli are tempered and refined terrify him so that he cannot step through them until Virgil calls Beatrice to his mind.[7] And then:

> *Si com fui dentro, in un bogliente vetro*
> *gittato mi sarei per rinfrescarmi,*
> *tant'era ivi lo 'ncendio sanza metro.*

(As soon as I was in it I would have cast myself into boiling glass to cool me, so beyond measure was the burning there) (*Purgatorio* 27:49–51).

The excruciating flames claim their sinner for a moment, but then Dante passes beyond this last barrier of torment into the flowery garden where he will be united with Beatrice. "It is not easy to see," writes Sinclair, "how Dante would have told us more convincingly of his own peculiar agony of repentance for the sin that is purged here. What may have been the circumstances of his offending we do not know, and it must be remembered that the passage was written by a man of stern and lofty moral judgement, reflecting, near his fiftieth year, on his own manhood; but the evidence is as plain as he could make it that here on the terrace of carnal lust, he is a penitent."[8]

Sensual joy would have disfigured Dante's love for Beatrice: he was far too steeped in the Christian ethic to think otherwise. But he was too profound and noble a thinker to fall into dualism and use the perfection of Beatrice to denigrate the human race or the rest of the female sex, even though no one could, in his eyes, match her excellence. And he was too subtle a moralist and too sympathetic a soul to confuse chastity and virginity. In the *Convito,* he stated: "In religion, God requires nothing of us but the heart," and on the terrace of the lustful in Purgatory, as the souls troop past, they cry out examples of chastity; among them are married couples who lived together virtuously (*Purgatorio* 25:134–5). *Lo naturale è sempre sanza errore* (The natural is always without error) (*Purgatorio* 17:94) was the cornerstone of his faith, and he had assembled his faith like a master mason. It was a lonely, healthy cry in a world that had been brought to its knees under the weight of its own natural sinfulness—a protest on behalf of Francesca lost in the whirlwind. For Dante, a miracle had taken place: a new incarnation of supreme love in an ordinary Florentine woman.

Beatrice dei Portinari was born in 1266, died in 1290, and was the wife of Simone dei Bardi, a merchant. Even these biographical scraps are not to be gleaned from Dante, but from another eminent Florentine, Boccaccio. Dante never even tells us the colour of those eyes that sustained him through the ascent to the empyrean. Yet for all this, Beatrice is not a shade from the nether world of Dante's fantasy, a neurotic phantasm like the troubadour Rudel's *amor de lonh*. Beatrice can be imperious and even curt; she is learned and expounds the knottier strands of theology and astronomy with scholastic skill. Some readers find her lengthy discourses in Paradise tedious, and see her as the desiccated mouthpiece of Dante at his most pedantic. Consequently there has been much debate about the "reality" of Beatrice, whether she is simply an allegory of moral perfection. The notion that allegory must necessarily exclude personal experience is absurd; also, Dante naturally saw things in Beatrice no one else did.

Writing about the *Vita Nuova,* T. S. Eliot defined the kind of spiritual adventure that is anchored in material events and characters:

I find it an account of a particular kind of experience: that is, of something which had actual experience (the experience of the "confession" in the modern sense) *and* intellectual and imaginative experience (the experience of thought and the experience of dream) as its materials; and which became a third kind. It seems to me of importance to grasp the simple fact that the *Vita Nuova* is neither a "confession" nor an indiscretion in the modern sense. . . . If you have that sense of intellectual and spiritual realities that Dante had, then a form of expression like the *Vita Nuova* cannot be classed either as "truth" or "fiction."[9]

There could be no alchemy more powerful than Dante's, which transformed a vision of the afterlife into palpable reality. Indeed, it is difficult reading the *Divine Comedy* to remember that in one sense at least Dante made this all up. Beatrice belongs in that reality, and never more so than in the scene in the earthly paradise when she calls Dante to her by his name and he, crushed with the shame of his forsaking her, weeps like a child.

But the experience of the Virgin in the *Divine Comedy* is of an altogether different order. There are points of similarity with Beatrice: both are filled with *bellezza* and *letizia,* both are described as mothers, and when Dante first looks on the Virgin, he sees:

> *il quale e il quanto della viva stella*
> *che là su vince, come qua giù vinse . . .*

(The quality and the magnitude of the living star who surpasses there above as she surpasses here below . . .) (*Paradiso* 23:92–3), just as when he lifted his eyes to gaze at Beatrice in the earthly paradise, he evoked her in the same comparison:

> *vincer parìemi più sè stessa antica,*
> *vincer che l'altre qui, quand' ella c'era.*

(She seemed to me to surpass her former self more than she surpassed the others here when she was with us) (*Purgatorio* 31:83–4).

But the Virgin, in Dante, is not the exalted beloved of the love lyric, and certainly no surrogate sweetheart. She appears twice to him in Paradise, first in the heaven of the fixed stars, and again in the empyrean. She is:

> *la faccia che a Cristo*
> *più si somiglia.*

(the face that most resembles Christ) (*Paradiso* 32:85–6). But when she stands before him, Dante cannot tear his eyes from the contemplation of the full power of Beatrice's smile, which he is able to bear unflinchingly for the first time. Rapt in this delight, he ignores the vision of the Mother of God before him, and Beatrice, once again, chides him:

> *Perchè la faccia mia sì t'innamora*
> *che tu non ti rivolgi al bel giardino*
> *che sotto i raggi di Cristo s'infiora?*

(Why does my face so enamour thee that thou dost not turn to the fair garden that flowers under the rays of Christ?) (*Paradiso* 23:70–3). Mary is there, the "rose" in which the Word became flesh, the lovely sapphire that dyes the heavens blue (*Paradiso* 23:73, 102). Gabriel, a firebrand ablaze with love, circles around her and sings a hymn to the Mother of God and the Lady of Heaven. As the saints in the heavenly throng take up the chant, the Virgin streams upwards to the highest heaven, and they rise up yearningly after her, like children reaching for their mother's breast (*Paradiso* 23:121–3). Dante remains transfigured with joy at the sweetness of their song—the *Regina Caeli.*

In the empyrean, Dante's eyes scan the tiers of the Mystic Rose's incandescent petals until they alight on a flame that, on the rose's highest rim, burns more brightly than the thousand angels round it with outspread wings:

> *Vidi a' lor giochi quivi ed a' lor canti*
> *ridere una bellezza, che letizia*
> *era nelli occhi a tutti li altri santi.*

(I saw there, smiling at their sports and songs, a beauty which was joy in the eyes of all the other saints) (*Paradiso* 31:133–6). She is, Dante says again, the Queen of Heaven,

> *cui questo regno è suddito e devoto*

(to whom this realm is subject and devoted) (*Paradiso* 31:117), and her court praises her without cease in the words of the "angelic versicle," the *Ave Maria.*

When Bernard later prays to her on Dante's behalf in the famous majestic plea Chaucer borrowed to place on the lips of the Prioress in the *Canterbury Tales,* he focusses on the mystery of the Incarnation:

> *Vergine madre, figlia del tuo figlio . . .*

(Mother maid, daughter of thy son . . .) and on the perfection of human nature found in her:

> *tu se' colei che l'umana natura*
> *nobilitasti sì, che 'l suo fattore*
> *non disdegnò di farsi sua fattura.*

(Thou art she who didst so ennoble human nature that its maker did not disdain to be made its making) (*Paradiso* 33:4–6). Above all, she is the universal mediatrix of mankind, the "noonday torch of charity" and the "living spring of hope." It is through her intercession that Dante will be granted the vision of God that crowns his poem and his journey:

> *Riguarda omai nella faccia che a Cristo*
> *più si somiglia, chè la sua chiarezza*
> *sola ti può disporre a veder Cristo.*

(Look now on the face that most resembles Christ, for only its brightness can fit thee to see Christ) (*Paradiso* 32:85–7).

Dante's Mariology is sober-minded, solid, and even cautious. Although he appoints Bernard, Mary's most extravagant bard, to sing her loveliness in *Paradiso,* he borrows next to nothing from Bernard's writings, avoiding the erotic rapture of the great preacher's tone and imagery. Instead, Dante works the orthodox theme of Mary's dignity as the instrument of the Incarnation, which makes her the most efficient intercessor in heaven. Through her divine motherhood, first of Jesus, and second of the whole fellowship of saints, Mary has won sovereignty of paradise. In the *Purgatorio,* Buonconte da Montefeltro tells Dante how he called on her aid as he fled wounded from the battle of Campaldino in 1289, and through his weak cry, his *lacrimetta,* he was spared the fires of hell (*Purgatorio* 5:94–108). The princes in the flowery valley of neglectful rulers sing the antiphon the *Salve Regina,* wailing and sighing from the vale of woe for her pity (*Purgatorio* 7:82). In the *Paradiso,* the gentle Piccarda Donati, who was forced to leave the cloister of her choice to make an unhappy marriage, ends her tale singing the *Ave Maria,* the first song Dante hears in heaven. She has defined for Dante that suspension of all self that is the monastic ideal:

> *E'n la sua volontade è nostra pace*

(In his will is our peace) (*Paradiso* 3:85), and her prayer to the Virgin recalls the Annunciation, when Mary also consented to the divine purpose. The *Ave Maria* is sung again, as we have seen, by the heavenly company in the Mystic Rose, those gay courtiers around their lady; and the *Regina Caeli* by the saints in the starry sphere.

Dante bears witness thereby to the growing popularity of the Marian liturgy of his time and its ranking importance beside the psalms and established hymns like the *Te Deum,* also sung in Paradise (24:113). But Dante never probes Mariological problems: he avoids altogether the issue of the Immaculate Conception, already flickering to life in his day, and all definition of the exact nature of Mary's presence in heaven. Indeed the Virgin is described no more fully than Beatrice, whose "fair members are scattered." As a Christian of the late Duecento and early Trecento, Dante undoubtedly believed the Virgin had been preserved from corruption in the grave, but he remains wary on the subject of her bodily assumption, and hazy about her preservation from original sin.

Profound and loving as Dante's reverence is, the Virgin Mary of the *Divine Comedy* remains a celestially exalted figure, who has passed from the time scale of this world into that of the next. He cannot approach her as an intimate, indeed requires a series of mediators—Lucy, Beatrice, and Bernard. His Madonna or Lady is Beatrice, a full-blooded and hot-tempered woman he knew and loved on this earth. In her, he had decided moral goodness was incarnate. To achieve this miracle Dante did not segregate her from the human crowd by denying her the fullness of the human condition. In his eyes, she surpasses all in fairness, wisdom, goodness, gentleness, and light, but she still belongs to mankind, and the supernatural resplendence she has attained is accessible to others, given the sustaining, elevating love of creatures like her.

Beatrice, however sublime, is still human; the Virgin represents humanity transfigured by its wildest and most hopeless dreams. Although it is the Virgin who obtains the final boon for Dante, love of her did not impel him through Hell and Purgatory to Heaven. Dante had an actual experience of personal love that he fused with an heroic adventure and an unequalled vision to accomplish his own redemption. He achieved it, but the tragedy for the western intellectual system was that the magnitude of his achievement inspired others to emulate him, only to arrive at that crippled travesty of both Plato and love termed Platonic love. Dante was aware of the sublime potential in the things of this world, and he therefore used them to turn his eyes heavenwards instead of following the growing tradition of eschewing altogether the visible world in pursuit of the invisible. Dante never retracted his remarkable argument that through human love one could reach the plenitude of the beatific vision. The boldness of his quest and the grandeur of his claims leave the reader marvelling, as in the empyrean he comes face to face with the hidden God through the mediation of his beloved Beatrice.

Petrarch's Laura is, for instance, often paired with Dante's Beatrice, but Petrarch's deepening faith and his increased reading in the Christian philosophers, particularly Augustine and John Chrysostom, inspired him to retract his claim that the love of a fellow creature could pitch the mind from the mundane to the sublime. In the *Secretum,* an imaginary conversation between Petrarch and Augustine written during the years 1342–58, the saint chastises the scholar for his passion. Petrarch says that it was pure at first, but then admits that his love for Laura deflected his will from the true pursuit of the good, and that it is blasphemy to claim at all that the love of God can be obtained by love of one of his creatures, for God should be loved for himself alone.[10]

The last poem of the *Canzoniere* is a masterpiece that can move to tears, so powerful, so magnificent is the poet's plea for mercy. But the object of his prayer is the Virgin: after a lifetime in bondage to Laura, and a sonnet cycle chronicling the finest movements of his psyche, Petrarch sinks to his knees before the mother of God and begs forgiveness for his weakness:

> *Mortal bellezza, atti e parole m'hanno*
> *Tutta ingombrata l'alma.*
> *Vergine sacra et alma,*
> *Non tardar, ch'i' son forse a l'ultimo anno.*

(Mortal beauty, acts and words have encumbered all my soul. Holy and gentle virgin, do not delay, for perhaps I've reached the last of my years.) Then he asks, counterposing spirit and matter with the true heart of a Christian:

> *Chè se poca mortal terra caduca*
> *Amar con sì mirabil fede soglio,*
> *Che devrò far di te, cosa gentile?*

(And if I used to love with such wonderful faith a little mortal dust, what should I feel for thee, sweet thing?)[11]

Such a palinode is to some extent convention, tribute to the prevailing idea that man is only of value when the world is of no value to him. Petrarch also capitulated to this orthodoxy in his *Letter to Posterity,* in which he paints his life and character as he would like to be remembered. It is an extraordinary and painful tissue of desires and deceit, and in it the poet who could never free himself from the thought of Laura writes: "I struggled in my younger days with a keen but constant and pure attachment, and would have struggled with it longer had not the sinking flames been extinguished by death—premature and bitter, but salutary." With that single word "salutary" Petrarch almost wipes out the *Canzoniere.* He goes on: "As I approached the age of forty, while my powers were unimpaired and my passions were still strong, I not only threw off my bad habits, but even the recollection of them, as if I had never looked on a woman."[12]

For this reason, he preferred among his works his punishing Latin epic on the second Punic war.

Dante avoided the comparison between Beatrice and the Virgin because pure love for him was pure enough to erase the line between this world and the next. Petrarch, however "constant and pure" his attachment, mended the dividing barrier.

The strange thing is that Petrarch was at least a precursor of the Renaissance, if not a Renaissance man, while Dante's system, though affected by the classics available to him, belongs to medieval cosmology. Yet the breach between the individual and God gapes wider in Petrarch's palinode than in Dante's vision of Beatrice. The classicism that penetrated the thought of the Renaissance was steeped in the dualism that the Church Fathers had themselves absorbed from ancient writers. The concept of Platonic love developed and the ideal took root that "a man overcomes sensuality when his reason makes him realise that beauty is all the more perfect the more it is removed from corruptible matter."[13]

The ramifications of neoplatonism are impossible to discuss here, but the Renaissance saw it reach into the minds of Europe and set there a stereotyped quest for salvation: perfect knights in Arcadian groves die for love of spotless maidens, tormented by the sweet agony of a passion that only a brute would seek to satisfy. Love is further kindled by denial and atrocious excesses of servitude, and always the spectre of the savage, the demon of lust, stalks on the perimeter. Civilization became synonymous with sexual restraint; and women were to be loved but not loving. So although Dante's exalted love of Beatrice had depended on chastity, this aspect acquired a disproportionate importance in the concept of earthly love after him.

The obsession that love must be chaste to be worthy of the name was the culmination of the Church's takeover of the collective intellect of Christendom. Naturally, it would be a mistake to confuse words with deeds: the triumph may well have taken place chiefly on paper. An unbroken chain of complaints about the levity and hedonism of the people from the clergy, and about the luxury, indolence, and corruption of the clergy from the people testifies that everyone had a good time just the same. But they considered their actions in a different and reprehensible light, and guilt made them the Church's captives.

The Virgin's role as the beloved in heaven diminished in the fifteenth century, when hymns of love are sung to her by angels, and not by the poets themselves.[14] But she had done her work. The heresy of the troubadours—the innocence and nobility of carnal love—had been trampled underfoot, and her name invoked in the battle.

Sometimes this long and durable obsession with chastity perpetuated by the Church appears to be an incomprehensible attack of mass lunacy. When applied to women, however, it served an evident social purpose, which was reinforced by chastity's correlative among the Christian virtues: humility, interpreted as submissiveness.

# Part Four
# MOTHER

## Chapter Twelve

# LET IT BE

*How sublime is this humility, which is incapable of
yielding to the weight of honours, or of being rendered proud by them! The Mother of God is chosen,
and she declares herself His handmaid.*[1]

—St. Bernard of Clairvaux

"Ecce ancilla Dei," said Mary. "Behold the handmaid of the Lord.
Be it unto me according to thy word" (Luke 1:38). In Christian theology
Mary's consent to the Incarnation, her *Fiat,* exemplifies the most sublime
fusion of man's free will with the divine plan. The free cooperation of
man and God for salvation bears the metaphysical name of synergy, but
this magnificent and lofty view of Mary's act of acceptance came to epitomize a restricted moral notion quite unworthy of the term: that of
feminine submissiveness.

The Christian revolution from earliest times centred on egalitarian-
ism, on the universal application of the Gospel, the welcome offered to
all men, and particularly as Christ himself stressed, to the poor and the
humble. But in the case of the Church's moral teaching to women, humility, the greatest of the Christian virtues, acquired a different connotation.

The two cultures, classical and Judaic, flowed together in the new
religion, bearing a heavy burden of long prejudice against women.
Woman was subordinate to man: in the *Timaeus,* Plato considered that a
man who led a good life might return to his native star; but if he did not,
he might come back to earth a woman.[2] Aristotle in the *Politics* casually
asserts woman's natural inferiority during a discussion of slavery:

"Again, the same holds good between man and the other animals: tame animals are superior in their nature to wild animals, yet for all the former it is advantageous to be ruled by man, since this gives them security. Also as between the sexes, the male is by nature superior, and the female inferior, the male ruler and the female subject . . ."[3] The *Timaeus* and the *Politics* were prominent among the Greek philosophical works commented on by the medieval schoolmen.

The Bible meshed with Greek opinion. In Exodus 20:17 women are listed among a man's possessions, along with his slaves, cattle, and donkeys. But the principal scriptural argument hinged on the story of the Creation in Genesis. For if the Fall illustrated woman's wickedness, the Creation proved man's precedence.

Modern scholarship has sifted Genesis and separated earlier and later strata, so that it is now generally known that the story of Adam's rib is the first primitive account; and that the seven-day version of the Creation, which precedes it in the book, was written several hundred years later, after the Babylonian exile had profoundly coloured Jewish thought and mythology. In the early account, Eve issues from the sleeping Adam's side, fashioned from his rib to be his helpmate. In the later version of the Creation God commands, "Let us make man in our image, after our likeness: and let them have dominion. . . . So God created man in his own image, in the image of God created he him; male and female created he them" (Genesis 1:26–7). This simple statement of the equality of the sexes, made together in God's image, was overlooked in favour of the folklore of the tale of Adam's rib, partly because it described graphically the creation of a specific individual and partly because it fitted traditional interpretations of women's place.[4] In Christian iconography the double creation of mankind, male and female, has never, in my experience, been attempted. The illuminations of medieval Bibles, the magnificent creation cycle of twelfth-century mosaics at Monreale, Michelangelo's painting on the Sistine chapel ceiling first wake Adam to life and then picture Eve rising naked from his side.

But this beautiful image was made of treacherous stuff: it permitted the interpretation that woman, as man's helper, was his subordinate; and as the afterthought of God she was not made in the divine image. Paul, heir to both Greek and Jewish thought, wrote that women should keep their heads veiled because they were not, like men, made in the image of God, but were the glory of their husbands—the reflection of the reflection of the ideal. "Neither was the man created for the woman; but the woman for the man" (1 Corinthians 11:9). They should hold their tongues in church, and if they had questions, ask their husbands at home.

They should be submissive and obedient. For St. Paul, the ideal union of a docile and faithful Church with her bridegroom Christ is the paradigm of Christian marriage: "Wives, submit yourselves unto your own husbands, as unto the Lord. . . . Therefore as the church is subject unto Christ, so let the wives be to their own husbands in every thing. Husbands, love your wives, even as Christ also loved the church . . ." (Ephesians 5:22; 24–5). Only through man could a woman become herself the mirror of God; and man, the purpose and fulfilment of her life at a spiritual level, became her master in society. As the Church's views on the sanctity of matrimony developed in the middle ages (see Chapter 9), this interpretation of Genesis and St. Paul hardened until Aquinas could state quite plainly: "In a secondary sense the image of God is found in man, and not in woman: for man is the beginning and end of woman; as God is the beginning and end of every creature."[5]

Although the ancient prejudice is of course heartily denied in ecclesiastical circles now, it continues to underpin the Christian ideal of woman. The legends of the Bible are translated into ethics; myths become morals; stories precepts. Just as the virgin birth provided an argument for virginity, so the creation of the first Eve and the wondering acceptance of her successor at the Annunciation corroborated a social order that deemed women underlings.

The Virgin Mary herself was not identified with women in their subject aspect until the Franciscan order wrought a revolution in Christian thinking on the Incarnation in the thirteenth and early fourteenth centuries. It is true that her silence, modesty, and self-effacement had previously been extolled by the Fathers and held up as an example to the female sex. Bernard, for whom humility was the root of ideal love, and the very image of Christ himself, had sung the perfection of Mary's humbleness when she called herself the Lord's handmaid; "The whole world prostrate at your feet waits for your consent. . . ."[6] And the Cistercian mood of intimate meditation created the climate in which Mary could be brought down from her plinth. But the translation of the spiritual state into a physical and social condition was accomplished by the peculiar, inflamed genius of the founder of the Franciscans, Francis of Assisi (1181–1226).

Francis had a unique thespian ability to turn thoughts into vivid gestures. From the moment he stripped himself of his patrimony by taking off his clothes before his merchant father in the public square in Assisi, to his death on the bare ground, the dust from which he came to which he would return, his life was an inspired sequence of dramatic, non-verbal parables. The focus of his mysticism was the humanity of

Christ, which he and his followers tried to emulate in what they understood to be a historical way: by being as poor, as homeless, as accessible to all as Christ the preacher himself had been. Thomas of Celano, who wrote Francis' life after his death, describes the saint's reaction when, "at a meal, a brother recalled her [Mary's] and Christ's poverty saying that the Blessed Virgin Mary was such a poor little woman that she had nothing to give her little son to eat. When St. Francis heard this, he immediately rose from the table, sighing with intense grief and groaning and sobbing with pain. He left the table and ate the rest of his bread on the bare ground, weeping very much."[7] The *humus*, the humble earth: Francis' mind unceasingly returned to this matrix symbol, the eternal reminder of the frailty of mortal clay, the sacrifice of the God made man.

*Humilitas,* lowliness in the image of the bare ground's lowliness, was the core of the Franciscan revolution. Francis identified with the creatures that also live on it, and like many ascetics, for whom the body is an obstacle to spiritual perfection, Francis himself felt a deep sympathy with other creatures who share the common plight of subjection to nature's laws. The popular legend of St. Jerome, who drew the thorn from a lion's paw and shared his desert solitude with him, perceives this fellowship of man and beast when man mortifies his flesh as a useless burden. Francis combined enmity and sweetness, though, in a way that Jerome, with all his ferocity, could never have achieved. When Francis lay down on the earth to die, he apologized to his body—"dear brother donkey"— for ill-using him so. In his marvellous *Canticle of the Sun* he praises the whole of natural creation in strongly pantheistic terms. But his celebration of the cosmos was slanted through a poignant and intense conviction of the material world's transience and inferiority; and this coloured the values that he and his order after him proclaimed.

In a Franciscan hymn to the Christian virtues, attributed to Francis himself, he sings of wisdom, simplicity, poverty, humility, and charity, in turn. Then he comes to obedience, and his prayer assumes an extreme quietism that is almost Taoist:

> Holy Obedience
> Confounds all self-will and all sensual will,
> And keeps its body
> Obedient to the spirit
> And obedient to its neighbour
> And makes men subject
> To all the men of this world,

And not only to the men
But also to all animals and wild beasts,
So that they can do with him
Whatever they wish,
As far as God above allows them.[8]

Francis' thought in this verse is desperately twisted: for in order to overcome the animal in him man subjects himself, by an effort of willed
submission, to the animal world.

The heterodoxy of Francis' ideal of self-abnegation is even clearer in
one of the only two letters we have that can definitely be attributed to
him. In 1223, he wrote to one of his brothers that he should welcome
pain and injustice for the sake of humility. He tells him, in his spontaneous, colloquial way:

All persons who obstruct your path—be they brethren or others—even if they
beat you, you must consider it all a grace. And will it thus and not otherwise.
And that you must consider your true obedience toward the Lord God and me,
for I know for certain that it is the true obedience. And love those who do
these things to you, and do not desire anything else from them, but what God
may give to you. And love them for this and do not desire that they be
better Christians. . . .[9]

Thus Francis welcomes the wrongdoing of others to accomplish the
dissolution of personal desire, to balk that "sensual will."

The Franciscans spoke for the wretched of the earth, the men and
women who during that violent epoch suffered unending injustice, ill-
treatment, famine, epidemics, poverty, and the toll of recruitment for the
quarrels of noblemen and the crusades of the Church. Any well-heeled
follower was stripped of all worldliness, of rank, possessions, power.
The friars swore poverty, chastity, and obedience, and owned nothing but
a robe and a girdle. They lived by begging. A few men who were, like
Francis, members of a prospering bourgeoisie were attracted to this radical brand of Christianity. But the new order also absorbed men who were
already dispossessed and footloose. The luminaries of the two mendicant
orders—the Dominicans were founded shortly after—were not vagrants,
but the rank and file was drawn from the explosive remnant of medieval
society, transformed, at a stroke, from a potential outcast class into a
caste of holy men. The recognition of the order of the Friars Minor by
Pope Innocent III in 1210 was the outcome of a genuine appreciation of
its founder's saintliness; but it was also a political master-stroke. It enfolded thousands of possible renegades in the bosom of the Church and

renewed Rome's weakening popularity among its flock. At the general chapter of 1219, only a few years after the official recognition of the order, there were five thousand friars present.

The Franciscan spirit continues to be considered, by agnostics and atheists as well as believers, as the most genuine expression of Christ's teaching ever approved by the Vatican. The Dominicans, approved some six years later, were also vowed to poverty, but their connection with the Inquisition gave them a more intellectual and more sinister character than their Franciscan counterparts. The Franciscans' gentle love of flowers and birds and animals, their compassion for the weak and the poor, the sick and the distressed, their emotionalism and their homage to Lady Poverty strike the modern man and woman as the epitome of the Gospel. St. Francis is loved by middle-class Americans who have hardly heard of another saint and who aspire to reject their backgrounds and opt for a life on the margins of society.

The impact of the friars' new ethic on the cult of the Virgin was profound, for they remoulded her to their revolutionary ideals. In Italy and France, the Virgin left her starry throne in the heavens and laid aside her robes and insignia and diadem to sit cross-legged on the bare earth like a peasant mother with her child. The Madonna of Humility first appears in a panel now in Palermo, painted in 1346; but Millard Meiss has authoritatively argued that Simone Martini (d. 1344), the great Sienese artist of the Trecento, was inspired by the Franciscan pseudo-Bonaventure's *Meditations on the Life of Christ* (c. 1300) to paint the prototype, which is now lost. Wrapped in simple blue homespun, seated on a tussock, with the baby often nursing at her breast, and only the stars and moon of the Woman of the Apocalypse sometimes about her to identify her divinity, the image of the Virgin of Humility compresses the new strain of poignant intimacy that men were then feeling about the highest mysteries of Christianity.[10] In a panel in the National Gallery, Washington, D.C., attributed—wrongly—to Masaccio, Mary appears as a blunt-featured, very young girl with coarse bare feet and a strapping baby on her knee (figure 23). In a painting now in the National Gallery of London, one of the followers of Fra Angelico (d. 1445), the Dominican friar, also seated her on the ground below a canopy held aloft by angels, but with greater delicacy made this canopy brocaded.

The image formed part of a movement towards direct, emotional involvement such as Francis himself experienced. It was Francis who placed a manger in the woods at Greccio with an ox and ass beside it, and so inaugurated the practice of the Christmas crib, transforming the mythological symbolism of the Byzantine nativity into a touching story of a struggling and roofless family.[11] The star, once the sign of a Greek hero's birth, became the exciting lure of an exotic caravan of eastern merchants: Franciscan writings, like the *Meditations on the Life of Christ*, attributed until recently to the order's General, St. Bonaventure, but now ascribed to Giovanni da San Gimignano, focus on the sweetness of the Virgin's character, on her youthful loveliness, her gentleness, her meekness, her mildness, the tenderness she shows to her child, the lullabies she sings as she rocks him in the cradle. Scores of English lyrics of the thirteenth and fourteenth centuries are placed on the lips of the young virgin mother or her loving son and describe the pleasant years together before the cruel fate of the Passion overtook them. Giovanni/pseudo-Bonaventure even contemplates with awed amazement the Mother of God spinning cotton in Egypt to help the family finances.[12]

The heart of the mystery was the child and so, with a crib, the climax came at Christmas, when the baby was introduced into the manger. It was a logical development of Franciscan piety that the Virgin should kneel in adoration before her newborn child: one icon of sublime humility before another. St. Bridget of Sweden (d. 1373), a member of the Franciscan Tertiaries and founder of an order of the Bridgettine nuns in the friars' spirit, received visions of the birth of Christ, in which the Virgin gave birth to the child on her knees and then worshipped him.[13] Bridget's visions, which swept medieval Europe, influenced some of the loveliest fifteenth-century paintings of the Nativity (see colour plate II, figure 2), including Piero della Francesca's masterpiece in the National Gallery, London, and several Botticellis in which the Virgin kneels. In motherhood Mary was glorified, and through her prostration before her child, became more glorious for her humility. As Simone de Beauvoir has written: "For the first time in human history the mother kneels before her son; she freely accepts her inferiority. This is the supreme masculine victory, consummated in the cult of the Virgin—it is the rehabilitation of woman through the accomplishment of her defeat."[14]

Although Jesus and Mary exemplified the virtues of poverty, humility, and obedience in equal measure, and although Christians of both sexes were exhorted to imitate them, the characteristics of these virtues—gentleness, docility, forbearance—are immediately classifiable as feminine, especially in Mediterranean Catholic countries. The more fervently religious the country—Spain, for instance—the more the menfolk swagger and command, the more the women submit and withdraw and are praised for their Christian goodness. *Machismo*, ironically enough, is the sweet and gentle Virgin's other face.

The Franciscans are obviously not responsible single-handedly for the ideal of the gentle housewife—that would be a preposterous charge. Francis himself was completely uninterested in promoting virtues that oiled the social machinery, and never made any distinctions between the sexes and their proper behaviour. His was a total ideal of renunciation. But the interweaving of the religious ethic into the social fabric transferred the values he had advocated for the monastery into the home. From the foundation of the mendicant orders and the mass preaching of their philosophy, the virtue of humility was fostered in the female sex in particular. But it was interpreted along social, not spiritual, lines and turned into a recipe for "feminine" qualities that have a kinship with humility—modesty, silence, obedience. The Franciscan preacher Berthold von Regensburg (d. 1272), who rarely minced his words, rounded on the women in his audience and ordered them to wear unassuming dress: "Yea, Our Lady was far fairer than thou, yet she was exceedingly humble of heart . . . if he (thy goodman) be a lewd fellow, then all thy crimple-crispings and christy-crosties and thy gold thread are of no avail, and they help thee only to hell for ever and ever. . . ."[15] In the thirteenth-century homily on Holy Maidenhead, the young girl is instructed in a social ideal that has little to do with the theological and cardinal virtues: "Take thyself to him [Christ], under whom thou shalt, in thy maidenhood, bring forth sons and daughters of spiritual teamings . . . virtues . . . such as righteousness and wariness against vices; moderation and temperance and spiritual strength . . . simplicity of manner and obedience and tranquillity, endurance and sympathy for every man's sorrow . . . meekness and mildness and sweetness of heart, that belongeth of all things best to maidenhood's virtues."[16]

In two secular fourteenth-century handbooks for women, obedience to their menfolk and long-suffering compliance with their wishes are advised as religious duties. In the *Livre du Chevalier de la Tour Landry,* a manual written around 1372 by a father for his daughters, the chevalier quotes approvingly the monstrous unpleasantness of the story of Patient Griselda—whose virtue was tried by every cunning form of cruelty by her husband—and when discussing womanly obedience, describes as exemplary the reaction of a wife who, when ordered by her husband, *"Sal sur la table,"* leapt on the table when he was merely asking her to pass the salt.[17]

In *Le Ménagier de Paris,* written in 1392–4, an old, rich husband teaches his child bride her daily tasks. Spiritual matters concern this meticulous and often broad-minded bourgeois very little. He only warns her she must always go to church chaperoned by a maid. Yet his moral counsel would tally with that of the friars: she is to be humble and obedient. Fortitude and justice, the most self-assertive of the Christian cardinal virtues, are passed over, while fear of the Lord and patience—both self-effacing—are encouraged. He recommends that she show her husband animal-like devotion.[18]

The convergence of a social code of behaviour with a spiritual ideal becomes more pronounced during the course of the later middle ages and the growth of the prosperous urban class, which permitted an exclusively domestic life to the wives of merchants and tradesmen. The Christian virtues were not only advocated for women; they were also thought to be naturally characteristic of the sex. St. Bernardino of Siena (d. 1444), a Franciscan and the most famous and coruscating preacher of his day, was one of the few men perceptive enough to criticize the double standard obtaining in society. In a sermon, he lashed out at the husbands in his congregation for their hypocrisy:

How wouldst thou have this thy wife?—I will have her an honest woman —and thou art dishonest: that again is not well. . . . I would have her temperate and thou art never out of the tavern: thou shalt not have her! O, how wouldst thou have this wife of thine?—I would not have her gluttonous—and thou art ever at thy pig's liver: that is not well. I would have her active—and thou art a very sluggard. Peaceful—and thou wouldst storm at a straw if it crossed thy feet. Obedient—and thou obeyest neither father nor mother nor any man; thou deservest her not. . . . I would have her good and fair and wise and bred in all virtue. I answer if thou wouldst have her thus, it is fitting that thou shouldst be the same.[19]

The cult of the Virgin mirrored the feminine ideal of the Catholic ethic. For instance, in an enamel plaque in the Gardner Museum in Boston, attributed to the Limoges craftsman Nardon Pénicaud (d. 1542), the Virgin and Child stand in the centre of a branching tree in which are perched the Virtues carrying phylacteries. Of the theological virtues only charity is present (faith and hope omitted); of the cardinal, only prudence (no fortitude, justice, temperance). Humility, patience, obedience, compassion, purity, truth, praise, and poverty all take their place around Mary (figure 24). Unimpeachable qualities, no doubt, in themselves, they nevertheless speak eloquently of the gentle personality Mary had acquired by the fifteenth century. The Pénicaud family of enamellers, because they were prolific, popular artisans who drew on current stories and ideas, often reveal a great deal about contemporary assumptions. This lovely, cobalt-coloured plaque demonstrates the cleavage between feminine and masculine, between passive and active that had divided society into symbolic camps along sexual lines.

Yet how could religion that averred the female sex's greater inclination to evil attribute to them all the Christian virtues in greater measure than men? Naturally, any reasons for this can only be suggested. According to the division of labour in the Garden of Eden, women's purpose was breeding. Augustine and Aquinas, pondering the problem of women's creation, had decided, as we have seen, that childbearing was the sole reason, as for any other task a man would have made a better helpmate. Woman was debarred from participating in the social process outside the domestic sphere. Handbooks like *Le Ménagier de Paris* express vividly the strictness of the social code of the late fourteenth century, which decreed the double purpose of women: "the salvation of your soul and the comfort of your husband." In pursuit of these goals was the life of the Ménagier's wife, a round of parlour games, food preparation, and personal attention to her appearance and dress. Reading his handbook conjures up contemporary American suburbia, where the prosperous woman is queen of the home, just as clearly as in the Paris of the middle ages.[20]

The paradox is that women's greater sin and consequently greater penance had thrust them "out of the world" into the private sphere, where greed and cruelty were less necessary to survive. The opposition between vice and virtue reflected the ancient conflict between those who are in the world and those who are not; to some extent this was in turn reflected by the polarization of the public and private, professional and domestic sectors.

Fallen man's special penalty—"to work in the sweat of thy brow"— was shared by women under feudalism; but with rising prosperity, the wife in a fourteenth-century urban household, like Le Ménagier's in Paris, no longer played a major productive role in the family economy—a situation she probably welcomed, for the dignity of work was not then a prevalent philosophical concept. However trivial and frivolous and futile such a life might be considered today, it was then intended to shield women from the corruption of the avaricious, self-seeking commerce of the world, and for this as well as reasons of snobbery was considered desirable. Until the nineteenth century, it was Mary at Christ's feet, not Martha at work, who had decidedly chosen the better part, as the parable itself made plain.

In order to protect women further from evil outside influences, their education in any but the traditional subjects—music, embroidery—was frowned upon, for ignorance was equated with innocence. In the view of a Father of the Greek Church, St. Gregory of Nyssa, men were capable of coping with the consequences of knowledge, but the greater weakness of the female sex, as epitomized by Eve's frailty in the garden, ill-suited women for study. This prejudice has proved tenacious in Christian Europe. At the same time as Le Ménagier in Paris was outlining his wife's ideal life of piety and leisure, the intelligent and rebarbative poetess Christine de Pisan (d. *c.* 1431) composed a treatise on women's education, *Le Livre des Trois Vertus,* and elsewhere remembered: *Si comme une fois respondis à un homme qui réprouvait mon désir de savoir disant qu'il n'appartient à femme avoir science, comme il en soit pou, lui dis que moins appartient à homme avoir ignorance, comme il en soit beaucoup.* (As I once answered a man who reproved my desire for learning, saying that it does not befit women to be learned as few of them are—I told him that it befits men even less to be ignorant, as many of them are.) [21]

Christine was a woman of unusual temperament, almost unique for her times. The ideas she attacked persisted: the weaker sex must not be exposed to "reality" or the outside world, female education was therefore dangerous, and men and women could not read the same books (Sir John Paston was advised not to let his lady's eyes fall on Ovid's *Technique of Love*). As late as the seventeenth century, when Mary Ward in England opened schools for girls, she incurred the anger and finally the condemnation of the pope for her horrifying independence and unwomanly enterprise.

The stirrings of the ideal bourgeois wife were already perceptible in the middle ages, because the Church wanted to keep women in the domestic role; sheltered from the world. Medieval culture demanded certain virtues in the female sex—gentleness, sweetness, and innocence—and it nurtured a womanly type that came to be seen as the natural character of the sex, and more virtuous than the male. In this symbolic unworldly region of dependence and obedience, women had their counterparts: the friars.

Naturally, the friars, being self-elected, had an identity as a group that women could not have, since Christian society classified them according to their fathers or husbands or sons. But women and friars shared something important in common: they could both practise, without jeopardizing their state in society, those Christian ideals that of themselves deny the possibility of worldly success. Poverty and humility and obedience presuppose a certain way of life; they cannot, like the theological virtues of faith, hope, and charity, be practised invisibly by prince and pauper, merchant and monk alike. The ideals St. Francis proclaimed attack at their very heart the laws by which western society still prospers, as the saint himself dramatized when he stood naked before his father.

Francis posed with dazzling clarity the central religious dilemma of renunciation or acceptance of the world. But his example was impracticable, except for the few mystics who chose to follow him, or for the
sections of society already so split off from the central machinery that
they could afford ideals that would *ipso facto* forfeit them wealth and
power and independence. For triumph in the realm of the spirit, the
pauper could win respect in a friar's cowl; and the woman, sweet and
submissive to her husband, could be honoured at the cradle, kitchen, and,
in medieval times, the spinning wheel.

The resemblance between the conditions of men of the Church and
women was recognized. Henry Adams maintains that priests were
counted as women in medieval society. (Both were exempt from military
service, for instance.) The Dominican witch hunter Johann Nider (d.
1438) harangued with some humour: "For there are three things in
nature, which, if they transgress the limits of their own conditions,
whether by diminution or by excess, attain to the highest pinnacle
whether of goodness or of evil. These are the tongue, the ecclesiastic and
the woman; all these are commonly best of all, so long as they are guided
by a good spirit, but worst of all, if guided by an evil spirit."[22]

More seriously, the constitution of the Second Vatican Council counselled priests to emulate the Virgin, "the protectress of their ministry,"
for "they can always find a wondrous model of such docility in the
Blessed Virgin Mary."[23]

From feudal times, men have endowed monasteries and enriched
individual churchmen—Catholics still make offerings to priests today—
so that prayer and masses will be offered to God on their behalf by men
closer to him in their way of life. The double standard that expects a
woman to be more virtuous than a man places her in the monk's relation
to his feudal benefactor, or the friar's to the rich burghers who tried to
save their souls by giving their profits to the *poverelli*. The woman in the
home can be seen as the keeper of her husband's conscience, the vicarious
Christian who is humble and obedient—and chaste—enough for two.

The new domestic idealism was projected onto the Holy Family as
part of the same movement that attributed the social customs of earth to
heaven (as in the wedding of St. Catherine), that disrobed the Virgin of
her regalia, and exchanged typology and metaphysics for anecdote. The
cult of humility, understood as female submissiveness to the head of the
house, set the seal on the Virgin's eclipse as a matriarchal symbol. Nowhere can this be seen more clearly than in the rise of Joseph in importance from the end of the fourteenth century onwards.

Previously a background figure in Byzantine nativities, fast asleep beside a rock, his back turned to the miracle, Joseph begins to occupy the centre stage and to inspire a cult in his own right. His restraint towards his bride had been singled out for praise and emulation by the Fathers of the Latin Church, like Jerome and Augustine; in the Greek calendar, his memory had been kept on July 20. But in the western Church, no feast celebrated him. Jean Gerson, the brilliant and influential chancellor of Paris, proposed at the Council of Constance in 1414 that this omission be rectified. He wrote a paean of three thousand lines to St. Joseph, which was one of the first printed books published. A feast was instituted after Gerson's death, and has wandered about the liturgical calendar ever since. It is now fixed on March 19, but another feast pays Jesus' father and Mary's husband further tribute with a gallant but clumsy gesture on May 1, and is called "Joseph the Worker."

Fresh and tender attention was paid, in Christian art from the fifteenth century on, to the details of the Holy Family's daily domestic life. The exquisite Books of Hours of the period, like Anne of Cleves', now in the Pierpont Morgan Library in New York, or the series of miniatures attributed to the Fleming Simon Benin in the Walters Gallery in Baltimore, portray Mary, Joseph, and the child by the fireside, while Joseph rocks in a chair and draws on a homely pipe, or feeds the baby from a bowl of warmed milk with a wooden spoon. In other illuminations, the infant Jesus takes his first hesitant steps in a walking frame, while Joseph supervises with proud benignity. The carpenter's shop at Nazareth provided a new and fertile source of inspiration to artists and writers who celebrate the diligence and obedience of Jesus as he fetches and carries for his father, a master craftsman. Luke's phrase, after Jesus was found among the doctors in the temple, summed up the correct attitude of a child towards his parents: "And he went down with them, and came to Nazareth, and was subject unto them . . ." (Luke 2:51).

St. Teresa of Ávila adopted Joseph as her personal patron—"the father of my soul." By the eighteenth century, he was the presiding saint of two hundred convents of her Carmelite order. St. Cajetan (d. 1547) had a vision of St. Joseph carrying the child Jesus in his arms, as the Virgin had always done before. The militant Catholic reformer of iconography, Molanus, who tried to cleanse Catholic painting after the Reformation of paganism and superstition, pointed out that the Gospels gave no indication that Joseph was aged and hoary-headed. Joseph therefore begins in Counter-Reformation painting to metamorphose from the venerable patriarch of Byzantine-influenced art into a young, raven-haired dynamic workman (figure 25). His virginity stemmed from a holy purpose, not the debility of old age. The Holy Family formed a second trinity, the earthly mirror of the heavenly triad. Murillo's *Two Trinities,* in the National Gallery in London, places Mary and Joseph on either side of Jesus with the Triune God above.

In France, the Catholic revival in the seventeenth century spawned a morass of sentimental literature about the Holy Family. Written by teachers and founders like St. Jean Eudes (d. 1680). Jean-Jacques Olier (d. 1657), Jean de Bérulle (d. 1629), and Louis-Marie Grignon de Montfort (d. 1716), pious books churned out appeals to young women to imitate the Virgin in the Nazareth household. Her purity and submissiveness and poverty became quintessential motherliness. Joseph protects her and works to keep her and the child; she is obedient, respectful, humble, quiet, and modest, simple in her tastes and demeanour, compliant, and gentle. Even her silence in the Gospels is turned to good account, becoming an example to all women to hold their tongues.

The rise of Joseph's cult as the head of the Holy Family illustrates how Christian devotion can reflect and affirm the prevailing social mode. Today in Catholic countries statues of Joseph encircling Mary with a paternal arm, can be bought in magnet form to stick on the dashboard of the family car. In Knock, now the most popular shrine of the Virgin in Ireland, the devotions focus on the hardships of Irish mothers in their family kitchens. One fast-selling holy picture at the shrine shows a wan, young mother in an apron stirring a bowl by a steaming stove. It is inscribed with the "Kitchen Prayer":

> Lord of all pots and pans and things,
> Since I've not time to be a saint
> By doing lovely things
> Or watching late with Thee
> Or dreaming in the dawn light
> Or storming heaven's gates
> Make me a saint by getting
> Meals and washing up the plates.[24]

The virtues that the Virgin Mary came to represent under the influence of the cult of poverty and humility in the middle ages are not to be scorned in themselves. But the web of social approval and religious taboo forced women in particular to cultivate those virtues or forfeit the name of women. For men in Catholic countries, the same qualities would lose them the name of man. And the type of virtues decreed feminine degenerate easily: obedience becomes docility; gentleness, irresolution; humility, cringing; forbearance, long-suffering.

Modern images of the Virgin Mary are vapid and savourless, especially when compared to the exalted matriarchs of early Christian art. But it is this very cult of the Virgin's "femininity," expressed by her sweetness, submissiveness, and passivity that permits her to survive, a goddess in a patriarchal society. For her cult flourishes in countries where women rarely participate in public life and are relegated to the domestic domain. In countries like Ireland, Spain, Portugal, Italy, and Belgium, women are not rallying for comfort to a symbol that holds out hope of something different from their lives. Mary is worshipped in places where the symbol of the subject housewife applies more readily, and therefore both reinforces and justifies the ruling state of affairs, in which women are expected to be, and are, men's devoted mothers and wives. As the anthropologist Mary Douglas has written:

If compensation theory were valid, the masses who experience control by objects would in reaction seek to differentiate more effectively. But instead they rush to adopt symbols of non-differentiation and so accentuate the condition from which they suffer. This is the dangerous backlash in symbolic experience of which we should beware. The man who has been raised up seeks symbols of his high estate; the one who has been degraded seeks symbols of debasement.[25]

The pope in eighth-century Rome worshipped *Maria Regina;* the kings and particularly the queens of thirteenth-century France looked to Our Lady of France, crowned and sceptred; the Florentine artisan of the Renaissance and the Irish housewife today find a tragically flawed consolation in the sweet maid of Nazareth, who bowed her head and submitted unmurmuringly to her destiny.

By defining the limits of womanliness as shrinking, retiring acquiescence, and by reinforcing that behaviour in the sex with praise, the myth of female inferiority and dependence could be and was perpetuated. The two arms of the Christian view of woman—the contempt and hatred evident in interpretations of the Creation and the Fall, and idealization of her more "Christian" submissive nature—meet and interlock in the advocacy of humility for the sex. The Church can therefore continue to deny women an active and independent role in its ministry. The priesthood is closed to women because they are considered a secondary image of the maker, too gentle and timid by nature, and destined to serve either their husbands and children as wives and mothers or priests and children as nuns.

*Chapter Thirteen*

# THE MILK OF PARADISE

*Tua sunt ubera
vino redolentia,
candor superat lac et lilia,
odor flores vincit et balsama.*

(*Your breasts are as fragrant
as wine; their whiteness whiter
than milk and lilies, their scent
lovelier than flowers and
balsam wood.*)[1]

—ANONYMOUS, TWELFTH CENTURY

THE VIRGIN in the Catholic Church represents motherhood in its fullness and perfection. Yet the Virgin as mother is exempt by special privilege from intercourse, from labour, and from other physical processes of ordinary childbearing. One natural biological function, however, was permitted the Virgin in Christian cult—suckling. From her earliest images onwards, the mother of God has been represented nursing her child. But the milk of the Virgin has not been a symbol of a constant, fixed content, and its varying and often extraordinary shifts of meaning contain a microcosmic history of Christian attitudes to the physicality of the female.

At a junction in the long tunnels of the catacombs of S. Priscilla in Rome, above the empty niches of the dead, a few wall paintings remain, disfigured by damp and fallen plaster. In a corner, set at right angles, is an inconspicuous ochre sketch of two figures—a prophet pointing to a star, and a mother who with a protective gesture cradles a wriggling baby in her arms and offers him her breast. This is the first known image of the Madonna and child. Painted before the third century, it looks like a Christian artisan's afterthought, a private reverie. The Virgin is drawn as the painter's contemporary, an ordinary Roman mother like many others, suckling her child on her knees (figure 3).

The theme of the nursing Virgin, *Maria Lactans,* probably originated in Egypt, where the goddess Isis had been portrayed suckling the infant Horus for over a thousand years before Christ. But the images of Isis are often remote and hieratic, very different in mood from the spontaneous catacomb painting. Enthroned, crowned with the sun disk clasped between the horns of the moon, Isis commands awe as with a frozen gesture, she offers her breast to her son (figure 32). In Egypt itself this tradition influenced the iconography of the Virgin: in two remarkable Coptic manuscripts from Fayum, dated 893 and 895 or 898 respectively, and now in the Pierpont Morgan Library, Mary also imposes her majesty and dignity on the reader as with huge, black-rimmed eyes she gazes forward above the head of the child on her knee, to whom she proffers her exposed breast (figure 33).[2]

But a less grandiose treatment of the theme existed, in the terracotta figurines that have been excavated from Egyptian tombs of mortal women kneeling on one knee and supporting the head of their babies on the other as they nourish them at the breast.[3] This type of image is intimate and almost anecdotal. By the third century, Isis was portrayed in this gentler vein, while two or three hundred years later, on a stele also found at Fayum, the Virgin nurses the child, tilting her head to one side with more human involvement and emotion.

Goddesses have suckled their divine offspring as far back as discovered civilization. Two thousand years before Christ, the goddess of Ur offered her son her breast; in Mexico in statues carved around 1000 B.C., in Liberia, the Lower Congo, the Ivory Coast, and the Gold Coast, female deities nurse their babies. In India later sculptures show the infant Krishna with his mother Dewaki.[4]

But for the Christian the mystery of the incarnate God was concentrated with unique intensity in the symbol of Mary's milk. The *Book of James,* after describing with awe the dazzling appearance of Christ on earth, then adds simply: "And it (the child) went and took the breast of his mother Mary."[5] That he, on whom all creation hangs, should hang from the breast of his human mother—it was a paradox cast on that particular dye of sublime humility that delights the Christian spirit. The Syrian poet Ephrem of Nisibin (d. 373) wrote one of Mary's first extant lullabies: "Since my son thou art, with my nursery rhymes will I soothe thee. . . . Lo, thou art with me, and whole thou art hidden in thy father. All heights of heaven are full of thy majesty, and yet my bosom is not too straitened for thee. . . ."[6]

Milk symbolized the full humanity of Jesus at one level, but it also belonged in an ancient and complex symbolic language. For milk was a crucial metaphor of the gift of life. Without it, a child had little or no chance of survival before the days of baby foods, and its almost miraculous appearance seemed as providential as the conception and birth of the child itself. The milk of the Mother of God became even more highly charged with the symbolism of life, for the life of life's own source depended on it. When the medieval mystic meditated on the Incarnation, he saw not only a mother nursing her baby—an event in historical time—but an eternal mystery whereby the Christian soul is perpetually nourished and sustained by grace, of which Mary's milk is a sublime epiphany. Thus the Church too, *Ecclesia,* associated with Mary, is depicted as a mother, as in Isaiah's passage on Jerusalem, which is now read in the mass of the feast of Our Lady of Lourdes: "Behold, I will extend peace to her like a river, and the glory of the Gentiles like a flowing stream: then shall ye suck, ye shall be borne upon her sides, and be dandled upon her knees" (Isaiah 66:12).

In the Old Testament, milk and honey form the twin images of the promised land, which to men and women of the New Covenant is the paradise of the afterlife. Tertullian in the third century describes an early Christian version of baptism in which the neophytes are given milk and honey to eat, as pledges of their rebirth into a new world, where they will acquire wisdom. Mystery cults of the early Christian period, through which the initiates sought knowledge, also used milk and honey.[7] As attributes of new life and wisdom, milk and honey were associated with the Messiah, who would, prophesied Isaiah, live on them in the wilderness (Isaiah 7:14–22). The honey the Jews ate was wild, for bee-keeping is not mentioned in the Bible, and Isaiah's imagery foretells that the Jews will overcome their subjection by abandoning the settled lives of agriculturalists and reverting to pastoral nomadism and survival off the natural bounty of the land.[8] Neither milk nor honey require any preparation to eat, but appear spontaneously in full perfection. No rites of purification attend their consumption: they are pristine. Eaten raw, they taste cooked. As symbols of nature's goodness, they are kin to sap and dew, which are also wild, but they are also nutritious in themselves. Unlike wine, another prime symbol of fertility and life, they undergo no process at the hand of man, and in their innocence are thus distinguished from other sources of nourishment. In the catalogue of effluvia milk therefore occupies a very different place.

The Wisdom books of the Old Testament constantly return to the twin symbol, and particularly to honey. "My son," says the Book of Proverbs, "eat thou honey, because it is good; and the honeycomb, which is sweet to thy taste: So shall the knowledge of Wisdom be unto thy soul . . ." (Proverbs 24:13–14). In Ecclesiasticus, the figure of Wisdom describes herself in a passage included in the Virgin's liturgy: "I am the mother of fair love, and fear, and knowledge and holy hope . . . my memorial is sweeter than honey and mine inheritance than the honeycomb" (Ecclesiasticus 24:18–20).

Proverbs, written in the fourth to third century B.C., and Ecclesiasticus, written around 200 B.C., were both influenced in their conception of Sophia—or Wisdom—by Alexandrian philosophy. In the crucible of Alexandria various religious philosophies sparkled and fused. Philo Judaeus had inspired a school of ecstatic mysticism dedicated to acquiring wisdom, personified, as in the Bible, as a female figure. In her embrace the seeker could obtain knowledge. The symbolism of milk and honey combined with the Egyptian religious tradition, in which the goddess Isis suckled her devotees. In a fine Nubian temple wall painting, Isis stands before the legendary Pharaoh Sesostris, offering him her breast. It flows with milk like a pitcher, while the inscription reads: "With my milk pure life shall pass into thy members."[9] The essence of the goddess infuses her votary with new strength—it is a eucharistic idea that returns, as we shall see, in medieval mysticism.

In Gnostic-tinged writings of the early Christian period, like the *Passion of Saints Perpetua and Felicity,* milk symbolizes in an even more pronounced way this cluster of ideas, uniting knowledge, new life, and paradise. In the apocryphal *Odes of Solomon,* written before the third century, milk is the vehicle of the conception of the Logos. Mary describes the virgin birth as a series of exchanges of wisdom and power: "A cup of milk was offered to me: and I drank it in the sweetness of the delight of the Lord. The son is the cup, and He who is milked is the Father, and the Holy Spirit milked him, because his breasts were full, and it was necessary for him that his milk should be sufficiently released."[10]

The classical Greek myths also lent their weight to the metaphysical significance of milk and of honey. Zeus was suckled by Amaltheia, who in some versions of the myth was a nanny goat and in others a mortal, the wife of Melisseus, father of Ida. Melisseus, from the Greek word for bee, *melissa,* means the bee-man; while Ida is a mountain in Greece famous for its wild honey. So Zeus's nurse provided him with milk; her husband with honey. In some accounts of the infancy of Dionysus, another pastoral god, the nymph Macris raised him on milk and honey.

The Romans also connected both with the eternity of the heavens. For on one night Juno's milk, when she was nursing Hercules, sprayed across the sky and created the Milky Way, our galaxy. The Greek *galaktos* means milk; *lac,* the Latin for milk, derives from the same root. The philosopher Macrobius (d. first century) who held the neoplatonist view that the soul descended from a high pure state among the stars into the lower material element of the body, wrote that the heavenly origins of infants accounted for the milk that first nourished them: "The nutriment of milk is first offered to infants, because their first motion commences from the galaxy, when they begin to fall into terrene bodies."[11] Macrobius' work was known to Bede, who apostrophized the breasts of the Virgin, using the same cosmology:

> *Beata cujus ubera*
> *Summo repleta munere*
> *Terris alebant unicam*
> *Terrae polique gloriam . . .*

(Thou whose blessed breasts, filled with a gift from on high, fed for all lands the unique glory of earth and heaven . . .).[12]

Thus the highest life was expressed by the milk of a mother—white, gleaming, and moist, a pure equivalent of astral light.

Within this cluster of images, the imagination of the great medieval saints Anselm of Canterbury (1033–1109) and Bernard of Clairvaux crystallized one of the most original devotions of the Christian Church.

As in the *Odes of Solomon,* the symbol of motherhood was not restricted to its prime historical level but was used typologically with rare flexibility and inventiveness, leaping the barrier of sexual polarity until God himself becomes a nursing mother, the epitome of *caritas,* love.

In his "Prayer to St. Paul," Anselm sustains for verse after verse a highly wrought and emotional plea to the saint to love him and shelter him as a mother would:

> Do, mother of my soul,
> what the mother of my flesh would do.

He turns rapidly from Paul to Christ and back again, begging him with anguished repentance to take him under his wings as a broody hen and warm his inanimate soul back to life again:

> Christ, my mother,
> you gather your chickens under your wings;
> this dead chicken of yours puts himself under
> > those wings.

The inverted imagery is used to maximum dramatic effect, and with such daring that the traditional language of God gains enormous fresh-ness and vitality:

> So you, Lord God, are the great mother.[13]

Bernard developed this same element of surprise in his invocations of Christ. But, with Cistercian starkness, Bernard tempered the imagery. No broody hen for him, but the naked embrace of the bloody body of the crucified God: "Suck not the wounds, but rather the breasts of the cruci-fied. He shall be as a mother to you, and you as a son to him."[14]

The imagery of milk as the sustenance of the Christian soul returns again in his sermons on the Canticle, where he characteristically applies it on many gliding and overlapping levels. He takes the text: "Thy lips, my spouse, drop as the honeycomb; honey and milk are under thy tongue . . ." (Song of Solomon 4:11) and paints the kiss of the Church and Christ her bridegroom:

> He gives her the kiss she had longed for . . . and so great is the power of that kiss that she at once conceives and her bosom swells with milk. . . . So too we approach the altar of God and pray, and, if we but persevere, despite our own dryness and tepidity, grace will overpower us, our bosom will swell, love will fill our hearts . . . and the milk of sweetness will overflow everywhere in a torrent.[15]

It is a remarkable passage, brimming with Bernard's magnificent in-temperateness. But milk for him was not only a learned symbol, used after study of the Bible and the classics. Bernard also took its meaning personally, and remarked angrily on women who did not nurse their own children. His own mother had suckled all seven of her offspring: "the noble lady disdained to commit them to another's breasts, but infused into them something of her own goodness with this mother's milk."[16]

The nursing Virgin is not the focus of Bernard's Marian rhapsodies, but the love of her that enlivened all his work quickly and logically developed a legend: Bernard was reciting the *Ave Maris Stella* before a statue of the Virgin in the church of St. Vorles at Châtillon-sur-Seine, and when he came to the words *Monstra esse matrem* (Show thyself a mother), the Virgin appeared before him and, pressing her breast, let three drops of milk fall onto his lips (figure 31).

The legend, which was painted by Perugino (d. 1523) in a graceful, lyrical altarpiece now in Munich and frescoed by Filippino Lippi (d. 1504) in the Badia church in Florence, was in wide circulation in the Renaissance, and was recorded in Manrique's *Annals of the Cistercian Order*, published in 1642, which inspired Murillo's enraptured version of the vision.[17] It encapsulates vividly the intimacy with which a holy man can expect to experience God, and the nearness of heaven on earth. The Virgin gives her faithful saint a material pledge of her reality and of her love, three drops of the milk that nourished the Redeemer. This short, short step between the material and the spiritual gives Catholics their adamantine sense of certainty. Mary's milk is an emanation of heaven, spun as it were in the silk of the Redeemer himself, and Bernard tasted it on his lips.

Bernard was not alone. The complex of symbolism that associated the Virgin with Wisdom and with the Church transformed her into the nursing mother of many penitents, visionaries, and saints. In the east, her identification with Wisdom is very close: Sophia appears, for instance, in an Armenian Gospel miniature of 1323 suckling the apostles Peter and Paul. In the west, her adventures are less metaphysical. The story of Bernard's vision was also told of the mystic Henry Suso (d. 1365) and of the promoter of the rosary, Alanus de Rupe (d. 1475).[18]

In the earliest collection of miracles of the Virgin, a story is told that reappears again and again in the later compilations—made principally by Cistercians and Dominicans—which were the medieval man's most popular reading matter. A monk is dying of a putrid disease of the mouth, and his nose and lips have been eaten away by ulcers. His fellow monks have given him up for dead. He reproaches the Madonna, reminding her with bitterness that he has faithfully invoked her daily in the words of the woman of the Gospels: "Blessed is the womb that bare thee and the paps which thou hast sucked" (Luke 11:27). The Virgin, suitably chastened by her swain's reproof, appears at his bedside and, as described by Gautier de Coincy, who wrote down the story in French in 1223:

> *Moult doucement et par grant delit*
> *De son douz sain trait sa mamele*
> *Qui tant est douce, sade et bele,*
> *Et li boute dedenz la bouche,*
> *Moult doucement partout li touche,*
> *Et arouse de son douz lait.*

1

Joseph is chosen as the Virgin's husband and guardian, and the defeated suitors break their staffs, which failed to flower. In the miniatures, St. Joachim prays for a child, embraces St. Anne at the Golden Gate, who gives birth to the Virgin, dedicates her to the temple, where she leads an exemplary life of prayer, and weaves the purple veil of the sanctuary. Master of the Duke of Bedford, Book of Hours, fifteenth century. (Chapter 2)

2

As in St. Bridget of Sweden's visions, the Virgin Mary looses her blond hair, and on her knees gives birth to Jesus, whose radiance eclipses the taper St. Joseph holds in his hands; the midwife Salome (*right*), who doubted Mary's virginity, extends the hand that withered when she blasphemously examined her. Robert Campin (d. 1444), *The Nativity,* Dijon. (Chapters 2 and 3)

3

The cycle of Redemption: the first Eve is thrown out of Eden and closes paradise to mankind, but the Virgin Mary, the Second Eve, accepts the words of the angel and conceives the redeemer who will restore humanity to the grace of God and reopen the gates of heaven. Giovanni di Paolo, *The Annunciation*, detail, *c.* 1445. (Chapter 4)

The three kings symbolize earthly power, and their homage to the humble baby in his ruined stall signifies the capitulation of worldly monarchs to the ruler of all. Sandro Botticelli (d. 1482), *The Adoration of the Magi.* (Chapter 7)

4

At the Virgin's Dormition, or death, St. John lays his head on her breast, St. Peter mourns at her feet, and Christ holds up her childlike soul. La Martorana, Palermo, 1143. (Chapter 6)

5

The lover in the Song of Songs, Christ embraces his mother, enthroned by his side as his queen and his bride in a twelfth-century mosaic in S. Maria in Trastevere, Rome. (Chapter 8)

6

The supreme image of promised transfiguration after death: Titian's *Assumption of the Virgin,* in which the apostles on earth reach out in awe and ecstasy towards the barefoot Madonna, who rises, borne upwards by angels and cherubim, into the golden corona of heaven, where God awaits her. S. Maria Gloriosa dei Frari, Venice, 1518. (Chapter 6)

The immaculate conception of Mary: a ray from heaven illuminates in St. Anne's womb the child she conceived without the stain of original sin. Hours of the Virgin, Bruges ?, *c.* 1515, by the Master of the Grimani Breviary. (Chapter 16)

Opposite, above: conceived "before the beginning" in the mind of the Creator, the ideal of womanhood floats on the moon with the twelve stars of the Apocalypse around her head. Diego Velásquez, *The Immaculate Conception,* seventeenth century. (Chapter 16)

Opposite, below: in Giovanni Bellini's *Pietà,* the Virgin laments over the dead body of her son. But the image of sorrow holds the promise of joy and resurrection: the winter landscape blossoms with the first flowers of spring. Accademia, Venice, sixteenth century. (Chapter 14)

9

10

VII

11

Piero della Francesca, *Madonna della Misericordia:* the Virgin Mary, an independent and monumental *magna mater,* spreads her cloak to shelter lay men and women who have sought her protection. *C.* 1445–8. (Chapter 21)

(With much sweetness and much delight, from her sweet bosom she drew forth her breast, that is so sweet, so soft, so beautiful, and placed it in his mouth, [and] gently touched him all about and sprinkled him with her sweet milk.)[19]

Needless to say, the monk was miraculously rendered whole again (figure 30).

Gautier thoroughly enjoyed his miracle stories, and he fails to draw an edifying moral from the cure of the monk. John of Garland, who gathered together many of the same miracles in his *Stella Maris* collection twenty years or so later, strives manfully to bring out the story's spiritual content. His monk is a worldly rascal, who in the delirium of illness has bitten away his lips and tongue. The Virgin appears and applies the healing balm of her milk:

> *Lac est vere virginale*
> *Nectar vite spiritale*
> *Quo mors victa commit.*

(Her milk is truly virginal, nectar of the spiritual life, through which death meets its defeat.)[20] The monk is not only healed in body, but repents as well.

The Blessed Paula of Florence, an anchorite, was rewarded for her sanctity around the year 1368 by the gift of the Virgin's milk in a vision.[21] But in her case the meaning of the symbol has shifted from wisdom to mercy, and the Virgin's milk has come to represent her intercession on behalf of mankind. The Cistercian Arnaud de Chartres (d. 1156), abbot of Bonneval, and St. Bernard's contemporary, described in a sermon the gesture of Hecuba when in the *Iliad* she bares her breasts and implores her son Hector not to fight Achilles; and after him the image passed into popular usage.[22]

In French miracle plays and Italian *laude,* Jesus displays the wounds he received to save humanity; Mary exposes the breasts with which she nourished him to encourage his mediation with God the Father. For, as a dutiful and loving son, Jesus can refuse his mother nothing. She says to him:

> *Doulz chier filz, vez cy la mamelle*
> *Dont je te norry bonnement.*

> Dear sweet son, regard the breast,
> with which I nursed you well.[23]

An early fifteenth-century painting from the cathedral in Florence, now in the Cloisters in New York, presents this dramatic scene. Mary, baring her breast, kneels beside Christ, who uncovers the stigmata of his passion, and in this attitude of supplication she begs him to intercede with the Father for the sinners huddled on their knees around her mantle: "Dearest son," reads the Italian inscription, "because of the milk I gave you, have mercy on them." God the Father above, in a flaming aureole, grants the prayers of mother and son (figure 26). A late fifteenth-century painting in the Palazzo Comunale, Chieti, extends the metaphor even further: streams of milk flow from Mary's breasts into the mouths of sufferers in Purgatory.[24]

The association of Mary's milk with her powers of intercession and healing inspired an extraordinary quantity of relics in Europe. From the thirteenth century, phials in which her milk was preserved were venerated all over Christendom in shrines that attracted pilgrims by the thousands. Walsingham, Chartres, Genoa, Rome, Venice, Avignon, Padua, Aix-en-Provence, Toulon, Paris, Naples, all possessed the precious and efficacious substance. Sometimes the relic purported to be a piece of the ground of the grotto at Bethlehem where a few drops had spilt while Mary was nursing. This place, known as the Milk Grotto, can still be visited by tourists to the Holy Land.

At other times the Virgin's milk had appeared miraculously, transcendental milk from heaven. It sometimes liquefied on certain feastdays, as if it were fresh. And it had the advantage, unlike a saint's head or body, of being almost infinitely divisible. Calvin gave the subject a withering paragraph in his *Treatise on Relics:* "There is no town so small, nor convent . . . so mean that it does not display some of the Virgin's milk. . . . There is so much that if the holy Virgin had been a cow, or a wet nurse all her life she would have been hard put to it to yield such a great quantity."[25]

A yet more curious development in the cult of the Madonna's milk was the application of the legend of the unicorn to the mystery of the Incarnation. According to the widely read and much loved bestiary, the *Physiologus,* the unicorn was a beast of fabulous swiftness, strength, and beauty, and could only be captured by a virgin. If huntsmen wished to seize a unicorn, they had to lure him with a spotless maid, whose scent would overpower all the animal's natural ferocity. Docile as a lamb, he would then lie in her lap and suckle at her breast. It would so intoxicate him that the huntsmen could move in on him unawares, to lead him off captive to the palace of their king. The story's origins are mysterious, and probably eastern. Pope Gregory the Great (d. 604) was the first to apply it to Jesus. By the fourteenth century it was an established allegory, not only of human love (the troubadours used it) but of the love of Christ for mankind. The unicorn is a type of the incarnate Redeemer who raised "a horn of salvation" for our sins; and the virgin who ensnares him is Mary his mother, whose virtue he could not resist. And once he has succumbed to her, become her baby, and suckled at her breast, he is doomed to die, hunted and buffeted so that he can lead the throng of the redeemed into the "king's palace" of paradise.[26]

From the beginning of the thirteenth century the *significatio* of the allegory was expounded in art along scholastic lines. Mary sits in the *hortus conclusus,* surrounded by other biblical types of her virginity: pots of lilies, of manna, of gold. Gabriel, dressed as a huntsman, appears with a pack of hounds in full cry. They are often labelled Mercy, Truth, Justice, and Peace, and they assault the unicorn, who has laid his head in the Virgin's lap, and claim him for mankind (see figure 29).[27]

A learned English poem of the early fourteenth century, attributed to the Franciscan William of Shoreham, invokes Mary under her multifarious biblical titles, including such recherché images as David's sling— "thy son the stone"—which slew Goliath. In one verse he uses the unicorn legend:

> That unicorn that was so wild
> Aleyd is of a cheaste;
> Thou has itamed and istild
> With milke of thy breste.[28]

Unsurprisingly, the hunt was outlawed as an allegory of the Incarnation in Christian art by the Council of Trent in 1563. But by then medieval taste for outlandish and extended metaphors had long been superseded, and the nursing Virgin become a simple human mother, not a metaphysical type. The shift from twelfth-century high-flown philosophy to the violence and despair of the late middle ages can even be perceived in a symbol like the milk of the Virgin. For by the fourteenth century the profound associations of milk with paradise and wisdom had yielded before the new concept of the nursing Virgin's humility.

The suckling of Christ by his mother served as the supreme example of her exemplary lowliness. The Madonna of Humility, painted sitting on the ground, sometimes with bare feet, often nurses the child at her breast. Such a connection obviously depended on social prejudices that made breast-feeding an act of humiliation. But the prejudices themselves were bound up with Christian teaching. Womankind had been especially punished for Eve's sin by the sufferings of childbearing in all its biological aspects, from menstruation to lactation. One result of the Fall, depicted in medieval illuminations of Adam and Eve, was suckling. After the expulsion from Eden, Adam delves and Eve, nursing, spins (figure 27). In the fourteenth and the first half of the fifteenth century the loss of paradise weighed especially on a fearful and credulous populace. Eustache Deschamps (d. *c.* 1406), the French balladeer and poet, wrote Adam's lament on the wretchedness of mankind:

> *Perpetuel puis eusmes soif et faim,*
> *Labour, dolour, et enfans en tristesce;*
> *Pour noz pechiez enfantent a destresce*
> *Toutes femmes; vilment estes concuz.*

(Afterwards we were perpetually thirsty and hungry. We laboured, we suffered, children were born in sorrow; For our sins, all women bear children in pain; vilely you are conceived.)[29] Preachers encouraging women to follow lives of virginity take up the old motif of the Fathers, that the celibate life spares a woman the sorrows and hardships of childbirth and children.

It was a message that had repercussions in the cult of the Virgin. For, if woman was considered inferior because of her greater subjection to biology, then the Virgin, by accepting that female destiny, by bearing and suckling a child, revealed her model humility as touchingly to medieval contemplatives as did Christ when he consented to become man.

However, because the Virgin had become like other mothers, the Incarnation itself could be depicted as a gentle domestic drama, and the mystery distilled into the sweet phrases of folksong and lullabies. English medieval poetry contains hundreds of examples of this new mood. In one particularly poignant song written around 1375, the Virgin asks the baby's forgiveness:

> Jesu, sweete, be not wroth,
> Though I n'ave clout ne cloth
> Thee on for to fold,
> Thee on for to folde ne to wrap,
> For I n'ave clout ne lap;
> But lay thou thy feet to my pap
> And wite thee from the cold.[30]

The same strain is caught in European paintings of the nursing Virgin, particularly in the fourteenth century. The earliest western example of Maria Lactans appears in a twelfth-century mosaic on the façade of S. Maria Trastevere in Rome, but it is regal and imposing in character, like the statues of the goddess Isis. In the Trecento, the new intimacy and tenderness soften the image, and in Sassetta's exquisite version in the Metropolitan in New York, the Virgin is the sweetest blonde young mother holding a new baby to her immaculate breast, against an azure field. During the course of the next hundred years, the background becomes more concrete and anecdotal. In Robert Campin's masterpiece in the National Gallery in London, the mother and child sit in a meticulously conceived contemporary parlour; and in Joos van Cleve's *Nursing Virgin*, Mary's half smile and the drowsy child epitomize domestic happiness (figure 34).

But as the Renaissance advanced, the image of the nursing Virgin waned in popularity. Molanus, the most prominent Catholic reformer of iconography, tried to defend its use, but he could not single-handedly alter prejudice.[31] The Virgin was already moving back onto her pedestal in the fifteenth century, and a century later the distinction between a lady and a peasant in the matter of breast-feeding was so unambiguously established that Clouet painted the king's favourite, Diane de Poitiers, naked in her bath, displaying her cool small rosy bosom while in the background a coarse wetnurse with a jolly and vulgar smile gives suck to a child from her swelling breast.

Snobbery, however, was not the only reason for the virtual disappearance of the nursing Madonna. Purity's alliance with modesty, and shame at the naked female body's beauty, contributed. It became indecorous for the Virgin to bare her breast. For when, at the orders of Pope Paul IV (1555-9), the painter Daniele da Volterra began clothing the nudes in the Sistine Chapel—hence his nickname *il Braghettone* (the Trouserer) —he represented most eloquently the renewed asceticism of the Catholic Church. Puritanism was not only the province of the Reformers. And the Counter-Reformers had reasons for their concern over voluptuousness in Christian art. For instance, it was reputed that Jean Fouquet had painted King Charles VII's mistress, Agnès Sorel, as the Mother of God. Against a backdrop of scarlet and sapphire seraphim—spirits of day and night— Agnès sits enthroned, her small petulant mouth pursed, her preternaturally high forehead (shaven, as was the fashion) crowned with jewels, while from her flirtatious bodice a round firm breast bursts forth (figure 28).[32] Savonarola's bonfire of vanities at the end of the fifteenth century had consumed just such blasphemies as this—likenesses by Botticelli and others of pretty young Italians dressed up as the Virgin—and no doubt the enraged Dominican would have itched to burn Fouquet's portrait too if he had laid eyes on it.

Another growing idea of more importance also led to the decline of the symbol of Mary's milk. For the controversy over her Immaculate Conception was in full swing in the fifteenth century. Mary had been spared, according to many among the faithful, the stain of original sin (see Chapter 16). One of the consequences of the Fall had been the suffering of women in parturition, and suckling was traditionally considered an integral part of this penalty.

The image of the Virgin suckling Christ represented women's humility in accepting the full human condition. It is interesting, however, that, as Millard Meiss has emphasized, the Dominicans were particularly instrumental in fostering the cult of the nursing Virgin. They were the only order in the Church that continually and vehemently opposed the growing belief in the Immaculate Conception of Mary. And if Mary was free from all stain of original sin, then lactation might not be her inheritance. The opposition of the Dominicans was eventually overcome, as we shall see, and the milk of the Virgin disappears from the Christian symbolic repertory. One of the few contemporary survivals of this unique metaphor of wisdom, paradise, mercy, and humility is a popular German wine—Liebfraumilch; it is the end of the road of one of Christian mysticism's more potent images.

Although the Virgin herself has become too exalted to suckle her child, many of the ideas that contributed to the cult of her milk still endure in Catholic countries' attitudes to breast-feeding. As the Spanish contemporary writer Lidia Falcon points out in her book *Cartas a una Idiota Espanola* (Letters to a Stupid Spanish Woman), mothers in Spain are prevailed upon to breast-feed, even when it is difficult and painful. The Catholic notion of the "natural" being good, which makes rhythm an acceptable form of contraception while any other is not, underlies this enthusiasm for natural suckling; but more sinisterly, the idea that women must submit to the biological destiny of the Fall also lends its support. Lactation, as well as the pain of labour, is a prime part of that penalty.

With vehement passion, Falcon accuses Spanish gynaecologists of retaining women in the reproductive role by refusing to prescribe contraceptives and by increasing maternal suffering by insisting on "natural" childbirth and mother's milk.[33] As in the case of the virgin birth and virginity, a mystical idea—the suckling of the incarnate God—is translated onto a sociological plane, where its import becomes very different and oppressive. Paradoxically when this, a Christian affirmation of the created world and its processes, symbolized by the cult of Mary's milk, is applied to the female sex in particular, it becomes a means of underpinning women's subjection to their biology, and of denying them freedom to reject it or overcome it through the medical means available.

Apart from her milk, the Virgin was allowed another human activity, another source of physical effluvia that expressed her motherhood of men: she wept. For at the same time as her maternal love of the infant Christ was celebrated in poetry and art, her grief at the grown Christ's death inspired a passionate cult of the *Mater Dolorosa*.

## Chapter Fourteen

# MATER DOLOROSA

*Holy Mary, pierce me through*
*In my heart each wound renew*
*Of my saviour crucified.*[1]

—POPULAR PRAYER

F IVE THOUSAND YEARS AGO, in the dust-blown plain of Sumer or south-ern Mesopotamia, during the month of August, when nature's anger was most pitiless and the scorched earth and relentless drought held the farmer captive, a chant went up as the priests invoked the life-giving powers of the new season and recited the annual liturgies of Dumuzi, the shepherd, and Inanna, the queen of heaven, his mother and his bride. Dumuzi had been sacrificed to the underworld, tortured and afflicted by demons, just as Christ suffered the tortures of his passion and then descended into hell. Inanna the goddess weeps for him:

> Into his face she stares, seeing
> what she has lost—his mother
> who has lost him to death's kingdom.
> O the agony she bears,
>     shuddering in the wilderness,
>     she is the mother suffering so much.[2]

It could be a poem on a Christian icon of the Pietà: the dead Christ laid out on his grieving mother's knees (colour plate VII, figure 10).

In the religion of Sumer, Inanna was the "Lady of Heaven," the presiding genius of the earth, and Dumuzi the guardian of flocks, the god of the sap and waters of spring, a shepherd "in love with the song of flutes." His name means "true son," and in some Sumerian laments he is called Damu, the child.[3] In the liturgical poem *Inanna's Journey* the goddess yields him up to the powers of the underworld as her surrogate:

> And the seven devils gripped his thighs
>> like mortal sickness.
> The flute-song of the shepherd
>> is broken, the pipes are shattered
>>> in front of him,
> for on him Inanna has fastened
>> the eyes of death . . .[4]

Dumuzi, pursued by monsters of drought and death and sterility, is abandoned to the merciless desert sun in the burning wasteland that is the Sumerian hell. He escapes, but they come at him again:

> They flew at his face with hooks and bits
> and bodkins, they slashed his body with a heavy-axe . . .

He escapes them again, but the devils seek him out, and after this, the Sumerian Way of the Cross, Dumuzi is taken down into death.[5]

Inanna, his spouse, then weeps for him, and his mother and sister Geshtinanna keen with her. His sister's name means "Lady of Desolation," and in the songs the singers are not distinguished, but a triad symbolizing woman in her relation to man under the one aspect of Lady of Sorrows. For Inanna is his wife, but he is also her "Child." Inanna's ritual grief is described:

> My heart is piping in the wilderness
> where the young man once went free.
> He is a prisoner now in death's kingdom,
>> lies bound where once he lived . . .
> My heart is piping in the wilderness
>> an instrument of grief . . .
> she is the mother desolate
> in a desolate place; where once
> he was alive, now he lies
> like a young bull felled to the ground.[6]

Inanna weeps, though she herself delivered Dumuzi to his fate; in Christian belief the Virgin Mary mourns, though she consented to the Incarnation and the Atonement, and knows that Christ will rise again.

The parallels between pagan and Christian mythology have been ex-
haustively discussed early this century by eminent anthropologists and
historians, like Frazer, who saw the Christian atonement as the last version of the ancient sacrifice of the fertility god. This subject is too broad
to discuss here. But it is occasionally possible to pinpoint an exact location of interchange in the cult of the Virgin Mary, as in Ephesus or Rome
or the Nile Valley, where one pagan goddess was supplanted by the
Christian mother; and it is always easy to perceive psychological anal-
ogies between the *magna mater* worship of the middle east and the
Mariolatry of the Mediterranean now.[7] But it is startling and profoundly
moving when the words of the world's oldest surviving literature—the
liturgies of Sumer, written around 3000 B.C.—correspond so closely to
Christian cult that an actual historical chain of descent can be postulated.

When Abraham left Ur of the Chaldees after the fall of the Sumero-
Akkadian empire of the Third Dynasty of Ur (2170–2062 B.C.), he took
with him memories of its culture and rituals that deeply affected the
development of the Bible and the practices of the Jews.[8] The funeral
lamentations of women mourners endured as a characteristic custom of
the middle east into biblical times and after. When Yahweh thunders at
Ezekiel, a prophet writing among the Babylonian exiles, after the fall
of Jerusalem in 587 B.C., he includes among the chief abominations of
this world "the women weeping for Tammuz" (Ezekiel 8:14). (Dumuzi
becomes Tammuz, Inanna Ishtar in the Babylonian inheritance of Sumerian religion). In other prophetic books of the Bible, the cult of Tammuz,
with its ritual prostitution and worship of trees, comes in for further
abuse. (See Daniel 11:37; Hosea 4:14; Isaiah 1:29; 17:10.) As late as
the tenth century A.D., a traveller in Arab countries observed: "All the
Sabaeans of our time, those of Babylonia as well as those of Harran,
lament and weep to this day over Tammuz at a festival which they, more
particularly the women, hold in the month of the same name."[9]

Similarly, in Egypt, the cult of Isis centred on the death of her spouse
and son Osiris, for whom the goddess weeps bitterly before she triumphantly resuscitates him, using the Egyptian rites of embalmment and
mummification she invented for the purpose. Plutarch has left us a full
account of this Egyptian myth, which was recounted and celebrated
every year at the autumn festival. Osiris is killed, and Isis, keening for her
lost love, wanders the world in search of his body; when she finds it,
"the Goddess threw herself upon the coffin with . . . dreadful wailing. . . ." Then, "when she was quite by herself, she opened the chest
and laid her face upon the face within it and caressed it and wept."[10]

The image of the goddess with the miniature mummy of the dead

Osiris across her knees, of which there are examples in the British Museum (figure 35), forms a diptych with the image of the goddess nursing Horus, Osiris' son, just as in countless Gothic and Renaissance treatments of the Pietà, the slumped body of Christ is disproportionately small and the face of the Virgin anachronistically young in order to recall, with tragic irony, the mother who once held a baby in her arms (figure 36). Although there exist no Christian examples before the middle ages, the image of the Pietà may have been influenced by the image of Isis and the dead Osiris. The cult of Isis lasted in Egypt well into the Christian period: Justinian closed her last temple at Philae, in the south, in the sixth century.

The weeping of the Virgin Mary for the dead Christ was dramatized in poetry at the same date. In Syria, where the tradition of loud public lamentation at death had never ceased, Jacob of Sarug (d. 521) and the gifted poet and hymn-writer Romanos Melodos, a converted Jew from Syria, both wrote on Mary's compassion at the foot of the Cross in vivid personal terms.[11] In Romanos' lament, written for the Emperor Justinian in Constantinople for the feast of Good Friday, Mary asks bitterly why God himself should have to suffer such a cruel death. Christ gently persuades her that it is his will, to which she must submit.

The poem is written in an acrostic form called *kontakion*, which Romanos himself invented. The stanzas are tossed back and forth between a soloist in the pulpit and the choir below in an urgent and rapid dialogue, punctuated by a repeated profession of faith. Mary cries out:

> I am overwhelmed, o my son
> I am overwhelmed by love
> And I cannot endure
> That I should be in the chamber
> And you on the wood of the cross
> I in the house
> And you in the tomb.[12]

The *kontakion* is a highly energetic form, beautifully suited to dramatic use. It appears in the Good Friday liturgy in the west as early as the ninth or tenth century, in the striking and tragic Reproaches or *improperia*. At the moment in the ceremony that symbolizes the hours of Christ on the Cross, he cries out against mankind for their cruelty towards him. Two deacons, concealed in the shadows behind the crucifix, sing in the voice of Jesus and bitterly castigate humanity for betraying him unto death. As the cross is gradually advanced for adoration by the chanting deacons, the celebrants and the congregation stand and watch, like a Greek chorus, the witnesses and also the accomplices of the tragedy, interjecting after each fresh reproach an acclamation of Christ's divinity.[13]

The eastern intensity of feeling created these living forms of expression, in which the mystery of the atonement was powerfully conveyed in immediate personal terms. And although, as in the case of the Easter liturgy, exchanges of ideas, legends, and iconography between the Greek Church and the Latin took place before the middle ages, it was at the time of the crusades that the halves of Christendom truly interacted and the west was infused with a new, vibrant spirit of religious faith and was inspired to a more immediate fashion of worship.

The cult of the *Mater Dolorosa* begins to rise in Italy, France, England, the Netherlands, and Spain from the end of the eleventh century, to reach full flowering in the fourteenth, from the time when the holy places were recaptured and the pilgrim traffic to the Holy Land became a constant stream.

Exposure to the passionate religious psyche of the east stimulated the new mystical mood of medieval western Christendom. In the thought of Bernard and the Cistercians, and later of Francis and the friars, the humanity of Christ—first as a helpless baby clinging to his mother or sleeping in a wooden cradle, and later as the Man of Sorrows, bloodied and bullied on man's account—was the single most important catalyst to the experience of love and faith. Bernard focussed on the wounds of Christ, which bathed the sinner in purifying water and nourishing blood. He preached that Mary was martyred, not in the body but in the spirit, and that the sword Simeon prophesied would pierce her soul drew forth spiritual graces for mankind. Like the beloved in the Canticle, Mary is wounded with the sweet pain of love. The mother of love (*caritas*) itself is herself transfixed with love in order that its sweetness may flow over the faithful.[14]

But the spontaneous vernacular character that the cult of the mourning mother acquired was really the creation of the Franciscans. A hundred years after Bernard, Francis of Assisi carried mystical Cistercian involvement with the Passion to a logical, but awe-inspiring climax, when, on Mount Alvernia on September 24, 1224, two years before his death, the saint was contemplating the sufferings of Christ with such pity and intensity that the marks of Christ's wounds appeared on his own body, stigmatizing him on side and hands and feet.

Francis' flair for the simple visual parable or gesture, and his order's determination to preach the Gospel among the lowest, hitherto cut off by ignorance of Latin and neglected by the clergy, inspired cult practices in a vernacular more universal than speech itself—the language of drama and image. The mystical typology of Christian devotion, so characteristic even of Bernard's passionate sermons, was abandoned in favour of the most literal, concrete, and emotional interpretation. As we have seen, the practice of the crib brought the Gospels to vivid life; similarly, the Stations of the Cross dramatized the Passion with stirring realism. Pilgrims and crusaders returning from the Holy Land brought back memories of the *Via Dolorosa*, the very path Jesus himself had trod, as laid out in Jerusalem. The friars in Europe re-created the scene and the events so that the thousands of Christians who could not afford the long, dangerous, and expensive journey could experience the Passion for themselves at home. The Stations of the Cross were a cycle of meditations that operated as satellite television of some great international event does now: it reported the drama of Christ's sufferings at first hand.

The Virgin, however, does not play a great part in the Passion as described by the four evangelists. Only the Fourth Gospel mentions her vigil at the Cross (John 19:2); the Synoptics do not describe her participation at any stage along the way. But the impetus of love for the Virgin, the intense belief in the mother and son's communion inspired a series of stories contained in the Stations of the Cross and innumerable paintings and sculptures: of Mary meeting Jesus on the way to Calvary, of Mary staunching Christ's wounds (figure 38), of Mary taking the body in her arms after the descent from the Cross (figure 37), of her helping to lay out, anoint, and bind the body before the burial. Through her, the Crucifixion, the Deposition, and the Entombment came to life. Through her sorrow, the man or woman in prayer could feel the stab of loss and agony. The Virgin was the instrument mediating bafflement at the mystery of the Redemption into emotional understanding. She made the sacrifice on Golgotha seem real, for she focussed human feeling in a comprehensible and accessible way (colour plate VII, figure 10).

The momentum of Mary's myth, which always seeks out a parallel to Christ's life in hers, made her Calvary the nodal point of his Passion. In one of the earliest and greatest of Italian vernacular poems, the Franciscan Jacopone da Todi (*c*. 1230–1306) gave unique voice to her sufferings in the Easter tradition. As in the *kontakion*, the narrative is tossed between a messenger, the clamorous crowd, and the Virgin, in verses describing each stage of Christ's torments until Christ himself appears, and in febrile and broken colloquialisms addresses his stricken mother.

The language is so intimate and immediate that when Jesus cries out to his mother he calls her "mamma."

Jacopone was a successful lawyer who, according to the fifteenth-century account of his life, experienced a sudden agony of repentance when he discovered on the body of his dead young wife, a penitential hair shirt under her rich brocades. Ten years later, he became a member of the radical spiritual wing of the Franciscan movement, a holy fool, dedicated to imitating the humility and shame of the son of God on this earth. He was the genius among the writers of *laude,* a form of religious poetry written and sung in public to educate and inspire the laity.[15]

Although Jacopone himself is not known to have travelled in the Greek east, he wrote in a tradition deeply influenced by the rediscovery of the holy places. Francis of Assisi himself had, in 1219, tried to make peace with the Sultan of Egypt in person, after the third crusade's disastrous attempt to recover Egypt from Islam. As Steven Runciman so eloquently described:

The Moslem guards were suspicious at first but soon decided that anyone so simple, so gentle and so dirty must be mad, and treated him with the respect due to a man who had been touched by God. He was taken to the Sultan al-Kamil who was charmed by him and listened patiently to his appeal, but who was too kind and too highly civilised to allow him to give witness to his faith in an ordeal by fire; nor would he risk the acrimony that a public discussion on religion would now arouse. Francis was offered many gifts, which he refused, and was sent back with an honourable escort to the Christians.[16]

It was in the context of this kind of mobility and exchange, which we associate with modern times, that the friars, the *joculatores dei* (God's minstrels), incited the faith of the Christian flock. Jacopone's dramatic hymn on the Passion, *Donna del Paradiso,* is very close to the east in feeling, and is the masterwork of the genre.

"Lady of Paradise," begins the messenger, "your little son has been taken." He tells her to run, to ask the crowd. Mary cries out for Mary Magdalene to help her, and then invokes Pilate, begging his mercy. The crowd howls, *"Crucifige, crucifige,"* and against their cry, Mary weeps and calls out for her son. The messenger, in broken sentences, tells her Jesus is being flogged and stripped and nailed to the Cross. She cries out in pain, wishing that her heart had rather been torn from her body than she should witness such a Crucifixion.

Then she and Christ meet, and he speaks to her:

> *Mamma, ove sei venuta?*
> *Mortal mi dai feruta*
> *Il tuo pianger mi stuta*
> *Che 'l veggio si afferrato.*

(Mamma, why have you come? You cause me a mortal wound, for your weeping pierces me and seems to me the sharpest sword.)

The Virgin replies, the syncopated rhythm and ceaseless, restless repetition compounding the overwhelming nature of her grief:

> *Figlio bianco e vermiglio*
> *Figlio senza somiglio:*
> *Figlio, a chi m'appiglio?*
> *Figlio, pur m'hai lassato?*
> *Figlio, bianco e biondo,*
> *Figlio, volto giocondo,*
> *Figlio, perchè t'ha el mondo,*
> *Figlio così sprezzato?*

(Son, white and ruddy, Son without compare, Son, on whom shall I rely? Son, have you also forsaken me? Son, white and fair, Son of the laughing face, Son, why has the world so despised thee?)

Mary's lament at its conclusion flows more quietly, and she turns to John, the new son Jesus gives her from the cross, and tells him that now she feels Simeon's sword, that now she and her son are in each other's arms, *abbracciati* on the same crucifix.[17]

Jacopone's poem is a lament, yet its energy, its sheer force of transport and ecstasy bear little relation to a dirge. The *Donna del Paradiso* rings with life, an antinomy that is, as we shall see, the heart of the primitive religious mystery at the heart of Our Lady of Sorrows' cult.

Another thirteenth-century masterpiece, the *Stabat Mater,* is a Latin sequence of technical and emotional perfection, with the same typical Franciscan tone of passion and intimacy.[18] It has long been attributed to Jacopone da Todi, though this is now in doubt. It has been set by Palestrina, Pergolese, Haydn, and Rossini: Palestrina's is one of the Church's most moving and powerful pieces of liturgical music. The genius of the sequence lies in its use of the first person. Jacopone saw the saviour's Passion through the eyes of his afflicted mother; the Franciscan who must have written the *Stabat Mater* wrote also from the vantage point of an eyewitness, and contemplates Mary standing by the Cross and shares her grief:

*Quis est homo qui non fleret*
*Matrem Christi si videret*
*In tanto supplicio?*

(Who is he who would not weep to see the mother of Christ in such torment?)

He then moves into direct, first-person communion with Christ, who is dying *pro me* (for me) on the Cross, and his fervour recalls that of Francis who received the stigmata:

*Sancta mater, illud agas:*
*Crucifixi fige plagas*
*Cordi meo valide.*

(Holy mother, do this for me: fix the wounds of the crucified deeply in my heart.)

*Fac me plagis vulnerari,*
*Cruce hac inebriari*
*Ob amorem filii.*

(Grant me to be wounded by his wounds, to be inebriated by his cross, for love of thy son.)

He closes with a prayer that, united with her lamentations and marked by Christ's wounds, he might enter into the glory of paradise.[19]

The legacy handed down from Egyptian to Copt, from mystery cult to Christian practice, would not have been sufficient to implant the cult of the Virgin's sorrows in western Europe; and the imagery of desolation, of drought, winter, and death could not have conserved its potency for the peoples of the west, who did not suffer the severity of the desert or the whims of the Nile's tidal swell or the noonday sun of the middle east, if the mystery of rebirth enacted at Calvary had not been reinforced by a calamity that made the experience of violent death and of sin, its correlative, more real than any of the homilies of the friars.

The Black Death was an eastern import, different in kind but no less influential than the intellectual stimulus of the crusaders' tales. *Pasteurella pestis,* the bacillus that, living in the stomachs of fleas, parasites on shipboard rats, wiped out a fifth of the population of Europe. No phenomenon could have driven home more forcefully the moral message of the Crucifixion.[20]

The Black Death first struck at Asia Minor in 1346, then reaching western Europe from Sicilian and other ports moved inland to attack the whole continent. At its height, in 1348–50, it raged throughout Europe, and was viewed almost exclusively in those years of faith as the retribution of a just God on the wickedness of mankind.[21] The established Church was ridden with schism (it was the time of the so-called "Babylonian Captivity" of the Papacy in Avignon), with simony, with lust for power, and political intrigue, such as Dante had denounced nearly fifty years before with such vitriolic invective in the *Divine Comedy;* in reaction, new ardent religious groups sprang up, acceptable and unacceptable (like the Waldensians and later the Hussites) to renew the mandate of heaven and abate the need of such justice as the plague.

The plague was a goad to faith: a new violent group, the Flagellants, did public penance for their own wrong-doing and for the sins of others, with a bloody zeal the clergy could not control and did not know whether to condone. In Germany, they swarmed from town to town, unwittingly carrying the pestilence they were trying to propitiate with them as they went. As they scourged themselves, they sang of Christ's own Passion, and one of their favourite marching songs was the *Stabat Mater*. In Italy, they claimed to possess a letter from the Virgin herself, absolving their company of their sins. Her sufferings provided a mental image on which they could fasten in their fervour. Although their life was brief—they were stamped out by 1351—the impact of their frenzied cult of pain was profound, and outbreaks of their brand of penance mark the history of the later middle ages.[22]

Naturally, medieval Europe was not innocent of death and pain before the onslaught of the plague. Famine, drought, other epidemics like the *mal ardens* (the burning sickness)—quite apart from the sufferings inflicted by human war and oppression—had taken their toll for centuries. But the swiftness of the Black Death, which could take a man in a day, the horror of the buboes, or boils, the stench, the catastrophic numbers of dead, who had to be shovelled into mass graves by men pious and courageous enough to risk their lives at such work, made this pestilence a new and unforgettable terror. It aroused penitential fever in a way never seen before, and gave the image of the *Mater Dolorosa* weighty contemporary significance.

At Pisa, the coincidence between the plague, an expiatory death cult, eastern legend, and the cult of the Virgin can be exactly pinpointed. The *Camposanto,* the burial ground at Pisa, is decorated with frescoes painted about 1350 by local artists—that is a year or so after the plague struck the city, in early 1348. Pisa was hit after Venice and Sicily, and it was from there that the plague travelled to Rome and throughout Italy.

On the south wall, three ornamental lordlings out hunting with their ladies and their hawks and hounds come across three sarcophagi in a forest clearing. Three kings lie in them, all crowned. The bones of the first are picked clean, the second is decomposing still, the third is freshly dead. One huntsman holds his nose as he contemplates them with his companions. The dead warn them: "What you are we were, what we are you shall be." (As Hamlet, a few hundred years later would cry out over Yorick's skull: "Tell her, let her paint an inch thick, to this favour she must come.")

The story the fresco relates—"Three Living and Three Dead"—was imported from the east, and appeared in the west for the first time about a hundred years before the Pisans used it on the wall of their cemetery to instil awe into the survivors of the plague.[23] They cared so deeply about the *Camposanto* that the very earth was from the Holy Land and had been transported by order of the archbishop in fifty-three shiploads, so that the dead might rest in sacred ground. As she does in hundreds of mid-fourteenth-century and later paintings, the Virgin appears beside Christ the Judge, imploring his mercy. For it was to her that the Pisans directed their prayers against the plague. In Siena too they credited her with abating the disease's fury, and in 1348, after the pestilence had claimed sixty-five thousand people out of a population of eighty thousand, the chapel of the Palazzo Pubblico was dedicated to her and decorated with the cycle of her death and triumphal Assumption.

The intimate devotions of the last hundred years had made the Virgin an approachable, kindly figure who could be depended on for pity and comfort. The cult of the *Mater Dolorosa* stressed her participation in mankind's ordinary, painful lot, and so although the repercussions of the Black Death restored a degree of majesty and terror to the personality of Christ the Judge, the Virgin herself retained the common touch. Her sorrows became a commonplace of medieval preoccupations. The sombre visions and prayers of fourteenth-century saints linger on the spiritual sword that pierced Mary's side and caused the fount of her mercy to flow. Conrad of Saxony (d. 1279), in the *Speculum Beatae Mariae Virginis,* meditates on this theme; Bridget of Sweden (d. 1373) wrote that according to the evidence of her visions, "of all mothers Mary was the most afflicted, by reason of her foreknowledge of Christ's most bitter Passion." Small Italian statues made for private devotion show the blood from Christ's wounded side spurting onto her breast and transfixing her. Death with his scythe stalks the period's prayer books; rosary beads were carved as skulls; skeletons danced their macabre dance on the walls of graveyards.

The Man of Sorrows—*Ecce Homo*—on the balcony is surrounded by angels bearing the grim instruments of his Passion; in paintings of the Crucifixion, his hands and feet flow like scarlet ribbons while the Virgin swoons beneath him. In Germany, where the Flagellants were most popular and repentance most extravagant, the cult of the *Mater Dolorosa* inspired innumerable carved wooden and polychromed statues of unfettered goriness and anguish. One of the most popular poems of Italy, and one of the most widely read sources alongside the pseudo-Bonaventure's *Meditations on the Life of Christ,* was the lengthy "Passion of Our Lord Jesus Christ" by the Sienese Niccolò di Mino Cicerchia, which with intense sympathy and pathos paints the Passion as the private tragedy of a loving family. In England, the Virgin's lament inspired the most poignant accents of despair—there are no fewer than twenty-five versions of the *Planctus Mariae* extant in Middle English. One of the most moving of these lyrics is the fourteenth-century *Quia amore langueo* (quoted in Chapter 10). The poet, like a knight in a *chanson d'aventure,* stands "musing on the moon" when he sees "a crowned queen . . . in ghostly sight," grieving on man's unkindness towards her son, for whom she is sick with love. In lines that convey a genuine and passionate distress, she rebukes man bitterly for the sins that have tormented and killed her child:

> My child is outlawed for thy sin,
> Mankind is better for his trespass;
> Yet pricketh mine heart that no nigh my kin
> Should be deceased, o son, alas![24]

In the fourteenth century such reproaches are "old and plain"—the emotion leaps out of the bleached language. But by the fifteenth century, when the crisis of the plague was receding, the laments became historic and the paintings full of empty gestures. The Virgin sometimes recalls a *diva* indulging a fit of temperament; the sincerity of the years of the Black Death disappears:

> Her hair, her face, she all to-rent,
> She tugged and tore with great torment;
> She brake her skin both body and breast,
> And said these words ever as she went,
> "Filius regis mortuus est."[25]

The popular movement seeped very gradually through the stiff fibre of the established Church, and lay confraternities who employed *can-*

*tastorie* (storytellers) to recount the tale of the Passion, and dedicated themselves to Mary, like the *Disciplinati della Madonna* in Siena, slowly influenced official circles. In 1423, in Cologne, the Archbishop Thierry de Meurs ratified the cult by instituting a feast of Our Lady of Sorrows on the Friday after Palm Sunday. At the end of the century, the first confraternity specifically vowed to contemplation of the dolours of the Virgin was founded in Flanders by the priest Jean de Coudemburghe. But in 1506, when Pope Julius II received a petition for a universal feast of the Church, dedicated to Our Lady of Sorrows, under the particular aspect of *La Madonna della Spasimo* (*Notre Dame de la Pâmoison,* Our Lady of Swooning), he took the advice of Cardinal Cajetan and rejected the idea.

But the tide of popular feeling was not checked: the Servites, a monastic order founded in the mid-thirteenth century, claimed that the Virgin had revealed her Seven Sorrows to their seven founder saints in a vision in their oratory near Florence. Pope Paul V (1605–21), one of the leading Counter-Reformers, gave the order permission to spread the cult of the sorrows by setting up new confraternities.[26] The sorrows, previously varying between five and fifteen, were officially fixed at seven: the prophecy of Simeon, the flight into Egypt, the loss of Jesus in the temple, the meeting with Jesus on the road to Calvary, the Crucifixion, the Deposition, and the Entombment. The Servites' vision inspired the iconography of Our Lady of Sorrows, her breast pierced with seven swords. From the high altar of their church in Rome, S. Maria in Via Lata, a tall statue of the ecstatic Virgin, bristling with silver swords, still dominates the congregation. In the rosary prayer, which was beginning to exercise its wide appeal at the end of the fifteenth century (see Chapter 20), the sorrowful mysteries of the Virgin were the subject of intense contemplation.

In the seventeenth century, a controversy arose over a point of Mariology: with her gift of knowledge and her perfect sympathy with Christ, Mary could not have grieved, as she knew he would rise from the dead. Francis de Sales (d. 1662) reminded his audience that Mary was not faint-hearted, but stood stalwartly at the Cross, exhibiting no signs of feminine hysteria and weakness (figure 38). But in her book *City of God* Maria de Agreda de Jesus (d. 1665), the strange, prolix Spanish nun, returned to the medieval theme of Mary's compassionate martyrdom: "She prayed that she might be permitted to feel and participate in her virginal body all the pains of the wounds and tortures about to be undergone by Jesus. This petition was granted by the blessed Trinity, and the mother in consequence suffered all the torments of her most holy son in exact duplication."[27]

The feast was extended to the whole Church and the *Stabat Mater* included in the liturgy only in 1727, by Pope Benedict XIII—an example of the time lag between popular fervour and official recognition. In 1814, in protest against Napoleon's persecution of the Church, Pius VII created a second feast of Our Lady of Sorrows, on September 16, where it has now stayed, although the Servites still retain it in its more logical Lenten position. And the tradition continues to inspire religious poetry. In a pamphlet published in Florence in 1903, the vibrant spontaneity of Jacopone da Todi reached a wondrous nadir:

> *Sulla testa, e sul bel collo*
> *La gran Vergine beata*
> *Era tutta insanguinata,*
> *Del buon sangue di Gesù.*

(On her head and on her lovely neck, the great and blessed Virgin was all covered in blood, in the good blood of Jesus.)

The blood is good; just as the rhythm beating in Jacopone's *Donna del Paradiso* is the dithyramb of life; just as Michelangelo, in his Pietà in St. Peter's, contrasts the quick pulse in the Virgin's youthful face and figure with the stiff death of Christ's limbs and staring mask. The mystery of the *Mater Dolorosa* flourished on the tension between grief and joy, between the death of the Cross and the future Resurrection. Mary's cry of grief will become a shout of exultation; the agony will be followed by *peripeteia* and triumph; sadness will explode into joy.[28]

On Good Friday in the Duomo in Florence, the crucifix is laid at the feet of one of Michelangelo's Pietàs. It is unfinished and shows Christ contorted in death, half lifted by Joseph of Arimathea and a young woman. The Virgin, roughly etched into the marble, presses her face into her son's hair, her awkward intimate crouched position accentuating his weight in death. Men and women process up to the statue to pray before the crucifix throughout the night of Good Friday. From three o'clock onwards the Duomo itself is in darkness, as are churches all over the Catholic world that day. Mass itself is not said, and the Holy Eucharist is removed to a place of repose, symbolizing the tomb in which Christ lay three days. The images and statues are shrouded in purple. In Spain, mourners shuffle and weep through the streets, many of them barefoot and bleeding, some shouldering crosses in imitation of Christ. In Sicily the Way of the Cross is enacted through the towns with gigantic, gesturing wood carvings borne aloft in procession. In Florence many of the men and women who come up softly to kiss the feet of the crucified God are in tears.

The next night, the Easter vigil, the shrouds are torn from the images, a sea of candles blaze on the altar, the choir shouts for joy, and the faithful wipe the tears from their eyes as the risen Christ returns to the altar at midnight, accompanied by all the pomp and ingenuity of centuries of ritual and display. In the early Church, this was the moment when the catechumens, after the ordeal of vigil and examinations during Holy Week, were baptised and reborn into the Church.[29]

The Virgin's role in the mystery of the rebirth of Easter is that of a mother. In Mariology, the Virgin at the foot of the Cross receives the human race in trust when Christ gives her into John's keeping and John into hers, and at Pentecost she also personifies the Church, the mother of all the faithful, guided by the Holy Spirit, which suffers tribulations as it awaits its forthcoming triumph (figure 14). In the theology of the mystical body of the Church, by which all Christians became members in Christ, they also became children of Mary, who fashioned his body in her womb. Her double consent—to the Incarnation and to the Atonement—associate her in this supreme way in the scheme of salvation. The Second Vatican Council stressed the relationship of Mary and the Church in the Redemption:

In celebrating this annual cycle of Christ's mysteries, Holy Church honours with especial love the blessed Mary, Mother of God, who is joined by an inseparable bond to the saving work of her son. In her the Church holds up and admires the most excellent fruit of redemption and joyfully contemplates, as in a faultless model, that which she herself wholly desires and hopes to be.[30]

In 1964, Mary was given a new title: *Mater Ecclesiae,* Mother of the Church.

This ecclesiology develops an oddly flavoured aspect of Our Lady of Sorrows: Mary does not simply submit herself to the will of God and consent to the death of her son. She actively participates in it: "The most holy mother of God," wrote the great Counter-Reformation theologian Francisco Suarez (d. 1617), "has not only the honour of having given the substance of her flesh to the only-begotten God . . . hers was the task, as well, of caring for and nourishing this same victim and even of placing it near the altar at the appointed hour. . . . Nor was she merely engaged in witnessing the cruel spectacle; rather, she rejoiced utterly that her only begotten was being offered for the salvation of the human race."[31]

Catholic prejudice naturally rules out that Mary's role on Calvary should be considered priestly. Such an interpretation would give powerful ammunition to the lobby for the female priesthood, an idea that is anathema to the Church. But the Virgin as the *Mater Dolorosa* belongs in the tradition of the all-devouring and savage goddess of myth who, like Inanna, sacrifices a substitute to the powers of darkness to save herself and then weeps for him. The Virgin's title is not *sacerdotissa,* though that is the function she fills, but *diacona sacrificii,* the deacon of the sacrifice, and *socia redemptori,* the colleague of the Redeemer.[32] She thus takes part, but in a suitably passive way.

All statements about Mary's participation carry the rider that Christ himself is the only saviour, the only redeemer, the only mediator. No Catholic, if asked, would hold that without Mary the atonement would have been impossible. But popular sentiment, expressed independently of official theology, recognizes that Jesus could not have been born a man without a mother and without life could not have accomplished his destiny, and it therefore accords Mary a crucial place in the economy of salvation. Her involvement in Christ's Passion even accounts for such peripheral symbols as the goldfinch, which appears on her finger in many Renaissance paintings of the Madonna and Child. She gives her baby the bird to play with because it was known to love the cover of thorn bushes, and thus prefigures the future sufferings of Christ.

Under her aspect of the *Mater Dolorosa,* Mary most resembles the fertility goddesses of antiquity. For she receives the broken body of her son in her arms and gazes upon his features with such avidity not only because she mourns her loss—for she knows, as theology states most clearly, that he will rise from the dead—but also because she is propitiating those same forces of sterility and death that the sacrifice of her son is attempting to appease (colour plate VII, figure 10; figure 36). He is the blood offering, she the principle of the abiding earth. The tears she sheds are charged with the magic of her precious, incorruptible, undying body and have power to give life and make whole.

Contemporary prudishness has tabooed the Virgin's milk, but her tears have still escaped the category of forbidden symbols, and are collected as one of the most efficacious and holy relics of Christendom. All over the Catholic world, statues and images of the Virgin weep. In Syracuse in Sicily, a mass-produced plaster of Paris plaque cried from August 29 to September 1, 1953, on the wall above the marital bed of a communist worker and his wife. It is a vacuous artefact that shows Mary proffering her burning, immaculate heart, crowned with fire. Tears welled in her eyes, and soon crowds were flocking to the tiny house, miracles were acclaimed, the tears examined by scientists and pronounced human. The plaque—*La Madonnina delle Lacrime*—now hangs aloft in a vast underground garage of a shrine in Syracuse, the focus of a flourishing cult. The walls of the ramps that lead down into the church—to enable the crippled to enter—are festooned with the grisly trophies seen in all wonder-working shrines: braces, crutches, artificial limbs, surgical collars as well as lurid snapshots of wounds, sores, and growths. On the high altar, in an ugly and costly reliquary, cotton wool soaked in the tears the Virgin shed is carefully preserved. The faithful can take away tiny pieces of other cotton wool that has touched the Madonna's tear ducts. The relic comes in a transparent sachet clipped inside a small pamphlet. It is a marvel of totemism: so many degrees removed from the magic of the Virgin, it is still believed to be filled with her powers.

Syracuse is only one of a score of places where the Virgin recently cried. In 1972, a priest was touring America with a weeping statue of the Virgin, carved, he claimed, on the instructions of Lucia, the last survivor of the three children who saw Mary at Fatima in Portugal in 1917.[33] In 1975, when the Vietcong took Saigon, the Catholics in the city claimed the Virgin's statue inside the cathedral wept. Such stories are the staple of the popular press in Catholic countries, but a certain relish greets their appearance in Protestant countries as well.

Tears are the only bodily effluvium permitted in an age obsessed with physical well-being and with the influence of the body on the personality. Snot, spit, blood, milk, nail parings, hairs all inspire recoil. A "civilized" modern man who finds a hair in his soup sends it back; spitting in the streets is considered bad-mannered and insanitary, if not barbaric; but few people are revolted by the tears falling down someone's cheek. Tears flow from the body, but unlike everything else from that source, they are not considered polluting. In fact, they are thought of as pure, like water. And it is within this complex and overarching symbolism of water that the weeping statues of the Virgin find a marginal place. Mircea Eliade has written:

The waters symbolise the entire universe of the virtual; they are the *fons et origo,* the reservoir of all the potentialities of existence; they precede every form and sustain every creation. . . . Emergence repeats the cosmogonic act of formal manifestation; while immersion is equivalent to a dissolution of forms. That is why the symbolism of the waters includes death as well as rebirth.[34]

The Christian Church uses water as a symbol of life and purification. On Easter night, the catechumens were immersed in the waters of baptism in which they were reborn, so that like the universe in Genesis, they could rise, re-created in a new and better mould, from the waters of sin and chaos in which they lived before. Mary's tears do not simply flow in sorrow at the historical event of the Crucifixion, a mother's grief at the death of her child. They course down her cheeks as a symbol of the purifying sacrifice of the Cross, which washes sinners of all stain and gives them new life, just as the tears of Inanna over Dumuzi fell on the parched Sumerian soil and quickened it into flower. In the winter of her despair, spring is not far behind. The Archbishop of Syracuse rejoiced when the plaque wept in his diocese because he understood the phenomenon within this ancient symbolic structure. He wrote that Mary's tears were not a reprimand, but a blessing:

Mary has wept! Mary has wept! . . . Weeping is fecund. There has never been a sterile tear. As the rain that falls from on high irrigates the countryside and prepares it to receive, in all fertility, the crops and seed and fruit that will in time come to ripeness, so it happens in the realm of the spirit. A woman who weeps always becomes, in the very act, a mother. And if Mary weeps beside the Cross of Jesus—I can tell you that her weeping was fertile and made her a mother.[35]

The *Mater Dolorosa* consoles the bereaved because she shares their sorrow; but also, at a more profound level, she satisfies a hunger of the believer, for the tears that gush from her eyes belong to a universal language of cleansing and rebirth.

## Chapter Fifteen

# THE PENITENT WHORE

*And when Jehu was come to Jezreel, Jezebel heard
of it; and she painted her face, and tired her head,
and looked out at a window. And as Jehu entered in
at the gate, she said, Had Zimri peace, who slew his
master? And he lifted up his face to the window, and
said, Who is on my side? who? And there looked
out to him two or three eunuchs. And he said,
Throw her down. So they threw her down: and
some of her blood was sprinkled on the wall, and on
the horses, and he trode her underfoot. And when
he was come in, he did eat and drink, and said, Go,
see now this cursed woman, and bury her: for she
is a king's daughter. And they went to bury her:
but they found no more of her than the skull, and
the feet, and the palms of her hands. Wherefore
they came again, and told him. And he said, This is
the word of the Lord, which he spake by his servant
Elijah the Tishbite, saying "In the portion of Jezreel
shall dogs eat the flesh of Jezebel": And the carcase
of Jezebel shall be as dung upon the face of the field
in the portion of Jezreel; so they shall not say,
This is Jezebel.*

—2 KINGS 9:30–7

A MYTH BLENDS with the history of a people and a community,
and gives it a certain perspective on its origins and destiny. Hence the
kings of England claimed descent from Brutus, son of Aeneas, the
founder of Rome, and the kings of France from Paris, the prince of Troy;

the Bible gave the Jews a unique view of their condition as the chosen race; in Catholic teaching all members of the Church are one in Christ, and Mary is the mother of them all. Mythological gods and heroes are also seen as the personifications of natural forces, themselves divinely instituted and organized: Diana was associated with the moon, Apollo with the sun, Demeter with the corn, and, as we shall see, the Virgin Mary is identified with the moon and the stars' influence as well as with the forces of fertility and generation (Chapters 17 and 18). But on a third level, a deity or mythological figure represents an aspect of the human mind, and the story in which he or she lives and suffers or triumphs is a psychological drama with timeless application.

This view of myth has endured from the allegorical interpretations of the neoplatonists of such myths as Cupid and Psyche until the rich use to which psychoanalysis has put ancient myths in order to plumb the mysteries of human behaviour. The classical pantheon possessed such a wide variety of personalities, and the gods and goddesses were conceived in such anthropomorphic terms that they reflect almost every imaginable virtue or vice of human nature: love, hatred, jealousy, even humour and certainly humourlessness—the range of human emotion can be learned from them.

But the Catholic religion does not admit sins or even faults in its God, nor even in his mother. The image of human error is relegated to the lesser ranks of the fellowship of saints. Peter, who denied his god when he lied three times; Thomas, who doubted Christ; Paul, who persecuted the Christians until his dramatic conversion; and many later saints who committed sins and then did bitter penitence for them provide consoling points of identification for Christians who lapse and fall, and thus fulfil the psychological function of myth, though with much less subtlety and depth than classical mythology.

The Virgin Mary could not meet this condition, for in her absolute purity and her exemption from the common lot she was free from all sin. Another figure consequently developed to fill this important lacuna, that of St. Mary Magdalene, who, together with the Virgin Mary, typifies Christian society's attitudes to women and to sex. Both female figures are perceived in sexual terms: Mary as a virgin and Mary Magdalene as a whore—until her repentance. The Magdalene, like Eve, was brought into existence by the powerful undertow of misogyny in Christianity, which associates women with the dangers and degradation of the flesh. For this reason she became a prominent and beloved saint.

Her prominence was assisted but not caused by the frequency and significance of her appearances in the Gospels. There is some confusion about them, however, and the need for such a female heroine in Christian mythology constantly shaped the understanding of the passages that might concern her, just as the need for the virgin birth influenced the reading of the infancy narratives. A close scrutiny of the Gospels refuses to yield Mary Magdalene's identity, and challenges the traditional assumption that she was a woman of great beauty and amorousness, indeed a prostitute, who repented of her evil life after she encountered Jesus Christ and learned to love him instead.

Luke tells the story of Jesus' supper with a pharisee called Simon in the town of Nain at the beginning of his ministry. While he is dining, an unnamed woman enters and, kneeling at Christ's feet, washes them with her tears, dries them with her hair, and then anoints them with precious ointment. The pharisee is appalled that Jesus should allow such a woman to touch him, especially while he eats. For she defiles him, "she is a sinner" (Luke 7:39). Jesus turns to him and asks him if a creditor released one man from a large debt and another from a small one, which man "will love him most?" Simon the pharisee is trapped and has to admit that the debtor released from the large sum would be most grateful. Jesus sternly reminds his host that he did not wash his guest's feet, or kiss him, or anoint him with oil. But the woman did, so "her sins which are many, are forgiven, for she loved much . . ." (Luke 7:47).

Luke's account has served the Catholic argument that Christ himself instituted the sacrament of penance to absolve the truly contrite of their sins. It has always been assumed, without inquiry, that the sins of the woman are worldly, and specifically carnal. Indeed, in England, houses for the reclamation of prostitutes were called Magdalenes. The implication that Jesus would be polluted by her touch has never led Christians to think of her as a murderess, a thief, a liar, but only as a whore. Christ's explanation, "for she loved much . . ." which manifestly describes the generosity of her gesture towards him, has even been misread as a reference to her sins. This aptly reflects Christian ideas about sexual love, but misunderstands altogether Christ's use of the verb *diligere,* to love, or *agapo* in the Greek, which has no erotic connotation whatsoever.

Matthew and Mark tell the same story, but they both set it at the end of Jesus' ministry, just before the Last Supper, in the town of Bethany and in the house of a leper called Simon (Matthew 26:6–13; Mark 14:3–8). The woman is not named, she is not described as a sinner, and there is no mention of Jesus' forgiveness. She brings an alabaster casket of precious ointment and anoints Jesus' head, not his feet. Her gesture is more restrained and ceremonious, and has none of the highly wrought drama and gallantry of Luke's account. Jesus is marked, like David, with the chrism of sovereignty. In Matthew and Mark, the disciples reproach Jesus—but only for the waste of the expensive oil, which could have been sold to raise money for the poor. But Jesus defends the woman's action in the sombre words: "For ye have the poor always with you; but me ye have not always. For in that she has poured this ointment on my body, she did it for my burial" (Matthew 6:12). So Jesus transforms the holy chrism of kingship into the embalming oil of death.

Mary Magdalene appears by name elsewhere, in a wholly different context, which has been virtually effaced from her cult and her legend. Mark says that the risen Christ appeared first to Mary Magdalene "out of whom he had cast seven devils" (Mark 16:9). Luke also mentions that among the women who followed Jesus and who "had been healed of evil spirits and infirmities" was one called Mary, from the town of Magdala. Jesus, he says, had exorcised seven devils out of her (Luke 8:2). Luke mentions this just after his account of the dinner with the pharisee Simon, which encouraged conflation of the two women. In Luke, though Mary Magdalene is present by implication at the burial and deposition of the dead Christ, she does not see the risen Christ, but only the empty sepulchre (Luke 24:4). In Matthew, she keeps watch at the Crucifixion, helps to bury Jesus, and later returns to the tomb, where an angel tells her Christ is risen. On the way back she meets Jesus and falls at his feet and worships him (Matthew 28:16).

It is Mark's account that made possible the confusion of the "sinner" of Luke and the woman who anointed Christ with Mary Magdalene. For in his last chapter, Mary Magdalene who was present at the Crucifixion comes to the grave of Jesus with other women "and brought sweet spices, that they might come and anoint him" (Mark 16:1). The spices, together with Jesus' prophetic words in Matthew's and Mark's stories, that the woman "did it for my burial," transformed the exorcised Mary of Magdala into the sinner who anointed his feet and was forgiven.

The Fourth Gospel compounds the difficulty. John describes Mary of Bethany, the sister of Lazarus, whom Jesus raised from the dead as "that Mary which anointed the Lord with ointments and wiped his feet with her hair" (John 11:2). In the next chapter, he describes the scene: "then took Mary a pound of ointment of spikenard, very costly, and anointed the feet of Jesus, and wiped his feet with her hair: and the house was filled with the odour of the ointment" (John 12:3). Judas in this case is the one to object, "not that he cared for the poor," says the evangelist scornfully, "but because he was a thief" (John 12:6). Jesus remonstrates with him, in the same terms as in the stories of Matthew and Mark: "against the day of my burying hath she kept this" (John 12:7).

In this Fourth Gospel, the woman named as Mary Magdalene appears in a wholly different context, playing a role of far greater consequence. John tells the story of her vigil at the empty tomb and her meeting with the risen Christ. She has found the sepulchre open and abandoned, and rushed back to tell Peter and another apostle. They accompany her back to the grave, and leave her there. Weeping she waits and, mistaking Christ for the gardener, begs him to tell her where he has taken the body of her Lord. Jesus, in a scene of extraordinary power, then calls her by her name, and she turns and, seeing him, says to him: *"Rabboni"* (Master). *"Noli me tangere"* (Touch me not), he commands her (John 20:17).

Fra Angelico caught the enigma and the majesty of their encounter in the garden on the walls of the convent of San Marco in Florence, where Christ weightlessly turns away with an ethereal gesture of disdain while Mary Magdalene kneels in worship before him. Unequivocally in the last Gospel therefore, Mary Magdalene, a different woman from Lazarus' sister, is the first key witness of the Resurrection.

The Greek Church followed the exegesis of Origen and always distinguished three separate women: Mary of Bethany, Lazarus' sister; Mary Magdalene, the witness of the Resurrection; and the "sinner." In the Orthodox calendar, their feasts are kept on three different days. But in the west, ever since the interpretation of Pope Gregory the Great (590–604), the three have been combined under the name of Mary Magdalene, whose memory is celebrated on July 22.

Western folklore of the Magdalene has flourished ever since. In the *Golden Legend,* Jacobus de Varagine tells us that Mary was the proprietor of the town of Magdala, while her brother Lazarus owned "a large part of Jerusalem," and her sister Martha the town of Bethany. "And for so much as she shone in beauty greatly, and in riches, so much the more she submitted her body to delight."[1] But penitence led her to Christ, and after she had washed and anointed his feet, she became his close friend, to whom he chose first to appear. The mystery plays of the middle ages often present the Resurrection through her eyes, following her from the merchant's shop where she buys the embalming unguents to the garden where she sees Christ. Her cult flourished particularly in the south of France, for her body was miraculously discovered in the crypt of St. Maximin's church in Aix-en-Provence in 1279. (The abbey church at Vézelay also possessed the saint's relics, authenticated in 1265. But its claims were eventually trounced by Provence.) Her relics were known to be in the vicinity because, according to local legend, Mary Magdalene, Martha her sister, Lazarus her brother, as well as two other Marys from the Gospels— Maria Jacobi and Maria Salome (see Appendix B)—had all been washed up on the shores of Provence in a rudderless boat after they had fled persecution in the holy land. They brought with them the bones of the Holy Innocents and the head of James the Less. Mary of James and Mary of Salome remained by the sea, and their relics, unearthed in the fifteenth century at the town called after them, *Les Saintes Maries de la Mer,* are jubilantly exhibited each year to multitudes of gypsies who gather there, and carried in procession by the *gardians,* the cowboys of the Camargue.

Mary Magdalene moved inland to the forest of Sainte Baume, where she preached Christianity to the locals and expiated her wicked life in conditions of grim austerity (figure 40). At the canonical hours, angels raised her heavenwards in ecstasy.[2] Another story, reported in the *Golden Legend,* relates how she made a pilgrimage to Rome, and after a shipwreck on a desert island saved a child by enabling it to suckle the corpse of its mother for two years.

The witness of the risen Christ, who, veiled and carrying her jar of ointment, walks up silently to the empty sepulchre in so many early Christian representations of the Resurrection (figure 39), was transformed in the middle ages into a hermitess, the perfect embodiment of Christian repentance. As such, the Magdalene was considered a powerful and beneficent witch, a great and beloved saint. After the Reformation provoked closer study of Scripture, one Catholic scholar, Lefèvre of Etaples (d. 1536), provoked a bitter and long-drawn-out battle when he suggested that Mary Magdalene and Mary of Bethany were not the same person.[3] The distinction is widely accepted in Church circles now, but not yet installed in the western liturgy.

The suggestion of love between Christ and Mary Magdalene had been celebrated by the Gnostics in the second century. The apocryphal *Gospel of Mary* portrays her as a supreme initiate into Christ's mysteries and the teacher of the other apostles; while the Gnostic *Gospel of Philip,* which sees the union of man and woman as a symbol of healing and peace, dwells on the relationship of Christ and the Magdalene, who, it says, was often kissed by him.[4] Analagous mythology is on the increase with the contemporary interest in the historical life of Jesus. *Jesus Christ Superstar* pictures her as a harlot, reformed through her love of Jesus. An avant-garde scholar, William Phipps, speculates in a serious book, *Was Jesus Married?,* that Mary Magdalene may have been his wife. And a riot of fire-bombing was provoked in Rome against the Danish Embassy after Pope Paul objected to the news that a film to be called *The Loves of Jesus Christ* was being made with the financial support of the Danish government. According to the producer, Jens Joergen Thorsen, Christ would be depicted "as a warlord, love apostle, erotomaniac, drunkard, idealist and revolutionary," and he would include "direct and explicit portrayals of Jesus' relations with women mentioned in the Bible in group sex scenes."[5]

The scriptural prominence of the woman thought of as Mary Magdalene was in marked contrast to the treatment of the Virgin, which embarrassed the Fathers of the Church at an early stage. Inexplicably, the mother of Jesus disappears after the scene at the foot of the Cross described by John. She is mentioned once again only in the New Testament, in Jerusalem, just after the Ascension of Christ (Acts 1:14). No Gospel ever says that the risen Jesus appeared to his mother. To Mary Magdalene, to other women, to the disciples, but never to his mother.

The first witnesses to the empty tomb arrive on Sunday morning, after Jesus had lain in the sepulchre throughout the Sabbath. Their identities differ from Gospel to Gospel, and to add to the imbroglio, a lot of them are called Mary (figure 39) (Appendix B). According to Ephrem's commentary on the *Diatessaron of Tatian,* Tatian had identified the Virgin Mary with Mary Magdalene in the scene in the garden of the Fourth Gospel. Since this was a bare-faced and untenable error, it found little support, beyond the pages of apocryphal works like the *Book of the Resurrection of Christ* by Bartholomew the Apostle.[6] But the desire to prove that Jesus did appear to his mother after his Resurrection was tenacious, and attempts were made by scrupulous exegetes to demonstrate that "the other Mary" mentioned by Matthew as Mary Magdalene's companion at the burial and at the empty grave on Sunday was the Virgin.[7] "The other Mary" (Matthew 27:61; 28:1) appears to refer back to "Mary the mother of James and Joses" (Matthew 27:56) and, in the east, where it was held that Mary brought up Joseph's sons by his first marriage, such an interpretation was therefore possible (see Mark 6:3; Matthew 13:54; Luke 4:16). St. John Chrysostom, George of Nicomedia, and Simeon Metaphrastes all propounded this view. John Chrysostom also argued that it was only fitting Christ should have appeared in the glory of his resurrected body to his mother; Origen before him had commented that Mary Magdalene was a wholly unsuitable first witness. In the monastery of Mount Sinai there is an eighth-century icon that testifies to the Greek devotion: the risen Christ is shown before two holy women, one of whom is unequivocally labelled MR, the traditional Byzantine monogram for the Virgin Mary.

But in the west, the mother of James could not be equated with the Virgin unless the position on Joseph's virginity was reversed and it was admitted that he had been married before. Jerome's weighty authority to

Joseph's inviolate chastity ruled that out, so the west fell back on the eastern argument from appropriateness. As a filial son, Christ must have visited his mother. In the Coventry mystery plays and the Cornish *Resurrectio Domini,* Christ appears to her before the soldiers awake.

Sometimes, however, the absence of Mary at the tomb was explained away: Mary did not need to go, for she knew all that was going to happen. If she had accompanied the other women who were taking embalming spices and oils, she would have shown little faith in Christ's promised Resurrection. In some Catholic devotional works, Mary waits at home and prays until Christ appears to her. The *Golden Legend* and the *Meditation* of the pseudo-Bonaventure both describe the rapture of their meeting: *"Salve sancta parens,"* he greets her, in the words of the antiphon of one of her most popular masses. Very edifyingly, it is the Virgin who encourages Christ to take pity on the Magdalene's grief and to visit and console her. Rogier van der Weyden painted a majestic tableau of the scene around 1440–5, which now hangs in the Metropolitan Museum in New York. The composition echoes the Annunciation, for Mary sits reading a prayer book, while Christ, enveloped in a billowing red cloak and displaying his stigmata, alights beside her. In the background the three other Marys approach the empty sepulchre in Indian file. Large tears course down Mary's furrowed cheeks; pouches under her eyes testify to her sad vigil; her long, delicate hands are raised in surprise and greeting. It is one of the few paintings to show the Virgin old enough to have borne the thirty-three-year-old Christ.

As a subject of meditation, the apparition of Christ to his mother continued sporadically after the middle ages. Maria de Agreda de Jesus gave it a gushing paragraph:

In this context, which was more intimate than the contact with the humanity and the wounds of the Saviour sought by the Magdalene, the Virgin Mother participated in an extraordinary favour . . . the glorious body of the Son so closely united itself to that of this purest Mother that He penetrated into it and she into his. . . .[8]

The cult of her Joys, which paralleled those of her Sorrows, sometimes included "the joy she felt when she was visited and greeted personally by her son Jesus."

But the theme only crops up half-heartedly, for, whatever the view of Maria de Agreda de Jesus, the figure thought of as Mary Magdalene thoroughly eclipsed the Virgin both as the witness of the Resurrection and as the privileged friend of Christ during his ministry: "Now Jesus loved Martha, and her sister and Lazarus" (John 11:5), but it was of Mary that he said: "Mary hath chosen that good part, which shall not be taken away from her" (Luke 10:42). Human appetite for romance cannot wholly explain the attraction of the figure called the Magdalene. Other women of equal potential interest throng the Gospels. For instance, Jesus' longest conversation takes place with a woman of Samaria who has had five husbands and who recognizes him as the Messiah (John 4:7–42). However, though Christ privileged her with some of his most resonant revelations—"whosoever drinketh of the water that I shall give him shall never thirst . . ." (John 4:14)—she has exercised no comparable fascination.

Mary Magdalene was created from unrelated stories in the image of an earlier mould, itself cast in a Judaic tradition. She fits into the theme of the harlot, like Gomer, the faithless wife of Hosea, who prefigured Israel's stormy union with Yahweh (Hosea 1:2–3); like Jezebel, who was eaten by dogs (2 Kings 9:30–7); and like Rahab (Joshua 2 *passim*), who appears in Matthew's genealogy as an ancestress of Christ (Matthew 1:5). In the Epistle to the Hebrews, Rahab is cited as someone saved by faith (Hebrews 11:31); and in the Epistle of James as justified by works (James 2:25). Dante placed her in the sphere of Venus, and in one of his most beautiful images described her as "a sunbeam in clear water"— *come raggio di sole in acqua mera* (*Paradiso* 9:114). For Dante, repentance could purify all sin, especially the excusable sin of love in excess. (Jezebel's crime in the Bible was not harlotry, but treachery and deceit [see 1 Kings 21:5–25], but because she painted her face to appear at the window before Jehu, the new king of Israel, her name became a household word for female infamy with powerful sexual overtones, and her terrible end has been used by preachers over the centuries to instruct young women in the horror of their charms.)

Above all others, Mary Magdalene is the prototype of the penitent whore, but she has colleagues in this particular brand of hagiography, which so neatly condenses Christianity's fear of women, its identification of physical beauty with temptation, and its practice of bodily mortification. With the courtesan Thaïs (d. *c.* 348), about whom Anatole France wrote his savage indictment of asceticism; with the anchorite Mary the harlot, who lived outside her holy uncle's cell until she was debauched and then reclaimed; with Mary of Egypt; and with the actress Pelagia, Mary Magdalene leads a Christian company of harlot saints. James the Deacon, in the eighth century, wrote a story he claimed he had heard from the protagonist himself, Nonnus, Bishop of Edessa, about Pelagia:

First of all the actresses of Antioch . . . first of the dancers was she, and riding on an ass: and with all fantastic graces did she ride, so decked that naught could be seen upon her but gold and pearls and precious stones . . . of the beauty and loveliness of her there could be no wearying for a world of men.

She smelt ambrosially sweet, and her shoulders and limbs were bare, her face uncovered to the world. The other bishops with Nonnus turn away, sickened at the sight. But twice Nonnus asks them: "Did not the sight of her great beauty delight you?" And when his companions demur, he cries out in anguish that Pelagia is arrayed so beautifully for her earthly lovers, while "a single day's adorning of a harlot is far beyond the adorning of my soul."[9]

Pelagia, suddenly experiencing that dramatic change of heart that is the essence of the harlot myth, begs to see the new bishop. But he, fearful that her beauty might tempt him, refuses to see her alone. Before a gathering, then, she pleads to be baptised, gives away all her goods to the poor, frees her slaves, and, disguised as a man, becomes a hermit in the desert.

Years after, when Nonnus tells James the Deacon to go and seek out the holy hermit, James finds a creature "wasted and haggard with fasting. Her eyes were trenches in her face." Only later, after her death, does he discover that she is the woman Pelagia, who had once been the glory of all Antioch.

Probably the strangest legend of all is that of St. Mary of Egypt, which the Doctor and Saint John Damascene believed was authentic. Her cult spread rapidly in the west. The lovely small pseudo-peripteral temple of *Fortuna Virilis* in the square in front of S. Maria in Cosmedin in Rome, which dates from Republican times, was dedicated to S. Maria Egiziaca in 872 by the Greek monks who lived in the area.

Born around 344 in Alexandria, Mary of Egypt lived as a prostitute from the age of twelve to seventeen, but she determined to go on a pilgrimage to the holy land. Lacking the wherewithal, she worked her passage as whore to the entire ship's crew. When she reached the church of the Holy Sepulchre in Jerusalem, the holiest place of Christendom, an invisible force pressed her away. Only when she caught sight of an icon of the Virgin and promised to repent of her ways was she able to enter the church. She then kissed the relic of the True Cross, and decided to become a hermit in the desert, where she lived for forty-seven years. A priest called Zosimus met her and saw her walking on the water and levitating. She was clothed only in her long hair. He gave her holy communion, and her peaceful but desiccated corpse was found by him the following year.[10]

Mary of Egypt and Mary Magdalene are often indistinguishable in Christian iconography: lifted by angels, chastely wrapped in hair, receiving the Eucharist from the hand of St. Maximin (Mary Magdalene) or St. Zosimus at the hour of their death, the two harlots fused into a single symbol.

When the Reformers challenged the validity of the sacrament of penance and the doctrine of the forgiveness of sins, the Catholic Church retaliated by intensifying the cult of those saints who had been redeemed through penitence. St. Peter, who denied Christ and was forgiven, and the harlots who turned their backs on their former lives of pleasure and were saved became the subjects of huge propaganda canvases. The stories of Mary Magdalene and Mary of Egypt answered simultaneously the Lutheran attacks on penance and transubstantiation, and their last communion with the real presence of Christ in the Eucharist is a favourite theme of Counter-Reformation art. An enormous painting in Palermo portrays Mary of Egypt as a Neapolitan streetwalker, and clothes Zosimus in a magnificent figured cope, a fashionable post-Tridentine assertion of the power of the priesthood.

The penitent Magdalene was popular because, as the great art historian Emile Mâle has written:

Beauty consuming itself like incense burned before God in solitude far from the eyes of men became the most stirring image of penance conceivable. . . . The generosity of expiation, the gift of tears, were to the Christian a perpetual subject of meditation.[11]

In Spain, the writer Pedro Malon de Chaide (d. 1589) attempted to reconcile the eternal quarrel of the body and the soul in the figure of the Magdalene, who is the perfection of divine love, for she had tasted corruption and rejected it.

The Virgin's mediation through an icon moved Mary of Egypt to repentance. But the Virgin's role could only be intercessionary, for she was innocent of the experience of sin and failure altogether. The cult of harlot saints reflects one of the most attractive features of Catholic Christianity—the doctrine that no one, except Satan, is beyond the reach of grace. But a figure like Mary Magdalene also strengthens the characteristic Christian correlation between sin, the flesh, and the female. It is bitter to realize that among all the female saints in the liturgy, Mary Magdalene is one of the few not entitled "virgin." (Among others are Perpetua and Felicity, the martyrs; Monica, the mother of St. Augustine; a few queens—Elizabeth of Portugal, Margaret of Scotland, Elizabeth of Hungary; and Martha of Bethany, the perfect Christian type of the domestic woman.)

And in her myth, Mary Magdalene sins because she is not chaste, and not for any other reason that might be considered more grave.[12] The Christian harlot has absorbed to some extent the role of the classical goddesses of love. Aphrodite was sometimes surnamed *Porne,* or Courtesan. The name Pelagia actually belonged to Aphrodite in her aspect of goddess of the sea, from the Greek word for sea, *pelagos.* This facet of human personality could not be represented by the Virgin Mary, however beautifully and youthfully and enticingly she is portrayed. Her unspotted goodness prevents the sinner from identifying with her, and keeps her in the position of the Platonic ideal; but Mary Magdalene holds up a comforting mirror to those who sin again and again, and promises joy to human frailty. Although the Virgin is both the bride of Christ and of mankind, Mary Magdalene when she mourns and lays out Christ's body usurps that role, leaving the Virgin of Sorrows a more restricted maternal character.

Together, the Virgin and the Magdalene form a diptych of Christian patriarchy's idea of woman. There is no place in the conceptual architecture of Christian society for a single woman who is neither a virgin nor a whore. Indeed, in Catholic countries the unmarried woman who has not taken the veil is a pathetic figure of fun—the *zitella,* the old maid ridiculed in popular Italian songs. The Church venerates two ideals of the feminine—consecrated chastity in the Virgin Mary and regenerate sexuality in the Magdalene. Populous as the Catholic pantheon is, it is nevertheless so impoverished that it cannot conceive of a single female saint independently of her relations (or lack of relations) with men.

The rise of the cult of Mary Magdalene through the high middle ages and Counter-Reformation keeps pace with the growth of belief in the Immaculate Conception of the Virgin. For the more Mary was held to be free of all taint of sin, actual and original, the less the ordinary sinner could turn to her for consolation in his weakness, and the more he needed the individual saints whose own lapses held out hope for him. From the capricious goddess capable of angry quarrels with her faithless votaries, or the barefoot mother nursing her child, the Virgin Mary became from the fifteenth century onwards more and more remote, as she ascended to ever higher pinnacles of perfection.

# Chapter Sixteen

# THE IMMACULATE CONCEPTION

*Post dominum tu spes hominum, quos conscia mordet*
*Mens sceleris, quae per Veneris contagia sordet.*

*(After the Lord, thou art the hope of men whom*
*the mind conscious of sin consumes—the mind*
*which is foul through the contagion of Venus.)*[1]

—MARBOD OF RENNES

THE ASCETIC STRAIN in Catholic doctrine has struggled with its incarnational and life-affirming aspects for centuries marked by Pyrrhic victories on both sides. The Word made flesh was a positive and joyous statement on humanity's behalf, although Mary's virginity—the unnaturalness of Christ's birth—undermined it. In the nineteenth century, a final blow for dualism was struck. On December 8, 1854, Pope Pius IX proclaimed the Virgin Mary the Immaculate Conception, the only human creature ever to have been preserved from all taint of original sin. Pius' Bull, *Ineffabilis Deus,* now declared this to be dogma, a mandatory belief for all those who acknowledge the spiritual authority of Rome. Pius also thereby made impossible any interpretation of Christ's Incarnation as the full embrace of the ordinary condition of man. Not only he, Christ, was exceptional; but so was his mother, his only human parent.

The doctrine of the Immaculate Conception promulgated in the Bull means that Mary surpassed the beatitude of Adam and Eve in the Garden of Eden. They were capable of sin—as it indeed befell—whereas Mary was not.[2] Her free will was not impaired, however, by this unique privilege, for her inability to sin resulted from her perfected resistance. In life she was wholly free from concupiscence, the "incentive to sin," and therefore unburdened by a single sinful desire. In purity she excelled the angels, though not in intelligence. God had elected her his beloved daughter from the beginning of time and predestined her to be the mother of his only-begotten son. The consequence of her exemption from original sin was a completely unblemished life. The Virgin Mary was therefore the most perfect created being after Jesus Christ.

The vicissitudes the doctrine of the Immaculate Conception underwent from its origins in the early Christian belief that Mary was ever-virgin to its definition as dogma in the nineteenth century faithfully reflect the vicissitudes the Church itself was undergoing, and its turbulent story mirrors the changing fashions in philosophical opinion. The delicate scholastic arguments penned by medieval theologians like Duns Scotus (d. 1308) were the object of derision for the humanists of the Renaissance, who looked principally to Scripture for the grounds of their beliefs and repudiated the infinitely regressive speculations of the medieval schoolmen with disgust.

In the sixteenth century, in England, men at Oxford actually tore up folios of Duns Scotus to use them as wastepaper. Belief in the doctrine of the Immaculate Conception, of which Duns Scotus was a principal architect, did not crumble, but built new foundations that it found, according to the sixteenth-century principles, in the Bible, interpreted allegorically in the patristic tradition. But when, during the eighteenth century, the Church was abandoned altogether for the first time by the intellectual élite of Europe, belief in the Immaculate Conception became an act of defiance against rationalism on behalf of *a priori* methods of deduction, and a believer's blow struck for faith against empiricism and reason. Finally, when Pope Pius IX proclaimed *Ineffabilis Deus,* he was announcing that the pope's authority to command the beliefs of Christendom had not been shattered by the philosophical and political turmoil of the age of scepticism. By proclaiming dogma a belief that had been stormily discussed since the twelfth century, he also asserted the position of the pope as the single, divinely inspired head of the Church and implied that the Church alone was the true spiritual guide and not the individual conscience, as the men of the Reformation and their heirs had maintained. The Bull was therefore an important strategic move in the long battle of Rome against its detractors, and once again, as with the cult of *Maria Regina* in eighth-century Rome, the interests of the papacy were bound up with the cult of the Virgin. It was only logical that Pius IX followed up the Bull of 1854 with another, in 1870, proclaiming the infallibility of the pope a dogma of the Church.

By 1854, the doctrine of the Immaculate Conception had become the tranquil belief of the majority of Catholics. But it is an interesting phenomenon, nevertheless, because most Catholics, then and now, have only the vaguest idea of what the doctrine means. "The Immaculate Conception" conveys the perfection and purity of the Virgin; only Catholics with a decided theological bent grasp the exemption from original sin defined by the dogma. It is therefore an interesting Mariological hybrid: the union of a belief that has enjoyed immense popularity and stimulated fierce passions, as we shall see, with a difficult framework provided by theologians in order to accommodate the popular creed. The popular belief has never found the theology anything but superfluous to its continuing life; but the theology has placed enormous obstacles in the way of the ecumenical movement. The Reformed Churches recoil from the superhuman exaltation of Mary that the doctrine implies, and from the interpretation of Scripture and tradition necessary to "prove" the Immaculate Conception. Thus the characteristic Roman response to the fluid and volatile emotions of its members—to incorporate their beliefs in an inflexible set of propositions and conclusions—has failed to educate the members or to raise their belief from an emotional to an intellectual level, but it continues to alienate possible friends, who do understand the doctrine's significance.

Nothing in the New Testament refers to the absence of sin in the Virgin. The Fathers of the Church, while singling out for extravagant praise her miraculous virginity's power over evil, refrain from pronouncing her free from original sin. She is *achrantos* (undefiled) according to Marcellus of Anycra (d. *c.* 374) and Gregory Nazianzen; the latter also hails her as *amiantos* (unspotted). In the west, Ambrose and Augustine both maintained that Mary never committed a sin; and Augustine argued that all actual sin resulted from the original sin of Adam and Eve, which was transmitted from generation to generation. When rebutting Pelagius' heresy, he insisted that all men were born in sin, but added that he wished to make an exception regarding the Virgin:

of whom out of honour to the Lord I wish no question to be made where sins are treated of—for how do we know what mode of grace wholly to conquer sin may have been bestowed on her . . . ?[3]

'But he let the question dangle and never tackled the issue that if Mary was sinless in life, was it because she was conceived without sin? For centuries Mariologians have struggled with Augustine's enigmatic reservation.

In the east, the Greeks, while extolling her sublime purity, ascribed actual sin to her. St. John Chrysostom saw a mother's vainglory in Mary's intervention at Cana (Irenaeus also held this view); Origen, St. Basil, and St. Cyril of Alexandria glossed the prophecy of Simeon as the doubt that stabbed Mary to the heart as she stood by the Cross and watched her son die. Jesus' response to the message that his mother and his brethren were outside, and wished to see him—"Who is my mother, or my brethren?"—was interpreted by Tertullian and John Chrysostom as a deserved rebuke to the Virgin for her interference.

Such slurs were angrily dismissed in the west, which had traditionally used Mary's virginity as the premise for the moral perfection of her actions. But in the east, the problem had not been posed in the same way, because heresy had not forced the Greeks to scrutinize the exact nature of original sin, as it had St. Augustine. After Augustine, it seemed impossible to maintain that the Redeemer had been conceived and carried in a woman's womb that, like all others, was stained by sin.

In popular belief, far from these conundrums of theology, the conception and birth of Mary had from the second-century apocryphal *Book of James* been considered a special miracle of God. The threnody of the barren St. Anne under the flowering tree and its cosy nest of sparrows, the grief and flight of Joachim into the wilderness, the double annunciation to Joachim and Anne that the curse of childlessness had been lifted, the prodigy child Mary, who was dedicated to the temple—it all formed a familiar and beloved story that set Mary apart from all other human children. In iconography, the electric impulse of life miraculously passed between Joachim and Anne when they ran to meet each other after the angel's news and fell into each other's arms before the Golden Gate of Jerusalem (colour plate I, figure 1). The conception of Mary at that moment was celebrated as a feast—the conception of St. Anne—as early as the seventh century.[4] St. Andrew of Crete wrote a canon for the day praising the Virgin's purity; and in the tenth-century *Menologium* of the Emperor Basil, an illuminated liturgical calendar, the first surviving paintings of the embrace before the Golden Gate illustrate the feast.[5] For five hundred years afterwards the image continued to serve as the sign of the supernatural nature of Mary's arrival.

The message of the image, however, was imprecise. Like John the Baptist, Mary was a miracle child, born to parents in their old age. It was not a "virgin" birth, but another kind of direct and miraculous intervention. But the transition from a material to a spiritual prodigy, which is the essence of the doctrine of the Immaculate Conception, was not made in the east, but only in the medieval, Mariolatrous west.

The feast celebrating Mary's conception was imported from the east by monks fleeing the Iconoclast persecutions of the ninth century, and began to be kept in Italy and Rome and Sicily.⁶ The cult progressed smoothly, spreading to England before the Norman Conquest. But around 1150 the controversy first erupted into violence in the south of France, when Bernard of Clairvaux, with a sense of outrage, fired off a protest to the canons of Lyons because they were proposing to institute the feast of the Immaculate Conception on December 8 in their diocese. "Do you mean that the Holy Spirit was a partner to the sin of concupiscence," he thundered. "Or are we to assume that there was no sin where lust was not absent?"⁷ Veneration of Mary's conception by St. Anne seemed tantamount in Bernard's eyes to worshipping the copulation of her parents.

The canons of Lyons were probably inspired to celebrate the new feast by the Archbishop William of Corbeil and his companion Anselm the Younger, nephew of the great English scholar and saint, during a visit in 1123.⁸ Anselm the Younger described himself as *sanctae Dei genitricis servitio tota mente deditus* (dedicated with his whole mind to the service of the Mother of God),⁹ and as Robert Southern has demonstrated, he stimulated veneration of the Virgin by collecting the miracle stories that formed the fountainhead of this extraordinarily popular genre in the middle ages. The tales Anselm collected promote different practices in the Virgin's cult: the recitation of the *Ave Maria,* for instance. In one miracle, during a terrifying storm at sea, an English abbot called Elsinus is promised safety in a vision on condition that he establish the feast of the Conception of the Virgin on his return. In the vision, the office to be used in the mass for the day is described in detail. Naturally, when Elsinus reaches home he duly introduces the new feast in his church at Ramsey.

Bernard, in his missive to the Lyons canons, warns them against giving this story credence. But his sternness was of no avail: the miracle was even read in the day's service, and, in order to justify its novelty, the Virgin herself demanding this honour was substituted for the original bishop who had appeared in the vision. Elsinus was a historical character, the abbot of St. Augustine's in Canterbury in 1061; and when he returned from exile to England in 1087 or 1088 he did indeed reintroduce the feast of December 8, which had been kept in England but which the Norman conquerors had at first suppressed.¹⁰ Anselm the Younger was the inheritor of a particularly English strain of piety. His uncle St. Anselm of Canterbury had hymned the Virgin in grandiose and majestic verse, counterposing his sullied, tarnished sinfulness with her bright and healthy purity, begging for her intercession on the day of judgement, and invoking her as the source of all created things. He embroidered the theme of her uniqueness:

O Woman uniquely to be wondered at, and to be wondered at for your uniqueness, by you the elements are renewed, hell is redeemed, demons are trampled down and men are saved, even the fallen angels are restored to their place. O woman full and overflowing with grace, plenty flows from you to make all creatures green again.[11]

But Anselm emphatically thrust aside the conclusion he might have drawn from Mary's unique abundance of grace and purity. "The Virgin herself," he wrote, ". . . was conceived in iniquity, and in sin did her mother conceive her, and with original sin was she born, because she too sinned in Adam in whom all sinned."[12]

Anselm's nephew, his disciple and biographer Eadmer (d. 1124), and the English theologian Osbert of Clare (d. *c.* 1127) disagreed, and they proselytized enthusiastically for the feast of the immaculate Virgin's conception. They argued the appropriateness of the privilege, marshalling the celebrated syllogism—*potuit, decuit, ergo fecit* (He [God] could, it was fitting he should, so he did)—and cited the sanctification of John the Baptist, when, at the approach of Mary, he leapt in his mother's womb, a sure sign he had been freed from the burden of sin by her pure presence. If the Baptist's mother had been granted such a privilege, then the virgin mother of God must have been granted a greater one.

From England, the cult of the Immaculate Conception spread to France, where Norman students adopted December 8 as their special feast. The French in turn influenced the Italians, and by the end of the twelfth century, a few Italian monasteries and towns paid homage to Mary under her new title. But Rome itself hung back, and it was not until the third decade of the thirteenth century that the Curia was seen as a mass for the Immaculate Conception on December 8.[13]

Peter Lombard (d. 1164) author of the influential *Sentences,* achieved a cunning compromise to justify the growing cult. He said that Mary, as a human being, had been conceived in original sin, but as the Mother of God had been purified before she was born. St. Thomas Aquinas corroborated Peter Lombard's view, but fingered an excessively tender spot: Mary could not have been free of original sin at her conception because no one could have been redeemed before the Redemption. Indeed, the great sacrifice of the Cross would be diminished by its superfluousness in the case of Mary. Mary, like John the Baptist, had been sanctified only in her mother's womb. The Dominicans followed the

Angelic Doctor's line; but the Franciscans, whose less intellectual strain of piety kept them closer to the groundswell of popular feeling, endorsed the Immaculate Conception against the Black Friars.

It was Duns Scotus who sliced through casuistic objections with great sleight of hand: the mediation and sacrifice of Christ were not belittled by her sinlessness, he said, but rather enhanced, since prevention is better than cure. He suggested the Virgin had been *preserved* from sin from the moment of her conception until the Redemption of the Cross, when she, like all the human race, had been saved. He called this the *Praeredemptio* or Preredemption, and he relied on the argument of congruity to support it. As the perfect intercessor, and the perfect filial son, Jesus could hardly have failed to obtain total purity for his Mother. Gossamer light as it is, his argument was the make-weight in the subsequent turbulent controversy that continued to surround the doctrine of the Immaculate Conception.

From the fourteenth century onwards, the battle was joined with a zeal on both sides astonishing to the modern mind. Rival visions, rival miracles marked the contest of the friars as they preached their case up and down Europe. In the Vatican Pinacoteca, a Trecento diptych gives rare pictorial evidence of the conflict. In one panel, the Virgin appears before two men and stays their murderous fight; in the other, a Franciscan friar emerges unscathed from an ordeal by fire in the presence of confounded Dominicans and other doubters.[14] A book of sermons by the Franciscan John of Verden, which went through at least thirty editions after it was printed in 1517, described the fate of the Virgin's detractors. Bernard of Clairvaux, because of his opposition to the feast of her conception, appears an unquiet spirit "with a stain" on his otherwise spotless soul. St. Bonaventure, an early general of the order, laments to another Franciscan in a vision that he burns in purgatory for his scepticism; Alexander Neckham (d. 1227), an English scholar, falls ill, but the Virgin appears, lances his ulcers, sews up his wounds with silk, and tells him his sufferings arise from his little faith. Alexander is converted to her Immaculate Conception.[15]

The assault on the dissidents was marshalled on another front: the cult of St. Anne was assiduously fostered in art and devotions of the fifteenth and early sixteenth centuries, for by focussing on the exemplary life of Mary's mother, the special privileges attending Mary's conception could be more persuasively presented. The private Books of Hours of the period, sumptuously illuminated for noblemen's consumption and glory, include prayers to the mother of the Virgin, whose identity is known only from the apocryphal *Book of James*. In one *Hours of the Virgin,* painted possibly in Bruges around 1515, and now in the Pierpont Morgan Library in New York, St. Anne sits reading while in her womb the tiny Virgin glows like a firefly in a golden aureole (colour plate VI, figure 8). In more imposing canvases of the same period the propaganda crystallizes around an image of a second trinity. Like the three ages of man, St. Anne looms, a towering matriarch, over both her daughter Mary and a smaller Christ child in Mary's lap (compare figure 41). The triad asserts the sanctity of Christ's lineage, and by eliminating Joachim, implies the unsullied purity of Mary's conception. Leonardo treated this trinity three times.

The Carmelites, who claimed descent from the prophet Elijah and his band of hermits on Mount Carmel, developed a new type of the Immaculate Virgin. They saw the single rain-bearing cloud, which appeared miraculously over the sea to end the great drought after Elijah's sacrifice to Yahweh on Carmel (I Kings 18:44), as Mary, who appeared as the harbinger of the end of the great drought before the Messiah, and they therefore professed a special devotion to the cult of her conception.[16]

The virgin birth of Christ began to redound along the line of the Virgin's ancestors in infinite regression. St. Anne's parents, Stollanus and Esmeria, were also singled out by divine prodigies. Esmeria, it was said, had joined the Carmelite order, but after a vision, her colleagues realized she was to be the ancestress of the saviour and encouraged her to leave the monastic life and marry. After five different husbands, each struck down by the jealous and threatened Satan, Esmeria succeeded with Stollanus, and conceived St. Anne (see figure 41).[17] (Esmeria is sometimes known as Emerentia.) This bizarre ancestry was revealed to a carpenter's daughter from Corbie, Picardy, Colette Boilet (d. 1447), who had tried herself to become a nun with the Beguines but failed, and then tried again and became the superior of the female wing of the Franciscan order, the Poor Clares, whom she reformed and spread throughout France, Savoy, Germany, and Flanders, the countries where the cult of the Immaculate Conception was most pronounced.[18]

The undertow of popular piety began to tug at the higher levels of the Church. At the Council of Constance in 1414, where Jean Gerson, chancellor of Paris, had pleaded for a feast of St. Joseph, he was no less eloquent on the need to recognize officially the doctrine and feast of the Immaculate Conception and to propagate its cult. At the Council of Basle in 1439, Pope Felix V declared the belief the official teaching of the Church. Unfortunately, the Church was in schism, and he was deposed as an anti-pope. When Sixtus IV, a Franciscan, came to the papal throne the views of his order prevailed, and in 1476 he formally instituted an office of extravagant praise for the feast.

The continuing debate took place against a background of renewed scrutiny of Scripture. Renaissance scholars like Lorenzo Valla (d. 1457) and Erasmus (d. 1536) were using sophisticated linguistic techniques to expose forgeries, apocryphal documents, and errors in the sacrosanct Latin Vulgate translation of the Bible by St. Jerome. Their criticisms did not immediately drive Catholics back into an entrenched reaction, but rather sharpened their appetite for biblical studies. Luther himself was a product of the questing and ardent piety that had begun coursing through Europe before the Reformation in protest at the clergy's corruption, ignorance, and superstition. Naturally, the invention of printing sent shock waves through the new movement, seizing Reformers and diehards alike. The appetite of the educated for Scripture, freed from the accretions of preachers' twaddle, was almost ungovernable. Between 1457 and 1500 over a hundred Latin editions of the Bible were printed. Luther's German Bible alone, or parts of it, went through three hundred and seventy-seven editions between its completion in 1534 and his death in 1546. The established Church's opposition to vernacular Bibles did not inhibit Catholic scholarship: the first polyglot Bible in Hebrew, Aramaic, Greek, and Latin, a most beautiful object to behold, was directed by the Spanish Cardinal Ximenes and printed at his new university between 1514–17.[19]

Paradoxically, the definition of the Immaculate Conception, wholly anathema to the Reformer, was the product of renewed scrutiny of Scripture by Catholic apologists, employing time-honoured techniques of allegorical interpretation.

The movement away from such works as the *Book of James* towards the inspired word of God began as the cult of St. Anne climaxed, at the end of the fifteenth century. By then, propaganda paintings commissioned for Franciscan churches began abandoning the embrace at the Golden Gate in favour of the theme of the Virgin's prefiguration in Scripture.[20] Fathers and Doctors of the Church surround her and hold scrolls that either foretell her miraculous sinlessness in biblical typology or quote their own works in support. Augustine and Anselm are frequently included in these groups, their lukewarm or non-existent endorsements conveniently overlooked. In the Church of San Francesco in Fiesole, Piero di Cosimo painted around 1480 the Virgin kneeling in adoration before God the Father, who holds up a book that reads, in the words of King Artaxerxes to Queen Esther in the Vulgate: *"Non enim pro te sed pro omnibus haec lex constituta est"* (Thou shalt not die: for this law is not made for thee, but for all others) (Douay. Esther 15:13).

The most important passage used to define the Immaculate Conception of the Virgin was the so-called *Proto-evangelion*, God's curse of the serpent in the Garden of Eden after the Fall, which has been traditionally interpreted as the first promise of a Redeemer, the first shaft of light across the shadows of Adam and Eve's exile. In Jerome's Vulgate, God's words read: "I will put enmities between thee and the woman, and thy seed and her seed: *she* shall crush thy head, and thou shalt lie in wait for her heel" (Douay. Genesis 3:15; author's italics).

In the "woman," Christians had seen a prophecy of the Virgin Mary ever since the fourth century, and the promised victory over the serpent had been used to develop the image of the second Eve who triumphs where the first Eve failed, who refuses where the first Eve was tempted.[21] When the controversy over the question of the Virgin's original sin became inflamed, this victory over the devil was used to prove that Mary was from the time of the creation predestined to escape altogether the devil's power. A total victory over Satan entailed total absence of sin— the Immaculate Conception.

But in the fifteenth century, Jerome's translation was already questioned. The Authorized Version gives the more accurate rendition of the Hebrew: "And I will put enmity between thee and the woman, and between thy seed and her seed; *it* shall bruise thy head, and thou shalt bruise his heel." The seed of the woman, not the woman herself, attacks the serpent; and the blow—whatever it is, for different translations have "grasp" or "bruise" or "strike"—is exactly reciprocated, the verb being the same in both parts of the sentence. Thus God does not prophesy a decisive victory over Satan by a woman, but an indecisive contest between the serpent and her offspring. But the mistranslation stuck, because of the decisions of the greatest Council of the Catholic Church, at Trent, from 1545 to 1563.

The Council of Trent did not proclaim Mary's Immaculate Conception, but it did exempt her, following St. Augustine, from the decree of universal original sin.[22] Such hedging fitted with the conciliatory policy of the early stages of the Council, and did not force a fray with the Reformers. At the same time, it did not fall into disrespect to the Mother of God. Two other separate decisions of the Council were much more momentous in Mariology, however: that the unwritten traditions of the Church and its members were to be held in equal honour as Scripture; and that the Vulgate Bible was the only canonical text. Regarding the first of these decisions, Owen Chadwick has pointed out that "it is clear that some of those who framed it were thinking not of an unwritten heritage of doctrine, but of certain practices, like the keeping of Sunday or the baptism of infants."[23] But whatever the intention of the councillors, the decree gave traditional beliefs, like the legends and miracles that fleshed out the shadowy Mary of Nazareth, a claim to canonical authority.

The traditional belief in the Immaculate Conception was crucially affected by the decision concerning the Vulgate text. For on three Marian counts, the translation was flawed, and although the Council agreed to emendations of Jerome's scholarship, these three renderings were retained as accurate. 'Almah was, as we have seen, translated as "virgin" and this was taken at absolute value; ave gratia plena, the angel Gabriel's greeting, was also taken at maximum force, implying that at the time of the Annunciation, that is, before the atonement, Mary was full of grace, not sin; above all, Jerome's version of the curse of the serpent in Eden was retained. In the Bull Ineffabilis Deus of 1854, the pope still quoted the Vulgate error:

the most holy Virgin . . . in union with him (Christ) and through him, waging eternal hostilities against the poisonous serpent, and obtaining a decisive triumph over him, completely crushed his head under her immaculate foot.[24]

Catholic scholarship is now ashamed that the Church's teaching should be built on such inaccuracies, but still maintains that the Virgin conquered evil through and with her son, as prophesied. Their latest English translation of the Bible scrupulously readjusts the prophecy, while the constitution of Vatican Two in 1964 was careful to emphasize that the Virgin had only co-operated with her son in the victory over the devil, and had not acted alone. But for three hundred years in Christian art and devotion her personal conquest, as prophesied by God to the serpent, had been lavishly celebrated. The image of the Immaculate Conception is still a favourite one in southern Europe, in Sicily and Spain in particular, where in churches and marketplaces Mary tramples the serpent's crushed head underfoot.

The Immaculate Conception is the most sophisticated theological image in Marian art. Francisco Pacheco (d. 1654), Velásquez' father-in-law, laid down the orthodox iconography in his Arte de la Pintura, inspired by the visions of the Portuguese mystic Beatrice de Silva (d. 1490). The imagery compresses together the passages of Scripture that in Catholic exegesis apply to the spotlessness of the Virgin. Like the superimposition of successive images in silkscreen printing, the woman prophesied in Genesis was overlaid on the "great wonder" seen by John in the Apocalypse (Revelation 12 passim). Clothed with the sun and standing on the moon, she prefigured the Assumption of the Virgin, as we have seen. But she also stood for Mary's participation in the victory of Christ over Satan, for her appearance heralded the battle between Michael and "the dragon and all his angels," in which the dragon is seized and bound and cast down into a bottomless pit, while the woman flees to the wilderness in safety and her son is snatched up to heaven.

This sun-robed figure was also assimilated into the Church and the figure of Wisdom in the Bible. Wisdom is the beloved of God from all eternity and says of herself: "He created me from the beginning before the world and I shall never fail" (Ecclesiasticus 24:9). Predestined and incapable of error, Mary was conceived in all purity in the mind of the creator, like the birth of an idea—Athene from the splitting head of Zeus. The Immaculate Conception thus became a metaphysical virgin birth, of the kind that had once been suggested in Alexandrian mystical thought on the generation of the Logos: the issue of the ideal by the power of the spirit. Since patristic times the figures of the Church and Wisdom and the Virgin were all encompassed by the smitten Shulamite of the Song of Songs, as the pre-eminent type of the bride of God. One verse in particular, among the loveliest and most languorous lines of all, prophesied the immaculate beauty of the predestined Virgin: "Thou art all fair, my love; and there is no spot in thee" (Song of Solomon 4:7) (*Tota pulchra es, amica mea; et macula non est in te*).

The Jesuits, founded in 1534, applied themselves with the fierce militancy of their order to spread the belief in Mary's Immaculate Conception, for it was one of the special Catholic ideas that roused the Reformers' tempers, and therefore proclaimed Rome's defiance and fearlessness. In the Gesù, the remarkable Jesuit church in Rome, hosts of cherubim and seraphim swarm on the ceiling, kicking and beating and pressing against one another in the chaos of a thriving paradise, all painted and carved in ingenious *trompe l'œil* and relief. There is a side chapel dedicated to the Virgin, which blazes all day with votive candles and hums to the sound of rosaries. The chapel was finished in 1575, just after the Council of Trent, and it stands next to the Jesuit founder Ignatius of Loyola's lapis lazuli and golden effigy, which incorporates a marvellously jesuitical statue of Religion trampling Heresy, with a gleeful angel tearing Heresy's book to pieces. In the chapel, all the biblical passages thought to prefigure the Immaculate Conception are inlaid in coloured marbles on the walls and floor, a material and splendid catena of authorities.

The image of the Immaculate Conception did not reach visual perfection, however, until seventeenth-century Spanish artists like Velásquez (d. 1660) (colour plate VII, figure 9), Zurbarán (d. 1664), Ribera (d.

1652), and Murillo (d. 1682) excelled themselves in this particular devotion.

The traditional embrace of Joachim and Anne was obsolete because it focussed attention on the physical circumstances of Mary's conception. Indeed, the image was formally banned by Pope Innocent XI in 1677. The conception of the Virgin before time was expressed by an altogether new image. Murillo, in his *Aranjuez Conception* now in the Prado—one of a score of paintings he made of the Immaculate Conception—shows Mary as a young girl, neither child nor woman, abiding in the pleroma of youth and beauty, as she existed in the mind of God "before the beginning." The sun's radiance forms an aureole around her, her eyes roll upwards to gaze on the vast mysteries of the heavens, and the expression of her lips is gentle and sweet; her arms folded across her breasts show her prayerful submission to her unique and exalted destiny. Cherubim bear her aloft, one holding lilies, another an olive branch and a cornsheaf, the symbols of her purity, her wisdom, and her fruitfulness. Highly emotional, honey-flavoured, and devout in the full-blown manner of the seventeenth century, it is the kind of Counter-Reformation propaganda painting that makes aesthetes and non-Catholics alike shudder, although it succinctly synthesizes message and style in as remarkably communicative a way as the earliest code symbols of the Church, like the Cross and the fish.

The painters of the Counter-Reformation were often less concerned with beauty than engaged in the fight against blasphemy. Domenichino (d. 1641), in a fresco on the church of San Gennaro in Naples, sent Luther and Calvin sprawling under the foot of a young Catholic saint, while a woman, an allegory of Prayer, says her rosary, her *Ave Marias* winging their way heavenwards towards Mary, pictured as the Immaculate Conception, who receives them and intercedes with God. At one stroke, Domenichino vengefully replied to the Reformers' attacks on the mediation and the Immaculate Conception of the Virgin.[25]

The iconography of the Immaculate Conception can include other symbols: the twelve stars from the Apocalypse sometimes encircle her head; sometimes, rather startlingly, she contemplates herself, Venus-like, in a mirror—an image taken from the Book of Wisdom in which Wisdom is described as the *specula sine macula,* the unspotted mirror of God (Wisdom of Solomon 7:26).

But the widespread acclamation of the Immaculate Virgin in art of the seventeenth century obscures the true bitterness of the continuing conflict, particularly between Dominican and Jesuit. In one church, the preacher sighed that all who denied Mary's spotlessness would burn eternally; in the church next door, a priest fulminated the opposite. The clashes were so frequent, and so often bloody, that in 1616 Pope Paul V forbade all discussion of the subject from the pulpit. In 1622 Pope Gregory XV had to increase the ban of his predecessor. For, like the Christological quarrels of the early Church, the dispute had raged in the streets. Absolute silence was imposed on all parties, with the exception of the sceptical Dominicans, who were permitted by the pope to pursue the truth, but strictly within the walls of their convents. Ippolito Maracci (d. 1675), a fanatical Mariolater, was excommunicated for disobeying this law.

Societies of "the slavery of Mary" continued in France, where the proximity of Protestants whipped up Rome's supporters. Vows were taken and sealed in blood that the Virgin's honour would be defended unto death against detractors. Saints of the French seventeenth-century revival, like Jean Eudes (d. 1680), declared that Mary

was an exact counterpart to Jesus: He [God] would give this Virgin Mother to us. And as the Son is the figure of his substance . . . and the perfect image of the Divinity . . . so also Mary should bear a perfect resemblance to him.[26]

Christ was born without stain; then, so was Mary.

By the eighteenth century, the Jesuits had honeycombed Dominican arguments with objections and their resistance was crumbling. The penetrating, learned, and often inspiring theology of members of the Society like the Spaniard Francisco Suarez and Peter Canisius (d. 1597), who had deployed all their impressive machinery, finally persuaded the Dominican order that their most illustrious member, St. Thomas Aquinas, had refrained from pronouncing Mary immaculate only because he had misunderstood the character of human generation.

When Pius IX proclaimed the Immaculate Conception in 1854 he therefore closed a prolonged and epic struggle within the Catholic Church. Four years later, his dogma was ratified, in the true spirit of the Counter-Reformation, by the appearance of the Virgin in person.

In the Pyrenean mountain town of Lourdes, once fortified against Islamic invasion, a fourteen-year-old girl who could not read or write and who had suffered from cholera three years before and acute asthma all her life, saw a lady eighteen times in a grotto by the river. *Aquerò,* as she called her (which means "she" in the local dialect), was "a very young girl," wearing a veil and an azure sash, barefoot except for two roses "more gleaming than gold," with eyes "blue as forget-me-nots." A white light, "like sunlight on the ground," preceded her, and during the visions the young woman and the child would tell their beads together and talk. Bernadette Soubirous went into trance before the grotto as she prayed, while crowds, who by the end numbered thousands, watched her movements. On one occasion, she scraped the ground and uncovered a spring, from which she drank the muddy waters. She also ate some grass. She said later *Aquerò* had told her to do so as a penance. The local church hierarchy pressed Bernadette to ask *Aquerò* her name. Obediently she did, but it was not until the sixteenth vision, on the feast of the Annunciation, 1858, that in reply to Bernadette's fourth reiteration of the question, the vision answered in dialect: *"Que soy era Immaculata Counception."*

I went back to M. le Curé, to tell him that she had told me she was the Immaculate Conception. And he asked me if I was certain of it. I replied that I was, and that in order not to forget the phrase, I had repeated it to myself the whole way there.[27]

When pressed for the exact features of the lady of her visions, Bernadette always maintained that the parade of Raphaels and Botticellis shown her did the Virgin little justice. The statue eventually erected in the grotto of Massabielle pleased her even less. But in the church at Nevers, near the convent where she retired, there was a statue of the Virgin standing on a serpent with her arms outstretched, palms outwards at her sides, whom Bernadette innocently and stoutly maintained "was a perfect resemblance—in the face and the clothes."[28]

But if her vision was influenced by art she had seen, she was not the first among Christian saints to respond vividly to images. Millard Meiss has demonstrated the profound effect art had on Catherine of Siena and such visionaries in the fourteenth century,[29] while at Knock in Ireland in 1879 the witnesses ingenuously maintained they recognized the saints who appeared with the Virgin because they looked like their statues.

Bernadette had also been going to the local nuns for instruction in the catechism, a necessary preparation for the sacrament of First Communion, and it is likely, though not proved, that she would have heard the nuns discuss the four-year-old dogma proclaimed by the pope. Her sincerity is nevertheless unimpeachable: she believed in her visions. The Church, after submitting the young girl to involved interrogations, which she withstood with unflinching simplicity, chose to endorse her. The shrine at Lourdes was permitted to become a place of pilgrimage.

Bernadette wrote to Pope Pius IX eight years after the visions from the convent at Nevers, where she had become a nun:

It seems to me . . . that from heaven the Blessed Virgin must often look on you in her maternal way, most Holy Father, for you proclaimed her Immaculate. I like to think that you are very particularly loved by this good mother, because four years later she came in person on earth to say "I am the Immaculate Conception." I did not know what that meant, I had never heard the words. I have often said to myself: how good the blessed Virgin is. One would think she came to confirm the words of our Holy Father.[30]

It is surprising that the belief stirred so much rancour. For it extends with complete logic the doctrines of the virgin birth of Christ and the belief in the Virgin's Assumption, both of which resulted from her exemption from the natural law that was the penalty of the Fall: childbirth in pain and suffering, corruption in the grave. The only biological function she was allowed (apart from the asexual function of weeping) was lactation, and as we have seen, the Dominicans, who opposed the Immaculate Conception, fostered the cult of the Virgin's milk. As she had been, since earliest times, considered free of the consequences of the Fall, then it is only logical to argue she was free of the root of those consequences—original sin.

But a great problem arises for non-Catholic Christians, Greek Orthodox and Protestants alike, when they contemplate the mystery of the Immaculate Conception. For under this aspect Mary is worshipped alone. In Bernadette's vision, or in the established iconography, the child does not appear on her arm. Alone, Mary ceases to be the instrument of the Incarnation, worthy of reverence because she is the *Theotokos,* the god-bearer, a creature uniquely wonderful but only because she is the mother of the Redeemer. This had been the crux of the devotion to the Virgin since earliest times. The Reformers continued this strain of piety: for instance, the feast of the Annunciation was retained by the Reformed Churches as the feast of Christ's conception. One Reformer repeated the vulgar stricture of the Iconoclast Emperor Constantine V in the eighth century: "When she bore Christ within her womb, she was like a purse filled with gold. But after giving birth, she was no more than an empty purse."[31] Although the Greeks had led the way to the doctrine of the Immaculate Virgin by their cult of her miraculous birth, they opposed the veneration of her as anything but the mother of the Redeemer, and were followed in this by the Reformed Churches.

The continuing resistance of the Greek and Russian Orthodox Churches and the various Protestant denominations to the concept of the Immaculate Conception is also based on a very much more important and sympathetic argument. For by her exceptional freedom from original sin, Mary is set apart from the human race in a special and separate trans-human category. The Orthodox Churches accept the Assumption of the Virgin because it presages the glory of every man and woman's resurrection. But the Immaculate Conception denies the common bond of humanity between Mary and the rest of us. For them, the Virgin is a human creature who has attained a pinnacle of perfection that is in theory accessible to all of us if we cooperate with God's will. Original sin is not an inherited stain, but human weakness, and to deprive Mary of it robs her of her full humanity and also of the greatness of her achievement. So the danger recognized by the dissidents from the dogma of the Immaculate Conception, both then and now, is an ancient one: Gnostic dualism. Mary is proclaimed the most perfect created being next to Jesus, but only because she is exempted by special decree from the fullness of the human condition. The lesson of the doctrine is that the ideal cannot be incarnate in a creature who is like everyone else.

The dogma of the Assumption, proclaimed by Pius XII in 1950, was a logical development from the dogma of the Immaculate Conception: free from original sin, she was dogmatically free from putrefaction in the grave. And this privilege raised another question, now debated in the Vatican: did Mary die? Scholars are still sifting the patristic evidence for and against; and their deliberations depend on whether death itself, not only the mortality of the flesh, was a penalty of the Fall.[32] The Fathers disagree over the exact nature of the beatitude of Adam and Eve in Eden: a few maintain that they would have died, peacefully and painlessly, but more that immortal life and youth was the bliss they forfeited. Death, sex, and sin, as we have seen, were most commonly thought the bitter fruit of their disobedience. The difficulty is that if Mary escaped all the penalties of the Fall, including death, she would be exalted above her son, who tasted the grave for three days. John Damascene reminded his congregation: "We do not celebrate a goddess, as in the fantastic fables of the Greeks, since we proclaim her death."[33] Hera, Athene, Aphrodite, Diana, Cybele, or Isis do not age and do not die, but Mary lived a human life that ended in the human way.

In the Counter-Reformation, the manner and causes of the Virgin's death, if she did indeed experience it, were lengthily discussed: Francis de Sales (d. 1622) suggested Mary died of love, daily re-experiencing the

Crucifixion, and longing so intensely for reunion with her son that the pain killed her. Francis reached a pitch of ardour:

From then on this love assaulted her so many times, her heart leapt so many times, the wound became so inflamed that in the end it was impossible for her not to die of it. . . . *O amor vulneris, o vulnus amoris:* O passion of love, o love of the Passion. . . .[34]

Suarez was much more restrained, and resolved the problem in a cunning compromise: Mary had died only as an act of profound humility, renouncing the exemption from the grave to which her immaculate conception entitled her. Her consent to death completes, in his view, her cooperation in the redemption and crowns her compassion at Calvary.

No decision has yet been reached in the matter; the definitions of the Immaculate Conception and the Assumption, and the constitution of Vatican Two, skirt the question of Mary's death. Pius XII stated that "having completed the course of her earthly life, [she] was assumed body and soul into heavenly glory."[35] Paul VI's Constitution is equally circumspect: "the immaculate Virgin was taken up body and soul into heavenly glory upon the completion of her earthly sojourn."[36]

What is death but the separation of body from soul, and the dissolution of the flesh in the grave? If Mary conquered both, she conquered death. It is difficult to draw the line, after both the Immaculate Conception and the Assumption have been declared articles of faith.

Another analogous problem is that according to some Fathers of the Church, the entire process of parturition, from menstruation to lactation, was a penalty of the Fall. If Mary through her Immaculate Conception was spared all the Fall's consequences, then the doctrine opens onto perilous ground, for the full humanity of Jesus would be questionable. (Justin Martyr in the second century had already trespassed here when he maintained that Jesus' blood was not like other men's.[37]) One impracticable answer to this problem for those who wish to believe in both the full manhood of Jesus Christ and the Immaculate Conception would be to stand traditional Christian prejudice on its head and reject the idea of menstruation as a "curse" and accept it as a condition of Eden when man and woman were friends with the Creator. Another more common escape route from the quandary is to maintain that it is the effect, not the phenomenon, that is the penalty and the sign of original sin: thus putrefaction, not death; labour pains, not childbirth; cramp and discomfort, not menstruation in itself, are the consequences of Adam's sin.

However the reply is framed, the Immaculate Conception remains the dogma by which the Virgin Mary is set apart from the human race because she is not stained by the Fall. And if on one plane the perfection of Mary is defined as the conquest of the natural laws of childbearing and death, then the prevailing idea of perfection denies the goodness of the created world, and of the human body, and postulates another perfect destiny where such conditions do not obtain. This is dualistic, and the Virgin Mary is a symbol and an instrument of that dualism.

As the icon of the ideal, the Virgin affirms the inferiority of the human lot. Soaring above the men and women who pray to her, the Virgin conceived without sin underscores rather than alleviates pain and anxiety and accentuates the feeling of sinfulness. The state her votaries believe to be hers must always elude them, for all creatures except her are, they are told, born in sin. Mary is indeed Eve's other face: the two female symbols excite that very emotion that the story of the Fall sought to explain and the story of the Incarnate God sought to heal: the feeling that in its very nature humanity is fatally estranged from goodness, which, for a believer, is God. Any symbol that exacerbates that pain runs counter to the central Christian doctrine that mankind was made and redeemed by God, and, more important, it is a continuing enemy of hope and happiness.

## Chapter Seventeen

# THE MOON
# AND THE STARS

*The Roman Empire stood appalled:*
*It dropped the reins of peace and war*
*When that fierce virgin and her Star*
*Out of the fabulous darkness called.*[1]

—W. B. YEATS

FOR ALL WESTERN society's revival of astrology, for all our explorations and adventures in space, we look uncomprehendingly at the skies, if we look at them at all. Few people can distinguish a waxing moon from the sickle on the wane; and the unceasing rhythm of the heavenly bodies is barren of significance. The promise of a comet, like Kohoutek in 1974, can whip up a brief spasm of excitement, but only because our torpid powers of perception are roused by the sensational, by the aberrational. Perhaps neon light has so dimmed the lustre of the night sky in the cities that we are literally blinded; perhaps the imagery of the galaxy finally proved so disappointing and unsatisfying that we have justly forgotten it. For even adepts of astrology consult charts and calendars, and cannot pick out their native constellation in the sky itself.

But this was not so in the hellenistic world that nurtured Christianity. In its symbolism and philosophy, no comparable disjunction between the tangible and visible world of nature and the intangible and invisible world of spirit existed; rather, they were fused in a rich and multi-layered language soundly rooted in observation—sometimes scientific, sometimes not—of the planetary system in which the world moves.

When the Virgin Mary, as the Immaculate Conception, hangs suspended in the heavens on the orb or on the crescent of the moon (colour plate VII, figure 9), she recapitulates this language in a form that in some respects alters the original meaning, in others sustains it. For the moon at the Virgin's feet represents more than the "great wonder" of Revelation 12:1, who appeared "clothed with the sun, and the moon under her feet, and upon her head a crown of twelve stars," and the beloved of the Canticle who "looketh forth as the morning, fair as the moon, clear as the sun" (Song of Solomon 6:10). The moon has been the most constant attribute of female divinities in the western world, and was taken over by the Virgin Mary because of ancient beliefs about its functions and role, which Christianity inherited.

When Lucius, at the end of the *Golden Ass* of Apuleius, is initiated into the mysteries of Isis, he sees the goddess in a vision, which might equally describe the appearance of the Virgin Mary in Murillo's *Aranjuez Conception,* or in the revelations of Catherine Labouré, who saw her in 1830 as the Immaculate Conception. For Isis, in hellenistic Egypt, was an astral divinity:

Her hair, long and hanging in tapered ringlets, fell luxuriantly on her divine neck; a crown of varied form encircled the summit of her head, with a diversity of flowers, and in the middle of it, just over her forehead, there was a flat circlet, which resembled a mirror or rather emitted a white refulgent light, thus indicating that she was the moon. Vipers rising from furrows of the earth, supported this on the right hand and on the left, while ears of corn projected on either side. . . . And then, what rivetted my gaze far more than all, was her mantle of the deepest black, which shone with a glossy lustre. It was wrapped around her . . . while a part of the robe fell down in many folds, and gracefully floated with its little knots of fringe that edged its extremities. Glittering stars were dispersed along the embroidered extremities of the robe, and over its whole surface; and in the middle of them a moon of two weeks old breathed forth its flaming fires. . . . Such was the appearance of the mighty goddess.[2]

By the second century, when Apuleius (b. *c.* 114) wrote his remarkable tale of his hero's adventures, Isis had acquired characteristics that associated her with Diana and other classical sky goddesses, whose particular business was the gift and sustenance of life, by rendering women fertile, and easing their pain in childbirth, by bringing plenty to the earth or, as in the case of Apuleius, restoring him to human shape after an enchantress had turned him into an ass.

The Church absorbed the planetary symbolism of the neoplatonists to turn it to good Christian account.[3] The feminine moon, who nourishes life with her beams, was first identified with the Church and then by analogy with the Virgin Mary; the sun was identified with Christ. The most powerful threat to Christianity in its infancy was the worship of Helios the sun, which during the first four centuries A.D. was absorbing and superseding all other cults of the Roman empire. Squarely facing the menace, the Christians of the west fixed Christmas Day on the very feast of *Sol Invictus,* the Unconquered Sun, and invoked Christ by his name, as in St. Ambrose's Dawn hymns.[4] (In the east Christmas was kept on January 6, not December 25, until the fourth century, when St. Jerome introduced the western custom in Bethlehem.)

The pagan symbolism of the sun god also affected the celebration of Easter. For although local tradition held that Jesus rose from the dead on the fourteenth of the Jewish month Nisan, when the first full moon of spring occurs, western Christians kept the memory of his Resurrection on the first day of the sun—Sunday—following the first full moon after the spring equinox. Thus the Christian liturgical year commemorates the birth of its god after the winter solstice, on the day when the sun has ended its long hibernation and begun to rise towards the spring; and in the west, celebrates his rebirth from the dead on the day when the sun has finally triumphed over darkness and the days are drawing ahead, lasting longer than the nights. (There was a bitter struggle during the second century over the date of Easter, and east and west still keep it on different days. But the controversy does not concern us here.)

As well as solar imagery, pagan lunar symbolism has been assimilated into Christian thought. For the moon is filled with light by the sun in an eternal dance; and at Easter the moon is also growing towards its summer brilliance. In some Greek thought, the moon was believed to retain the sunlight, to preserve it for the following day, and thus to mother each new sun into being. The harmonious symmetry of the sun and moon's constant relations inspired Greek Christians to perceive the ideal of the Church's relations with Christ. Methodius of Olympus, in the *Symposium of Ten Virgins,* interprets the Woman Clothed with the Sun of Apocalypse 12 as the Church that, reflecting like the moon the dazzling light of Christ, pours forth more light on the souls of her members. The Church is Christ's bride, and the mother of his flock.[5]

Origen in Alexandria, and Ambrose and Augustine later in the west all perceived in the relations of the sun and moon the ideal model of the love and reciprocity between Christ and his bride the Church. Hugo Rahner, the great contemporary Jesuit theologian, describes these sacred mysteries:

Selene (the moon) becomes that heavenly star which hangs as an inter-
mediary between the sublime light of Helios (the sun) and the dark
earth, the great mediator between the world of pure spirit of the fixed
stars and the dark sensuality of earthly elements.[6]

By the middle ages, as we have seen, the Church and the Virgin were
closely identified, particularly with the symbol of the woman of the
Apocalypse and the beloved of the Canticle.[7] The Virgin thereby acquired the lunar imagery previously applied to the Church; and as belief
in her intercession with God became more profound, the idea crystallized
that Mary, through her mediation, bent the beams of God's grace into the
Christian soul, just as the Church stood before Christ, her bridegroom,
irradiated by his grace, or as the moon is filled with sunlight and sheds it
on the earth at night. Also through the Virgin, the sun was born at
Christmas.[8] Analogously, each Christian is reborn in the light of Christ,
which she deflects on them.

Hugo Rahner quotes a penitential song chanted by the Flagellants as
they marched in the fourteenth century:

> Ave Regina pure et gente
> Tres Haulte, ave maris stella
> Ave Précieuse jovante
> Lune, ou Dieu s'esconsa
> Se ne fust la Vierge Marie
> Le siècle fust pieça perdu.
>
> Ave Regina, pure and loving
> Most noble; Ave maris stella,
> Ave, dear Maid,
> Moon where God took hiding.
> But for the Virgin Mary
> The world had been lost.[9]

Pope Innocent III (1198–1216) exhorted the faithful:

Towards the Moon it is he should look, who is buried in the shades of sin
and iniquity. Having lost grace, the day disappears and there is no more
sun for him, but the Moon is still on the horizon. Let him address himself
to Mary; under her influence thousands every day find their way to God.[10]

The pope's use of the ancient symbols is learned and precise; but the
lore passed into the vernacular poetry of the faithful to surface poi-
gnantly in street and sailor songs. Cardinal Jean Daniélou (d. 1974)

himself heard Normandy fishermen invoking the help of the Virgin under her aspect as the tutelary moon:

> *Veillez toujours, belle lune*
> *Aux besoins de vos dévots.*
>
> Watch over always, lovely moon,
> the needs of those devoted to you.[11]

The association of the Virgin with the moon in seventeenth-century paintings of the Immaculate Conception had probably already impressed St. Catherine Labouré's imagination. Her own vision of the Virgin in Paris in 1830 did, however, strengthen the identification of Mary with the moon in the popular mind. The Virgin appeared to her in a white silken rustling dress, swathed in a white veil, with dazzling rays flashing from her extended hands. Her feet crushed the serpent and rested on a globe, which she informed Catherine was France or the whole world. She asked her to make a medal of the vision and institute its cult in her honour and for the protection of her votaries. Catherine's vision greatly helped the movement to define the Immaculate Conception; and her miraculous medal is the talisman of the Legion of Mary and is worn by Catholics all over the world.[12] Although the globe at Mary's feet is the earth, not the moon, the iconography so resembles the Immaculate Conception that the two spheres have been confused, and the saving activities of the Virgin are intimately intertwined with the imagery of the moon, whose silver light she pours from her hands onto the earth.

In the thought of late antiquity, the light of the moon not only dispelled the shadows of night, but also had all-important life-giving powers. The grace of God, mediated through Mary, as the light of the sun reflects off the disc of the moon, also gives life and quickens and nourishes and purifies, like water. Thus the imagery of light was intimately associated with the imagery of water, itself the foremost image of grace. The Egyptians of hellenistic times considered the moon the source of moisture, the "governess of floods" and hence the principle of fertility and life. Plutarch, in his description of the cult of Isis and Osiris, is clear on this score:

The moon, because it was light that is generative and productive of moisture, is kindly towards the young of animals and the burgeoning plants, whereas the sun, by its untempered and pitiless heat, makes all growing and flourishing vegetation hot and parched, and through its blazing light, renders a large part of the earth uninhabitable. . . . In fact, the actions of the moon are like the actions of reason and perfect wisdom, whereas those of the sun are like beatings administered through violence and brute strength.

Plutarch then moves from the Egyptians' view of the moon's functions to the Stoics, who "assert that the sun is kindled and fed from the sea, but that for the moon, the moving waters from the springs and lakes send up a sweet and mild exhalation."[13]

According to some systems of symbolic thought that arose in the dry lands of Egypt and Asia Minor, North Africa and Greece, the sun stood for ferocious energy and power, and its rays were only beneficent when converted, as it seemed, by the limpid light of the moon into the dew that irrigates the earth at night. Had Christianity not taken root in the sun-baked east, the astral images it employs might have been very different. (The religion is not always consistent in its use, however: the sun also corresponds to the highest principle or mind, and was often identified with Christ, as we have seen, while the moon mediates between the mind and the body, as the Church does between Christ the sun and the world of the faithful on earth.)

Dew was "moonwater" to the Greeks and to their intellectual followers; it imparted life. The moon also coincided with, and appeared to control, the menstrual cycle of women, which was widely considered the prime matter of human life. Because aridity was death and moisture quickened it; because the conception of a child depended on the fertility of a woman, and that in turn was, it appeared, governed by the moon, a nexus of images of water, moonlight, and birth bound together the Christian doctrine of the Redemption through an incarnate god with the relations of the cosmic galaxy and the earth, as perceived by the contemplative philosophies of neoplatonism and stoicism, and by their heirs in medieval and Renaissance thought.

The powers of the moon over fertility are maintained, for instance, in the popular but quack medical handbook *De Secretis Mulieribus* (On the Secrets of Women), long attributed to Albertus Magnus, Aquinas' teacher.[14] Shakespeare drew on the symbolism, particularly in *Midsummer Night's Dream,* where Titania, a moon spirit, laments the disarray of nature since her quarrel with Oberon, a sun figure:

> Therefore the moon, the governess of floods,
> Pale in her anger, washes all the air,
> That rheumatic diseases do abound.
> And through this distemperature we see

The seasons alter: hoary-headed frosts
Fall in the fresh lap of the crimson rose. . . .
(Act II, Sc. 1: 103–8)

In the iconography of the Virgin Mary, the connection between the moon and fecundity is alluded to in that loveliest and most sympathetic of images, the nursing Madonna of Humility in Trecento Italian art. Millard Meiss believes the lost Simone Martini prototype may have assembled the sun, moon, and stars around the Madonna, thus underlining the cosmological associations of milk (see Chapter 13). In many paintings the lowly Virgin, sitting on the ground, is set against an explosion of light: the aureole of the sun, the shimmering light of the moon, and the twelve dazzling stars either in a halo round her head, or on the dark blue field behind her.[15] The combination of the Virgin suckling and these astral symbols does not derive directly from Revelation 12, for the "great wonder" of John travails to give birth and cries out, but does not give suck, for the child is snatched away from her. Also, there is no scene more serene or more loving in Christian art than the nursing Madonna (figure 34). The juxtaposition of the supernatural signs with the natural act of a mother emphasizes, with a characteristic medieval love of polarity, the Mother of God's self-effacement. But it also springs from the classical analogy between the nutrient properties of both milk and lunar light.[16] Dürer, in the frontispiece of his popular cycle of engravings on the *Life of the Virgin,* later isolated the image, and seated the nursing Virgin in a sweeping sickle moon aloft above the clouds, a dynamic and impressive picture of the miracle of the Incarnation, very different in feeling from the original Madonna of Humility from which it is derived.[17]

The Virgin Mary was associated not only with the moon's fertility, but also with two other lunar properties: its constancy, which makes it nature's own most accurate timepiece, and its hegemony over the tides. In Indo-European languages, the word for "measure" and the word for "moon" stem from the same root: *mas* in Sanskrit; *mah* in Avestic and Old Prussian; *menu* in Lithuanian; *mena* in Gothic; *mene* in Greek; *mensis* in Latin.[18] Before chronometry, the moon marked the passage of time. In English, the pre-horological habit of counting by nights and not by days survives in the expression "fortnight" and in the lingering custom of keeping great feasts on what is now considered their vigil: Hallowe'en, Christmas Eve, and Easter Eve. Unchanging and precise, yet in constant flux, the moon vividly symbolizes the idea of eternity; therefore, when adopted by the Virgin, it stands for both her eternal predestination in the creator's scheme and for the undying and invincible existence of the Church.

Secondly, the moon moves the tides to her ebb and flow, as the Celts and the Greeks both noted. Posidonius, in the first century B.C., won renown in the empire when he travelled to Cadiz and ascertained from observation of the tidal Atlantic that, as he and others had intuited, the tides rose and fell to the rhythm of the moon.[19]

In this pattern of symbolism, Mary—like classical goddesses before her—emerged the eternal mistress of the waters, the protective deity of life, and especially the patroness of women in childbirth. In the Orphic mysteries' initiation prayers, the goddess Diana was addressed as *Prothyraea*, the Gate-keeper:

> Benignant nourisher; great Nature's key
> Belongs to no divinity but thee . . .
> Thine is the task to loose the virgin's zone . . .
> With births you sympathise, tho' pleas'd to see
> The numerous offspring of fertility;
> When rack'd with nature's pangs and sore distress'd,
> The sex invoke thee, as the soul's sure rest. . . .[20]

The Virgin Mary inherited these ancient responsibilities of the moon goddess, as we shall see in more detail later (Chapter 18).

As a lunar deity she was also closely associated with the sea. One interpretation of her name derives it from *mar*, Latin for sea. St. Jerome glossed the Hebrew Miriam of the Gospel as *stilla maris*, a drop of the sea. The sway of astronomy over the medieval imagination was so strong, and the Virgin so closely identified with the heavens, that the slip of a scribe's hand introduced into Marian literature and art one of its most suggestive and beautiful metaphors. For an early copyist wrote *stella maris*, star of the sea, instead of *stilla maris*, a mistake that persisted until the most recent edition of Jerome's *On the Interpretation of Hebrew Names*.[21] Thus the Virgin was associated not only with the moon, but also with other planets of the firmament. In the seventh- or eighth-century antiphon *Ave Maris Stella*, included in the Office of the Virgin, Mary appears as the ocean's guide, the pole star, winking benignly overhead to make life's journey safe. The dancing lines evoke her also as the gate of heaven, and the light-bearer, who purifies the sinner with her gentle fires.[22] Anselm uses the latter title;[23] Bernard loved it, as another perfect symbol of Mary's incorrupt virginity, because it seemed to him that a star burns and burns and is never consumed. Her splendour, he wrote, "both shines in the heavens and penetrates into hell;

and as it traverses the lands, it causes minds to glow with virtues more than bodies with heat, while vices it burns up and consumes." With the fine sustained use of metaphor at which Bernard excelled, he brings his sermon to its climax:

If the winds of temptation arise, if you are diving upon the rocks of tribulation, look to the star, invoke Mary. If you are tossed upon the waves of pride, of ambition, or envy, or rivalry, look to the star, invoke Mary.[24]

Painters placed the glittering star on the Virgin's shoulder in altarpieces of the middle ages; and poets worked the theme, stressing sometimes the nautical imagery, as in John of Garland's thirteenth-century collection of Miracles of the Virgin called *Stella Maris,* in which Mary figures as the mariners' guiding light, and sometimes exulting purely in the beauty of the image, as in the lovely line that recurs in a student song composed in Paris around 1300 in honour of the Virgin's birthday: *Stella maris hodie processit ad ortum* (The star of the sea moves today to its rising).[25]

Petrarch, in his most beautiful and stirring meditation on the Virgin, the final *canzone* of his cycle about Laura, gives the image its most anguished interior intensity, when he invokes her as the star that holds sway over his life, and pleads for her help:

> *Vergine chiara stabile in eterno,*
> *Di questo tempestoso mare stella,*
> *D'ogni fedel nocchier fidata guida,*
> *Pon' mente in che terribile procella*
> *I' mi ritrovo sol, senza governo. . . .*

> (Bright virgin, steadfast in eternity
> Star of this storm-tossed sea,
> Trusted guide of every trustful pilot
> Turn your thoughts to the terrifying squall
> In which I find myself, alone and rudderless. . . .)[26]

On the prow of fishing boats in Sicily, where once the protective eye of Horus was blazoned, the star of the sea emblem of the Virgin is now painted. So although the image is so familiar, a stock-in-trade of sermons —the Christian soul tossed on a sea of tribulation, with hope his anchor, and God his haven—it avoids that deadly ring of staleness in Petrarch's plea or on a Sicilian fisherman's amulet.

The *stella maris* was identified not only with the pole star, but also with the *stella matutina,* the morning star, which the ancients called

Phosphorus by day and Hesperus by night, the first star of evening and
the last star of morning, so dazzling that it casts a shadow in the darkness
and can still be seen with the naked eye in sunlight. The Babylonians had
named this planet after the sky goddess Ishtar, whom they also associated
with the moon, and the Romans renewed the Babylonian image when
they renamed it after the goddess Venus, who by then had absorbed the
character and functions of the Greek goddess of love Aphrodite.[27] Thus
Dante, who was steeped in the metaphysical topography of the heavens
as determined by Christian neoplatonism, placed the lovers in the sphere
of Venus in Paradise. It is as this star, *stella matutina,* not *stella maris,*
that the Virgin is invoked in the litany of Loreto, an anthology of her
titles and attributes.

Naturally, the Virgin was also associated with the constellation
Virgo; and the most interesting instance of this was the Christian interpretation of Virgil's *Fourth Eclogue,* in which he hails the birth of an
heroic child who will inaugurate a golden age. Christian mystics from the
twelfth century onwards understood this as a messianic text, and they can
hardly be reproached, since the eloquent and rapturous lines stir memories of God in the Garden of Eden and recall the impassioned luxuriance
of Isaiah's prophecies:

> *occidet et serpens, et fallax herba veneni*
> *occidet; Assyrium vulgo nascetur amomum.*
> *at simul heroum laudes et facta parentis*
> *iam legere et quae sit poteris cognoscere virtus,*
> *molli paulatim flavescet campus arista*
> *incultisque rubens pendebit sentibus uva*
> *et durae quercus sudabunt roscida mella.*

> (Destruction shall o'ertake the serpent's brood,
> The tree of poison seeming good for food
> Destruction shall o'ertake; and in its stead
> Assyrian spices in abundance spread.
> And then, O Child, as soon as thou canst read
> Of famous heroes, and of many a deed
> Wrought by thy father, and canst fully know
> Wherein consists true manliness below,
> A golden light from waving fields of grain
> Shall slowly broaden o'er the fertile plain,
> And pendent from the rough uncultured brake
> The ruddy grapes shall in the breezes shake
> While many a grove of cross-grained oaks at will
> Shall dewy honey from their trunks distil.)[28]

This age of gold will supersede the age of iron, Virgil prophesies, when the stars move into a new position in the wheeling heavens; and the conjunction he describes is Virgo with Saturn, the planet that the medieval schoolmen associated with contemplation:

> *iam redit et virgo, redeunt Saturnia regna,*
> *iam nova progenies caelo demittitur alto.*

(Now returns the Virgin also, and the rule of Saturn; now a new race is sent down from the highest heaven.) [29]

It has never been discovered for certain whom Virgil was in fact addressing. That Christian scholars should have read his apostrophe of a marvellous boy, the hero of a new and golden age, as a prophecy of Christ and of his birth from a virgin, is hardly surprising, for the Catholic Church has frequently sought to establish that it always existed in the mind of a provident creator who subtly prepared the world for its coming, and second that the Christian era does not represent a rupture with the civilization of the ancient past, but a continuation of its noblest feelings. It was partly because of the *Fourth Eclogue* that Dante chose Virgil for his guide in the Christian afterlife.

(Another early legend made a similar attempt to link the pagan past, symbolized by the Emperor Augustus, with the Christian era, symbolized by the Virgin in her apocalyptic splendour. The emperor, according to the story, consulted the Tiburtine sibyl on the day Jesus Christ was born. The Senate wished to elect him a god, for he had brought peace to the world, but the sibyl told him:"Today is born a king who will be more powerful than you." The heavens opened and the emperor saw the Virgin and child seated in the centre of a flaming sun. "Here is the altar of heaven," said a voice. Augustus therefore caused an altar to be built on the Capitol, which the church of S. Maria in Aracoeli claims it still preserves. The vision of the first Roman emperor was painted often in Italy, and after it appeared as a prophecy of Christ's triumph in the popular *Speculum Humanae Salvationis,* probably composed in 1324 in Strasbourg, it acquired widespread currency in medieval Europe.) [30]

Within the imagery of these planets and constellations, the Virgin's association with the sea must never be forgotten, for in a different age the night sky's principal practical function was navigation. Mary's astral character gives her, in medieval legend, hegemony over tempests, not only as the star that leads sailors to safety, but even more directly as a goddess with powers to still the wind and calm the waves. As we saw, the storm abated when the abbot Elsinus promised he would institute the feast of the Immaculate Conception on his safe return to England. Another of these early miracle stories of the Virgin illustrates her power over the element of water (three others tell of her equal powers over the other elements).

At the shrine of Mont St. Michel in Normandy, a woman who is just about to give birth is washed overboard in a storm. She calls on the Virgin and St. Michael to help her, and, as the version of the Dominican Jean Hérolt, written 1435–40, describes, "it seemed to the woman, a sleeve held above her so kept her safe and untouched by the dreadful sounding flood of the sea that not even the least drop of all that deep touched her garments. But she, as though she lay in the finest of all dwellings, brought forth her child without fear, remaining there until the sea, withdrawing its wave into itself, gave a free passage to the woman, and she came with the child to the shore."[31]

This miracle was so popular that it was retold and translated into many languages, from its first appearance in Dominic of Evesham's collection at the end of the eleventh century until the close of the middle ages. A pious anecdote about the Virgin's helpfulness to mothers in distress, it reveals the metaphysical analogy between the watery mass from which form emerges into life and the actual birth of a child, between the ocean and the maternal womb.

As a sky goddess, Mary's colour is blue. Her starry mantle is a figure of the sky, as in Apuleius' vision of Isis; as late as 1649, Francisco Pacheco in his *Art of Painting* still laid down that she should wear a blue cloak. Blue is the colour of space and light and eternity, of the sea and the sky. The reason for the symbolism is also economic, however, for blue was an expensive pigment, obtainable only from crushed lapis lazuli imported from Afghanistan, and, after gold, it thus became the medieval painter's most fitting and fervent tribute to the Queen of Heaven.[32] As Philip Hendy wrote in his book on Piero della Francesca:

From time immemorial blue has been the sacred colour, with magical properties, and in Constantinople, when the Byzantine capital was the centre of Christian art, blue became the Virgin's colour, celestial blue, the colour of heaven. So in the Italian altarpieces before Piero came upon the scene, and indeed for long afterwards, ultramarine blue tends to dominate and to have a special quality—hieratic or, in modern parlance, abstract.[33]

In the Renaissance, the heavenly attributes of Mary were increased, although the medieval appetite for allegory and typology declined. The Virgin's governance of the oceans was adapted to a practical purpose: she was prayed to by the missionaries who set out across the Atlantic and other oceans to conquer new territories for Christ. Christopher Columbus placed his ship under her aegis; and Spanish and Portuguese explorers after him invoked the protection of Our Lady of the Navigators, whom painters like Alejo Fernandez (d. 1543) depicted as a towering Queen of Heaven, illuminated by the sun, floating on banks of clouds over the sea. Under the folds of her sky-blue mantle she gathers together all involved in the enterprise, from the fur-robed patrons and sponsors of the expedition to the armoured knights and the ragged crew, while beneath them the tall ships float ready to weigh anchor.

Sanctuaries all along the shores of the Mediterranean celebrate her relation with the sea. At Tindari, in Sicily, on a spectacular bluff overlooking the azure, sparkling waves, a Black Madonna is enshrined. According to local legend, she was found washed up like sea-born Aphrodite on the shore in a casket during the Iconoclast heresy in the east. At Crotone, on the promontory overlooking the stormy gulf of Taranto, once one of Magna Graecia's most prosperous cities, there used to stand a great temple to Hera Lacinia, the specific patroness of marriage. All that remains now is a single Doric column. But nearby, twenty-five centuries later, the church of Our Lady of Capo Colonna draws pilgrims, and nubile girls—*le verginelle*—used to process barefoot every Saturday to the windy cliff overhanging the sea. But now the cult chiefly comes to life on the second Sunday in May, when the venerated statue—also a Black Madonna—is carried from the cathedral at Crotone to the church on the headland and then, by night, brought back over the sea to the town in a torchlight procession of fishing boats whose masters hope to secure the Virgin's protection.[84]

It is principally as the Immaculate Conception that the Virgin is associated with the moon and the sky, and thereby with the sea. It is therefore interesting that at the time—the mid-seventeenth century—there was much debate about the best visual expression of the belief, one priest suggested that the most apposite symbol would be a pearl, enclosed in a shell, because a pearl is pure and imperishable.[35] Pearls are also glistening, white, and spherical, an exact epiphany of the moon, and a fruit of the sea. The suggestion was not acted upon, principally because there is no biblical foundation for associating the Virgin with a pearl. But in some places in the world, the connection of images has led to the pearl's appearance. In Macao, at the heart of the oriental pearl trade, the Virgin Mary bears a distinct resemblance to the ancient local goddess of the seed pearls, whose cult declined after the Portuguese took over Macao in the sixteenth century.[36] In Saragossa, some souvenirs represent

the Virgin standing on a half-shell to remind the pilgrim that St. James
—whose emblem is the scallop—saw the Virgin at Saragossa in a vision.
It is nevertheless startling to contemplate the Virgin standing like Venus
on a shell.[37]

Lunar symbolism is bewilderingly complex and it is all too easy to
fall foul of it. With regard to the Virgin's Immaculate Conception, however, one further relationship should be noted. For the association of the
snake and the moon has proved one of the most ancient and enduring
mysteries.[38] It is impossible to describe here the myriad snake cults and
legends, but, in brief, a snake appears to be reborn each time it sloughs
its skin, and thus it became for many peoples in different places in the
world an analogue of the moon, which is also reborn each month. By
principle of association, both the snake and the moon become symbols of
immortal life. In the ancient epic of Gilgamesh, for instance, as well as in
Chinese myth, it is the serpent who steals the fruit of immortality for
itself. The same significance lies deeply buried in the biblical story of the
Fall, in which mankind loses eternal life through the agency of the
serpent, "more subtil than all the beasts of the field," who professes to
know the secret of immortality.[39]

The lunar rhythm of renewal connects the snake with menstruation.
Various cultures all over the globe believe that the two are causally
linked and tell tales of women bitten or penetrated by snakes—an experience that brings on menstruation.[40] The penalty of eating the fruit of
knowledge offered by the snake was partly the curse of menstruation;
and the implication of the Immaculate Conception, whereby Mary con-
quers the serpent, is that she is spared it.

In Christianity, the serpent has lost its primary character as a source
of wisdom and eternity. It is above all the principal Christian symbol of
evil, and when it sprawls under the Virgin's foot, it is not her direct
attribute, representing her knowledge and power as it does in the snake-
brandishing statue of the goddess of Minoan Crete, but illustrates her
victory over evil.

Christian theology identified the serpent of the Garden of Eden with
the devil by taking Genesis with the Apocalypse of John, in which John
sees the triumph of the Redeemer: "And the great dragon was cast out,
that old serpent, called the Devil, and Satan, which deceiveth the whole
world" (Revelation 20:2). But the symbol of the snake has not, in spite
of John's neat bundle of identifications, been successfully confined within
Christian moral categories. Some of the beast's oracular and regenerative
powers have survived from its classical past. Christ himself said his Crucifixion was prefigured when God sent a plague of snakes and Moses

changed one of them into brass, and "set it upon a pole," where it healed anyone who had been bitten (Numbers 21:8–9; John 3:14). He also advised his followers: to "Be ye therefore wise as serpents, and harmless as doves" (Matthew 10:16). And on the shield of the medical profession, the symbol has survived all Christian prejudice: the snakes of Asclepius are still intertwined on Hermes' magic staff—a curious relic, when one considers that most people's immediate association with snakes is fatal poisoning.

By far the most fascinating survival of snake-worship, however, is the Easter egg. During the first decades of Christianity, the Orphic mystery cult, which was deeply involved in lunar and astral symbolism, gained great popularity. According to the Orphic mystery religion, the world was created when the great goddess, in the shape of a snake, coupled with the sacred serpent Ophion, who, his tail in his mouth, encircles the world in an image of abiding eternity. At the vernal equinox—which coincides with the Christian Annunciation—the light of the growing sun Helios began to warm the egg the goddess had laid after their union. When it later hatched, the world came into being. Easter, which celebrates the rebirth of the world in the person of the resurrected Christ, is also observed after the vernal equinox, when the sun is gaining over the darkness. The Easter egg, which Europeans, Russians, and Americans give each other at this time, is the same Orphic symbol of the birth of the new world.[41]

The serpent the immaculate Virgin treads underfoot is therefore a much more complex symbol, and has undergone more transformations than the moon beneath her or the stars round her head. For, at an immediate level, the serpent has lost its connotations of knowledge and power and simply become a loathsome emblem of wickedness that the Virgin's purity and wisdom have overcome; but at another level it has retained its ancient meaning, for it represents a kind of heterodox knowledge and sexuality that Christianity has spurned. Furthermore, although its presence in images of the Immaculate Conception is negative, it continues to form with the moon and the stars and the waters an elaborate code of the mysteries of life, growth, and birth over which the woman—the Virgin Mary—is believed to hold sway.

A pivotal contradiction therefore exists at the centre of the figure of the immaculately conceived Virgin because, assembling about her the symbols wielded by Isis in Apuleius' remarkable vision, she is, at the very moment of her most complete triumph over carnality, a goddess of vegetable and animal and human fertility.

*Part Five*

# INTERCESSOR

*Chapter Eighteen*

# GROWTH IN EVERY THING

*Witness those rings and roundelays*
*Of theirs which yet remain*
*Were footed in Queen Mary's days*
*On many a grassy plain.*
*But since of late Elizabeth*
*And later James came in,*
*They never dance on any heath*
*As when the time had been.*
*By which we note the fairies*
*Were of the old profession*
*Their songs were Ave Maries*
*Their dances were procession . . .*[1]

—RICHARD CORBET, *"Farewell, Rewards and Fairies"*

THE PINNACLES OF THE MOUNTAIN of Montserrat rise out of the Catalonian plain like watchtowers and gaze over towards Barcelona. From the depths of a prehistoric lake, a cataclysm threw up these enormous crags, and since then wind and rain have eroded fantastic shapes out of them, needles and spires and jags and cones. Locals called it *mons serrata,* the serrated mountain, and the device of the monastery that crowns its peaks shows an angel plying a saw back and forth over the mountain top. The smooth rocks are hollow, and the whole mass is honeycombed with caves; water rises only in the valley below. So it is something of a miracle that the mountain bears flowers and fruit and trees and shrubs with irrepressible exuberance. Wild violets, carnations, honeysuckle, roses, orchids, lilies carpet its face in spring; even in winter vegetation clings to it and clothes it, while clouds drift over the rim of the mountain and spill down into the valley, giving the plain below the seething look of hell, and the pinnacles of rock the character of a refuge, an eyrie paradise.

With the medieval man's ability to see through the visible phenomena of nature into the spiritual meaning beneath, the Benedictines of Montserrat saw in their mountain's remarkable fertility an image of the Virgin herself. For while Mary provides a focus for the steeliest asceticism, she is also the ultimate of fertility symbols. The mountain blossoms spontaneously; so does the mother maid. The old significance of the moon and the serpent as divine attributes survives in such sanctuaries as Montserrat, for there she is venerated as a source of fertility and delight. Her intercession with her son is still begged by women who want children or fear the pain of birth, just as it was in the middle ages, when the cult of the humanity of Jesus and Mary transformed her into a gentle, tender, and ordinary mother caring for her helpless baby. Montserrat, the site of one of the longest continuous cults of the Virgin, retains its ancient popularity, not particularly as a shrine of healing (though the sick do make the pilgrimage once a year) but as a shrine for newly married couples.[2] The monks have built a large new hospice to accommodate them, for *no es ben casat qui no duu la dona a Montserrat* (a man's not properly set up until he's taken his wife to Montserrat). After mass on her feastdays, the congregation dances the *Sardana* in a ring before the church and sings roundelays in Catalan. The Virgin of Montserrat presides especially over marriage and sex, pregnancy and childbirth, and has inspired a host of bizarre, chthonic legends. In one gruesome variation on a recurrent theme, a barren woman gives birth to a lump of dead flesh, but she wraps it up in a handkerchief, and prays to Our Lady of Montserrat until it begins to move and turn into a beautiful baby boy.[3]

The image worshipped there is a Black Madonna, as in so many shrines (at Chartres, Rocamadour, Loreto, Le Puy, Orléans, S. Maria Maggiore in Rome—to name only the most famous). The Church often explains their blackness in allegorical terms from the Song of Songs: "I am black, but comely, O ye daughters of Jerusalem" (Song of Solomon 1:5), but this does not illuminate the mystery of their origins. Some images are carved in ebony, but another theory about their colour is even more prosaic: that the smoke of votive candles for centuries has blackened the wood or the pigment, and when artists restored the images, they repainted the robes and jewels that clothed the Madonna and Child but out of awe left their faces black. Awe, however, did not arise only from simple veneration of their sacred image—many icons have been wholly repainted many times—but also probably because the mysterious and exotic darkness of the countenances had rapidly inspired a special cult. In Catholic countries, where blackness is the climate of the devils, not the angels, and is associated almost exclusively with magic and the occult, Black Madonnas are considered especially wonder-working, as the possessors of hermetic knowledge and power.

The Madonna of Montserrat is known as *La Moreneta,* "the little black one," and was found, according to legend, by a group of shepherds in A.D. 888—after the Moors had been driven out of Barcelona. It had lain in a cave since a Goth bishop had hidden it from the heathen, and had been brought to Spain by St. Peter in A.D. 50. Peter had been given it by the sculptor, St. Luke. A choir of angels led the shepherds to the spot, and when the local bishop tried to move it to Manresa, it refused to budge from the heights on which the shrine now stands.[4]

The statue of the aquiline and severe Madonna enthroned with Jesus in her lap holding a pinecone is in fact twelfth-century and Byzantine, but its full history is not known. A Benedictine convent was founded in 976, and since the middle ages the shrine has prospered as one of the holy places of Christendom. The counts of Barcelona and the kings and queens of Aragon and Castile have lavished treasure on Our Lady of Montserrat; popes, especially the Spaniards like Alexander VI Borgia (1492–1503), have enriched her cult with indulgences. Her most famous votary was St. Ignatius of Loyola, who, in 1522, spent the night in vigil before her and, hanging up his sword and dagger, dedicated himself a soldier of Christ.

Montserrat is by no means unique in fostering the Virgin's maternal and midwife aspect. Though it would seem natural in one sense for women to pray to the highest woman in the Christian pantheon for help, it remains ironical that the mother who brought forth virginally and without pain should be invoked in sympathy. It is of course her very immunity that women plead to obtain, especially in Catholic countries, where the ban on contraception condemns them to childbearing without respite. Mary's powers over fertility were celebrated in the first recorded act of homage paid to her, when Epiphanius, in a list of heresies, noted with outrage that some women of the Arab Collyridian sect in the neighbouring countryside were offering the Virgin cakes and liquor at the shrine where their ancestors had worshipped the goddess of heaven Ashtaroth. "Others in their folly," he wrote, "wishing to exalt the Ever-Blessed Virgin, have put her in the place of God."[5] Just as Jeremiah had inveighed against Ashtaroth's cult—"the children gather wood and the fathers kindle the fire, and the women knead the dough, to make cakes for the queen of heaven . . ." (Jeremiah 7:18)—so Epiphanius turned his scorn on the Collyridians. But the multiple associations of the Virgin with fruitfulness—animal and vegetable—survived all ecclesiastical injunctions.

In Milan the Virgin Mary appeared as a corn goddess to a medieval merchant. Her robe was sewn with ears of wheat, and he was so grateful for this promise of plenty that he commissioned a painting of the vision for the Duomo of Milan, where the faithful hung garlands of flowers in order to secure the image's fertility for themselves. During the fifteenth century, the corn maiden of Milan became an extremely popular votive image in Germany and the Tyrol, where numerous woodcut copies of it were circulated.[6]

Christianity has of course profoundly spiritualized the meaning of such ancient pagan symbols of fertility; when Dionysus' grapes or Ceres' wheat appear in Christian artefacts, their eucharistic significance is plain, and the cymbals and flutes of the Dionysiac train are far and faint. Yet the assimilation of pagan imagery into the polymorphous figure of the Virgin is interesting if only for its extraordinary endurance: the pinecone the Christ child on La Moreneta's knees holds in his hand, a symbol of potency because of the multiplicity of its concealed nuts, used to crown the ivy-wreathed staff, or thyrsus, of Dionysus.

Similarly, the pomegranate, an ancient image of abundance and fertility, was revived in Renaissance images of the Virgin and child. In Paestum, near Naples, the Madonna of the Pomegranate recalls directly the famous statue of Hera at Argos, Polycletus' long-lost masterpiece, known to us from coins. Argive Hera, like the Virgin at Paestum, held a pomegranate in her left hand, and in her right a staff surmounted by a cuckoo, the form in which Zeus wooed her. As the first cuckoo is the herald of spring, Hera in this aspect presided over the season of new life, which in Christianity begins on March 25, the spring equinox, and the feast of the Annunciation. Argive Hera was worshipped at Paestum, for many votive figurines have been recovered from the site, and it is possible that the Madonna of the Pomegranate echoes over the centuries the ivory and gold splendour of Polycletus' statue.[7]

In Sicily, the cult of the corn goddess Demeter flourished, and statuettes have been excavated showing her dandling her infant daughter Kore-Persephone in her arms, or supporting her, asleep on her shoulder—an image so close to the Madonna and child that at Enna (formerly Castrogiovanni) near Lake Pergusa, where Persephone was swallowed up into the underworld, the cathedral used to display a Greek statue of Demeter and her daughter on the altar.[8]

The quickening and obstetric functions of the classical goddesses like Hera and Demeter have been taken over by the Virgin in Catholic cult, not only in the iconography of sacred images and their use of symbols, but also in the emotive folklore and usages of her following. Thomas of Celano, for instance, reported that a woman of Arezzo, who had been a week in labour and was turning black in agony, was told by St. Francis to recite the *Salve Regina.* Immediately the pain ceased and she was safely delivered of a handsome son.[9]

In the large and popular corpus of medieval miracles ascribed to the Virgin, one of the most dubious and entertaining is the story of an abbess who in spite of her extreme strictness over her charges, "fell into wantonness" with her page, and conceived a child. Her delighted flock were quick to notice her pregnancy and denounced her to the bishop, who appeared at the convent to investigate. The abbess implored the Virgin to help her. As in most medieval miracles the Virgin plays an utterly amoral role, her loyalty outweighing all justice. In this case she duly spirits away the child while the abbess lies asleep and gives him into the care of a hermit. The bishop rebukes the nuns for their tale-bearing and the abbess is cleared. Later, under the seal of the confessional, she tells him that her slanderers had in fact spoken true but that the Virgin had helped her. Suitably impressed, the bishop sends for the child, who in due course becomes bishop of the area himself.[10]

In miracle plays, which by the fourteenth century used much ingenious stagecraft—real pools for crusaders' boats and real fire for martyrs' pyres—the stories of the Virgin's midwifery were extremely popular and vividly enacted. The actor would heave and groan, while the Virgin Mary in attendance encouraged him roundly. At the appropriate moment, she would bend down and draw from between the actor's legs a doll wrapped in swaddling clothes.[11]

Her motherly concern for the happiness of young couples was justified by Christian preachers from her concern at the marriage feast of Cana. And although the model of the ascetic life was transformed into a marriage broker and midwife during the middle ages, when as we have seen human life was projected into the divine sector, this character of the Virgin has lasted into modern times. In Châtillon-sur-Seine in France the small grey stone church of St. Vorles on the hill (where St. Bernard received the Virgin's milk, according to legend) is scrawled all over with the pun that was the thirteenth-century monk Gautier de Coincy's great delight. *Chère Marie, faîtes que je me marie,* read the graffiti. Sometimes the name of the boy, and less often of the girl, is included for all to see; sometimes, the prayer, like a lonely-hearts advertisement, merely begs for any marriage partner.

The practice of providing dowries for poverty-stricken or orphaned girls out of church funds continued in Europe until the last century. In S. Maria sopra Minerva in Rome, there is an altarpiece of the Annunciation painted by Antoniazzo Romano (d. 1508): Mary ignores the presence of the angel Gabriel in order to bestow a silken purse of gold on the three young girls in simple white shifts and loose tresses who kneel before her. The painting was commissioned by Cardinal Juan de Torquemada (who appears in it, presenting the three girls to the Virgin) in order to commemorate the confraternity of the Annunciation founded in 1460 to furnish the poor with dowries (see figure 42, a stone relief on the same theme). The pope himself, in default of the Virgin, distributed the largesse in a solemn ceremony on the feast of the Annunciation. Augustus Hare describes how the Eucharist was borne through the streets on the back of the white papal mule, while the young recipients waited in front of the Minerva. The girls wearing white wreaths received a double portion, for they were to be brides of Christ.[12]

The choice of the Annunciation itself is significant, for it is the feast of Christ's conception and thus reveals the indissoluble link (forgotten in these days of contraception) between union and pregnancy, which in Catholic thought provides the only moral justification for sexual intercourse in the first place. The Virgin can never therefore be said to be the tutelary goddess of sex; for sex in Catholic terminology means procreation, and the Virgin when she blesses wedlock remains first and foremost a mother blessing the future mother and child.

Of all the relics and images of the Virgin imbued with the power to quicken the womb, the most efficacious was the sash she had worn round her waist. According to a medieval legend, she had let it fall to earth at her Assumption to convince doubting Thomas of her ascent. Although the story is probably eastern, its origins are a matter of dispute. The first examples in art date from the first half of the fourteenth century and are found as widely scattered as Gracanica in Yugoslavia, Chalgrove in England, and Prato in Tuscany. Throughout the fifteenth century and afterwards the girdle, falling from the Virgin's hand into Thomas' arms, is a staple image in Assumption iconography (figure 10). Prato's devotion to the legend was particularly eager, because la sacratissima cintola itself was preserved in the cathedral, where it is still exhibited to the faithful on special feasts. In Prato this obvious plagiarism of the Gospel story of doubting Thomas was expanded into an almost Arthurian romance about a young local called Michele Dagomari, who left on the first crusade. Like many Italian fortune-hunters, he remained in the holy land after the war as a merchant, and in Jerusalem fell in love with the beautiful daughter of a Greek priest (*sic*) whose family had faithfully kept the relic of the Virgin's belt for over a thousand years—indeed ever since St. Thomas himself, before his departure to convert India, had entrusted it to their keeping. When the father refused permission to Michele to marry his daughter, Michele turned to her mother, who was won over and gave him the girdle as the girl's dowry to boot. The happy couple sailed back to Italy, where they jealously guarded their treasure until Michele on his deathbed revealed his secret to the bishop of Prato and made him promise to build a cathedral to house it.

The gift of St. Thomas, the love affair, the fugitive couple, their sea journey back to Prato are all illustrated on the walls of Prato cathedral in an exquisite cycle of frescoes painted by Agnolo Gaddi, around 1365. It is impossible to retrieve history from fairytale, but it is not improbable that a returning crusader did believe he possessed the true relic of the Virgin.[13] Prato was not the only shrine, however, that venerated the relic of the girdle. Paris, Chartres, Constantinople, Le Puy and Assisi all boasted other examples. But the Prato legend seizes unerringly on the erotic association of the Virgin's sash, for it actually describes it as the young girl's marriage portion, the apt image of her changing state.[14]

The girdle that encircles the loins of a goddess has direct mythological antecedents in the west. At the judgement of Paris, after Hera promised Paris power and Athene victory, Aphrodite unfastened the belt of her tunic and let it fall. Then she promised Paris the most beautiful of mortal women, and he, enraptured by her loveliness, presented her with the apple of discord.[15] Hera herself used to borrow Aphrodite's girdle as a love charm—for, according to Homer, not even the wisest among the wise was proof against it.[16] In Rome, Juno Cinxia (Juno of the Belt) presided especially over the unknotting of the bride's girdle.[17]

The sexuality of the symbol derives from its tantalizing ambivalence: loosed, the girdle gives promise; fastened, it denies. In that sense, it is a mirror image of the symbol of the virgin-bride. But its predominant association with fecundity is preserved in the Romance languages, in which the word "engirdled," *enceinte* or *incinta,* means pregnant with child.

The origins of the relic in Christian cult can only be guessed, but it is interesting that another cult of a magic girdle existed at Ephesus in classical times. For Ephesus was the centre of the worship of the Amazons, who, it was believed, had founded the city. Ares, the god of war, gave their queen Hippolyte a sacred golden belt as the mark of her sovereignty over her warrior tribe, and Herakles, as one of his twelve labours, massacred the Amazons in order to seize this magic talisman of their queen and thus shear her of her powers.[18] The cult of the Amazons flourished in Cappadocia, where Diana of Ephesus was still worshipped in Christian times.

In the figure of Diana of Ephesus a number of different divinities were conflated: by the reign of Artaxerxes II (404–358 B.C.), the Iranian goddess of the waters, Anahita, had been coalesced with the Greek goddess of the moon, Artemis.[19] By Roman times, Artemis had in turn been identified with Diana, an Italian maiden goddess of springs and fruitfulness who was invoked with Juno to bless marriages with fertility and ease childbirth. However, a single glance at the votive statue of Diana of Ephesus as she was in the days of early Christianity reveals that she bears no resemblance to the virgin huntress who was Apollo's twin. A grapevine of breasts falling from her chin to her waist and the turreted crown she wears mark her a *magna mater,* more kin to Cybele than to Anahita and Artemis. The heroine who does resemble Artemis-Diana in her chaste, huntress aspect, however, is Hippolyte, the queen of the Amazons, who also imposed a vow of chastity on all her followers. Thus it is possible that the Amazon queen venerated in Cappadocia was subsumed into the fertility goddess Diana of Ephesus, and that the memories of her emblem the girdle survived in the city where the Virgin Mary was proclaimed *Theotokos* three hundred and fifty years after the silversmiths, who lived by making statuettes of Diana, rebelled against the preaching of St. Paul and shouted "Great is Diana of the Ephesians" (Acts 19:23–40). There could be, therefore, a chain of descent from Hippolyte to Diana to the Virgin, for one tradition also holds that Mary was assumed into heaven from Ephesus, where she spent the last years of her life, and where St. Thomas, according to the legend, received her heavenly girdle as proof.

For centuries Christians have prayed over the various relics of the Virgin's girdle that the curse of infertility be lifted from them. The Cathedral at Chartres was a veritable arsenal of relics, and for the childless the favourite, the most famous and most powerful, was the shift Mary had worn at the Annunciation when she conceived Christ. Henri III and Louise of Lorraine dressed themselves in sackcloth every winter to walk barefoot fifty miles to Chartres to beg the Virgin for children. But Henri and Louise died without issue, murdered in 1589, the last of the house of Valois.

Anne of Austria, the wife of Louis XIII, was the open-handed benefactress of several shrines of the Virgin in France. She singled out Le Puy, where one of the girdles was preserved, for particular devotion. After twenty-two years of marriage, with the girdle brought in its casket from the cathedral to her bedroom, she gave birth in 1638 to the future

Sun King, Louis XIV.[20] His father, in gratitude, dedicated the whole of his kingdom that year to the Virgin, a gesture that exactly caught the fanatical spirit of Catholic piety in the country at that time.

Louis XIV himself was more cynical. On his ascent to the throne, he converted the prodigious treasure amassed by the shrine at Le Puy into liquidities for the coffers of Versailles.

For every queen who felt her barrenness dissolved by the Virgin's power, a thousand unrecorded suppliants must have shared that emotion and that trust. In contemporary Mediterranean shrines, the phenomenon is still very much in evidence. In Sant' Agostino in Rome, Jacopo Sansovino's statue of the Virgin as Capitoline Juno (carved in 1521) blazes with candles behind banks of flowers while the walls around are encrusted with silver *ex voto* plaques giving thanks for the conception or birth of a child. The inscription above each reads: *Virgo tua gloria partus.* She is the Madonna of Childbirth and her foot is encased in gold so that the kisses of the faithful will not wear it away. With Catholic prudishness, a bronze drape over the baby's genitals has been added to Sansovino's work.

At Montevergine, a mountain south of Naples where there once stood a sanctuary of the *magna mater* Cybele, a shrine of the Virgin now incorporates the former temple. In the Brides' Corner in the church, hundreds of wedding dresses that have been dedicated to the Virgin are preserved. Dust catches in the yards of tulle, the white silks and satins and lace are yellowing with age; and the desiccated bouquets are disintegrating.[21] It looks like Miss Haversham's room in *Great Expectations* when Pip first saw it, shrouded in cobwebs. But it is a solid Italian tradition, carried on by women in what they consider to be their best interests, during pilgrimages of much wild and bawdy gaiety. At Syracuse, in the shrine of *La Madonnina delle Lacrime,* there are wardrobes filled to overflowing alongside other propitiatory and thanksgiving offerings, like china and plastic dolls, to commemorate the birth of a baby.

These *ex voto* offerings record gratitude, and the Virgin Mary, as a source of fertility, is often a source of rejoicing. As a mother, she is associated with joy, with songs, with dancing and flowers. May, morning of the year, is dedicated to her. It became Mary's month only in the eighteenth century, in Naples, whence it spread to Italy, to Ireland, and all over the Catholic world, encouraged chiefly by the Jesuits.[22] Gerard Manley Hopkins in the *May Magnificat* captured all the bursting joy of spring and its promise of fruitfulness in lines so rich and beautiful they stand for all that is best and happiest in the cult of the Virgin:

May is Mary's month and I
Muse at that and wonder why:
　　Her feasts follow reason,
　　Dated due to season—

Candlemas, Lady Day;
But the Lady Month, May,
　　Why fasten that upon her,
　　With a feasting in her honour? . . .

Ask of her, the mighty mother:
Her reply puts this other
　　Question: What is spring?—
　　Growth in every thing—

Flesh and fleece, fur and feather,
Grass and greenworld altogether;
　　Star-eyed strawberry-breasted
　　Throstle above her nested

Cluster of bugle blue eggs thin
Forms and warms the life within;
　　And bird and blossom swell
　　In sod or sheath or shell.

All things rising, all things sizing
Mary sees, sympathising
　　With that world of good,
　　Nature's motherhood. . . .[23]

The absorption of this fertility role by the Virgin represents yet another late but successful attempt to draw the teeth of secular and originally pagan rites by incorporating them into Catholic worship. For May is
named after Maia, the Greek nymph who was the mother of Hermes by
Zeus, and was transformed with her sisters into the seven stars of the
Pleiades constellation. Harbingers of summer, they appear in the sky in
the month of May. In Rome, the nymph Maia was first assimilated to a
minor fertility deity, like Diana a patroness of fresh-water springs, and
then she was identified with the *Bona Dea*, an earth goddess of plenty
who was popular in the later years of the empire. Romans pelted each
other with flowers during the licentious *Ludi Floreales* from April 23 to
May 3 in honour of Flora, a Roman goddess of the harvest and of
fruitfulness whose cult was particularly associated with the heady flower
of the hawthorn tree—mayblossom. All over medieval Europe on May
Day, the Queen of the May was crowned and sometimes married to the

Green Man, in an ancient fertility rite, that in some places, including England, has survived all bans, Catholic and Protestant alike. The arrival of summer was celebrated with junketing and merrymaking, as Frazer has chronicled in *The Golden Bough*.[24] In the Limbourg Brothers' most sumptuous illumination for the month of May, in *Les Très Riches Heures du Duc de Berry*, a hunting party of elegant and decorative young courtiers set out in a wood bright with new young leaf. They wear budding branches in their broad-brimmed hats, and some wear bright green surcoats too—the *vert gai*—the traditional leit-motif for the beginning of summer on the first of May.[25]

This was a frivolous aspect of Catholicism the Reformers loathed, and struggled to stamp out in northern Europe. However, churchmen had inveighed against the levity of their chattering, dancing, and carousing flocks for centuries, and the Jesuit drive to sanctify the secular custom and transform the Queen of the May into the Virgin Mary—another symptom of Rome's puritanism—was largely successful. In Catholic countries, statues of the Virgin are bedecked in flowers and crowned on May 1, and carried in gay processions through flower-strewn streets and squares carpeted with blossoms. In Ireland, the may or thorn tree, which has a peculiar erotic aroma, is considered powerful magic, and is sacred to the Virgin in many of her sanctuaries.

The fact that the cult of the Virgin was capable of assimilating so much classical fertility worship reveals that much thinking on the connection between mother goddesses and matriarchs is erroneous: it is conventional wisdom among some mythographers and feminists to invoke a golden age when the social power and position of women were recognized and reflected in mythology and worship. The Eleusinian mysteries, performed exclusively by priestesses in honour of Demeter and Kore, are often held up as an example of an ancient matriarchal religious rite that granted women an equal, if not superior, place, and was suppressed in the interests of male hegemony. In fact, Alaric the Goth razed the temple at Eleusis only in A.D. 410, several centuries after patriarchal authority had been undisputed in Greece, and, given the enormous body of analogous evidence from the Virgin's cult, it is not daring to suggest that the mysteries performed there in honour of Demeter in no way reflected the standing of women. There is no logical equivalence in any society between exalted female objects of worship and a high position for women.[26]

The powers of Demeter and Kore over life and over death are attributed to the Christian mother goddess too. She quickens and heals; and she reigns over the afterlife and the realm of the dead (as we shall see).

Yet this veneration provokes no corresponding rise in the status of women. On the contrary, the fertility ascribed to her reinforces the mythology that motherhood is the central point of a woman's life, where all the streams of her nature converge and prosper. For it is in Catholic countries above all, from Italy to Latin America, that women are subjugated to the ideal of maternity. Therefore, although the Virgin's fruitfulness inspires the gayest and most joyful side of her cult, affirming rather than denying the world, and although in some senses it excites pleasure in love and humanity against a backdrop of blossom and springtime and dance and song, it does not transform her into a divinity who restores the equilibrium between the sexes, or looses women from the bonds of tedious biological teleology. The ideal of fruitfulness, combined with the other Catholic interpretations of purity and humility, as epitomized by the Virgin, do on the contrary bind those bonds tighter.

# Chapter Nineteen

# ICONS AND RELICS

*We ought to imitate the man who has incurred the King's anger. What does he do? He goes secretly to the Queen and promises a present, then to the earls and barons and does the same, then to the freemen of the household and lastly to the footmen. So when we have offended Christ we should first go to the Queen of heaven and offer her, instead of a present, prayers, fasting, vigils and alms; then she, like a mother, will come between thee and Christ, the father who wishes to beat us, and she will throw the cloak of her mercy between the rod of punishment and us and soften the king's anger against us. Afterwards we should go to the earls and barons, that is, the apostles and ask them to intercede for us; then to the knights and squires, that is, martyrs and confessors; then to the ladies of the Queen's chamber, that is, the women saints; and lastly to the footmen, that is, the poor, for the poor should be persuaded by gifts of alms to intercede for us with Christ.*[1]

—FRANCISCAN EXEMPLUM (FOURTEENTH CENTURY)

PRAYER FORMED THE FIGURE of the Virgin Mary, and it is the chief function of her myth to answer it. She mediates between heaven and earth, for in her glorified body she belongs in both realms. She listens to the implorations of mankind, "groaning and weeping in this valley of tears"—as the *Salve Regina* sings—and promises to ease their pain with heavenly medicine.

The theology of the Virgin's intercession maintains very strictly that the Virgin does not have the power to grant any boon by herself, but only intercedes with her son, who as God is the only source of salvation. But the powers of mediation attributed to her throughout Christianity are considered sovereign: the son can refuse his mother nothing. So a prayer to Mary, made in a spirit of repentance and resolve, is wonder-working; and men and women gathered together to pray to the Virgin forget the distinction between direct and indirect power.

Patristic symbolism concentrates on her mediation, and the concept that two distinct and almost irreconcilable worlds are bridged by Mary lies at the heart of Christian imagery of her intercession. The sixth-century *Akathistos* hymn hails her as Jacob's ladder (Genesis 28:12) on which he saw the angels of the Lord ascending and descending between heaven and earth, for Mary is the ladder that Christ used to descend to earth and that man can use to ascend to heaven.[2]

The medieval schoolmen, meditating on the Pauline idea of the mystical body of Christ, called the Virgin the neck that joins Christ, the head of the Church, to the body of the faithful. The ugly anatomical image, first found in Hermann of Tournai (d. 1147), was enthusiastically propounded by later popularizers like Jacobus de Varagine and San Bernardino of Siena, and even by later and more sober sages like Robert Bellarmine (d. 1621), who described in lingering detail the blood of grace flowing down from the head through the neck into the Church's body. Bernard of Clairvaux, with the natural eloquence that won him the title of *Doctor Mellifluus,* compared the Virgin to an aqueduct that brings the grace of God coursing down through the city of the faithful; or to the perfume of a ripe fruit that lingers on the hands and scents them long after the fruit itself has been eaten. Thus do the gifts received through Mary, said the saint, sweeten the soul.[3]

The most consistent theme in the theology of the Virgin's intercession, however, is her motherhood. She is approached as a human mother who brims over with a mother's love. This element in her cult is present in earliest Byzantine times, recedes in the early middle ages, when she is at her most queenly and hieratic, and then re-emerges in the thirteenth century, to last undiminished to the present day. Her love of mankind is maternal, and her qualities of mercy, gentleness, loving kindness, indulgence, forgiveness, are all seen as motherly. All men are her children through Christ her son, who gave her to them from the Cross; and so she lavishes a mother's love and pity on all her brood.

Her actions in the Gospels were interpreted to support this idea of the Virgin's salvific effect. Her visit to Elisabeth—which Dante used as the perfect example of zealous love—caused the infant John the Baptist to leap in his mother's womb, freed from the burden of sin by the Virgin's radiant presence. Out of kindliness at Cana, she had prompted her son to change water into wine so that their hosts should not be shamed; but at a deeper level she had attended, even instigated, the first miracle, which both revealed the divinity of her son and prefigured the transubstantiation of bread and wine in the Eucharist. On Calvary she consented to the holocaust, and therefore cooperated in a special way in the Redemption. Above all, her role in the Incarnation made the Atonement possible. Taken all together, her collaboration with the will of God entitled her to the glory of heaven, where, as the first fruit of the Resurrection, assumed in her transfigured eschatological body, she stands like the Queen of Ophir at Christ's right hand to entreat his mercy for mankind.

One of the most ancient Christian prayers—much older than the medieval Hail Mary (see next chapter)—is the *Sub tuum praesidium*, dated from the late third to the eighth century by different scholars, which contains a plea for the Virgin's help:

We seek refuge under the protection of your mercies, oh Mother of God; do not reject our supplication in need but save us from perdition, oh you who alone are blessed.[4]

The medieval antiphons—the *Alma Redemptoris Mater* (eleventh century) and the *Salve Regina* (also eleventh century)—plead for her help in obtaining God's mercy.

The people's prayers have always found support among papal pronouncements, and never more so than in the past two hundred years, when the Vatican has continuously hymned the Virgin in her aspect of Mediatrix. Leo XIII (1878–1903) declared in 1891: "We can receive absolutely nothing . . . nothing, unless, God willing, it is bestowed on us through Mary."[5] Most of his successors have embroidered on this theme, and the special chapter on Mary in *Lumen Gentium* focusses closely on the kin ideas that the Virgin, like the Church, is the mother of all Christians, and that through her, as through the Church, grace is channelled into each individual soul. The 1964 Constitution does include, however, a strongly expressed caveat:

We have but one Mediator [Jesus Christ] . . . The maternal duty of Mary towards men in no way obscures or diminishes this unique mediation of Christ. . . . For all the saving influences of the Blessed Virgin originate, not from some inner necessity, but from the divine pleasure. They flow forth from the superabundance of the merits of Christ, rest on his mediation, depend entirely on it, and derive all their power from it.[6]

For this reason, the prayers of the Catholic Church are generally worded with care: Mary and the saints are begged to "pray for us" and not to act directly and grant the ultimate object of the prayer.

This scheme seems crystalline yet sturdy, consistent with past tradition, and firm in its outline and conception. But it is based on several assumptions. First, the economy of the Catholic salvation is completely anthropomorphic: the model of the human family is projected twice onto the divine realm, once in the filial relation of Jesus and Mary, and again in the motherhood of Mary and sinners. Such anthropomorphism runs smoothly with the grain of Christian theology, in which God is the "Father" and Christ the "Son." In the case of the Virgin's mediation, it does beg a serious question: that the natural role of a mother is intercession.

This premise was carried so far that in this century the Dominicans even proposed that the doctrine of the Virgin's intercession be tackled from the angle of "the Queen's influence over the heart of the King."[7] The mediation of Mary could be understood by extending not only the metaphor of the family, but of a theoretical royal family in which the Queen Mother is "the power behind the throne." This line of attack has fortunately been abandoned, but the fact that it could be suggested at all reveals how profoundly man–woman relations, assumed from prevailing social conditions, influence Mariology in its vital aspects.

At one level, the argument that Mary and the saints intercede with God rather than wield power in their own right is necessitated by monotheism. The jurisdiction of the One True God cannot be encroached upon by other powers. But at another level the doctrine of Mary's intercession coheres with other characteristics that establish her as the ideal *woman*—with her submission and her purity and her gentleness. She acts positively only through the principal man in her life, who is, in this case of a virgin birth, her son. Such a concept mirrors faithfully the patriarchal family as it exists in the Mediterranean, and in southern Ireland, where a woman is considered to have sovereign powers in the family (and depending on her character, sometimes exercises them) and yet has little or no rights beyond her role as a mother. It is not as a wife or lover that a woman acquires authority in a Spanish or Italian or Irish household, but only as the origin of the heir's life. Almost naïvely, therefore, the theology of the Virgin's intercession assumes the state of affairs in heaven to resemble the conditions in, say, a Neapolitan artisan's family. And by doing so, it reinforces society's belief in mothers' moderating and merciful influence, in the woman's role as the hen who really rules the roost but lets the cock think he does. The natural order for the female sex is ordained as motherhood and, through motherhood, domestic dominion. The idea that a woman might direct matters in her own right as an independent individual is not even entertained. In Catholic societies, such a state of affairs is general, and finds approval in the religion's chief female figure. But that does not mean that feminine mediation is innate or natural or unalterable.

There is tension, nevertheless, between the theory of the Virgin's intercession and the cult practices that attempt to secure it. For the flowers arrayed before her image or her statue, the smoking candles and sanctuary lamps, the rising incense swung from censers, the implorations of the choir, the numberless paintings and churches, poems and songs made in her honour are offered to her, for her own glorious sake, because the beauty and perfection of womanhood she represents has enchanted men and women for centuries. And underneath all this undiluted flattery runs the courtier's usual ulterior motive.

She is prayed to as the Queen of Heaven, an eschatological figure who holds the key to eternal life and can fling open the gates of paradise (see Chapter 21). But she is also petitioned for more mundane favours and terrestrial benefits with little compunction on the part of the devout and little restraint from the clergy. The prayers that guarantee her continuing life rise up to heaven to plead for anything from the cure of a loved one's illness, the conversion of an agnostic or Protestant friend, the coveted job, possession, or holiday, the sudden flowering of love in someone's hitherto indifferent heart. Even the (just) downfall of an enemy or a rival finds its place in prayer, while, as we have seen, the conception and safe birth of a child is the particular business of certain Madonnas. And in countries where contraception is forbidden through the collusion of Church and state, there are many women who also pray fervently and bitterly that they might be spared another pregnancy.

Ideally prayer is less pragmatic or self-seeking. Yet to scoff at the Catholic attitude to their saint's personal usefulness, as the Reformers and rationalists have done since the sixteenth century, is to miss its sympathetic side. For such prayers give evidence of the intimacy of sinner and saint, and are equivalent, in their concern with daily problems, to conversations between family and friends.

The prayers of the great saints did not run on such petty preoccupations, and there are moments in every believer's life when the miracle of true prayer—communion with the divine—can happen as the spirit rises towards its maker and, as Bernard described, is fused, almost liquefied in the experience of God's love. But to feel this love in the numb, constantly trespassing soul—that is the problem. Prayer is an emotional experience that demands the totality of the self, as Claudius knew when he groaned:

> My words fly up, my thoughts remain below.
> Words without thoughts never to heaven go.
> (*Hamlet*, Act III, Sc. 3:97–9)

The gift of all-consuming involvement in contemplation of the Godhead is very rare, and the Catholic Church, recognizing this, has enthusiastically endorsed the use of external stimuli to prayer: the sacred drama of the mass excites each of the senses, with its spectacular display and pageantry, its music and perfumes, even the taste of the Eucharist on the tongue; and holy places and holy things, as a piece of Mycenaean gold in the hand can conjure all the fury and splendour of Agamemnon's house, can pierce the carapace of the insensible soul and fill it to the brim with the certainty of divinity's closeness. So pictures, relics, and sanctuaries are all component parts of the same language of prayer that communicates heaven to earthlings and makes addressing a saint much easier. The image or simulacrum of someone's face, the clothes once worn, the possessions once used, the ground once trodden are highly charged with the qualities that made him holy, and retain long after he is gone his sacred and powerful imprint.[8]

The psychological reality of this hardly needs emphasizing, for it is an obvious human characteristic, even outside the spiritual sphere: crowds still tear the clothes off the backs of their idols, and pop magazines offer Elvis Presley's bath water to his fans. Anyone who has kept a snapshot of a lover and felt moved to kiss it, or anyone who has opened the cupboards of a dead friend and felt the onrush of despair evoked by his or her presence in all that jumble of personal possessions has in a different way had the same experience sought by the pilgrim when he gazed on Christ's face printed on Veronica's veil or worshipped before a relic of the True Cross.

These are commonplaces of the human heart, and need describing at all only because the legacy of Reformation horror has branded the Catholic method as myopic superstition and empty externals, missing its simple humanity. The Virgin's help has long been sought through relics and images. However, because her body had disappeared from earth there were no tangible relics of her person for early Christians to venerate. As Christian cult in the first centuries focussed on the remains of the martyrs and the sites of their sufferings, this lack is considered the major reason for the slow development of the Virgin's cult. But by the fifth century veneration for the Virgin was becoming established, and later legends date the first discovery of relics to that time. The Empress Eudocia (408–50), wife of Theodosius II (d. 450), retired after an unhappy experience of court life to live piously in Jerusalem, where she became, like the Empress Helena before her, an enthusiastic amateur archaeologist and relic-hunter.[9] According to one legend, she asked for the Virgin's body and was sent her shroud (see Chapter 6). According to another, in 438 Eudocia sent her husband's equally devout sister Pulcheria an icon of the Virgin that had been painted by St. Luke. The *Theotokos Hodegetria,* the Mother of God, Guide of Wayfarers (so called because the Virgin points the way with her finger to the child on her arm), was enshrined after its arrival in Constantinople in the convent of Blachernae next to the imperial palace at a time of mounting popular devotion to the Virgin, as the Council of Ephesus a few years before had demonstrated.[10]

Another related legend, which cannot be traced further back than the seventh century, describes how Pulcheria, at the time of the Council of Chalcedon in 451, asked the patriarch of Jerusalem if the body of the Virgin could be sent to her. He replied—in one of the first hints at Mary's Assumption—that her body had never been found on earth, but that instead he was sending Pulcheria the Virgin's grave-clothes. Pulcheria also deposited these at Blachernae. In yet another story of the same date, Mary's dress was discovered by Greek soldiers in a golden reliquary during a battle against the Mongols in 619. They took it to the patriarch of Constantinople, who found that inside the coffer the relic was miraculously intact: Mary's incorruptibility had been communicated to the material of her clothes. A feast commemorating the deposition of the relic at Blachernae was instituted on July 2 between 620 and 625, which led the eminent Catholic Byzantinist Wenger to believe this story was authentic.

The chapel at Blachernae also boasted, alongside Luke's portrait and the Virgin's grave-clothes, the *maphorion,* or long blue veil, of Syrian women that the Virgin wore and that has remained her abiding signature. This had been enshrined in the treasure house of the Blachernae convent by the Empress Verina, wife of Leo I (457–74), who were both so devoted to the *Theotokos* that they were portrayed there in mosaic with their family all aligned beside the Virgin. In the church of Chalkoprateia another infinitely precious relic of the Virgin—yet another example of her girdle additionally sanctified by a few drops of her milk—had been preserved, according to tradition, since the fourth century, when the Emperor Arcadius had deposited it there. In Salonika, a basilica was built in 470 to house a miraculous icon of the Virgin *Hodegetria,* which had been painted by angels this time, and was therefore *acheiropoieton,* "untouched by human hand."[11]

Clothes the Virgin had worn were steeped in her holiness by direct communication with her pure and incorruptible body. Images of her, which lacked the blessing of immediate contact, were provided with holy origins by ascribing them to St. Luke or to angels. The prolific Luke is still credited with hundreds of statues and paintings all over the Catholic world (figure 43); and there are still many *acheiropoietoi* images in Catholic churches. It seems pathetically childish to believe such tales, but they perform a crucial function that should not really be mocked. For the all-important lifeline, the direct chain of descent from God to man, is not broken if the images appeared miraculously or were painted by Luke in the presence of the Virgin (figure 44). The time continuum is not interrupted, for the believer finds himself contemplating the face of the Virgin as she really was, living in an eternal present in which she still abides. As Peter Brown has brilliantly described in a paper on the Iconoclast heresy, images and relics were not simply instruments to excite piety and religious emotion, but were considered actively holy in themselves because, like the Gospels themselves, they had been handed down from God to men:

An icon or a wall painting might be known to have made St. Gregory of Nyssa weep; it had reminded St. Anastasius, at a crucial moment, of the courage of the martyrs; it might lead the mystical devotee, in a more subtle way, "by the hand" to contemplate the incarnation of Christ; but it could do more than this. The icon was a hole in the dyke separating the visible world from the divine, and through this hole there oozed precious driblets from the great sea of God's mercy: icons were active. . . .[12]

A sacred image was not an illusion but the possessor of reality itself, and the beneficent forces that flow through icons and relics of a holy personage like the Virgin bring them to life. A homily attributed to Theophilus, bishop of Alexandria, tells a typical Catholic story about an icon of the Virgin. A Jew orders some Christian workmen to destroy the picture. They refuse, so he smashes it himself and tells the workmen to throw it in the river. But the image is bleeding, and when the workmen put it in a basket, the blood seeps through and soaks the carriers. The

Jew, horrified at the sight of this, is converted and builds a church to house the icon, where countless miracles of healing and exorcism take place.[13]

In medieval miracle stories, statues and paintings, in accordance with iconodule belief, are constantly coming to life. In many the Virgin weeps, as she did in 1953 in Syracuse and elsewhere more recently; in one, a Saracen is converted when her breasts become flesh and flow with oil;[14] in a very popular tale, a woman begs the Virgin to spare her dying child, and to make sure seizes the Christ child from her arms as a hostage and only returns him to his mother on the recovery of her own child.[15] In yet another miracle, the Virgin breaks out in sweat as she tries to restrain her son's almighty and vengeful arm from striking a sinner down.[16]

The dynamic holiness of icons and relics did not just stir the soul to the contemplation of higher things, they also physically communicated the properties of their subject or owner. Images were alive, and so they could breathe life into the dying. Mary's peculiar qualities of bodily and spiritual integrity made her the supreme medium of healing and rendering whole again, and her shrines have always been thronged, since early Christian times, when, according to a tenth-century legend, the Empress Zoe had been cured by touching the girdle preserved in the Chalkoprateia church.[17]

Surprisingly, the mediation of sacred objects does have the imprimatur of the New Testament. The intercession of the saints, on the other hand, has little authority in Scripture, as Luther pointed out. There is an allusion in Revelation to an angel offering the Lamb incense with the prayers of the saints (Revelation 5:8, 8:3–4); and prayers for the dead are mentioned in the Old Testament (see Tobit 12:12; 2 Maccabees 15:11–16). But the power of holy men to heal the body and the spirit by their touch as well as by indirect means is attested in the Acts of the Apostles. After Peter had raised the lame man at the gate of the temple in Jerusalem, the sick flock to line his path "that at the least the shadow of Peter passing might overshadow some of them . . . and they were healed every one" (Acts 5:15–16). Paul cures by the laying on of hands; but he also works miracles through the possessions he leaves behind: "from his body were brought unto the sick handkerchiefs or aprons, and the diseases departed from them, and the evil spirits went out of them" (Acts 19:12). The Virgin's relics had analogous powers: in Byzantium stories of wonders performed at the shrines of Blachernae and Chalkoprateia circulated widely, and influenced in turn innumerable stories of prodigies associated with certain treasured objects brought back from the holy land by pilgrims, merchants, and returning crusaders. According to a strong tradition, the tunic the Virgin had worn at the Annunciation was brought from Constantinople by Charles the Bald, Charlemagne's son, and after his death in 877 this most treasured relic passed to the cathedral chapter of Notre Dame at Chartres (see Chapter 18).[18] It was to provide a fitting setting for the wondrous and powerful dress that Chartres was rebuilt in its present rainbow beauty and grace after a fire swept through the old church in 1194. For the relic was spared by a miracle, or so it seemed to the medieval mind, who saw in the Virgin's shift a material image of the imperishable Virgin herself.

The appetite for relics and for the powers they conferred could overcome worldly covetousness in the most ambitious princelings of the middle ages. When Roger Borsa, the Norman duke of Apulia, housed and fed the armies of Robert II of Flanders and of his cousin, Robert, duke of Normandy, as they passed through his territories in 1096 on their way to fight the first crusade, he turned down all the costly gifts he was offered in gratitude—except for the bones of Saints Matthew and Nicolas (still in Bari) and some of the Virgin's hair.[19]

Throughout the twelfth century, the flow of Marian relics increased prodigiously, and clergymen all over western Christendom discovered sacred and hitherto unknown remains of the Virgin in their sacristy treasuries. The canons of Coutances marvelled when their bishop, Geoffrey de Montbray (d. 1110), found some neatly labelled Virgin's hair, protesting that "no relics of the Virgin were known to exist on earth."[20]

By the high middle ages, no scruple about the Virgin's assumed body impeded the discovery and veneration of physical relics. Whereas the Byzantines had concentrated on clothes the Virgin wore, western Christians revered her hair, her milk, and even her nail parings, which were kept in a red satin purse at Poitou. Our Lady's hair was preserved at St. John Lateran and S. Maria sopra Minerva as well as in lesser churches throughout Rome; there was some in Venice, Bologna, Padua, Oviedo, Bruges, Assisi, St. Omer, Mâcon, in the Sainte Chapelle in Paris, at Montserrat, and at St. Denis, in shades of gold to red to blonde to black and in quantities that would have made a grizzly bear look hirsute. Her wardrobe took on fabulous dimensions, and fragments of her clothing or richly embroidered medieval dresses that had belonged to her hung in shrines in Rome, San Salvador, Marseilles, Toulon, Assisi, Arles, Novgorod, the Escorial palace, Limbourg, and Brussels. Soissons kept her slipper, which worked many miracles. The wedding ring she had worn as Joseph's wife was kept at Chiusi in Tuscany.[21] And it was not the only one in Europe.

25

The marriage of Joseph and Mary remained chaste because Joseph respected Mary's virginity, not because he was old. In paintings like Murillo's *Marriage of the Virgin*, St. Joseph therefore sheds his traditional decrepitude. Seventeenth century. (Chapter 12)

Jesus displays his wounds and Mary bares her breast in order to win the mercy of God the Father towards the sinners who kneel at their feet. Florentine, *c.* 1402. (Chapters 13 and 21)

"When Adam delved / And Eve span . . . / Where was then / The pride of man?" asks the poem. Labour was one consequence of the Fall, another was woman's curse—"in sorrow thou shalt bring forth children"—which in the medieval view embraced the complete biological cycle, including suckling. Liège, thirteenth century. Detail. (Chapter 13)

Agnès Sorel, the mistress of Charles VII of France and mother of four of his daughters, so bewitched his treasurer Étienne Chevalier that he commissioned her portrait as the enthroned Virgin. Jean Fouquet, the Melun Diptych, *c.* 1450. Detail. (Chapter 13)

The Mystic Hunt. Christ the unicorn, hunted by the angel Gabriel and his hounds, lays his head in the lap of the Virgin, whom he cannot resist as she sits in the enclosed garden, surrounded by other biblical symbols of her inviolate virginity: *left to right,* the burning bush, the tower of ivory, the ark of the covenant, the closed gate, at her side the pot that held the manna safe from corruption. Dutch, sixteenth century. (Chapter 13)

The miracle of the Virgin's milk is a recurrent image to be found even in Ethiopia. "How a monk with an ulcerated mouth was laid out as dead, and how the Virgin healed him with milk from her breast," illustrated in the fourteenth-century English Queen Mary Psalter. (Chapter 13)

The Virgin rewarded the zeal of St. Bernard her "Troubadour" with three drops of milk from her breast. Filippino Lippi, *The Vision of St. Bernard.* (Chapter 13)

31

Opposite—top left: Isis suckles Horus in an ancient Egyptian bronze; top right: the Virgin Mary nurses the child Jesus in a painting by the Coptic artist Isaac from a manuscript written in 893 in Fayum, Egypt; bottom: Joos van Cleve, nearly seven hundred years later, treats the theme, but with a new sense of domestic intimacy and deep affection. (Chapter 13)

32

33

34

Left: in an ancient Egyptian statuette, Isis holds Osiris across her knees after his cruel death. Below, in the marble carving by the Master of Rimini, c. 1430, the Virgin cradles in her lap the lifeless body of her son. (Chapter 14)

35

36

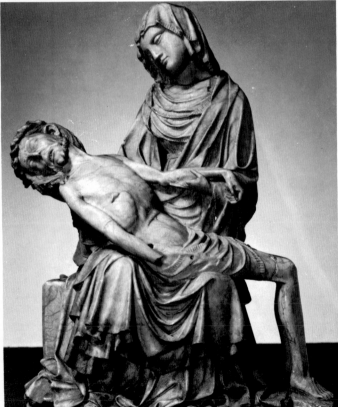

## 37

The Virgin receives the body of Christ from the Cross, in an English ivory of about 1150. (Chapter 14)

Left: the sun and moon cover their faces while Mary and St. John keep vigil in a pre–Norman Conquest illumination from the English Gospels of Judith of Flanders. (Chapter 14)

Below, right: in repentance for her wickedness, Mary Magdalene chastised her sinful flesh with a life of total self-denial, but her hair grew miraculously to cover her wasted limbs. Donatello, *La Maddalena,* the Baptistry, Florence, fifteenth century. (Chapter 15)

38

39

Above: the identity and number of the first witnesses of Christ's Resurrection vary, but they were known to medieval tradition as the Three Marys or, as in this ivory of the mid-fourteenth century, as the Two Marys. (Chapter 15 and Appendix B)

40

Speculation about the matrilineal ancestry of Christ was particularly popular in northern Europe. Polychrome statue of Christ, the Virgin, St. Anne, her mother, and St. Emerentia (or Esmeria), her grandmother, by the Urban Master from Hildesheim, Lower Saxony. (Chapter 16)

The patroness of marriages and the protectress of brides, Mary distributes dowries to two young paupers. Mid-fifteenth century, Rome. (Chapter 18)

43

44

Opposite: the wonder-working Black Madonna of Montserrat in Spain is twelfth-century Byzantine, but according to tradition it is believed to have been carved from life by St. Luke, who also painted the Virgin many times, as imagined by Rogier van der Weyden in his masterpiece (above), *c*. 1440. (Chapters 18 and 19)

Rosary propaganda: the Apocalyptic Madonna is surrounded by five decades of beads. Woodcut, Savoy, France (?), c. 1490. (Chapter 20)

Idyllically surrounded by the roses that are her symbol, the Virgin sits in a paradise or garden. Stefan Lochner (d. 1451), *Madonna in a Rose Arbour*. (Chapter 20)

An angel pierced the heart of St. Teresa of Ávila and left her "utterly consumed by the great love of God." Bernini, *The Ecstasy,* S. Maria della Vittoria,
Rome. 1645–52. (Chapter 20)

The monster Leviathan's mouth of "burning lamps" where "sparks of fire leap" was identified with the mouth of hell, Satan's domain, where the damned can find reprieve only through the intercession of the Virgin, who therefore becomes queen of hell. Fourteenth century. (Chapter 21)

49

50

Theophilus, "lover of God," sold his soul to the Devil, but the Virgin heard his prayers, and in the twelfth-century tympanum of the abbey church at Souillac (top), she flies down to return the deed to him as he sleeps (centre, detail). On the north portal of Notre Dame in Paris, about a hundred years later, she despatches the craven Satan with a righteous thrust (bottom). (Chapter 21)

51

52

The Madonna and Child, painted by a follower of Giotto, filled with the profound and gentle humanity that master infused into western painting, epitomizes the Christian ideal of motherhood. Italian, early fourteenth century. (Epilogue)

At Walsingham in England there was a replica of the Holy House at Nazareth, which drew pilgrims from all England and Europe for three hundred years and fattened the local clergy. During the reign of Edward the Confessor, the Virgin had appeared to a devout widow of Walsingham called Richeldis de Faverches and had led her in spirit to Nazareth, given her the measurements of the house in which she had received the angel Gabriel and lived with the Holy Family, and asked her to build "England's Nazareth." The construction of the wooden house around 1130 was accompanied by many wonders; thereafter the shrine saw further miracles. As the fifteenth-century ballad printed by Richard Pynson and widely circulated describes:

> Many seke ben here cured by our Lady's myghte
> Dede agayne revyved of this no dought
> Lame made whole and blynded restored to syghte
> Lo here the chyef solace agaynst all tribulacyon
> To all that be seke bodely or goostly
> Callin to Our Lady devoutly.[22]

In 1538 Henry VIII despoiled Walsingham—which, as a young man, he had generously endowed—and the miraculous statue was taken to London and burned; the Holy House was razed, the luxurious buildings of the monastery and the numerous dependencies of the exceedingly prosperous pilgrimage were levelled. But by that date Walsingham had a formidable rival: the Holy House of Loreto.

The Virgin's actual house, not a copy, had been miraculously transported by angels from Nazareth after the fall of the Christian kingdom of Jerusalem to the infidel in 1291. The angels had set it down many times in different places, in Yugoslavia and in Italy, but were dissatisfied by the lukewarm response the major relic received until they deposited it at Loreto in 1296. There, in a dream, the Virgin revealed to a holy man that it was her house, where the Annunciation had taken place.

The legend is first recorded in Italian around the year 1472, and any evidence corroborating the house's earlier origins is of the flimsiest nature. A deputation visited the holy land and found the house had mysteriously disappeared; they came back, measured the dimensions of the Loreto version, and pronounced them identical. Miracles accumulated at the shrine, and in 1507 Julius II (1503–13), the most sophisticated and urbane of Renaissance popes, approved the *Santa Casa* as a place of pilgrimage. He added the reservation *ut pie creditur et fama est* (as it is piously and traditionally believed), and the faithful since then have displayed little reserve. Crowds have flocked to Loreto for four hundred years, and in 1936 a visit to the shrine was granted lavish indulgences, which placed it on a par with Lourdes and the holy land. In 1920, Our Lady of Loreto, whose house took flight, was proclaimed the patroness of airmen.

Erasmus addressed himself to the nonsense and vulgarity of Catholic cult with trenchant intelligence and biting scorn. His was the most formidable voice in the clamour for Church reform that rose in Europe from the end of the fifteenth century onwards. Christians of all orders of life knew the rottenness in the Church, and cried out for change. One of the particular areas that demanded cure was cult, for it was obvious to any thinking Christian with a sincere religious conviction that the reliance on externals—on relics, processions, pilgrimages, and various rituals that earned indulgences and reprieve from purgatorial fire—was altogether unbalanced and abused, while purity of the heart, moral rectitude, and above all the inner man had been forgotten under the dross.

The Virgin Mary was not an important figure in the theological issues raised by the Reformers; she had, for instance, no direct bearing on papal supremacy or the doctrine of the True Presence in the Eucharist. But her cult excited precisely those excesses of external idolatry, with their accompanying hollowness of the spirit, that horrified the men who pressed for reformation; and she was the chief guarantor of a safe conduct to heaven for sinners, however wicked, who performed the right ceremonies (see Chapter 21). Erasmus was scathing about the shrine at Walsingham and others; and in countries turning towards the Reformers her images, relics, and churches came under attack.

The Lutherans, who kept some of the traditional liturgical rites and vestments and adornments in their churches, were less zealous in their cleansing, and their devotion to the Virgin was the keenest among the Reformers, for they continued to revere her as the instrument of the Incarnation, the biblical mother of the man Jesus of Nazareth. But in England, the idols were swept away: as mentioned earlier the statue of Our Lady of Walsingham was taken to London and burnt; the Lady Chapel at Ely Cathedral, the largest of its kind in England, with the complete cycle of the life and miracles of the Virgin carved by John de Wisbech (d. 1349) under the direction of the genius master-builder Alan de Walsingham, was completely mutilated in 1539, during the dissolution of the monasteries. The scenes can barely be deciphered, and the beautiful chapel stands now as a tragic monument to iconoclastic passion.

The Catholics responded to the Protestant Reformation of cult practices by purging their sacristies of the rubbish that Chaucer had mocked so skilfully many years before, when he described the indulgence seller, the pardoner:

> There was no pardoner of equal grace,
> For in his trunk he had a pillow-case
> Which he asserted was Our Lady's veil.
> He said he had a gobbet of the sail
> Saint Peter had the time when he made bold
> To walk the waves, till Jesu Christ took hold.
> He had a cross of metal set with stones
> And, in a glass, a rubble of pigs' bones.[23]

But when the Catholic reformers set their house in order, they did not reject the principles on which it had always been run; rather, they insisted on the efficacious intercession of the Virgin and saints more vehemently than before, and did not put an end to the use of images and relics as a channel of communication with heaven. If some holy things through which men had tried to contact God had now been declared spurious, it only made the genuine articles rarer, more sacred, and more worthy of veneration. Thus in the sixteenth century all the energy of the baroque Catholic style was poured molten into the aggrandizement of sacred objects that were, in the Catholic view, indubitably authentic. St. Charles Borromeo (d. 1584), one of the most impressive of the men of the Counter-Reformation, a young blood who became an unflagging, austere, and kindly prelate and the beloved cardinal-archbishop of Milan, was learned and zealous in his defence of Catholic iconodulia. It was his opinion that prevailed at the Council of Trent and influenced its whole-hearted justification of the use of images in Christian worship. In Rome, where as a young man he was bishop of S. Prassede, Borromeo followed in the footsteps of his noble mentor, St. Philip Neri (d. 1595), and advocated the return to legacies from the Church's earliest years. Icons and relics were almost fetishes from this past, and were rehabilitated with pomp and display. In S. Maria Maggiore, for instance, Borromeo's enthusiasm inspired the Borghese chapel, a seventeenth-century shrine for an ancient *acheiropoieton* icon of the Virgin that exactly captures the passion with which the Counter-Reformers addressed themselves to re-opening of the lines of communication with the Christian tradition and reasserting themselves as the legitimate heirs of Jesus Christ.[24] High in the centre of a treasury of jasper, agate, lapis lazuli, and amethyst, the icon of the Virgin and child looks down. Overburdened with excrescent precious stones that not only stud the frame but also adorn the neck, head, and shoulders of the icon, the veiled and aquiline-featured Virgin gazes steadfastly out with that grave, introspective thoughtfulness typical of fine Byzantine art.

This icon is called the *Salus Populi Romani* (the salvation of the Roman people). Before it on August 5 clouds of petals from white roses are loosed from the ceiling in commemoration of the miracle of the basilica's foundation. For according to legend, Pope Liberius (352–66) dreamed that the Virgin commanded him to build her a church on the Esquiline hill on a site marked out by a freak snowfall in August. The white petals of the roses evoke this signal gesture of the Virgin.

The icon used to be assigned to the twelfth century, but experts now date it much earlier—to the ninth or even the eighth century. Its present Aladdin's cave setting celebrates not only the holy *acheiropoieton* icon itself, but also the military victories of Popes Clement VIII (1592–1605) and Paul V (1605–21), who gave his family name Borghese to the chapel he commissioned. The serene Madonna contemplates from her encrusted heights the splendid mayhem of her champions as they defended the truly revealed faith against blasphemy and iconoclasm.

At S. Maria in Trastevere, where Borromeo's uncle Sittico Altemps was cardinal, John VII's magnificent icon of *Maria Regina* (see Chapter 7 and figure 12) was translated with full ceremony in 1593 to a new chapel of glittering opulence, in which the cardinal's participation in the Council of Trent is also commemorated in a painting on the side wall. Both the Borghese and the Altemps chapels, baroque extravaganzas in the oldest churches dedicated to the Virgin in Rome, bear witness to the epic effort of the Counter-Reformation to renew the Church's dialogue with God through holy things. The time machine was to be arrested and turned back, and contact with the past to be forged anew. Objects from that past, like the icons of S. Maria Maggiore and S. Maria in Trastevere, were media through which the new Catholic Church could communicate. But every convulsed line of the art that enshrines them, the grappling angels and the surging saints, the plethora of bosses and stars and roses and bows and garlands, gives tragic evidence of the cataclysm Rome had suffered and the desperation of its remedies, for in neither chapel is there space for the eye to rest or the mind to breathe.

The antiquities of the Christian tradition did not therefore suffice; and from the sixteenth century onwards, another way a creature could address his God was explored, another way by which the historical time continuum could be slashed and the years of increasing distance and alienation be made to disappear; and that was through intense personal prayer, for sometimes it could conjure visions.

## Chapter Twenty

# VISIONS, THE ROSARY, AND WAR

*Mock on, mock on, Voltaire, Rousseau:*
*Mock on, mock on: 'tis all in vain!*
*You throw the sand against the wind,*
*And the wind blows it back again.*

*And every sand becomes a gem*
*Reflected in the beams divine;*
*Blown back they blind the mocking eye,*
*But still in Israel's paths they shine.*

*The atoms of Democritus*
*And Newton's particles of light*
*Are sands upon the Red Sea shore,*
*Where Israel's tents do shine so bright.*[1]

—WILLIAM BLAKE, "Mock on! Mock on!"

S<small>T. TERESA OF ÁVILA</small>, a woman of indomitable hard sense, was also an ecstatic and a visionary, and no one has better described the experience of communion with the divine than she did in her autobiography, when she told how she had tasted "the great love of God":

An angel in bodily form, such as I am not in the habit of seeing except very rarely . . . not tall, but short, and very beautiful. . . . In his hands I saw a great golden spear, and at the iron tip there appeared to be a point of fire. This he plunged into my heart several times so that it penetrated to my entrails. When he pulled it out, I felt that he took them with it, and left me utterly consumed by the great love of God. The pain was so severe that it made me utter several moans. The sweetness caused by this intense pain is so extreme that one cannot possibly wish it to cease, nor is one's soul content then with anything but God. . . .[2]

Bernini sculpted the saint nearly a hundred years later. In the church of S. Maria della Vittoria in Rome, she falls back in a swoon, transfixed by a smiling seraph. Her lips are parted, her foot hangs bare below the hem of her full robes. The Cornaro family, who commissioned the chapel in which Bernini's statue stands, gaze on the supernatural visitation from the wings, as if the saint's vision were still taking place and the breach between the human and the divine were closed and healed in the single ardent point of the pretty angel's spearhead (figure 47).

One wag looking at Bernini's masterpiece commented: "If this is divine love, I know what it is."[3] The post-Freudian reader might well say the same of Teresa's own description. But psychoanalysis cannot really diminish the spiritual reality of the experience for the visionaries themselves; and cannot obliterate the impact the vision as a mediating instrument between heaven and earth had on the development of Catholic cult after the Reformation.

Through visions, the experience of the Incarnation and the Redemption was re-enacted. The art of the time captures the dramatic realism of the encounter: Parmigianino hurls Jerome to the ground before the high-lit, foreshortened glory of the Madonna and child; in a sculpture by Louisa Ignacia Roldan, San Diego of Alcalá shoulders the cross handed him by the infant Christ in his mother's arms.[4] The Fathers of the Church, who in fifteenth-century paintings were decorously grouped around the enthroned Virgin and child, now reel back as the full glory of the divine presence hits them.

Aquinas, and seers like Teresa herself, distinguished between an imaginary vision, which took place in the mind's eye but was nonetheless real for that, and an apparition, which, like Christ's appearances to the disciples after the Resurrection, was apprehensible to the eyes of the flesh. Both visions and apparitions conferred extraordinary grace on the visionaries and through them on the members of the Church to which they belonged. For in a vision heaven and earth collided in a piece of time and space and suspended both of them; its occurrence furnished vivid proof of God's continuing colloquium with Rome, of the continuing approval of a heaven that had allowed half of Europe to fall into the hands of Lutherans, Calvinists, and Protestants of other persuasions;

above all, a vision designated a new saint, in communication with the supernatural, while an apparition sanctified that portion of the terrestrial sphere where it took place with lasting salvific effect. Therefore, at the moment when much of the legacy of early Christian times—especially relics—had been declared bogus and the Roman Church had been thereby discredited, a new and fertile seam of holy things was discovered and richly mined. St. Teresa of Avila's left hand was severed from her body (which exuded a sweet odour and did not decompose in death) and during subsequent exhumations and displays of her earthly remains, the rest of her left arm, her heart, and other parts of her body were removed as relics by ecclesiastics and the faithful.[5] It seems incomprehensibly ghoulish, yet it would happen again today in Italy or Spain on the death of someone as celebrated for holiness as was St. Teresa. The hunger for direct messages from heaven in visionary form has not been appeased, and the continuing faith with which such manifestations are treated still forms one of the most precise images of the Catholic Church's anxiety to renew intimacy with the Godhead.

The Virgin outstrips all other saints in frequency and popularity. She appeared to Teresa of Ávila, and although that saint insists that a vision is seen with the eyes of the soul in an ineffable manner, she describes her experience of the Virgin with her customary vividness. With St. Joseph at her side, the Virgin appeared to St. Teresa on the feast of her Assumption and clothed her "in a robe of great whiteness and clarity. . . ." She was purified of her sins, and felt "the greatest joy and bliss" when

Our Lady seemed suddenly to seize me by the hands. She told me that I was giving her great pleasure by serving the glorious St. Joseph, and promised me that my plans for the convent would be fulfilled. . . . Then she seemed to hang around my neck a very beautiful gold collar from which hung a cross of great value. The gold and the stones were so different from those of this world that there is no comparing them; their beauty is quite unlike anything we can imagine here. Nor can the imagination rise to any understanding of the nature of the robe, or to any conception of its whiteness. Such was the vision that the Lord was pleased to send to me that by comparison everything here on earth seems, as you might say, a smudge of soot.

The beauty that I saw in Our Lady was wonderful, though I could make out no particular detail, only the general shape of her face and the whiteness and amazing splendour of her robes, which was not dazzling but quite soft. . . . Our Lady looked to me almost like a child. When they had stayed with me for a little while, bringing me the greatest joy and bliss—

more I believe than I had ever known before, and I wished it would last for ever—I seemed to see them ascend into the sky with a great multitude of angels. . . .[6]

St. Teresa's vision surpasses others in its serene and simple communication of a joy beyond all earthly joy; but the characteristics of many appearances of the Virgin in this century and the last are already present in her narrative—the soft but overwhelming radiance, the sweetness and reassurance of Our Lady, the intimacy with which she treats the visionary, and, above all, the childlikeness of her appearance. As the idea of the innocence of childhood grew up in Europe, the Virgin's youth became the visible sign of her purity, and her visionaries were often children themselves, particularly in nineteenth-century France, where a sentimental view of both children and religion was rampant.

From the Church's point of view, the most important aspect of a vision was not the private ecstasy, but the public message of divine approval that the descent of Christ or the Virgin on earth communicated to all the faithful. Through the experience of an individual mystic a whole locality, where the vision had taken place, was thereby blessed. Just as touching a relic, contemplating an icon painted by St. Luke, or treading the *Via Dolorosa* in Jerusalem could make the pilgrim feel in touch with the divine, so visiting places hallowed by the recent presence of the Virgin strengthens faith in the religion's continuity and endurance and efficiency.

Of all the post-Reformation shrines of the Virgin, one in particular reveals the mechanism by which a vision becomes the mark of a people's favour with God and thus boosts their confidence in the Church. At the shrine of Our Lady of Guadalupe, all the strands of Catholic devotion since the departure of the Reformed Churches are gathered together in their most characteristic form, so that although Latin America is beyond the scope of this book, this particular cult does illumine western Catholicism.

In 1531, a converted Indian called Juan Diego was walking through the mountains near Tepeyac when he heard

a singing like that when many choice birds sing together, their voices resounding as if echoing through the hills . . . their song gave him rapture. . . .

Then he saw

on the tip of the peak . . . a lady . . . he was struck with wonder at the radiance of her exceeding great beauty, her garments shining like the sun; and the stones of the hill, and the caves, reflecting the brightness of her light were like precious gold; and he saw how the rainbow clothed the land so that the cactus and other things that grew there seemed like celestial plants, their leaves and thorns shining like gold in her presence.

After this explosion of music and light, the vision asks him to tell the bishop to build a church in her honour. The peasant went to the bishop, but he would not listen. In a later apparition, the Lady promised Juan Diego a sign: he is to climb the mountain to a certain place and gather the roses that he finds there and bring them back to her. It was December, when nothing but the naked thorn covered the mountainside. But the Indian trusted her and found the spot in bloom. When he brought the roses back to her "she gathered them into her immaculate hands and then put them again into my mantle."[7]

Juan Diego returned to the bishop, and in his presence opened his mantle and let fall the shower of roses. On his cloak, the image of the Lady appeared, miraculously imprinted on the homely cloth. At this prodigy, the bishop believed and enshrined the *vera icon,* the new *acheiropoieton,* in the church. The Virgin is called Our Lady of Guadalupe (the origins of this name are debated).[8] Her shrine is the best loved of Catholic Mexico. She was declared patroness of the country in 1754 by Pope Benedict XIV, and of the Americas in 1910. Her image appears on magnets for car dashboards, in amulets and medals and statues and portable shrines of every type. She is dark-complexioned like an Indian, and her lustrous black eyes are often adorned with false eyelashes.

During the Mexican revolution, the Royalists fought under the standard of *La Virgen de los Remedios,* the ancient palladium of Cortes' conquering army, which he had brought with him from Alcantara. The independents marched under the banner of Our Lady of Guadalupe.[9] The progression from vision to sacred object (Juan Diego's cloak) to cult site (the shrine church, now in a suburb of Mexico City), to palladium of a people and a nation and a cause—a progression that occurs in many stories of Catholic attempts to contact the eternal—is crystal clear from the tale of Guadalupe. Within this, an important pattern can be discerned: the private ecstatic experience—Juan Diego's moment of rapture when he was encircled by music sweeter than bird song, by December roses in full bloom, by a vision of more than mortal beauty that transfixed his soul with light—is translated over the years into a communal experience whereby a whole people is blessed. The possession of a sacred event or object fills that people with power, and that divine badge of favour confers moral authority in the temporal realm: the Indian's vision later flutters from the bayonets of his countrymen.

The Virgin, like Athene, presides over peace and over war. She exists on earth and through the places and things she has consecrated by her touch, and gives those things the right to victory. Mexico was not the first nor indeed the only theatre of war in which the Virgin presided. In the ninth century the defenders of Chartres against the Norsemen had flown the Virgin's tunic from the staff of their bishop, and in local legend the wonder-working relic singlehandedly turned back and defeated the invaders. (The timely arrival of allied troops on the enemy's unprotected flank was overlooked.)[10] Before that, in Byzantium, the emperors Maurice and Phocas and Heraclius and Constant II in the sixth and seventh centuries had struck the image of Nike, Goddess of Victory, from the imperial seals and replaced her with the Virgin and child.[11] At the turn of the seventh century, the Emperor Heraclius had called his enemy Phocas "that Gorgon's head," and had turned against him another different magic face—"the awe-inspiring image of the pure Virgin," flying her image from the mastheads of his ships as he sailed into battle. During the siege of Constantinople by the Avars in 626, the patriarch had the Virgin and child painted on the west gates to commend the city into her hands, for the emperor and his army were far away; in 717, when the Arabs were attacking Constantinople, a picture of the Virgin and child and a relic of the True Cross were carried around the city walls as a charm against the besiegers.[12]

During the crusades, when archangels and warrior saints like Michael and George were seen by the soldiery fighting alongside them, the Virgin also played her part, putting in a judicious appearance to hearten her champions, or intervening with an earthquake or similar prodigy to help them to victory. Joinville, biographer of St. Louis IX, reports a primitive anecdote about the crusaders' faith. Joinville went on a pilgrimage to the great Syrian shrine of Our Lady of Tortosa, and heard the story of a miracle she had performed: a man possessed by the devil was taken to Tortosa to be cured, and as his friends prayed for him they suddenly heard the devil speak within him, saying, "Our Lady is not here. She is in Egypt giving help to the King of France and the Christians, who will land this very day to fight on foot against the mounted forces of the heathen." The date was correct, says Joinville, and "I can assure you," he adds, "that Our Lady did indeed help us that day and would have helped us still more if . . . we had not angered her and her son."[13]

In Byzantium and during the crusades, Christian was generally (but not always) fighting heathen; in medieval Europe, the armies who invoked the Virgin were simply fighting fellow-Catholics; and in the Counter-Reformation's holy wars, internecine horrors were perpetrated by Christian upon Christian, again in the name of the same God. At the battle of White Mountain near Prague on November 8, 1620, the Catholic army of the Holy Roman Emperor Ferdinand of Austria advanced crying, "St. Mary!" and defeated the Calvinist enemy in one of the first military coups of the Thirty Years' War, which turned the tide of the Protestant Reformation in Europe and started the recovery of Bohemia (now Czechoslovakia) for Rome. After the victory of White Mountain, Austrian armies established Catholic authority over the country. The Jesuits assumed control of the universities; thirty thousand Protestant families were banished; and those that remained were deprived of their civil rights.[14]

The same church in Rome where St. Teresa is smitten by God's fiery dart was renamed S. Maria della Vittoria—after an icon of the Madonna that had, it was believed, secured the triumph of White Mountain. The ecstasy of a saint and the palladium of a war together in this church form a bitter diptych of the spirit of the Counter-Reformation.[15]

That spirit found another, even more resonant and enduring echo: the hunger for a private experience of God, the need to assert the legitimacy of Rome against the heretics, and the use of a religious practice as a battle standard were all combined in the Church's fostering of devotion to the rosary, the necklace of beads on which the Hail Mary is recited over and over again with hypnotic insistence.

In 1041, Lady Godiva of Coventry left in her will a circlet of gems on which she used to say her prayers. It was, she specified, to be hung round a statue of the Virgin. William of Malmesbury tells this story in his history of England, and it is one of the earliest and most intriguing mentions of the method of telling beads on a rosary.[16]

The chain of beads or knops originated in Brahmanic India, where it is still current in the worship of Vishnu and Shiva. Through Hinduism its use spreads to Buddhism, and later to Islam, where it is referred to as early as the ninth century. The necklace resembles the tasselled amber worry beads that men at café tables all over Greece and Asia Minor and North Africa click through their fingers to soothe the nerves, like a cigarette, but whereas in those countries it has acquired a secular character, it became in the west an exclusively religious habit.

Although the exact point and date of entry of the rosary into western Christendom is not known, the crusaders are generally given the credit for spreading a habit picked up from their Moslem adversaries. But, as the legacy of Lady Godiva shows, the practice of counting one's prayers was known in England before the first crusade and may therefore have arisen spontaneously, or been imported by pilgrims to the holy land.[17]

The combination of Gabriel's greeting—"Hail full of grace, the Lord is with thee"—with Elisabeth's—"Blessed art thou amongst women and blessed is the fruit of thy womb"—is found in the ancient eastern liturgies of James and Mark, in the seventh-century offertory for the feast of the Annunciation and Ember Wednesday in Advent, but it was not widespread until Peter Damian (d. 1072), who called it the "angelic versicle," recommended its use. It was becoming popular at this time in England and the Netherlands, and by the end of the twelfth century a Church synod told the clergy to recite it alongside the scriptural prayer, the Our Father, and the ancient profession of faith, the Creed. The Franciscans and Dominicans spread its use among the laity and encouraged the illiterate to recite it several times over to themselves as "the Psalter of Our Lady," a substitute for more sophisticated prayers. Although Bernardino of Siena had added "pray for us" to the opening praises of the Virgin, the rosary first used the short version of the prayer, without the petition. It was only when the Lutherans criticized the medieval form of the *Ave Maria* that Catholics began including the imploration that now closes the prayer: "Pray for us sinners, now and at the hour of our death." This formula was officially recognized by Pope Pius V in 1568, when he included it in the reformed breviary. By then the rosary, the garland of *Aves* for the Queen of Heaven, had been popular for nearly a hundred years.[18]

Around 1470, the Dominican priest Alanus de Rupe (d. 1475) published the *De Utilitate Psalterii Mariae,* which instantly awakened fervent belief in the powers of the rosary to obtain the Virgin's mercy and protection, particularly in Cologne and Augsburg. His book was followed, before the end of the century, by others no less zealous, and the example of his ardour inspired preachers, particularly Dominicans of his order, to encourage the devotion. In 1495, Pope Alexander VI—the first pope to mention the rosary—gave the Holy See's approval. The practice thereafter spread like wildfire. The notorious witch-hunter Jacob Sprenger had formed the first lay confraternity devoted to the rosary in Germany in 1475; by the sixteenth century it would have been difficult to find a church in Italy that did not boast a confraternity dedicated to reciting it.[19] The full rosary now consists of one hundred and fifty Hail Marys arranged in fifteen decades. For ten Hail Marys the reciter meditates on one mystery of the life of Jesus and Mary, then one Our Father, followed by the doxology "Glory be to the Father. . . ." In practice, one cycle of either the Sorrowful, Joyful, or Glorious Mysteries (fifty Hail Marys) is considered enough.[20] The beads are actively holy in themselves, and are often lovingly carved and jewelled and numbered among a person's most treasured possessions. In the sixteenth century it was fashionable to carve one large bead with a loving couple on one side and a death's head on the reverse, as a bitter *memento mori* to the wearer.

The use of repetition in meditation is of course world-wide, and common in Christian rite. The Reproaches of Good Friday or the litanies chanted by the choir and answered by the congregation are intended, like the rosary, to lull the believer into a trance-like state in which spiritual light may more easily flood the soul. In the rosary, the use of incantatory prayers blended with the medieval symbolism of the rose, until the beads themselves were seen to be chaplets to crown the Queen of Heaven, as garlands for the rose without thorn (Ecclesiasticus 24:14), the rose of Sharon (Song of Solomon 2:1), the rose of Jericho, the rose in which the Word became flesh, as Dante wrote, which flowers at the centre of the arrayed petals of the mystic rose in the empyrean (*Paradiso* 23). The flower that had been a symbol in medieval poetry of the lover's quest was, like so much profane imagery, translated and applied to the Lady of Paradise (figure 46).

Woodcuts of the late fifteenth century—mostly German—are among the earliest signs of mass devotion to the rosary (figure 45), and, in some of them, the image is still fresh, for the Virgin appears ringed with roses. One woodcut from Augsburg shows God the Father above with the arrows of pestilence in his clenched fists, while below Mary shelters kings and cardinals from his wrath under her mantle. The woodcut itself is round, which leads some experts to suggest that it was pasted on an apothecary's jar of ointment against plague.[21] In 1506, Dürer was commissioned by German merchants working in Venice to paint the idyllic *Festival of the Rose Garlands* (now in the National Gallery, Prague); it shows Dürer himself, as well as the Emperor Maximilian and Pope Julius II and other figures offering wreaths of roses to the Virgin.

Devotion to the rosary rises when the Church feels weak and insecure; the prayer, therefore, often indicates an embattled mood among Catholics. When Alanus de Rupe popularized it at the end of the fifteenth century, the cry for Church reform was anguished and widespread; the new meditation was designed to restore an element of sincerity and interior contemplation to the prayers of the faithful, who had come to rely more and more on external acts of piety and particularly the purchase of indulgences to win them forgiveness. The rosary was directly invoked in the politics of Counter-Reformation Rome at the end of the sixteenth century, when Pius V, the same towering pope who reformed the Breviary, promulgated a Bull endorsing its use. Then, in 1573, he instituted a feast of Our Lady of Victory to commemorate the defeat of the Turks at the battle of Lepanto in 1571 by the Holy League under Don John of Austria, brother of the greatest Catholic monarch in the world, Philip II of Spain, a victory that effectively destroyed the power of the heathen Turks in the Mediterranean. The battle had been given to God's side, said the pope, through the intercession of the Virgin obtained by the rosaries offered to her on earth by confraternities of Rome.

This was the most glorious affirmation of the rosary's sacred power; but what is much more interesting is the evidence the pope cited for the authenticity of the devotion: a vision of the Madonna to St. Dominic. According to tradition, Dominic, while conducting the Inquisition against the Albigensian heretics at the beginning of the thirteenth century, had been given the rosary in a vision by the Virgin herself, who told him that Christian men and women should invoke her aid on the beads. This direct intervention of the divine in human affairs gave the rosary a vital claim to divine ordinance and hence validity. A dozen popes since Pius V have, in their encouragement of the rosary, ascribed its origins to this vision;[22] hundreds of artefacts and paintings, including German propaganda woodcuts of the late fifteenth century, depict the friar at the Virgin's feet, receiving the string of beads just as gratefully as St. Thomas caught her falling girdle.

The story cannot be traced further back than the enthusiasm of the Dominican Alanus de Rupe, who, in an access of pious imagination, seems to have invented it. But a sacred character had been conferred on the rosary by its visionary origin. And the process, unfolded in the cult of Our Lady of Guadalupe, is repeated: a holy object originates in heaven, is given to humanity through a vision, is disseminated over the Catholic world, and becomes a mighty thaumaturge, the emblem of solidarity and God-given right in a battle against the enemy.[23]

The victory of Lepanto has lived on in Catholic legend as the last, heroic crusade fought by man for God's kingdom on earth. In this century, G. K. Chesterton's *Ballad of Lepanto,* a splendid piece of bluster, evoked Don John of Austria, the battle's champion, and the great assault made by ascetic chivalry against the exotic and luxurious heathen.[24] Although the pope attributed the victory to the rosary, the rosary itself, unlike Juan Diego's cloak, was not produced as the palladium of Don John's warriors. Indeed, the actual string of beads the Virgin gave Dominic has never been produced as a sacred relic—a difference between the concrete, almost medieval spirit of the American missions and the more abstract grasp of post-Reformation religious feeling in Europe.

But in keeping with this spiritual renascence, visions of the Virgin confirmed her special love of the rosary. There have been several authenticated visitations of the Virgin in the nineteenth and twentieth centuries, and over two hundred that have not been officially approved by the Church.[25] The majority somehow include the theme of the rosary's signal worth. Bernadette Soubirous at Lourdes recited it with her vision many times; at Fatima in 1917, the apparition urged the children to say their rosaries and called herself Our Lady of the Rosary. Both pilgrimages are now committed to the recital of the Hail Mary. At La Salette in France in 1846, she appeared, arrayed in light and roses, to an eleven-year-old boy, Maximin Giraud (d. 1875), and a fourteen-year-old girl, Melanie Calvat (d. 1904). Both Melanie and Maximin led troubled, feckless lives after the vision—to the Church's horror, Maximin franchised a liqueur called Salettine—and the pilgrimage to La Salette, though officially endorsed, is in decline.[26]

In 1871 the Virgin again appeared in France, at Pontmain, to a twelve-year-old cowherd and his ten-year-old brother and two other children, and while the vision doubled in size and the stars on her robe multiplied, the entire village recited the rosary before the spot.[27] In Ireland, in the tiny impoverished village of Knock, County Mayo, the Virgin, surrounded by a group of saints, materialized during a driving rainstorm on the wall of the parish church in 1879. Again, the visionaries —who numbered fifteen or more in this case—recited the rosary before the prodigy, and the shrine, the most popular Marian pilgrimage in a country devoted to the Virgin, hums every Sunday with the *Ave Marias* of Catholics praying for peace in their country.[28] In 1933, the Virgin, dressed in white and azure, with roses on her toes and the beads at her waist, appeared to twelve-year-old Mariette Beco at Banneux in Belgium as she recited her rosary.[29]

The visions both hallowed the place in which they took place and increased devotion to the rosary as the miracle-working prayer. The shrine at Lourdes drew nearly three and a half million pilgrims in 1971, of whom three hundred and ninety-four thousand were sick and travelled there in specially equipped hospital trains; Fatima was visited by more than a million people in 1973.[30] In both places the official keynote is penitence for sin: pilgrims win plenary indulgences for the journey, remitting all the punishment in purgatory due for their sins. But for the visitor the dominant motif is not repentance. The millions of beads run through millions of fervent fingers daily in quest of earthly miracle. The rose garlands of *Aves* rise in the candle-blazing plaza before the ugly modern churches at Lourdes and Fatima to beg for the cure of earthly ills. This is the dominant tragedy of contemporary Marian shrines. Everyone has seen the photographs of stretchers after stretchers in serried phalanx before the grotto where the young and shining lady stood and talked to Bernadette and said the rosary with her. But unless one has been there, one cannot feel the stark desolation of that scene.

Since the pilgrimage began in the middle of the last century until 1959, when the most recent miracle took place, the Church and Lourdes' two medical committees have officially recognised sixty-two miraculous cures. Scores of unofficial cures have been claimed by delighted pilgrims, however, as the crutches and braces hung up on the grotto testify. Anatole France commented when he saw this display: "What, no wooden legs?"[31]

As the Catholic definition of a mystery is "a truth above reason but revealed by God," the cures at Lourdes and elsewhere are pronounced miraculous only if they defy explanation according to the state of medical and scientific knowledge. Thus the operations of God are restricted to the area of the inexplicable and the unnatural. As scientific inquiry learns more, this area shrinks. For instance, it is known now that *sacer ignis* (holy fire) or *le mal des ardents* (the burning sickness), which swept medieval France before the Black Death, was ergotism, the consequence of eating fungus-infested rye bread. In the eleventh century, however, the pestilence was thought to be divine retribution for sin, and its alleviation the direct and particular result of the Virgin's mercy.[32]

By insisting that the supernatural is only manifest in the unnatural, the Church renders itself extremely vulnerable to scientific discovery, which can make its decisions look foolish. It could instead adopt the position of absolute faith and maintain that as God is everywhere, his miraculous work informs all natural phenomena—including cures, both startling and otherwise. Miracles would then increase a hundredfold. This would correspond to the conviction of most Catholics, who are men of great faith (most pilgrims to Lourdes see a miracle cure while they are there). It would also put an end to the lip-service that scientific bodies like the Medical Records Office at Lourdes pay to nineteenth-century rationalism as they attempt the impossible task of reconciling the religious and scientific systems of thought.

It is difficult, nevertheless, to pinpoint why Lourdes should leave so many visitors hollow and dry, and the experience raises problematic and ultimately insoluble questions about the religious response and its mechanism. Does Lourdes fail to uplift because, unlike St. Peter's in Rome or the Duomo in Florence, it does not bear witness to the artistic greatness of its followers? Because the thousands of pilgrims worship in a concrete cavern that resembles an underground carpark, and the nineteenth-century church is adorned with mosaics of singular weakness and vulgarity? Does the sublime have to be beautiful? But to admit this would mistake form for content altogether and indict contemporary piety for failing to meet aesthetic standards. And yet because the Catholic Church has always sought to reach the soul through the senses, its new failure in that sphere contributes to the emptiness of a shrine like Lourdes. There is also at Lourdes the horror of the town's commercialization: the piles of tinsel and plastic amulets, the dross of holy water bottles shaped like the Virgin (her crown the stopper), cocoa-bean rosaries, grottoes in snow-storm globes, Bernadettes wreathed in roses that light up, while all around hotels dedicated to saints pin edifying mottoes to the walls ("If I have not charity . . .") and charge inflated prices. Yet the buyers and sellers only transgressed against the temple's holiness; they did not invalidate the temple itself.

It is understandable if the people of Lourdes exploit the prosperity the pilgrimage has brought them: it is the single boom industry of a remote Pyrenean town. And yet it is undeniable that the souvenir shops and bric-à-brac undermine the spiritual experience to be expected from the greatest Marian shrine in the world. In spite of all the selflessness of the nuns and nurses who look after the sick, and the sincerity of the priests who minister to the pilgrims, Lourdes has become a cynical enterprise: on February 2, the feast of the Purification of the Virgin, there was to be no commemoration in the church at Lourdes, but only a daily mass in the crypt, because the main church was full of workmen redecorating for the coming summer season. Like a seaside hotel in winter, Lourdes was refurbishing in time for the rush, and meanwhile the rest of the liturgical year laid little claim on its resources or its time.

The confidence that Catholics place in the visions of children like Bernadette and the others who were mostly illiterate and often neurasthenic brutally reveals the desperate thirst believers have for assurances that the faith is still credit-worthy. The pressures that the Reformation brought on the Catholic Church erupted into the volcanic activity of the missionary saints and Catholic reformers like St. Ignatius of Loyola, founder of the Jesuits, and St. Francis Xavier, apostle of India and Japan. But in the eighteenth century, the rationalism of the *philosophes* attacked religion itself on a different front, and mocked in particular the sensuous rituals and complex beliefs of the Catholics, which were seen as rank superstition and hocus pocus (perhaps derived from the actual words of the priest at the moment of transubstantiation—*"Hoc est corpus"*). The Reformation had challenged the virtue of Rome; the Age of Reason questioned something that had never before been doubted—its intelligence. The fountainhead of European culture and knowledge, the curators of world history, were ridiculed as ignorant and credulous. The Counter-Reformation had been a revolt: the Church would prove the Reformers wrong by exceeding them in moral courage; but the assaults that stemmed from rationalism and its legacy and continued from the eighteenth century until the present day did not produce such a muscular response, but a form of acquiescence to their critics, as the Church relaxed its claim to intellectual leadership and Catholic piety throughout Europe became more saccharin, more prettified, more emotional.

This sentimentality and quest for simplicity were themselves products of the affective streak in eighteenth-century thought, and they permeated Catholicism, especially in France, until very recently. As Vita Sackville-West pointed out in her biographical studies *The Eagle and the Dove,* the capable and fiery St. Teresa of Avila was the saint of the Counter-Reformation; the sweet, indeed glutinous, St. Thérèse of Lisieux (d. 1897), who entitled her autobiography *L'Histoire d'une Ame—Histoire printanière d'une petite fleur blanche* (The story of a soul—the springtime story of a little white flower), inflamed the hearts and minds of the entire Catholic world at the beginning of this century with her naïve and simple mixture of excessive egoism and emotional self-sacrifice. The Little Flower of Jesus, as she came to be known, also saw the Virgin in a vision when she was a child in bed with a fever; she marked it, along with her first communion and her entry into Carmel at the age of fifteen, as one of the important days in her brief and unexceptional life.[33] Other children saw the Virgin, as we have noted, throughout the nineteenth century and the beginning of this; it is a belief in the freshness, the native goodness of the simple and uncorrupted nature of the child (ironically a direct inheritance from Rousseau) that makes their testimony acceptable to a Church that now chiefly exercises its sphere of influence over parts of southern Europe, Latin America, and Africa, where progress towards industrialization has been comparatively slow. The Curé d'Ars (d. 1859), a parish priest of simple mind and intense feeling, represents like St. Thérèse of Lisieux the way the Church in the nineteenth century and today identifies itself with humble men and their message. And when the Virgin appears to Catholics in obscure places, clinging to an old way of life that has come under strain, proof is thereby given that God has not altogether hidden his face.

Each vision represents a rearguard action against the forces of "progress" or "reason" that deny God and religion. When he reveals himself through his appearance or, as happens more frequently, that of his mother, he confirms the embattled Church's legitimacy. And therefore, as at Guadalupe and Lepanto, a vision can easily be translated into another victory in the long battle of the Church and its assailants.

Since the battle of Lepanto, the Virgin and her special prayer, the rosary, have continued to be particularly associated with the Catholic struggle against its enemies. In 1717 the feast of the Rosary was extended to the whole Church after the Turks were once again defeated by Catholic armies at Petrovaradin (now in Yugoslavia). In the visions at Fatima in Portugal in 1917, Our Lady of the Rosary spoke of an Anti-Christ. In the propaganda that followed the visions, this Anti-Christ was identified with communism and used to inflame fanatical and widespread paranoia. Lucia dos Santos, one of the three children who spoke with the Virgin, revealed in 1927 that she had told them:

I shall come to ask for the consecration of Russia to my Immaculate Heart. . . . If my requests are heard, Russia will be converted and there will be peace. If not, she will spread her errors throughout the entire world, provoking wars and persecution of the Church. . . . But in the end, my Immaculate Heart will triumph.[34]

In 1942, Pope Pius XII dedicated the world to the Immaculate Heart of Mary, and soon afterwards instituted a new feast of that name, which is kept on August 22. It is not impossible that the horror with which Rome, the Vatican, viewed Russia, contributed to its reaction to Nazi Germany, Russia's enemy, and that the Fatima vision, which many Catholics believed had prophesied the Second World War, influenced the pope's attitude, which at best was pusillanimous and at worst criminal.

The jingoism of this period of Marian worship is sometimes shameful: "The modern Red menace," wrote one Catholic author,

got its first hold west of Russia in Spain. But under the banner of Our Lady of Mount Carmel and the Sacred Heart, Catholicity had defeated it there. Yes, despite the cooperation of the great bear, despite the advantage of holding the reins of government, Communism has gone down into the dust before the meagre armies struggling for religious independence. . . . Against Satan in his red threats, we have Mary. . . .[35]

Although the political wind in the Catholic Church is now very changeable, the militant associations of the rosary have survived. In 1966, on the feast of Our Lady of Sorrows, and again in 1974, Pope Paul

. VI urged a universal rosary crusade to bring peace to the world, and particularly to Indo-China. The ecumenical movement has softened the Virgin's militant side, and many popes, particularly Leo XIII, the "Pope of the Rosary," have pleaded for more rosaries to win the unification of Christendom and bring peace to the Church.[36]

As guardian of cities and nations and peoples, as the bringer of peace or victory, her image the palladium of royal armies, the Virgin resembles Athene. She did indeed usurp the Greek goddess of peace in Athens, where the Parthenon was dedicated to her in the sixth century and where the Emperor Basil II paid homage to her in 1017 for his victory over the Bulgars; and in Syracuse, where the honey-coloured Doric columns of Athene's ancient temple are visibly incorporated into the fabric of a sumptuous baroque cathedral that was converted into a Christian place of worship before the seventh century and later dedicated to the Assumption of the Virgin.

But this Virgin's duties towards defence and war represent only a tiny fraction of her huge responsibility, and the thousands of rosaries recited in the Catholic world appeal to her protection not only in the daily business of living but also, above all, in the future, in the experience of death and its eternal aftermath.

## Chapter Twenty-One

# THE HOUR OF OUR DEATH

*Dame du ciel, regente terrienne*
*Emperiere des infernaux palus,*
*Recevez moy, vostre humble chrestienne . . .*
*A vostre Filz dictes que je suis sienne;*
*De luy soyent mes pechiez abolus;*
*Pardonne moy comme a l'Egipcienne,*
*Ou comme il feist au clerc Theophilus,*
*Lequel par vous fut quitte et absolus,*
*Combien qu'il eust au deable fait promesse.*

*(Lady of heaven, regent of earth, Empress of the*
*marshes of hell, Receive me, your humble Christian*
*. . . Tell your son that I am his; (Ask him) to*
*absolve me of my sins; Forgive me as the Egyptian*
*was forgiven, Or as he forgave the clerk Theophilus,*
*Who was acquitted and absolved by you, Although*
*he'd sworn himself the devil's man.)*[1]

—FRANCOIS VILLON

THE LEARNED and ardent St. Anselm, in his prayer written to be recited to the Virgin, "when the mind is anxious with fear," describes the sinner's refuge:

So the accused flees from the just God
To the good mother of the merciful God.[2]

The Virgin's intercession with her son can bring healing and fertility and consolation to the living; but by far her greatest function in the Catholic scheme of salvation is to reprieve the sufferings of sinners after death. She is "the mother of mercy," the "life, sweetness, and hope" of the fallen, the advocate who pleads humanity's cause before the judgement seat of God. As Christ cannot find it in his heart to refuse his mother, her merciful role helps in part to solve the racking dilemma that a God who is goodness, love, and forgiveness could be so harsh as to consign any of his creatures to hell for all eternity. The Virgin gives Christ the Judge his human face; as Anselm's prayer conveys, she transforms him, by a magician's sweep of her hand, from the God of justice to the God of mercy.

The paintings and music and poems; the hymns and prayers and liturgies, the churches and cathedrals—between 1170 and 1270 the French alone built eighty cathedrals and over a hundred churches— the cornucopia overflows for Mary's glory. But an ulterior aim sustains it: to invest in Mary's gilt-edged stock with God.

The intercession of the Virgin and the saints depends on the peculiarly Catholic doctrine of true repentance, which washes away all sin in the sacrament of penance. The Virgin and saints stand in a landscape of the Christian afterlife: a real and awesome place where hell's bonfires burn and the luminous and serried ranks of angels and the fellowship of saints assemble in eternal elation round the throne of God above. A vivid drama follows the passage across the gulf into this landscape of the nether world; a drama peopled with familiar characters—Peter, Michael, the guardian angel—who each plays his part in the particular judgement after death, when each individual soul is assessed on his own, pending the final sentence of the day of doom.

Hell is burned into the brain of every Catholic child, who, like the poet Rutebeuf shakes like a leaf in a storm at the thought of death[3] or like Stephen Dedalus in our time is licked already by the many-tongued flames of hell.[4] Christian ideas of the Last Judgement, however primitive they seem, have the authority of Scripture. In Paul, the last day casts a terrifying, running shadow across the world. He warns it will come suddenly like a thunder-clap, in the twinkling of an eye (1 Thessalonians 4:12–17; 5:1–11; 2 Thessalonians 1:7–11; 2:1–11). In Matthew, the Lord's justice has a devastating simplicity: Christ will welcome the elect, "For I was hungry and ye gave me to eat; I was naked and ye clothed me." But the damned he will thrust into everlasting fire (Matthew 25:31–6). Christ at the *parousia* will snatch up each soul like a thief in the night, without mercy for those who, like the foolish virgins, have fallen asleep over untrimmed lamps and run out of oil, or those who, like the guest at the wedding feast, have not adorned their souls in the raiment of grace (Matthew 25:1–3; 22:1–14).

In Mark, Christ will come again "in the clouds with great power and glory" (Mark 13:26–7). But it is of course in John's Apocalypse (in Revelation) that the world-encompassing cataclysm, the full blood-curdling vengeance of the Lamb, and primeval chaos are unleashed once more on the world, in a smoking, charred, pestilential, and murderous sequence of mayhem and catastrophe.

The early and medieval Church expected this Second Coming of Christ, if not hourly, at least at the turn of each century. Millenarian fever still grips some Christian sects, but in general Catholic and Protestant have now reorganized their time scale, and each man's judgement is now thought to occur at death, while the Last Day itself recedes into infinity, where it stands as the last full stop to the last syllable of recorded time. But this crack of doom has not lost its reality: theologians do not consider the last day a mere metaphor of the end of the world. The resurrection of the body, which will take place on doomsday, is an article of the Christian faith, contained in the creed. At the blast of the last trump, the dead will rise again in their bodies and each man and woman, reunited with his or her transfigured mortal coil, will be assigned a place in heaven or in hell for all eternity. From that moment, linear time will cease.

In Catholic doctrine, the slope of time running down between the point of death and this eternity of timelessness contains a foothold and a haven, a let-out clause in the inexorable charter that metes out justice to each soul: purgatory.

Purgatory is the Catholic halfway house, neither in heaven nor in hell, where sinners are confined for a space of time to purify their souls of all stain. There is no way down to hell, only the way up; once allotted a sojourn in purgatory, the soul is destined, eventually, for paradise. The sentences vary, and theologians continue to disagree, as they have done for nearly two millennia, about the nature of the punishment: some insist that material fire tempers the sinners' souls to the pure love of God, which alone can equip them for the beatific vision in heaven; others that the mere abstract deprivation of the sight of God, and the yearning to look upon his face, is punishment in itself. All are agreed, however, that the souls in purgatory do not cry out in pain or remonstrate, as they do in hell, but, as Dante described, bask lovingly in the pain that cleanses them and will lead to heaven.

Catholic doctrine is also in a state of indecision over what exactly can be expiated in purgatory. A man who in a spirit of contrition has confessed and repented his mortal sins (which blot all grace from the soul) is delivered from the guilt of them and therefore spared hell's torments.

But he still must be punished for a time in purgatory in order to abolish his sinful debt and extirpate the sinfulness that has vitiated and warped his soul. Regarding venial sins—which only nibble at the store of grace in the soul—there has been much debate; but the prevailing theological view now is that the guilt itself can be wiped out in purgatory, and that therefore a man who dies unconfessed in a state of venial sin does not go to hell, although his soul is in a state of disorder. Only the unrepentant and unforgiven diehard sinner is inevitably damned to hell forever.

Purgatory, pictured by Dante as a mountain leading upwards to the stars, is the antechamber of paradise, and just as a court favourite who has the emperor's confidence can arrange a pardon for a suppliant, so the prayers of the saints to God, besought by the living on behalf of the dead, can commute the sentence or even pluck a soul from purgatory and transfer it to eternal bliss. So can all good works offered for the dead: pilgrimages and their related indulgences, acts of self-denial—fasting, hair shirts, scourging—and acts of charity like giving alms. The living can also of course deposit such prayers and good deeds to their own account, for the future hour of their own death. But the pleas of the Virgin, the Mother of God, are considered more certain of fulfilment than those of any other saint, and so purgatory, that time continuum of expiatory pain that stretches between death and the end of the world, is her special sphere of influence.

This cosmology of the afterlife has naturally been reassessed by progressive theologians who point out that it originated in a world devoid of our present scientific knowledge. So the realism of clouds of angels and ovens fed by devils with pitchforks has been firmly attributed to the naïve primitiveness of the medieval mind. But it is all too facile to smile patronizingly at the middle ages: the eschatological landscape of the Christian afterlife was an inescapable reality to believers of varying levels of sophistication for hundreds of years and continues today to excite terror.

In the prayer the fifteenth-century scapegrace genius François Villon wrote for his mother, he catches with an exact ear the mixture of learned theological jargon heard in the pulpit and the simple words of faith and fear that spring from the heart. And it is interesting that as heartfelt as the prayer is, the afterlife is conceptualized in visual terms only, in the vivid imagery of French reliefs and paintings of the day of reckoning. For when Villon's mother prays to the Virgin she begs understanding of her illiteracy and her ignorance—and her prayer sends a shaft of light into the mind of the ordinary Christian who until this century was un- lettered and learned his religion from the walls of his places of worship.

*Femme je suis povrette et ancienne*
*Qui riens ne scay; oncques lettre ne lus.*
*Au moustier voy dont suis paroissienne*
*Paradis paint, ou sont harpes et lus,*
*Et ung enfer ou dampnez sont boullus:*
*L'ung me fait paour, l'autre joye et liesse.*
*La joye avoir me fay, haulte deesse . . .*

(I am a little poor old woman who knows nothing, Who's never read a word. In my parish church I see a painting of paradise, where there are harps and lutes, And of hell too, where the damned boil: One fills me with fear, the other with joy and delight. Grant me that joy, high Goddess. . . .)[5]

Thus Villon opens a casement on the religious mind of the fifteenth century. Since the fierce torments depicted on Romanesque churches like Conques, images of terror have borne down on the faithful. In France, the last day was usually carved over the main doorway, so that the faithful streamed in under the majestic and implacable figure of Christ the Judge. The bloated and loathsome figure of Satan mangled sinners in his jaws and claws while his minions shovelled them into flames stoked enthusiastically by other demons; above the scene of hell's torments, Christ displayed the wounds engraved on his sacred body day by day through man's incorrigible wickedness. Like the magistrate of a tribunal in imperial Rome, he listens to the entreaties of the advocates on his left and right—the Virgin and St. John the Baptist, first fruits of the Redemption, who lift their hands in supplication.[6] Sometimes a river of fire flows molten from his throne itself, engulfing the damned along its course. Below them, Michael the archangel holds up the scales of justice in which he sometimes weighs one naked trembling soul. At Chartres, the devil sneakily presses down the scales with his thumb, but as Émile Mâle has written: "the shabbiness of this grocery store rascality leaves St. Michael unmoved."[7] In Italy the same violence appears. One of the most resplendent masterpieces of mosaic work, executed between 1100 and 1150 in the cathedral at Torcello, shows Christ straddling the world, a colossus ransacking hell to free the just, while below, he reappears again in glory, parting the elect from the damned above a river of flame and wheels of fire.

The apocalyptic violence of the motifs are Christian in conception; but the central drama of judgement appears in ancient Egypt, where it was believed that Osiris ruled in the judgement hall of the dead, and that each man at his death was brought before him and his heart weighed in the scales held by the god Anubis. Maat, goddess of truth and justice, or her ideogram, the feather, was placed in the scales' other pan, and if the dishes balanced Osiris spoke: "Let the deceased depart victorious. Let him go wherever he wishes to mingle freely with the gods and spirits of the dead." If the man's heart were light in the balance, Ahemait, the "Devourer," part lion, part hippopotamus, part crocodile, swallowed him up.[8]

The image of the scales of judgement appears—such are the cross-cultural leaps of history—on the beautiful Celtic Muirdach's Cross, which dates from the early tenth century and still stands in the cemetery of Monasterboice, County Louth, in Ireland, and in the eleventh and twelfth centuries in places as scattered as Chaldon in Surrey, in a faded, bizarre wall painting, of around 1200; in a fresco in the church of S. Maria in Grotta at Rongolise near Naples; in Byzantine Gospels; and sculpted on many twelfth-century French churches. It is one of the most direct and most assimilated importations from ancient pagan belief.

Egyptian eschatological justice allowed of no appeal. The Christian plan, on the other hand, was characteristically anthropomorphic and the human social state, both public and private, was mirrored by the other world, where a mother's indulgence softened the father's righteous rage.

As the Reformers pointed out, there is very little about the intercession of the saints and nothing at all about purgatory in Scripture. On the other hand, hell (Gehenna, Shiloh), the abyss where men wail and gnash their teeth, has Jesus Christ's own authority. The Bible therefore raised the question, could a soul be saved from hell by the intercession of the saints? The Catholics say no, that hell is "everlasting fire" and the damned can win no respite. But since the thirteenth century the Greek Orthodox Church has openly contested the Roman view of purgatory; and permitted the hope that everyone might be saved. Therefore, according to their belief, the prayers of the living and of the saints in heaven can win diminution of the expiatory pain of the damned.

The difficulty is exacerbated because of the ancient Christian tenet, still incorporated in the creed, that Christ himself "descended into hell." There he tussled with death and broke its fetters and rose again; there he trampled the devil underfoot and overcame evil's dominion; there he grasped by the hand the just who had died before the Redemption and caught them up to eternal glory by his side in heaven.

According to the Church Fathers as early as the second century, the purpose of the harrowing of hell was the liberation of the righteous dead like Abraham and David and John the Baptist. But the problem for

Catholics is that the belief implies souls can be delivered from hell—which has been heresy since Augustine laid down the firm distinction between purgatory and hell. The Council of Trent cautiously left aside the question of the release of the just, and decreed that the harrowing should simply be seen as a metaphor of Christ's victory over death and evil.

In order to accommodate the problem, however, another region of the afterlife, limbo, a shadowy world of neither pain nor joy, has been accepted since the age of Aquinas. There, according to contemporary teaching, the righteous who died before Christ (or some of them—John the Baptist, for instance, is definitely in heaven) and the innocent who have not been redeemed, like unbaptized babies, spin out eternity in a kind of numb nirvana. But only one papal document—the Bull *Auctorem Fidei* of 1794—mentions limbo, and belief is not mandatory.

The harrowing of hell recalls other gods' epic tussles with the forces of destruction: the underworld raided by Herakles and Orpheus; the victory of Osiris over Set and his triumph as judge over the living and the dead. It is a belief in marked contrast to the Assumption of the Virgin, which pointedly spares her the throes of death, and it therefore highlights the polarity between the two major Christian figures: the one fully human, the other idealized beyond humanity.

Nevertheless, the principle of analogy that had formed so much of Marian doctrine held again in the case of the harrowing of hell. For in many eastern Apocalypses, the Virgin Mary descends into the underworld.[9] She does not enter the underworld to wrestle with death, but to see the fate of the wicked. Such apocryphal revelations open with Mary praying on Golgotha before her death. Michael appears and transports her to the infernal regions, where she sees blasphemers, murderers, abortioners, adulterers, usurers, and all manner of other sinners foully and ingeniously tortured. Some drown in a lake of fire or boil in a river of pitch; others, like meat in a butcher's shop, are hooked up by their ears, tongues, and feet; yet others are relentlessly devoured by serpents and worms; monsters gnaw at the breasts of prostitutes.

The Virgin is aghast at the spectacle, and cries out to Jesus for mercy. He at first points angrily to the wounds in his hands and side and feet, saying mankind has inflicted them on him. But he later relents, grants his mother's prayers, and allows the tormented souls to rest during the season of Pentecost.

The Greek version, recounted above, exists in many manuscripts, in many forms, and from varying times, none earlier than the ninth century. The Ethiopic version, which carries the same message, has simply transferred to the Virgin the *Apocalypse of Paul,* a document that was current in the fourth century and remained very popular, in spite of St. Augustine's scathing dismissal. Dante, for instance, refers to Paul's descent into hell, and was influenced, it is thought, by the vision his *Apocalypse* describes.[10]

The differences between the various Apocalypses of the Virgin are of trifling importance—embellishments of the penalties, and varying lengths of reprieve gained by the Virgin. In some she obtains almost half the year as respite for the damned. In another, the Virgin does not rest content at a mere interval of relief, but begs her son on her breasts, her womb, and her motherhood always to grant her prayers for sinners (figure 26). Jesus agrees, and the Covenant of Mercy between them, which also appears at the end of some of the Dormition stories (see Chapter 6), is again compacted.[11] A semi-legal charter, it expands the courtroom metaphor of the Last Judgement.

No early Latin version of the *Apocalypse of the Virgin* is extant, yet the idea that Mary and the saints by their merciful prayers could win rest for the eternally damned crops up in the Irish legend of St. Brandon, a ninth-century or even earlier document, in which the saint meets Judas sitting comfortably on a rock in mid-Atlantic. Lapped by the waves, Judas informs the saint that his usual torture by fire in the depths of the pit of hell is waived at week-ends, and from Christmas to Epiphany, from Easter to Whitsun, and on two feast days of the Virgin.[12] Although such an idea could have been derived from the *Apocalypse of Paul,* there is some evidence that the tale of the Virgin's descent into hell and appeal on behalf of the damned had reached Ireland by that early date.

Yet even if the story of a formal compact of mercy for the damned was not current in the west, there was an overwhelming, widespread, and complete confidence that the Virgin's pity could pierce, like the light of Bernard's star, into the abysses of darkness, illuminate even the blackest soul, and save him from damnation by inspiring a deathbed repentance (figure 48). Thus the theological distinction laid down by St. Augustine between an invincible hell and purgatory became blurred in practice; and the strict moral rule that a good life alone merited a happy afterlife was overthrown by the specifically Catholic trust in God's forgiveness and the expiation of guilt in purgatory.

Mary's descent into hell may not have been known as such in the west, but the ideas contained in the tale were common change: she was a chthonic divinity who had met death and defeated it; the dark trough of sin into which all humanity had fallen had not claimed her; the underworld of sterility and dryness had not asserted its dominion over her.

Like Isis, who snatched Osiris' dismembered body from the powers of evil by reanimating his corpse and conceiving his child, Mary through the virgin birth had defeated the death of sin; like Ishtar, who sent Tammuz down into the dustbowl of shadows and ghosts as her substitute, Mary participated in the immolation of her son, the conqueror of death. Consequently, the Virgin becomes an eschatological figure of a promised eternal life in which the powers of darkness with all their correlatives of death and torment are brought to nothing.

In theology, the intercession of the Virgin with her almighty son brings about this salvation. She never works on her own, but only through Christ; in practice, in the myriad stories that star the Virgin as all-powerful sorceress with dominion over angels and devils alike, this qualification is forgotten.

In the folktales and miracle stories that chronicle the Virgin's unfailing assistance to her devotees, she undeniably usurps the unique privileges of Christ. One of the best-loved tales of the middle ages concerns the treasurer and archdeacon of the bishop of Ardana in Cilicia, Asia Minor, a man called Theophilus, "lover of God," who, it seems, really existed and died around 538. When Theophilus' bishop dies, he is elected in his place by popular acclaim, but is too humble to accept, and finds himself dismissed altogether from his post by the bishop's eventual successor. So the worm of envy fastens upon him, and he begins to thirst for worldly power. Driven by the devil, he seeks out a Jewish necromancer and signs away his soul in blood in exchange for riches and success. They duly come to him, but remorse gnaws at him and prevents him finding any joy. He rails against the devil's bargain he has made, but the devil is adamant and gloats over his prize. Praying for help to the Virgin, Theophilus falls asleep and dreams. The Virgin appears to him and gives him back the deed he signed in blood. She has wrested it from the devil himself, she tells him, and he is pardoned. When Theophilus awakes, he finds his dream come true: the deed lies there beside him. He confesses his wrongdoing publicly and dies in peace a few days later.[13]

Paul the Deacon (d. *c.* 799), a monk of Monte Cassino, translated the *Miracle of Theophilus* into Latin and from then on it circulated throughout Christendom, merging with the legends of Simon Magus, who flew in the Forum before St. Peter's eyes and, of course, with the figure of Doctor Faustus, hero of Marlowe and Goethe's masterworks. Hroswitha of Gandersheim first wrote the story in verse in the tenth century; in the eleventh it was included in the office of Our Lady of France. The vivid impact of the liturgy on the visual imagination, which Émile Mâle has demonstrated, inspired the theatrical portal of the abbey church of Souillac, which told the story in the twelfth century. It was the first time an action of the Virgin, independent of her role in the Incarnation, had been depicted in monumental art (figures 49, 50).[14] In the thirteenth century Theophilus' tale appeared in stained glass, in illuminated manuscripts and songs (as in Alfonso el Sabio's *Cantigas*), in Books of Hours, and paintings and sculptures. It formed part of the multi-coloured *tour de force* of medieval carving in the Lady Chapel of Ely Cathedral. The northern portal of Notre Dame of Paris tells the story in vigorous strip cartoon style: Theophilus kneels to the cloven-hoofed, pointy-eared Satan on the left, receives money from a devilish hobgoblin, implores a delicate Gothic statue of the Virgin for help, and then, on the right, watches as Mary, with a graceful but practised lunge, holds the devil down at the point of her cross-hilted sword and seizes the contract from his claw (figure 51). At this point in the play by the marvellous *jongleur* Rutebeuf, the Virgin cries out: *"Et je te foulerai la pance"* (And I'll trample on your gut).[15]

The Virgin had a dozen other ruses to cheat the devil of his rightful prey. When a knight promised Satan to deliver up to him his own wife in return for wealth and fame, the Virgin assumed not only her place but also her features and speech and dress, and travelled unrecognized with the knight to his rendezvous with the devil in the forest. Of course, at her approach the devil screams in torment and takes to his heels (figure 20).[16]

A most important group of miracle stories feature the Virgin circumventing God's justice altogether, by resurrecting her votaries so that they can make a good confession and then die again in grace. Her powers both over evil and over death are thus intertwined. A pilgrim on his way to Compostela makes love to a woman—a nice historical touch—and then encounters the devil, who has disguised himself as St. James. He tells the pilgrim that because of his foul sin, he would do better to castrate himself and then cut his throat. The victim of this deviltry weeps, but obeys and is triumphantly snatched off to hell. But as the devil bears him off, Saints Peter and James bar the way, seize the pilgrim, and take him before Mary. She restores him to life, and he rises from the dead a eunuch, with a red thread around his neck. He lives just long enough to do penance for his sin and then dies again, at peace with his maker.[17]

Resuscitating sinners so that they can confess is one of the Virgin's prerogatives; another is sustaining the damned in life until they can repent. A thief hanging on the gallows finds he swings three days and nights and still does not expire. The executioner takes a swipe at him but cannot hurt him, and the crowd marvel. When they take him down, he tells them the Virgin held him up so his neck should not break, and then caught the executioner's sword. In the exquisitely illuminated manuscript of Gautier de Coincy's version of this miracle, the Virgin appears with a determined look on her face, holding up a most rueful thief on the tip of her finger.[18]

The devil's wrath at such brazen cheating on the Virgin's part is mighty: the miracle plays and stories ring with his righteous indignation and remonstrations before Christ's judgement seat that she should be prevented from subverting the course of justice. "It is she who does us most harm," says the devil in one tale. "Those whom the Son in his justice casts away, the mother in her superfluity of mercy brings back again to indulgence."[19] In some stories, she holds up St. Michael's scales (figure 22).

The more raffish the Virgin's suppliant, the better she likes him. The miracles' heroes are liars, thieves, adulterers, and fornicators, footloose students, pregnant nuns, unruly and lazy clerics, and eloping monks. On the single condition that they sing her praises, usually by reciting the *Ave Maria,* and show due respect for the miracle of the Incarnation wrought in her, they can do no wrong. Her justice is loyalty to her own: whatever his conduct, anyone pledged to her protection is her liegeman and she his responsible suzerain. Through her the whole gay crew of wanton, loving, weak humanity finds its way to paradise. No wonder the devils are puzzled as, in Gautier de Coincy:

> *Au ciel va toute la ringaille*
> *Le grain avons et Diex la paille.*

> Heaven's the place for all the riff–raff:
> We've got the wheat, and God the chaff.

It was not only in the vernacular diet of miracle and folktale that the Virgin's all-powerful intercession for the sinner was stressed and celebrated. The severe Peter Damian extolled Mary's powers to deliver souls from purgatory, as he had seen her do in visions.[21] In a sequence for an Annunciation mass, attributed to Peter Abelard, there appears the heretical idea that Mary shares the Father's dominion in paradise:

> *matremque faciat*
> *secum partecipem*
> *patris imperii.*

and he [Christ] made his mother
share with him in the power of the
father.[22]

Adam of St. Victor (d. *c.* 1180) hailed her as the *superatrix infernorum.*[23] Visions received by Saints Dominic, Bridget of Sweden, Gertrude (d. 1302), and Simon Stock (d. 1265) confirmed the Virgin's purposeful support.[24] The *Meditations on the Life of Christ* described the efficiency of the Hail Mary; St. Bernardino of Siena (d. 1444), with barnstorming eloquence, painted the everflowing mercy of the Virgin mother.[25] Brother Leo, a Franciscan monk, saw the last judgement in a dream that neatly reveals the recurrent idea of the Lord's justice and the Lady's pity. Leo saw two ladders leading up to heaven, one as red as blood, the other as white as lilies. At the top of the red ladder there appeared Christ, his face full of wrath. St. Francis beckoned to his brothers not to fear and to climb the ladder. They try, but fall. Francis prays, but Christ displays his wounds and thunders,"Your brothers have done this to me." So St. Francis runs down and leads his brethren to the white ladder, which they scale effortlessly and without mishap, to find Mary at the top, all smiles, to welcome them.[26]

In the cruel upheavals and violence of life in the fourteenth century and after, when suffering in this life and damnation afterwards seemed the deserved lot of every man, and a barren pessimism informed the spirit of a contorted age, the *Ars Moriendi,* a book about a dying man assaulted by demons, had a tremendous following. Doubt and despair assail the protagonist, but after manifold diabolical attacks, a vision of the Virgin in the midst of the Trinity—also wholly heretical—saves him for the faith and paradise.[27]

As the only haven from the sure terror of eternal damnation, the interceding Virgin acquired a new and imposing aspect in the iconography of the west. The traditional Byzantine group—the Deesis—of John the Baptist and the Virgin as litigants before the Judge's throne, was stately and serene and it therefore failed to capture the dynamic completeness of the Virgin's protection in the minds of medieval men and women. At the end of the thirteenth century, a new image was developed in Umbria that corresponded far more skilfully to the mixture of intense supplication and fervent trust expressed in the prayers and stories of that critical epoch.[28] The *Madonna della Misericordia,* Our Lady of Mercy, spreads her star-spangled cloak over men and women huddled at her feet on their knees. Exactly as Christ spoke of a mother hen gathering her brood under her wing, so Mary shelters her flock. One of the earliest examples of the image, attributed to Rainaldictus Ranucci of Spoleto, and now in the Pitcairn Collection in Philadelphia, combines it with a Last Judgement scene—the sinners crowd for shelter from Christ's wrath under Mary's outspread mantle.

After the Black Death of the late 1340s, the Mother of Mercy became the most popular votive figure on her own, a detached image of an independent tutelary goddess adopted in particular by monastic orders and lay confraternities to bless them with her special protection. The ecclesiastics and laymen who worked during the horrors of the pestilence, gathering up and laying out and burying the purulent dead, often addressed their prayers to the Virgin in this aspect, and sometimes, in the paintings of the period, two or three small figures under her mantle wear white or black cloaks with steeple-like cowls, pierced only by a slit for the eyes. This costume—horrifying now, for it recalls to mind the Ku Klux Klan—was both the penitential dress of the Flagellants and of the few compassionate and courageous people who worked with the victims of the plague.

One work of art in particular made the Mother of Mercy an unforgettable figure: Piero della Francesca's first known painting, the polyptych of the *Madonna della Misericordia,* which he executed in 1445–8 for the eponymous confraternity in the small town of Borgo Sansepolcro (colour plate VIII, figure 11). In the centre panel, the Virgin towers over the men and women who on her right and left respectively gaze up at her in prayer. One wears the black hood this confraternity wore when looking after the dead. The Virgin's face is strong and brooding, and her mouth is set in a distant, almost deprecatory expression of gravity, because for Piero, unlike the authors of some of the miracles, there was nothing frivolous in the clemency she accorded. The greenish otherworldly light often cast by Piero across the countenances of his subjects suffuses her. She is monumental, so tall and imposing that the halo above her head is seen in perspective from below. All this emphasizes the supernatural forces that her serene and static figure can unleash at will. Almost terrifying in her immensity and her stillness, Piero's *Madonna della Misericordia* is truly, in the words of a fifteenth-century English *Stabat Mater,* the "Emparyse of helle . . . [whose] name is kouthe/To be the joye of all mankynde."[29]

The image, of course, omitted Christ altogether and inspired veneration for the Virgin for her own sake, suggesting that her mercy, directly given, could save sinners. This conformed to medieval faith, though it always remained technically heterodox. The image of the Mother of Mercy travelled throughout Europe during the fourteenth and fifteenth centuries and enjoyed an unprecedentedly wide circulation. But at the Council of Trent, the heterodoxy of the Madonna of Mercy was formally proclaimed and the iconography banned because it implied the Virgin's autonomous sovereignty.

However, the symbol of the Virgin's mantle survived its proscription in art. Like the rosary, the scapular (or cloak) of the Virgin was believed to have originated in the vision of a saint, and to have special prophylactic powers against death and evil. In 1251 the Virgin appeared to St. Simon, an English mystic, who had acquired the sobriquet Stock from the tree in which he liked to immure himself. She gave him the mantle: "Receive, my beloved son," she said, "this habit of thy order, this shall be to thee and to all Carmelites a privilege that whosoever dies clothed in this shall never suffer eternal fire."[30]

The garment the Virgin gave Simon is called the Brown Scapular, a narrow tunic that passes over the head and falls to the ground front and back, protecting the monks' habits while they laboured. Long before the supposed date of the vision some orders who did manual work—like the Cistercians—had adopted this type of apron and interpreted it, with medieval love of symbolism, as Christ's cross. By the thirteenth century, lay groups of men attaching themselves to the monastic life by making a limited promise to work and pray often wore the scapular as a token of their Third Order status.

The story of Simon's vision begins to appear only around the year 1500, in order to justify the growing belief in the powers of the garment. The popularity of the scapular as an amulet coincides with the crescendo of appeals to Mary's protection after death, and with the despair and sense of damnation universal in Europe at that time. Preachers like John Wycliffe (d. 1384) stormed at the friars for claiming that anyone wearing the scapular when he died would not go to hell, so the Church tried to correct the heterodoxy of the Virgin's "scapular promise" by inserting the word "piously": "whosoever dies (piously) clothed in this shall never suffer eternal fire."

In the sixteenth century, in order to enable ordinary men and women to wear it without encumbrance, the scapular shrunk to two tiny pieces of brown monastic homespun, embroidered with images of Christ and the Virgin, attached by threads and worn between the shoulder blades at the back and over the heart in the front, as if it were indeed an armoured breastplate. It has not declined in popularity since. During the First World War, the Vatican permitted the substitution of a metal image for the brown cloth, which is an intrinsic feature of the scapular, because the cloth was prone to vermin. At the Carmelite shrine at Aylesford in Kent, busloads of schoolchildren are still enrolled in the confraternity of the scapular, and promised our Lady's protection throughout their lives and especially at the point of death.

The survival of the scapular underlines the persistent value attached to the Virgin's mediation, and it would be a mistake wholly to attribute the Christian underworld, with all its Gothic horrors, to unsophisticated minds. For ideas have changed rather than progressed, and Dante's violent imagery of hell is much more valuable than the enlightened equivocations of up-to-date theologians. Damnation at the left hand of an all-conquering God of justice was a terrifying reality for Michelangelo too, and he can hardly be criticized for medieval drollery. Yet his *Last Judgement* in the Sistine Chapel, the outpouring of his final years' anguish, draws on the imagery of doom established since the so-called Dark Ages: the devils are as hairy, as bestial, as forked and cloven as any monstrous product of uncouth Romanesque fantasy. Christ, raising his right hand to strike down the damned, commands the full terror of absolute power so that even the elect seem to cower, while the fallen stream downwards convulsed in agony as the devils take them captive down to hell. Even the Virgin in this despairing painting cannot interpose, but curls herself under the figure of her son.

The Last Judgement has not been painted with anything approaching Michelangelo's vehemence since; and it was not a popular theme among Christian propagandists in the Enlightenment of the seventeenth century. But the intercession of the saints was, as we have seen, a hinge of the Counter-Reformation's attack on the dissidents, and invocations to the Virgin for aid, particularly through the rosary, increased in importance. The foremost thinkers stress Mary's powerful role in the salvation of each individual. Language and incident change: no more whore-mongers or thieves receive her bounty, for the new moral climate excludes them. But she is still, in the devotional works of men like Alphonsus of Liguori (d. 1787), "the most blessed Virgin [who] rules over the infernal regions . . . the sovereign mistress of the devils" (figure 48).[31]

In the *City of God* by Maria de Agreda de Jesus, the visionary imagines Christ on the Cross entrusting the universe to his mother:

The demons shall fear her and be subject to her. All the irrational creatures, the stars, the planets, the elements, with all the living beings, the birds, the fishes and the animals . . . shall likewise be subject to her. . . . Whatever she ordains and disposes in my Church for my children the sons of men shall be confirmed by the three divine persons, and whatever she asks for mortals now, afterwards and forever, we shall concede . . .[32]

The *City of God,* Maria's copious revelation, was admittedly placed on the Index many times, but it continued to be widely read and loved, and in its banal flourishes, it expresses aptly the faith of God-fearing times.

If travellers from another planet were to enter churches as far flung as the National Shrine of the Immaculate Conception in Washington, D.C., or the Catholic cathedral in Saigon, or the rococo phantasmagoria of New World churches, and see the Virgin's image on the altar, it would be exceedingly difficult for them to understand that she was only an intercessor and not a divinity in her own right. The spirit that informs Maria de Agreda's Crucifixion fantasy still walks abroad, and it thrives on the stigma of sinfulness inculcated by the Church, the fear of death, and the terror of hell. The Virgin Mary, either through her beads, or her scapular, or other methods, can be reached to quell this distress. For she can be good and merciful without being right, which is one reason why the stern moralists of the Reformation opposed her cult.

In the Trastevere quarter of Rome, not far from the basilica of S. Maria, there is a tranquil, grass-green walled garden where oranges and lemons and peaches bloom, cultivated by sisters for the old people whom they look after. At the door, a picture of the Virgin is subtitled "the guardian of the house," and in the eleventh-century chapel, S. Maria in Cappella, the men and women who live in the home pray between antique columns before an altar on which the Virgin stands. It is a modern statue carved in dead white marble, and it towers majestically over the tiny dark church. Mary is alone, crowned with gold and twelve silver stars in halo round her head. At her feet the serpent is coiled, and under him a globe of the world on which is engraved a relief map of Italy. The Madonna extends her hands towards the congregation, holding out to them another sphere, surmounted by a cross.

There she stands on the high altar, a queen in both worlds, the terrestrial sphere at her feet and the symbol of spiritual sovereignty, the orb of Christ the emperor and the judge in her hands. Mariology that restricts and limits her power, venerating her only as the mother of Jesus, has no meaning in this corner of the painful earth where men and women have come to die.

For although the Virgin is a healer, a midwife, a peacemaker, the protectress of virgins, and the patroness of monks and nuns in this world; although her polymorphous myth has myriad uses and functions for the living, it is the jurisdiction over death accorded her in popular belief that gives her such widespread supremacy. When Catholics contemplate the darkness of death stretching before them, they cling to a light on the horizon that seems to them no will-o'-the-wisp but as constant as the moon, which is the Virgin's attribute. At the moment the finite plane of a mortal life reaches its term it intersects with the timeless, undifferentiated, immortal beauty and bliss epitomized by the Virgin and makes death meaningless. At the moment the believer fears that step across the gulf, as every man who knows himself a sinner must fear, the promise of the Virgin's ungrudging, ever-flowing clemency sustains him. That is why the best-loved prayer of the Catholic world—the Hail Mary—ends with the plea that the Virgin should "pray for us sinners, now and at the hour of our death."

# EPILOGUE

In the sacred *Epic of Gilgamesh,* when Ishtar the goddess, queen of heaven, solicits the love of Gilgamesh, king of Uruk and greatest of mortal heroes, he turns on her in violence and reproaches her from the depths of his heart, not because she tempts his virtue, but because her love is a lie, a distortion, an illusion of splendour and beauty and security. Its aftertaste can only be wormwood and ashes, for it raises mortal aspirations far beyond any possible fulfilment, and so brings on despair.

As he bitterly rejects the goddess, Gilgamesh reminds her of her past lovers, including the hero Ishullanu, who also tried to withstand her blandishments. Ishullanu had told Ishtar: " 'What are you asking from me? My mother has baked and I have eaten; why should I come to such as you for food that is tainted and rotten? For when was a screen of rushes sufficient protection from frosts?' At this Ishtar struck Ishullanu and he was changed into a blind mole deep in the earth, one whose desire is always beyond his reach."

Then Gilgamesh asks the goddess if Ishullanu's fate does not await him also: "And if you and I should be lovers, should not I be served in the same fashion as all these others whom you loved once?"[1]

It is a wise and profound passage, and indicts in a remarkable manner the Platonic yearning towards the ideal, which is the core of the cult of the Virgin Mary. For Gilgamesh reproaches the goddess Ishtar, first because she provides only "a screen of rushes" and that is insufficient "protection against frosts," and secondly because her love condemns a mortal to the pit, to gaze up with a mole's unseeing eyes at the dazzling skies.

Gilgamesh rejects Ishtar, but not her reality. He "believes" in her, but he quarrels with her dominion over the mortal world. To him, and to Ishullanu, and to the authors and the audience of the epic, her love is unacceptable and cruel because it asserts heaven's superiority and man's incapacity. Because Gilgamesh speaks from the standpoint of belief, he is rebelling against the given order that distinguishes human from divine, mortal from immortal, and rejecting the goddess who will always make him yearn for heaven. But to the modern reader, who no longer believes in the Babylonian pantheon, the reproach of Gilgamesh expresses tragically the irony of the religious man who quarrels with the deities whom his culture has invented for not providing what he desires; and raises the tragic question, why do men, when they have purposely devised a mythological system that classifies them as separate and lower than the gods, seek to become like the gods?

Gilgamesh's words of bitterness do throw light on the worship of the Virgin Mary. For although to many of her devotees, like the old people in the home at S. Maria in Cappella, her love can seem a fortress against frosts, it is only a reed for the sinner who feels the frost-swollen wind of Christ's justice blowing down from heaven, while to the non-believer it seems a wretched placebo.

Gilgamesh also rails against Ishtar for transforming her lover into "a blind mole . . . whose desire is always beyond his reach." This is central to the myth of the Virgin Mary, who is theologically and doctrinally defined as wholly unique and yet set up as the model of Christian virtue. Of course the belief that man should constantly aspire to higher things has been fundamental to western moral philosophy since Plato; and to suggest otherwise could lead to accusations of antinomianism or quietism, neither of which do I hold. But it is worth considering the kind of ideal the Virgin represents.

First, she is presented as a fixed immutable absolute, and the historical process that changes the character of the Virgin is seen merely as a gradual discovery of a great and eternal mystery, progressively revealed. Mary did not become Mother of God at Ephesus in 431; nor was she assumed into heaven in 1950, when it first became an article of faith: these things always were. Indeed, the disregard of historical accretions with regard to the Virgin is so complete that it gives rise to tautology: the doctrine of the Immaculate Conception requires belief that Mary existed from all eternity, a fully-fledged concept in the eternal mind of the creator. When historical circumstances are admitted in evidence at all, they are treated as barnacles disguising the pure shape of the mystery. Pope Paul VI, in his 1974 apostolic exhortation on the cult of Mary, prises off the encrustations, saying that many difficulties modern women experience in modelling themselves on the Virgin spring from "popular writings":

They are not connected with the gospel image of Mary nor with the doctrinal data which have been made explicit through a slow and conscientious process of drawing from revelation. It should be considered quite normal for succeeding generations of Christians in differing socio-cultural contexts to have expressed their sentiments about the Mother of Jesus in a way and a manner that reflected their own age.[2]

This "slow and conscientious process" is therefore seen to operate independently of "socio-cultural contexts," and the accumulation of new history, altering the shape of the myth—of which the pope's own document is another instance—is viewed as a stripping down to an old and absolute truth.

Roland Barthes, the French semiologist or reader of signs, writes that "in myth, things lose the memory that they once were made."[3] In the case of the Virgin Mary, faith has simply wiped out the silt of history in her myth. It comes as a surprise to believers and non-believers alike that she is rarely mentioned in the Gospels, and is not even always called Mary.

There is another sector of thought that has nothing to do with the Catholic Church but also accepts the idea that the Virgin exists from all eternity. Under the influence of contemporary psychology—particularly Jungian—many people accept unquestioningly that the Virgin is an inevitable expression of the archetype of the Great Mother. Thus psychologists collude with and continue the Church's operations on the mind. While the Vatican proclaims that the Virgin Mother of God always existed, the Jungian determines that all men want a virgin mother, at least in symbolic form, and that the symbol is so powerful it has a dynamic and irrepressible life of its own. Roland Barthes again pinpoints this process with crystalline clarity: "We reach here the very principle of myth: it transforms history into nature."[4]

This is the crux of the matter: for the moral concepts the Virgin expresses are presented as quite natural. By emptying history from the figure of Mary, all the various silks interwoven for centuries on the sensitive loom of the mind are deprived of context, of motive, of circumstance, and therefore seem to be the spontaneous expression of enduring archetypal ideas. Once the combination of historical and social circumstances is ignored, the reasons for such a symbol are also obscured, and the distortions and assumptions the symbol perpetuates in our lives become invisible.

Nothing it seems, even to non-Catholics, could be more natural than this icon of feminine perfection, built on the equivalence between goodness, motherhood, purity, gentleness, and submission. To take a random, visual example: in the beautiful school of Giotto panel now at Oxford (figure 52), the Virgin is serene, sagacious, exquisitely fulfilled as the Christ child on her arm reaches up and touches her cheek with his tiny hand and clutches at the neckline of her dress. She tenderly hovers with delicate tapering fingers to catch him if he struggles too vigorously. Her eyes, as in so much Marian iconography, gaze out beyond the picture frame to dwell on an inner landscape of the soul, where tragedy and triumph are bound together, and her countenance is therefore wistful. Wistfulness seems also a natural quality of the feminine, a part of modesty and grace, a suitable expression of wonderment at her own beauty and mystery, a kind of hesitancy and humility that is hardly ever present in images of masculine beauty and goodness.

In such an icon as this school of Giotto painting—the beauty of which no one would deny, just as I am not saying that motherhood, purity, gentleness are evil or ugly in themselves—the interlocking of myth and ideology is camouflaged. Without any duplicity or malevolence on the painter's part, myriad assumptions are limpidly and luminously made. Assumptions about role satisfaction, sexual differences, beauty, and goodness are all wondrously compressed in this one icon, just as they are in every artefact produced by the cult of the Virgin Mary.

The concept expressed by the Catholic symbol of the Virgin extends further than the simple nobility of motherhood. She is the symbol of the ideal woman and has been held up as an example to women since Tertullian in the third century and John Chrysostom in the fourth lambasted the sex. The imitation of the perfected female type of humanity is still enthusiastically encouraged in Catholic families and schools from Ireland to Brazil. At one level, the purpose of woman and her fulfilment is seen to be motherhood, but at another the teleological argument is cut across by a major reservation, expressed succinctly in Canon Ten of the Council of Trent's twenty-fourth session: "virginity and celibacy are better and more blessed than the bond of matrimony" (*Melius ac beatus quam jungi in matrimonio*).[5]

Mary is mother and virgin; since the sixth century, when the marvellous *Akathistos* hymn hailed her as the one creature in whom all opposites are reconciled, her virgin motherhood has been the chief sign of her supernatural nature. Metaphysical mysteries must defy reason, for if the human mind could compass them, they would lose their sacred character. So Christ the God-Man and Mary the Virgin-Mother blot out antinomy, absolve contradiction, and manifest that the impossible is possible with God. But unlike the myth of the incarnate God, the myth of the Virgin Mother is translated into moral exhortation. Mary establishes the child as the destiny of woman, but escapes the sexual intercourse necessary for all other women to fulfil this destiny. Thus the very purpose of women established by the myth with one hand is slighted with the other. The Catholic religion therefore binds its female followers in particular on a double wheel, to be pulled one way and then the other, like Catherine of Alexandria during her martyrdom. Mary Douglas, the anthropologist, discussing the ways different religions keep their hold on the faithful, describes this method of changing tack and setting ambiguous and divided goals. At one moment, a religion of this type declares that by obeying one moral code and performing certain rites correctly, the believer will prosper; at another, it spirits away this book of rules and substitutes another, contradictory one.[6] Catholicism operates in a similar fashion, for on the one hand it affirms the beauty and goodness of the natural world and insists that man's purpose is to cultivate fully his God-given gifts on earth; but on the other it endorses the most pessimistic world-denying self-sacrifice as the state of the elect, and accords virginity, the symbol of renunciation, the highest accolade. When Pope Paul VI held up Mary as the New Woman, the model for all Christians, he expressed this impossibly divided aim without irony, in the immemorial manner of his predecessors. The Virgin is to be emulated as "the disciple who builds up the earthly and temporal city while a diligent pilgrim towards the heavenly and eternal city."[7]

The twin ideal the Virgin represents is of course unobtainable. Therefore, the effect the myth has on the mind of a Catholic girl cannot but be disturbing, and if it does not provoke revolt (as it often does) it deepens the need for religion's consolation, for the screen of rushes against the perpetual frost of being carnal and female. By setting up an impossible ideal the cult of the Virgin does drive the adherent into a position of acknowledged and hopeless yearning and inferiority, as Ishullanu so vindictively told Ishtar. The process is self-perpetuating: if the Virgin were not venerated, the dangers of sex, the fear of corruption, the sense of sin would not be woven together in this particular misogynist web, but would be articulated in a different way.

But the existence of the web prolongs the existence of the Virgin herself, who is represented as the only haven and the only solace. A. R. Radcliffe-Brown, the anthropologist, has pointed out the circular character of religious fear:

. . . and if it were not for the existence of the rite and the beliefs associated with it, the individual would feel no anxiety, . . . the psychological effect of the rite is to create in him a sense of insecurity or danger. It seems very unlikely that an Andaman islander would think it dangerous to eat dugong or pork or turtle meat if it were not for the existence of a specific body of ritual, the ostensible purpose of which is to protect him from these dangers. . . . Thus, while one anthropological theory is that magic and religion give men confidence, comfort and a sense of security, it could equally well be argued that they give men fears and anxieties from which they would otherwise be free.[8]

In Catholic countries a woman's dugong, pork and turtle meat, are sex and childbirth. Mary's virginity underlines the pollution of intercourse; her freedom from the pangs of birth focusses exaggerated attention on them. In addition, the Church's teaching on contraception and abortion, which stems directly from the same misogynist ideas about women's role contained in the myth of the Virgin, exacerbates the terrors of sex and childbirth by maintaining pregnancy as a constant and very real danger. In turn, this reinforces the believer's need for solace, and swells the Church's authority and power.

The Virgin Mary is not the innate archetype of female nature, the dream incarnate; she is the instrument of a dynamic argument from the Catholic Church about the structure of society, presented as a God-given code. The argument changes, according to contingencies. For instance, in 1974 Pope Paul VI, sensitive to a new mood among Catholic women, attempted to represent her as the steely champion of the oppressed and a woman of action and resolve. She should not be thought of, he wrote, "as a mother exclusively concerned with her own divine Son, but rather as a woman whose action helped to strengthen the apostolic community's faith in Christ."[9] But the Vatican cannot simply strip away a veil and reveal Mary's metamorphosis into the New Woman unless it dredges centuries of prejudice. Its incapacity to do this is complete: the teleological view that the natural law ordains that women must bear and suffer underpins the Church's continuing indefensible ban on contraception; a dualistic distaste for the material world reinforces the ideal of virginity; and an undiminished certainty that women are subordinate to men continues to make the priesthood of women unacceptable.

Although Mary cannot be a model for the New Woman, a goddess is better than no goddess at all, for the sombre-suited masculine world of the Protestant religion is altogether too much like a gentlemen's club to which the ladies are only admitted on special days. But it should not be necessary to have a goddess contrasted with a god, a divinity who stands for qualities considered the quintessence of femininity and who thus polarizes symbolic and religious thought into two irreconcilably opposed camps.

The Virgin Mary has inspired some of the loftiest architecture, some of the most moving poetry, some of the most beautiful paintings in the world; she has filled men and women with deep joy and fervent trust; she has been an image of the ideal that has entranced and stirred men and women to the noblest emotions of love and pity and awe. But the reality her myth describes is over; the moral code she affirms has been exhausted. The Catholic Church might succeed, with its natural resilience and craft, in accommodating her to the new circumstances of sexual equality, but it is more likely that, like Ishtar, the Virgin will recede into legend. For as Barthes has written:

Some objects become the prey of mythical speech for a while, then they disappear, others take their place and attain the status of myth. Are there objects which are inevitably a source of suggestiveness, as Baudelaire suggested about Woman? Certainly not: one can conceive of very ancient myths, but there are no eternal ones; for it is human history which converts reality into speech, and it alone rules the life and death of mythical language.[10]

As an acknowledged creation of Christian mythology, the Virgin's legend will endure in its splendour and lyricism, but it will be emptied of moral significance, and thus lose its present real powers to heal and to harm.

APPENDICES
CHRONOLOGY
NOTES
SELECT BIBLIOGRAPHY
INDEX

# Appendix A: St. Luke's Magnificat[1]

MARY (LUKE 1:46–55)

My soul doth magnify the Lord,
And my spirit hath rejoiced in God
my Saviour.

For he hath regarded the low
estate of his handmaiden:

for, behold, from henceforth
all generations shall call me blessed.

For he that is mighty hath done to
me great things; and holy is his name.

And his mercy is on them that
fear him from generation to generation.

He hath shewed strength with his
arm; he hath scattered the proud
in the imagination of their hearts.

He hath put down the mighty from their
seats, and exalted them of low degree.

He hath filled the hungry with
good things; and the rich he
hath sent empty away.

He hath holpen his servent Israel,
in remembrance of his mercy;

As he spake to our fathers, to
Abraham and to his seed for ever.

HANNAH

My heart rejoiceth in the Lord . . .
my mouth is enlarged over mine
enemies; because I rejoice in
thy salvation. (I Samuel 2:1)

O Lord of hosts, if thou wilt
indeed look on the affliction
of thine handmaid, and remember
me, and not forget thine handmaid . . .
(1 Samuel 1:11)

Let thine handmaid find grace in
thy sight. (1 Samuel 1:18)

and the Lord remembered her. (1 Samuel
1:19)

The bows of the mighty men are
broken, and they that stumbled
are girded with strength. (1 Samuel 2:4)

The Lord killeth, and maketh alive:
he bringeth down to the grave and
bringeth up. The Lord maketh
poor, and maketh rich: he bringeth low,
and lifteth up. He raiseth up
the poor out of the dust, and lifteth up
the beggar from the dunghill,
to set them among princes,
and to make them inherit the
throne of glory . . . (1 Samuel 2:6–8)

The adversaries of the Lord shall be
broken to pieces . . . (1 Samuel 2:10)

They that were full have hired out
themselves for bread; and they that
were hungry ceased . . . (1 Samuel 2:5)

He . . . sheweth mercy to his
anointed, unto David, and to
his seed for evermore. (2 Samuel 22:51)

I will rejoice in the Lord, I will joy in the God of my salvation. (Habakkuk 3:18)

And all nations shall call you blessed. (Malachi 3:12)

the daughters will call me blessed. (Genesis 30:13)

He hath visited and redeemed his people. (1 Kings 1:68)

He sent redemption unto his people: he hath commanded his covenant for ever: holy and reverend is his name. (Psalms 111:9)

Sing ye to the Lord, for he hath triumphed gloriously; the horse and his rider hath he thrown into the sea. (Exodus 15:21)

To give light to them that sit in darkness and in the shadow of death . . . (Luke 1:79)

For he satisfieth the longing soul, and filleth the hungry soul with goodness. Such as sit in darkness and in the shadow of death . . . (Psalms 107:9–10)

To perform the mercy promised to our fathers, and to remember his holy covenant; the oath which he sware to our father Abraham. (Luke 1:72–3)

Thou wilt perform the truth to Jacob, and the mercy to Abraham, which thou hast sworn unto our fathers from the days of old. (Micah 7:20)

# Appendix B: A Muddle of Marys

In Matthew, Mary Magdalene, "Mary the mother of James and Joses," and another unnamed woman, "the mother of Zebedee's children," keep watch at the Crucifixion (Matthew 27:56). The sons of Zebedee are James and John (Matthew 4:21; 10:2; Mark 3:17), but their mother is not named. At the burial, Mary Magdalene and "the other Mary" are also present (Matthew 27:61). And in the following chapter of Matthew, Mary Magdalene and "the other Mary" go to the sepulchre, where they meet one angel, radiant with light, sitting on the stone of the tomb which he has rolled back (Matthew 28:1). "He is risen, as he said," the angel, with a face like lightning, tells the two women, and orders them to inform the disciples (Matthew 28:5–7) (figure 39). On the way, they meet Jesus, and fall to their knees before him. Later, Jesus appears to the eleven apostles on a mountain in Galilee (Matthew 28:16).

In Mark, Mary Magdalene, Mary "the mother of James the Less and Joses," are also present at the Crucifixion, with another person called Salome (Mark 15:40) and "many other women which came up with him unto Jerusalem" (Mark 15:41). Bringing sweet spices to embalm the body, Mary Magdalene, "Mary the mother of James," and Salome come to the grave of Jesus on the Sunday and find a young man dressed in white inside the empty tomb (Mark 16:1), who tells them to give the good news to the disciples that Christ is risen. Unlike Matthew's account, the women tremble: "Neither said they anything to any man; for they were afraid" (Mark 16:8). Later, Jesus appears to Mary Magdalene, who tells his followers, and then to two of his companions in the country, and then to the eleven whom he reproaches with scepticism, and orders to preach his gospel "into all the world" (Mark 16:9–15).

In both Matthew and Mark, therefore, the Virgin Mary is not named as a witness at the sepulchre, unless one argues that she is the mother of James and Joses, or "the other Mary" and that the evangelists would refer to her in this way.

In Luke, "a great company of people, and of women," the daughters of Jerusalem, follow Jesus to Calvary (Luke 23:27), and at the Crucifixion, "all his acquaintance, and the women that followed him from Galilee, stood afar off" (Luke 23:49). Later, they watch the laying out and burial at the tomb (Luke 23:55) and then return home to prepare spices and ointments. Luke says, "they"—as yet unnamed—rested the next day, as it was the Sabbath, but went to the sepulchre early on Sunday with "certain others" (Luke 24:1). They find two men in "shining garments" (not one, as in Matthew and Mark), who tell them "he is risen" (Luke 24:4–6). They leave the sepulchre and tell the eleven apostles what they saw and heard. Only at this stage does Luke name them: Mary Magdalene, Joanna, "Mary the mother of James" and "other women" (Luke 24:10). Jesus appears to the disciples at Emmaus, to Simon Peter, and then to all the eleven together in Jerusalem (Luke 24:36). Again, the Virgin Mary, if she was present, is not mentioned.

In John, the confusion is exacerbated because there could be one or two women at the foot of the Cross besides the Virgin Mary and Mary Magdalene. His phrase, "and his mother's sister, Mary the wife of Cleopas," can be construed to mean either a single woman or two. At the burial of Jesus, John mentions no one except Nicodemus, who brings "a mixture of myrrh and aloes, about a hundred pound weight" to embalm the body (John 19:39). In his next chapter, John tells the magnificent story of Mary Magdalene's visit to the grave, her discovery, and her eventual encounter with the risen Christ, whom she mistakes for the gardener. Jesus then orders her to tell his brethren and she does so. Later, he appears among them. Eight days later he appears again, and Thomas, who had doubted the story, puts his fingers in his wounds (John 20 *passim*). In his last chapter, John describes three more appearances of Christ to the Apostles.

The most important discrepancies are those about Jesus' Resurrection, which is not my theme. The imbroglio about this Mary and that Mary is interesting only because of what Christian cult has made of it. Traditionally, Mary the mother of James and Joses is identified with "his mother's sister, Mary the wife of Cleopas" (John 19:25) as one person who is the half-sister of the Virgin Mary and the daughter of St. Anne. Far from being discomfited by two sisters in the same family with the same name, popular legend developed a taste for symmetry, and "Salome" of Mark's account is aligned with "Mary of James" (Maria Jacobi) and becomes Mary of Salome, that is, the wife of a man called Salome, and also the half-sister of the Virgin. As we have seen, the *Golden Legend* describes how St. Anne bore three daughters called Mary by three husbands, who died one after the other: first Cleopas, the father of Maria Jacobi; then Salome, the father of Maria Salome; and then Joachim, the father of the Virgin.[1] There are surprising paintings, principally fifteenth-century German and Flemish, showing the Virgin in St. Anne's lap, flanked by St. Anne's three husbands, two elder daughters, and their respective husbands. At their feet play numerous children, the first cousins of Jesus.[2]

Maria Jacobi, Maria Salome, and Mary Magdalene become the "Three Marys" who in the earliest iconography of the Resurrection approach the empty tomb bearing unguents and spices. At the mass of the Easter vigil, deacons enacted the Marys' visit to the grave, when the angel asked: *"Quem quaretis?"* (Whom do you seek?).[3] André Grabar has pointed out that two or three witnesses were required by Jewish law, and in the earliest version of the scene, painted around A.D. 230 at Dura-Europos, where a heterogenous community that included Christians has recently been uncovered, three holy women approach the tomb.[4] The sixth-century mosaic in S. Apollinare Nuovo in Ravenna shows only two Marys approaching, and from then on throughout the middle ages, until this representation of the Resurrection was superseded by the image of the risen Christ himself, the numbers of women witnesses vary (figure 39).

Some writers have seen the Marys as the Christian inheritance of the Greek *Moirai*, the three fates who attended birth and death.[5] But while the Marys do form a female trinity, they seem to have found their place in Christian mythology purely out of confusion. The only text to deal satisfactorily with the problem is the *Twentieth Discourse*, a spurious Coptic work attributed to Cyril of Jerusalem, in which the Virgin introduces herself as all possible Marys: "I am Mary Magdalene, because the name of the village wherein I was born was Magdalia. My name is Mary of Cleopa. I am Mary of James, the son of Joseph the carpenter."[6]

# Chronology

| Historical Background | Cult of the Virgin | Arts and Letters |
|---|---|---|
| | | 70–100 Gospels of Matthew, Mark, Luke, and John |
| | | 95 Apocalypse (Revelation) of John |
| A.D. 100 | 100–200 *Gospel of Thomas* | |
| | | c. 110 Death of Ignatius of Antioch |
| | | c. 140–202 Irenaeus |
| | c. 150 Book of James | c. 150 Apuleius: *The Golden Ass* |
| | | c. 165 Death of Justin Martyr |
| | | c. 185–254 Origen of Alexandria |
| | before 200 First paintings of Virgin in catacombs, Rome | |
| 200 | c. 200? *Obsequies of the Virgin* | 200–258 Cyprian of Carthage |
| | between 200–400 Prayer *Sub tuum praesidium* composed | 205–270 Plotinus |
| 216–277 Mani | 217 Legendary founding of S. Maria in Trastevere, Rome | |
| 250 Persecution under Decius | | c. 250–356 Antony Abbot |
| 250–336 Arius | | |
| | | 260–312 Methodius of Olympus |
| c. 285 Beginnings of monasticism in Egypt | | |
| 300 | | |
| 305–311 Persecution under Diocletian and Galerius | | |
| | | 306–373 Ephrem of Syria |
| 312–313 Constantine grants peace of the Church | | |
| 324 Founding of Constantinople | | |

| Historical Background | Cult of the Virgin | Arts and Letters |
|---|---|---|
| 325 Council of Nicaea | | |
| | | 339–397 Ambrose of Milan |
| | | c. 340 earliest version of *Apostles' Creed* |
| | | 342–419 Jerome |
| | | 347–407 John Chrysostom |
| | c. 350 First invocation of Virgin recorded (St. Justina) | |
| | c. 352–366 Legendary foundation of S. Maria Maggiore under Pope Liberius I | |
| | | 354–430 Augustine of Hippo |
| | c. 370 Earliest liturgy of Virgin composed, in Syria | |
| | | 384 Vulgate translation of New Testament, Rome |
| | | 397 *Confessions of Saint Augustine* |
| 400 | c. 400 Earliest version of Transitus of Virgin written | |
| | 400–500 Temple of Isis at Soissons dedicated to Blessed Virgin Mary; Feast of Commemoration of Virgin introduced around Christmas throughout Europe; Feast of Annunciation kept in Byzantium | |
| 410 Sack of Rome by Alaric the Goth | | |
| | | 413–426 Augustine: *City of God* |
| 417 Heresy of Pelagius condemned | | |
| | 431 Council of Ephesus —*Theotokos* | |
| 432–436 Patrick's mission to Ireland | 432–440 Papacy of Sixtus III, who dedicates S. Maria Maggiore | |
| | 450–453 Pulcheria, Empress of Byzantium, collects relics | |
| | 451 Council of Chalcedon—*Aeiparthenos* | |

| Historical Background | Cult of the Virgin | Arts and Letters |
|---|---|---|
| | *c.* 470 Basilica at Salonika dedicated to Blessed Virgin Mary | |
| 476 Deposition of last emperor in the west | | |
| 487–493 Theodoric, King of Goths, conquers Italy | | |
| 491 Theodosius closes last pagan temple in Rome | | |
| 496 Clovis, King of Franks, and subjects baptized | | |
| *500* | 500–600 Parthenon dedicated to Blessed Virgin Mary; S. Maria Antiqua, in Rome, consecrated; *Akathistos* hymn composed | *c.* 500 Gelasian decree condemns apocryphal books |
| | | 523 Boethius: *Consolation of Philosophy* |
| 527–556 Justinian, Emperor | | |
| | 543 Church of St. Mary, Jerusalem, dedicated | |
| | *c.* 550 Feasts of Nativity of the Virgin, Presentation of Christ, and Dormition kept in Byzantium; mosaics at Euphrasian Basilica, Poreč (first church where Virgin and Child, not Christ Pantocrator, appear in conch) | |
| | | after 555 Death of Romanos Melodos, author of *Akathistos* hymn? |
| 568 Lombard invasion of Italy | | |
| 589 Conversion of Visigoths | | |
| 590–604 Papacy of Gregory the Great | | |
| | | 594 Death of Gregory of Tours, author of *History of the Franks* |

| | *Historical Background* | *Cult of the Virgin* | *Arts and Letters* |
|---|---|---|---|
| | 597 Augustine of Canterbury arrives in England; King of Kent and subjects converted | | |
| *600* | | 600–700 Antiphon *Ave Maris Stella* composed; feasts of Presentation and Purification of Virgin kept in Byzantium<br>*c.* 600–800 Gospel of pseudo-Matthew<br>610 Emperor Heraclius flies Virgin's image from masts of his fleet | |
| | 614 Fall of Jerusalem to Persians<br>629 Heraclius recovers Jerusalem<br>632 Death of Mohammed<br>638 Fall of Jerusalem to Moslems<br>670 Arabs begin conquest of North Africa | | |
| | | | *c.* 675–*c.* 749 John Damascene |
| | | 687–710 Papacy of Sergius I, who introduces feasts of Annunciation, Dormition, Purification, and Nativity of Virgin to Rome | |
| *700* | | 705–707 Papacy of John VII, "servant of the Mother of God" | |
| | | | 731 Venerable Bede: *History of the Church*<br>*c.* 732 Death of Germanus of Constantinople<br>*c.* 740 Death of Andrew of Crete |
| | 741–775 Emperor Constantine V | | |

| Historical Background | Cult of the Virgin | Arts and Letters |
|---|---|---|
| | *c.* 750 *Theophilus* legend translated into Latin | *c.* 750 *Apostles' Creed*, final version |
| 753–754 Iconoclast Council | | |
| 754 Papal State created | | |
| 800 Coronation of Charlemagne | *c.* 800 Gospel of the Nativity of Mary | |
| | 800–900 Feast of Conception of St. Anne introduced in Byzantium | |
| | 817–824 Papacy of Paschal I, who adorns many churches in Rome | |
| 843 Triumph of Orthodoxy—end of Iconoclast heresy | | |
| | before 851 Story of the Birth of Mary | |
| | 876 According to legend, Charles the Bold gives Chartres the shift of the Virgin | |
| 910 Foundation of Cluny abbey | | |
| | | *c.* 960–980 Hroswitha of Gandersheim's plays |
| 962 Otto I crowned Emperor in Rome | | |
| | *c.* 975 Saturdays dedicated to the Virgin | |
| | 976 Abbey of Montserrat founded | |
| 987–996 Hugh Capet, King of France (line lasts until 1328) | | |
| | before 999 Antiphon *Regina caeli* composed | |
| | before 1000 Little Office of Blessed Virgin introduced; Transitus stories translated into Latin | |
| | *c.* 1000 Feast of Conception of Virgin kept in the west; Hroswitha: *Maria and Theophilus*, poems | 1000–1010 *Song of Roland* |

Left margin time markers: 800, 900, 1000

| Historical Background | Cult of the Virgin | Arts and Letters |
|---|---|---|
| | 1000–1100 Antiphons *Alma redemptoris mater* and *Salve regina* composed | |
| | | 1007–1072 Peter Damian |
| | | 1033–1109 Anselm of Aosta, Archbishop of Canterbury |
| 1035 Death of King Canute | | |
| | | 1050 Death of Ralph Glaber, chronicler |
| 1065 Westminster Abbey consecrated | | |
| 1066 William I crowned King of England | | |
| | | 1071–1127 William IX, Duke of Aquitaine, first troubadour |
| 1073–1085 Papacy of Gregory VII (Hildebrand) | | |
| | | 1079–1142 Peter Abelard |
| 1084 Normans sack Rome; Carthusian order founded | | |
| | | 1091–1153 Bernard of Clairvaux |
| | | 1093–1133 Durham cathedral built |
| 1096–1098 First crusade | | |
| 1098 Founding of Cîteaux | | |
| *1100* | 1100–1150 Mosaics of Virgin at Torcello | |
| 1108 Augustinian Canons of St. Victor founded | | |
| | | *c.* 1110–1180 Adam of St. Victor |
| 1115 Founding of Clairvaux | | |
| 1120 Praemonstratensian Canons founded | *c.* 1120 Anselm the Younger: *Miracles of Blessed Virgin Mary* | |
| | *c.* 1120–1130 Dominic of Evesham: *Miracles of Blessed Virgin Mary* | |

| Historical Background | Cult of the Virgin | Arts and Letters |
|---|---|---|
| 1122 Concordat at Worms | | |
| 1122–1152 Suger, Abbot of St. Denis | | |
| c. 1122–1204 Eleanor of Aquitaine | | |
| | 1130 Holy House built at Walsingham | |
| | | 1137–1144 St. Denis built |
| | c. 1140 William of Malmesbury: *Miracles of Blessed Virgin Mary* | c. 1140–before 1215 Bertran de Born, troubadour |
| | | 1145–50 Peter Lombard: *Sententiae* |
| 1147–1149 Second crusade | | |
| | c. 1150 Senlis cathedral —first dormition scene in the west; S. Maria dell' Ammiraglio (la Martorana) and Capella Palatina, Palermo | |
| | 1150–1155 Portail Royal, Chartres | |
| 1156 Carmelite order founded | | |
| | 1160–1205 Notre Dame, Laon | |
| | 1163–1235 Notre Dame, Paris | |
| | c. 1164 Notre Dame, Noyon | 1164–1198 Marie de Champagne |
| | 1164 Death of Elizabeth of Schonau (visions of Assumption) | |
| | | 1167–1168 Oxford University founded |
| 1170–1221 Dominic de Guzman | | 1170–1190 Chrétien de Troyes's major poems |
| 1182–1226 Francis of Assisi | | |
| 1187 Fall of Jerusalem | | |
| 1189–1193 Third crusade | | |
| | 1194–1220 Chartres cathedral rebuilt | |
| 1198–1216 Papacy of Innocent III | | |

| *Historical Background* | *Cult of the Virgin* | *Arts and Letters* |
|---|---|---|
| **1200** | | |
| | *c.* 1200 Notre Dame, Mantes | |
| | *c.* 1200–1250 Notre Dame, Coutances | |
| 1202–1204 Fourth crusade | | |
| | | 1203 Wolfram von Eschenbach: *Parsifal* |
| 1204 Fall of Constantinople | | |
| | | 1208 Godfrey of Strasbourg: *Tristan and Isolde* |
| 1209–1213 Albigensian crusade | | |
| 1210 Franciscan order approved | | |
| 1215 Fourth Lateran Council; Magna Carta | | |
| 1216 Dominican order approved | | |
| 1217–1221 Crusade against Egypt | | |
| | *c.* 1220 Notre Dame, Amiens | |
| | 1223–1224 Caesarius of Heisterbach: *Dialogus miraculorum* | |
| | | 1225 Guillaume de Lorris and Jean de Meun: *Le Roman de la Rose* |
| | | *c.* 1225–1274 Thomas Aquinas |
| 1226–1270 King Louis IX | | |
| 1233 Dominicans entrusted with Inquisition | | |
| | before 1236 Death of Gautier de Coincy, *Songs and Miracles of the Virgin* | |
| 1240 Order of Servites founded | | |
| 1244 Albigensian persecution ends | | |
| 1248–1254 Sixth crusade | | |
| | 1251 Virgin gives scapular to St. Simon Stock (legend) | |

| *Historical Background* | *Cult of the Virgin* | *Arts and Letters* |
|---|---|---|
| | | 1257 Sorbonne, Paris, founded |
| 1260–1261 First Flagellants in Italy and Germany | 1260 Cimabue: *Madonna* for S. Trinità, Florence; new Chartres cathedral consecrated | |
| | | 1265–1321 Dante Alighieri |
| | | 1265?–1308? Duns Scotus |
| 1270 Last crusade | | |
| | 1278–1350 S. Maria Novella, Florence | |
| | before 1284 Alfonso el Sabio, King of Castile: *Cantigas* to the Virgin | 1284 Peterhouse, Cambridge, founded |
| | | 1292 Dante Alighieri: *La Vita Nuova* |
| | 1296 S. Maria del Fiore (Duomo), Florence, begun; Holy House discovered at Loreto (legend) | |
| | | before 1298 Jacopus de Varagine: *The Golden Legend* |
| *1300* | c. 1300 *Meditations on the Life of Our Lord,* attributed to St. Bonaventure; legend of Virgin's girdle reaches the west | 1300 Death of Guido Cavalcanti |
| | 1300–1400 *Angelus* prayer introduced | |
| 1305–1378 Papacy at Avignon | | 1304–1374 Petrarch |
| | | 1305 Giotto: The Arena chapel, Padua |
| | before 1306 Jacopone da Todi: *Laude* | |
| | 1311 Duccio's polyptych, *La Maestà,* unveiled in Siena | |
| | | 1314–1321 Dante: *La Divina Commedia* |
| 1323 Thomas Aquinas canonized | | |
| | | 1324? *Speculum Humanae Salvationis* |
| | 1326 Oriel College founded at Oxford, dedicated to Virgin | |
| | | c. 1340–1400 Geoffrey Chaucer |

| Historical Background | Cult of the Virgin | Arts and Letters |
|---|---|---|
| 1347–1380 Catherine of Siena | | |
| 1348–1351 Height of the Black Death | | 1348–1353 Boccaccio: *Il Decamerone* |
| | 1355 St. Mary's, Nuremberg, begun | |
| 1370 Bridgettine order approved | | |
| | 1372 Feast of Presentation of Virgin instituted in west | |
| | before 1373 Visions of St. Bridget of Sweden | |
| | 1376–1386 Feast of Scapular established | |
| | 1379 New College, Oxford (St. Mary College), founded | |
| | | 1385 Chaucer: *Troilus and Crisseyde* |
| | | 1387–1400 Chaucer: *Canterbury Tales* |
| | 1389 Feast of Visitation recognized | |
| | | 1398 Confraternity of the Passion founded in Paris to perform religious plays |
| 1400 | 1400–1450 Herolt: *Miracles of Blessed Virgin Mary* | |
| 1405 Crusade against Turks proclaimed | | |
| | *c.* 1409–1411 John Lydgate: *Life of Our Lady* | |
| | | 1410 Limbourg Brothers: *Les Très Riches Heures du Duc de Berry* |
| 1414–1418 Council of Constance | | |
| 1415 Battle of Agincourt | | 1415 Thomas à Kempis: *The Imitation of Christ* |
| | | 1420–1434 Brunelleschi: Dome of Florence cathedral |
| | 1423 Feast of Our Lady's Dolours established | |
| | | 1428 Death of Masaccio |

| Historical Background | Cult of the Virgin | Arts and Letters |
|---|---|---|
| 1431 Joan of Arc burned | | |
| | | 1432 Jan van Eyck: *The Adoration of the Lamb*, Ghent |
| | | 1440 Gutenberg invents movable type |
| | 1440 Eton College (dedicated to Blessed Virgin Mary) founded | |
| | 1445 Piero della Francesca: *Madonna della Misericordia* | 1445 Piero della Francesca: *Madonna della Misericordia* |
| | before 1447 Colette of Corbie's visions of Virgin and family | |
| 1453 Fall of Constantinople to Turks | | |
| | | 1454–1456 Gutenberg Bible |
| | | 1455 Death of Fra Angelico |
| | 1457 Gutenberg's successor prints *Office of Our Lady* | |
| | | 1463 Death of François Villon |
| | | 1466 Death of Donatello |
| | | 1466–1536 Erasmus |
| | | 1469 Death of Fra Filippo Lippi |
| | c. 1470 Alanus de Rupe: *De Utilitate Psalterii Mariae* | |
| | c. 1470–1475 Martin Schongauer: *Life of the Virgin* (engravings) | |
| | 1475 First confraternity of rosary | |
| 1478–1535 Thomas More | | |
| 1479 Aragon and Castile united | | |
| 1480 Beginning of Spanish Inquisition | | |
| | 1481–1483 Leonardo: *Virgin of the Rocks* | |
| 1483–1546 Martin Luther | | 1483 *Golden Legend* printed in English |

| Historical Background | Cult of the Virgin | Arts and Letters |
|---|---|---|
| 1489–1556 Thomas Cranmer | | |
| 1491–1556 Ignatius of Loyola | | |
| 1492 Columbus discovers America | | |
| | | 1494 First pocket-sized books printed |
| 1498 Execution of Savonarola | | |
| *1500* | 1500–1510 Albrecht Dürer: *Life of the Virgin* (woodcuts) | |
| 1503–1513 Papacy of Julius II | | |
| | 1507 Pilgrimage to Loreto approved | |
| | | 1508–1512 Michelangelo: Sistine Chapel ceiling |
| 1509–1564 Jean Calvin | | 1509 Raphael: *Stanze della Segnatura*, Vatican |
| | | 1510 Death of Botticelli |
| 1513–1521 Papacy of Leo X | | |
| | | 1514 Giuseppe Castiglione: *Il Cortegiano* |
| | | 1514–1517 First polyglot Bible |
| 1515–1582 Teresa of Ávila | | |
| 1517 Luther: *95 Theses* | | |
| | 1518 Titian: *The Assumption*, Frari, Venice | |
| 1519–1521 Conquest of Mexico by Cortez | | |
| | 1522 Conversion of Ignatius of Loyola at Montserrat | |
| | | 1524–1594 Palestrina |
| | | 1525 Tyndale's translation of the New Testament |
| 1527 Sack of Rome by Spanish | | |
| 1531 Henry VIII recognized Head of English Church | 1531 Vision of Virgin of Guadalupe, Mexico | |

| Historical Background | Cult of the Virgin | Arts and Letters |
|---|---|---|
| 1531–1532 Conquest of Peru by Pizarro | | |
| 1534 Jesuit order founded; 1540 approved | | |
| 1534–1549 Papacy of Paul III | | |
| 1536 Dissolution of the monasteries begins in England | | 1536 Death of Erasmus |
| 1538–1584 Charles Borromeo | 1538 Shrine at Walsingham destroyed | |
| 1542–1552 Missions of Francis Xavier to India, Ceylon, Malaya, Japan | | 1542–1591 John of the Cross |
| 1545–1563 Council of Trent | | |
| 1558–1603 Elizabeth I of England | 1558 Litany of Loreto published | |
| 1562 Huguenots massacred on St. Bartholomew's Day | | |
| | 1563 Sodality of Our Lady founded | |
| | | 1564–1616 Shakespeare |
| | 1568 *Hail Mary* in present form officially introduced into Breviary | |
| 1571 Battle of Lepanto | | |
| | 1573 Feasts of Expectation of Virgin and of Our Lady of Victory and Rosary established | |
| | 1577 Peter Canisius: *De Maria Virgine Incomparabili* | |
| | 1584 Francisco Suarez lectures on Mariology in Rome | |
| | | 1590 Spenser: *The Faerie Queene* |
| | 1592 Suarez: *Mysteries of the Life of Christ* | 1592 Definitive edition of Vulgate |
| 1593 Henry IV of France becomes a Catholic | | |
| 1597–1602 Upper and Lower Austria reconverted to Catholicism | | |

| Historical Background | Cult of the Virgin | Arts and Letters |
|---|---|---|
| | | 1598–1664 Zurbarán |
| | | 1599–1660 Velásquez |
| *1600* | | |
| 1603 James I grants toleration to Catholics in England | | |
| | | 1606–1684 Corneille |
| | | 1608–1674 Milton |
| 1609 Catholic League founded in Bavaria | | |
| | | 1611 Authorized Version of the Bible |
| 1616–1648 Thirty Years' War | | |
| | | 1617–1682 Murillo |
| 1620 Mayflower lands in America; victory of White Mountain—Bohemia reconverted to Catholicism | | |
| | | 1622–1673 Molière |
| | | 1623–1662 Pascal |
| 1625 Vincent de Paul founds Sisters of Mercy | | |
| | | 1629 Bernini appointed architect of St. Peter's, Rome |
| 1634 Maryland, U.S.A., founded for Catholic settlers | | |
| | | 1639–1699 Racine |
| | 1644 Feast of Purest Heart of Mary established | |
| 1649 Charles I of England beheaded | | |
| 1654–1715 Reign of Louis XIV of France | | |
| 1660–1685 Reign of Charles II of England | | |
| | 1670 Maria de Agreda de Jesus: *The Mystical City of God* | |
| | before 1680 Jean Eudes preaches devotion to the Virgin's immaculate heart | |
| 1683 Vienna delivered from Turks | 1683 Feast of Holy Name of Mary extended to whole Church | |

|  |  |  |
|---|---|---|
| 1700 | | |
| 1716 Turks defeated at Petrovaradin | 1716 Feast of Rosary extended to whole Church | |
| | | 1727 Death of Isaac Newton |
| | | 1729 J. S. Bach: *The St. Matthew Passion* |
| | | 1741 Handel: *The Messiah* |
| | | 1749–1832 Goethe |
| | 1750 Alphonsus de Liguori: *The Glories of Mary* | |
| | 1754 Our Lady of Guadalupe proclaimed Patroness of Mexico | |
| | | 1759 Voltaire: *Candide;* British Museum opened |
| 1773 Pope Clement XIV suppresses Jesuits | | |
| 1774 Death of Clive of India | | |
| 1776 American Declaration of Independence | | |
| | | 1781 Rousseau: *Confessions* |
| 1789 Fall of the Bastille | | |
| | | 1792 Mary Wollstonecraft: *Vindication of the Rights of Women* |
| 1793 Execution of Louis XVI; Christianity abolished in France | | |
| | | 1798 Wordsworth and Coleridge: *Lyrical Ballads* |
| 1800 | | |
| 1801 Catholicism restored in France | | |
| 1804–1815 Napoleon I, Emperor of France | | |
| 1814 Pius VII restores the Inquisition, the Index, and the Jesuit order | | |
| 1815 Congress of Vienna | | |

| Historical Background | Cult of the Virgin | Arts and Letters |
|---|---|---|
| | | 1821 Death of Keats |
| | | 1822 Beethoven: *Missa Solemnis;* Death of Shelley |
| | before 1824 Catherine Emmerich's vision of Our Lady's house at Ephesus | 1824 Death of Byron |
| | 1830 Catherine Labouré's vision of the Miraculous Medal | |
| | | 1833 Oxford Movement begins |
| | 1842 Louis-Marie Grignon de Montfort's (d. 1716) *True Devotion* discovered, and Holy Slavery of Mary founded | |
| 1845 John Henry Newman converted to Catholicism | | |
| | 1846 Mary Immaculate declared Patroness of United States; visions at La Salette | |
| | before 1850 Society of Mary founded | 1850 Death of Wordsworth |
| | 1854 Dogma of Immaculate Conception proclaimed | |
| | 1858 Bernadette's visions at Lourdes | |
| | | 1859 Darwin: *The Origin of Species* |
| | | 1863 Renan: *Vie de Jésus* |
| | | 1867 Marx: *Das Kapital* |
| | | 1867 Death of Baudelaire |
| 1870 Dogma of Papal Infallibility proclaimed | | 1870 Death of Dickens |
| | 1871 Visions at Pontmain | |
| | | 1873 Death of John Stuart Mill |
| | 1878–1903 Papacy of Leo XIII, "Pope of the Rosary" | |
| | 1879 Vision at Knock | |

| Historical Background | Cult of the Virgin | Arts and Letters |
|---|---|---|
| | | 1880 Death of George Eliot; Death of Flaubert |
| | | 1883 Death of Wagner |
| | | 1883 Death of Karl Marx |
| | | 1885 Death of Victor Hugo |
| | | 1889 Death of Gerard Manley Hopkins |
| | | 1890–1915 Frazer: *The Golden Bough* |
| *1900* | 1900 Our Lady of Guadalupe proclaimed Patroness of the Americas | |
| | | 1910 Death of Tolstoy |
| 1914–1918 First World War | | |
| | 1917 Visions at Fatima | |
| | 1921 Legion of Mary founded in Dublin | |
| 1930 *Casti Connubi*, papal encyclical on contraception | | |
| | 1931 Feast of Divine Motherhood established | |
| | 1932–1933 Beauraing: visions | |
| | 1933 Banneux: visions | |
| 1936 Spanish Revolution | | |
| 1937 Guernica destroyed | | |
| 1939–1945 Second World War | | 1939 Death of Sigmund Freud |
| 1939–1958 Papacy of Pius XII | | 1939 Death of W. B. Yeats |
| | | 1941 Death of James Joyce |
| | 1942 World dedicated to Immaculate Heart of Mary | |
| | 1945 Marian Year proclaimed | |
| | 1950 Dogma of Assumption proclaimed | 1950 Death of G. B. Shaw |

|  | 1954 Queenship of Virgin proclaimed and feast established |  |
| 1957–    War in Southeast Asia |  |  |
| 1958–1963 Papacy of John XXIII | 1958 Centennial of Lourdes proclaimed | 1961 Death of C. G. Jung |
|  | 1961–1965 Visions at Garabandal, Spain |  |
| 1963 Papacy of Paul VI begins; assassination of John F. Kennedy |  |  |
| 1963–1965 Second Council of the Vatican |  |  |
|  | 1964 Mary proclaimed *Mater Ecclesiae* |  |
|  | 1974 *Marialis Cultus* papal encyclical |  |

# *Notes*

## *Quotation and Prologue*

1. Caelius Sedulius, "Paschalis Carminis," Book II, lines 68–9, *Sedulii Opera Omnia,* ed. John Huemer (Vienna, 1885). The original Latin reads: *Nec primam similem visa es nec habere sequentem: Sola sine exemplo placuisti femina Christo.* I have quoted it from the translation by Herbert Musurillo, S. J., who has changed it from the second to the third person, in *Symbolism and the Christian Imagination* (Baltimore and Dublin, 1962), pp. 112–13.

2. Claude Lévi-Strauss, *Totemism,* trans. Rodney Needham (Boston, 1963), p. 70.

3. My gratitude to Joanna Sturm for telling me this story from her convent education.

4. In 1415 Henry V made a will before he left England on his French campaign. In it he said that he hoped to go to Abraham's bosom "through the prayers of Mary, the High Mother of God." He ordered that an altar dedicated to the Annunciation should be built over his tomb; that all extravagance should be avoided at his funeral, and that thirty poor men, if they recited daily the office of the Virgin, were to be fed and clothed for a year; three masses were to be said daily for his soul, to commemorate her Assumption and her Nativity and other feasts, and five thousand masses were to be said in honour of her Five Joys. After his signature he wrote: "R.H. Jesu Mercy and Gremercy, Ladie Marie Help!" Joseph Lauritis, editor of John Lydgate's *Life of Our Lady* (Pittsburgh, 1961), believes that the king commissioned the poem in gratitude for the success of the ensuing campaign in France. Certainly Henry attributed the victory of Harfleur, which was fought on August 14, 1415, to the Assumption of the Virgin.

5. Oriel is the "House of the Blessed Virgin in Oxford" and was founded in 1326. New College is "St. Mary College of Winchester in Oxford," for it was founded by William of Wykeham in 1379, who also established Winchester School and dedicated it to the Virgin. Similarly Henry VI showed his devotion to the Virgin by dedicating to her his two great educational foundations: Eton College in 1440, and King's College, Cambridge, in 1443.

## *Chapter 1: Mary in the Gospels*

1. Helen Gardner, ed., *The New Oxford Book of English Verse* (Oxford, 1972), p. 13.

2. Catholic tradition holds that Matthew is the earliest Gospel, though decisive biblical scholarship argues that Mark precedes Matthew. Matthew was first written in Aramaic, and then translated into Greek. The contemporary Catholic position is that Matthew's Aramaic version was written before Mark, but the translator of his Gospel into Greek (who is known as Matthew Greek to the scholars) used Mark to amplify the original Aramaic version. It is Matthew Greek who is responsible for the addition of the first two chapters about the birth and infancy of Christ. *The Jerusalem Bible, Introduction to the Synoptic Gospels* (London, 1966), pp. 5–10, discusses the vexed question of sources and dates most clearly.

3. S. H. Hooke, *Middle Eastern Mythology* (London, 1963), p. 169.

4. *Ibid.,* pp. 167–8.

5. *Ibid.*, p. 169.

6. M. D. Goulder and M. H. Sanderson: "St. Luke's Genesis," *Journal of Theological Studies* (April 1957), pp. 12–13.

7. *New Catholic Encyclopaedia* (Washington, D.C., 1967), 2:562–3.

8. For the following analysis of Luke's infancy Gospel I am profoundly indebted to Goulder and Sanderson, "St. Luke's Genesis," pp. 12–15.

9. Both Irenaeus and Nicetas of Remesiana provide independent evidence for manuscripts in which Elisabeth, not Mary, recited the *Magnificat;* see Giovanni Miegge, *The Virgin Mary* (London and Toronto, 1955), p. 33.

10. Goulder and Sanderson, "St. Luke's Genesis," pp. 17–18.

11. *Ibid.*, p. 19.

12. *Ibid.*, pp. 20, 23.

13. *Ibid.*, p. 21.

14. A painting of the birth of John the Baptist by the Maestro dell'Incoronazione di Urbino, in the Galleria Nazionale, Palazzo Barberini, Rome, *c.* 1300, shows the Virgin bringing St. Elisabeth a bowl of soup as she lies in bed just after her confinement. It is the only picture I have ever seen in which the Virgin attends Elisabeth.

15. Hooke, *Middle Eastern Mythology,* p. 170; Goulder and Sanderson, "St. Luke's Genesis," pp. 18–19, 20–1.

16. Goulder and Sanderson, *ibid.*, pp. 20, 24.

17. *Ibid.*, p. 23.

18. Joseph Pohle, *Mariology, A Dogmatic Treatise on the Blessed Virgin Mary, Mother of God,* ed. Arthur Preuss (London, 1953), pp. 34–5.

19. Paul VI, *Marialis Cultus,* Devotion to the Blessed Virgin Mary (Washington, D.C., 1974), sec. 39, pp. 28–9.

20. A. Feuillet, "La Vierge Marie dans le Nouveau Testament," in H. Du Manoir de Juaye: *Maria: Études sur La Sainte Vierge* (Paris 1949–    ), 6:20.

21. *Lumen Gentium,* chap. VIII, pt. III, para. 61. Walter Abbott and Joseph Gallagher, *The Documents of Vatican Two* (New York, 1966), p. 91.

22. Hooke: *Middle Eastern Mythology,* p. 17.

23. In a fourth- or fifth-century Syriac version of the Gospel discovered at St. Catherine's monastery on Mount Sinai in 1892 by Mrs. Agnes Smith and Mrs. Margaret Dunlop, this passage runs as follows: "Jacob begat Joseph, Joseph with whom the Virgin Mary was affianced, begat Jesus who is called Christ." Miegge, *The Virgin Mary,* p. 30.

24. Edmund Leach, *Genesis as Myth and Other Essays* (London, 1969). See "Virgin Birth," pp. 97, 106.

25. James Rendel Harris, *Fragments of the Commentary of Ephrem Syrus upon the Diatessaron* (London, 1895), p. 30.

26. Roland Batey, *New Testament Nuptial Imagery* (Leiden, 1971), p. 13.

27. René Laurentin, *Jésus au Temple, Mystère de Pâques et Foi de Marie en Luc 2:48–50* (Paris, 1966), *passim.*

28. R. M. Grant, *The Earliest Lives of Jesus* (London, 1961), p. 2: "Ancient Christians had in mind a picture of a person with a 'historical' life, but they were not primarily interested in dealing with that life either by using psychological techniques or by employing historical tools to analyze the setting in time and place. They did not ask themselves, as we might ask ourselves of any historical character, what it was his nature to be and to do. They did not try to make Jesus comprehensible against his environment in the manner of a modern biographer. . . ."

29. Francis Suarez, "The Dignity and Virginity of the Mother of God," in *The Mysteries of the Life of Christ,* trans. Richard O'Brien (Indiana, 1954), pp. 63–5.

30. The controversy over the brethren question continues. The contemporary theologian John McHugh ingeniously argues the theory that the "brothers" were the

# VOB
EARNINGS
STATEMENT

# F L M DATAGRAPHICS CORPORATION
PAYROLL ACCOUNT
16 PASSAIC AVE. — FAIRFIELD, N.J. 07006

| RATE | HOURS | EARNINGS | TYPE | CLOCK NO./IDENT. | NAME |
|---|---|---|---|---|---|
| 81250 | 4000 | 32500 | REG | 72004 | JOHN DESALVO |

DEDUCTIONS

| | | | | FED. WITH. TAX | F.I.C.A. | S.U.I./DIS. | STATE WITH. |
|---|---|---|---|---|---|---|---|
| | | | | 6691 | 398 | 325 | 715 |

| GROSS PAY | NET PAY | GROSS PAY | FED. WITH. TAX | F.I.C.A. | S.U.I./DIS. | STATE WITH. TAX | CITY |
|---|---|---|---|---|---|---|---|
| 32500 | 24321 | 162500 | 33455 | 8366 | 1625 | 3575 | |

EARNINGS THIS PAY                    YEAR - TO - DATE TOTALS

DETACH
BEFORE
CASHING

sons of Joseph's brother and sister, and were therefore Jesus' first cousins on his father's side. He further explains the use of the word "brother" and not "cousin" by postulating that Joseph adopted the children as his foster-children after their respective fathers' deaths. See John McHugh, *The Mother of Jesus in the New Testament* (London, 1975), pp. 234–54.

31. Jacobus de Varagine, *The Golden Legend,* trans. and adapted from the Latin by Granger Ryan and Helmut Ripperger (New York, 1941), pp. 261–8.

32. *Ibid.,* as Englished by William Caxton (London, 1900), vol. 5, pp. 97–8.

### Chapter 2: Mary in the Apocrypha

1. E. B. Tylor, *Primitive Culture* (London, 1871), 1:416.

2. M. R. James, *The Apocryphal New Testament* (Oxford, 1926), the Book of James, pp. 39–40.

3. *Ibid.,* the Gospel of pseudo-Matthew, chap. 7, pp. 73–9.

4. *Ibid.,* the Gospel of the Birth of Mary, chap. 8, pp. 79–80.

5. The Marriage of the Virgin, BM MS. Cotton Vesp. D. 8 (London, 1836).

6. James, *The Apocryphal New Testament,* the Book of James, chaps. 22, 24.

7. *Ibid.,* Gospel of Thomas, pp. 49–65; Gospel of pseudo-Matthew, chaps. 18–24, pp. 74–9.

8. *Ibid.,* Gospel of pseudo-Matthew, pp. 70–1.

9. Christopher St. John, trans., *The Plays of Hroswitha* (New York, 1923), pp. xxxii–iii. For the poem "Maria," see *The Non-Dramatic Works of Hroswitha,* text, trans., and commentary by Sister M. Gonsalva Wiegand, O.S.F. (St. Louis, Mo., 1936).

10. See Robert Briffault, *The Mothers* (New York, 1927), 3:214–15.

11. James, *The Apocryphal New Testament,* p. 38.

### Chapter 3: Virgin Birth

1. W. B. Yeats, "The Mother of God," *The Collected Poems of W. B. Yeats* (London, 1973), pp. 281–2. Reproduced by permission of W. B. Yeats, Miss Anne Yeats, and Macmillan of London and Basingtoke. I am indebted to both John Rosselli and David Esterley for drawing my attention to this poem.

2. Ovid, *Metamorphoses,* trans. Mary M. Innes (London, 1973), p. 81.

3. Origen, *Contra Celsum,* 1:32; quoted in R. M. Grant, *The Earliest Lives of Jesus* (London, 1961), p. 72.

4. E. D. Nourry (Saint-Yves d'Alveydre), *Les Vierges-Mères et les Naissances Miraculeuses* (Paris, 1908), p. 260. The father of Jesus is called by a similar name in two Jewish documents. One says, "As for the Satada (Mary), her lover was Pandera, but her husband was Papos-ben-Johadan." In the Talmud of Jerusalem, a disciple heals a sick man "in the name of Jesus, son of Pandera." Christians have tried to explain away these references as obvious slanders based on the word *pandarus,* meaning pander or pimp, and have argued that Pantherus or Pandera was not therefore a historical character. Apart from etymological difficulties, the use of the name for a procurer is medieval, and derives from the character in the story of Troilus and Cressida, as told by Boccaccio, and later by Chaucer and Shakespeare. The Pandarus of the classical world was a distinguished Trojan archer and a companion of Aeneas.

It is obviously impossible now to prove or disprove the story that Pantherus, a Roman centurion, was the biological father of Jesus of Nazareth, and it is of little consequence.

5. H. Rahner, S.J.: *Greek Myths and Christian Mystery* (London, 1963), p. 96. He quotes Newman: "These things are in Christianity, therefore they are not heathen." And continues, "So far then from her creed being of doubtful merit because it re-

sembles foreign theologies, we even hold that one special way in which Providence has imparted divine knowledge to us has been by enabling her to draw and collect it together out of the world."

6. Clement of Alexandria, *Recognitiones,* vols. 1, part 2, chap. 14, quoted in Nourry, *Les Vierges-Mères,* p. 258.

7. Henry Chadwick, *The Early Church* (London, 1968), Penguin History of the Church, 2:87.

8. Origen, *Contra Celsum,* 1:37.

9. Grant, *The Earliest Lives of Jesus,* p. 72; Grant: *Miracle and Natural Law in Graeco-Roman and Early Christian Thought* (Amsterdam, 1952), pp. 26–7, 108, 207.

10. T. H. White, *The Book of Beasts, being a translation from a Latin bestiary of the twelfth century* (London, 1954), pp. 108–9.

11. Robert Graves, *The White Goddess* (London, 1962), p. 437.

12. Epiphanius, *Panarion* 51, 22, 3–11, quoted in Rahner, *Greek Myths and Christian Mystery,* p. 138.

13. Chadwick, *The Early Church,* p. 192.

14. H. W. Garrod, ed., *The Oxford Book of Latin Verse* (Oxford, 1921), pp. 23–4.

15. Carleton Brown, ed., *English Lyrics of the Thirteenth Century* (Oxford, 1932), pp. 32–3 (English translation of *"Gaude virgo mater Christi/que per aurem concepisti"*).

16. Quoted in T. D. Boslooper, *The Virgin Birth* (Philadelphia, 1962), p. 59.

17. White, *Bestiary,* pp. 92–3.

18. Ambrose, *Veni Redemptor Gentium,* in Frederick Brittain, ed., *Penguin Book of Latin Verse* (London, 1962), p. 91.

19. See Dorothy Penn, *The Staging of the Miracles de Notre Dame par Personnages of Ms. Cangé* (University of Wisconsin Ph.D. Thesis, 1932), publication of the Institute of French Studies, Columbia University, 1932, p. 32.

20. Graves, *The White Goddess,* p. 157.

21. Origen, *In Jeremiam,* Homily 15:4; Commentary on John 2:12; Jerome, Commentary on Micah 7:6; on Ezekiel 16:13; on Isaiah 11:9; see Briffault, *The Mothers,* 3:180.

22. James, *The Apocryphal New Testament,* the Acts of Thomas, p. 388.

23. Francisco Suarez, S.J., "The Dignity and Virginity of the Mother of God," p. 41.

24. Graves, *The White Goddess,* p. 157.

25. Galen, *De Usu Partium,* bk. 2; quoted in Walter Riese, intro. to Galen, *On the Passions and Errors of the Soul* (Ohio, 1963), p. 29.

26. R. M. Grant, *Miracle and Natural Law in Graeco-Roman and Early Christian Thought, passim.*

27. Tertullian, *Apologia* 9:8; quoted in Grant, *The Earliest Lives of Jesus,* pp. 118–21.

28. The Rohan Master, *A Book of Hours* (in the Bibliothèque Nationale, Paris); commented by Marcel Thomas (New York, 1973), fol. 212, pl. 83; cf. Hesychius of Jerusalem (d. after 451), comm. on Lev. 2:4.

29. Quoted in Michael Baxandall, *Painting and Experience in Fifteenth-Century Italy* (Oxford, 1972), p. 43.

30. Aristotle, *On the Generation of Animals,* trans. A. L. Peck (Harvard, 1943), bk. 1; quoted in Julia O'Faolain and Lauro Martines, eds., *Not in God's Image* (London, 1973), pp. 118–20.

31. Aeschylus, *Oresteia;* quoted in Briffault, *The Mothers,* 3:155.

32. Dante, *Purgatorio,* Canto XXV:47.

33. Albertus Magnus (attrib.), *Les Admirables Secrets d'Albert le Grand. Con-*

*tenant plusieurs Traitez sur la Conception des Femmes, et les Vertus des Herbes, des Pierres Précieuses, et les Animaux* (Paris, 1962), p. 25.

34. William Harvey, *On Conception,* from *The Works of William Harvey,* trans. R. Willis (London, 1847); quoted in O'Faolain and Martines, eds., *Not in God's Image,* pp. 122–3.

35. Plutarch, *Symposiac,* VIII; quoted in Nourry, *Les Vierges-Mères,* pp. 227–8.

36. Suarez, "Dignity and Virginity," p. 14.

37. Joseph Patsch, *Our Lady in the Gospels* (London, 1958), p. 37.

38. Eileen Hunter, *Christabel: The Russell Case and After* (London, 1973), *passim.*

39. Roy J. Harris, Jr., "The Birds and Bees Can't Explain the Birth of Certain Turkeys" (article about the studies of Edward Buss and M. W. Olsen), *Wall Street Journal,* July 1973.

40. Robert T. Francoeur, *Utopian Motherhood: New Trends in Human Reproduction* (New Jersey, 1973); quoted in Andrea Dworkin, *Woman Hating* (New York, 1974), p. 181.

41. Suarez, "Dignity and Virginity," p. 39.

42. Anon., twelfth-century hymn, "Laetabundus . . ."; in Brittain, ed., *Penguin Book of Latin Verse,* pp. 183–4.

43. Rutebeuf, *Le Miracle de Théophile,* ed. Grace Frank (1925).

44. St. Bonaventure (attrib.), *Meditations on the Life of Our Lord* (Paris, Bibliothèque Nationale MS. Ital. 115). Trans. Isa Ragusa, eds. Isa Ragusa and Rosalie B. Green (Princeton, 1961), pp. 32–3.

45. Hendrik Cornell, *The Iconography of the Nativity of Christ* (Uppsala, 1924), pp. 12–13.

46. Edmund Leach, *Genesis as Myth and Other Essays;* see "Virgin Birth," *passim.*

47. See Norman E. Himes, *Medical History of Contraception* (New York, 1970), pp. 30–41, for an interesting discussion of the contraceptive techniques possibly used by the Trobriand islanders, who nevertheless denied biological paternity.

48. One of the earliest depictions of the Actaeon myth, the fifth century B.C. *metope* from Temple E in Selinunte, Sicily, now in the Museo Nazionale Archeologico, Palermo, makes the original ritual sacrifice clear.

49. Fifth century B.C., now in the Museo Nazionale Romano, Rome.

50. Arthur Darby Nock, *Essays on Religion and the Ancient World,* 2 vols. (London, 1972), ed. Zeph Stewart. See "Eunuchs in Ancient Religion," 2:7–15.

51. David M. Schneider, in *Man,* vol. 3, no. 1 (1968). I am deeply grateful to Edmund Leach for drawing my attention to the correspondence provoked by his lecture "Virgin Birth." The Danish anthropologist Dr. Toben Monberg has since argued that the Bellonese natives of the Solomon Islands were genuinely ignorant of biological paternity and the function of sex in reproduction before the arrival of the Christian missionaries, and that they were assisted in their innocence by the absence of large mammals and livestock on the island and by their consequent ignorance of animal breeding—*Man,* vol. 10, no. 34 (1975).

52. Henry Adams, *Mont St. Michel and Chartres* (London, 1913), p. 198.

## Chapter 4: Second Eve

1. David Greene and Frank O'Connor, eds. and trans., *A Golden Treasury of Irish Poetry 600–1200* (London, 1967), p. 158. I am deeply grateful to Jo Radner for telling me of this poem, and offer my thanks to A. D. Peters for the right to reproduce it.

2. T. E. Crane, ed., *The Exempla or Illustrative Stories from the Sermones Vulgares of Jacques de Vitry* (New York, 1971), exemplum CCXLV, pp. 102, 236. The original is found in the *Vitae Patrum.*

3. The Canons and Decrees of the Council of Trent declared that concupiscence was "an incentive to sin . . . left for our exercise . . . of sin and inclines to sin . . . but cannot injure those who consent not, but resist manfully by the grace of Jesus Christ." See William Graham Cole, *Sex in Christianity and Psychoanalysis* (New York and Oxford, 1955) for the historical view of original sin; and Edward Yarnold, S.J., *The Theology of Original Sin* (Indiana, 1971), for a lucid contemporary account.

4. St. John Chrysostom, *On Virginity;* quoted in O'Faolain and Martines, eds., *Not in God's Image,* p. 138.

5. See Kari Elizabeth Børessen, *Subordination et Equivalence. Nature et Rôle de la Femme d'après Augustin et Thomas d'Aquin* (Oslo and Paris, 1968), pp. 43–7, 150–5. for the views of Augustine and Aquinas on sex in Eden. Many of the Fathers, like Irenaeus, took the view that Eve was a virgin before the Fall. The question has never been definitely resolved.

6. It is possible to read the story of the Fall in Genesis as the story of a jealous God seeking to withhold moral knowledge from mankind. Hooke, in *Middle Eastern Mythology*, p. 112, explores the similarities between the Fall and other myths about man's loss of immortality, like the ancient Epic of Gilgamesh.

7. See Børessen, *Nature et Rôle de la Femme,* p. 172.

8. Augustine, *De Nuptiis et Concupiscentia,* 1, 8 (7.); quoted in Mary Daly, *The Church and the Second Sex* (New York, 1968), p. 54.

9. Augustine, *Sermones de Tempore,* Sermon 2; quoted in Suarez, "Dignity and Virginity of the Mother of God," p. 52.

10. St. Jerome, Letter 22. *The Nicene and Post Nicene Fathers of the Christian Church,* trans. and annotated by Philip Schaff and Henry Wace, 6:30.

11. St. John Damascene, *De Fide Orthodoxa,* IV, 25. Quoted in Suarez, "Dignity and Virginity," p. 95.

12. The Fitzwilliam Museum in Cambridge has a fourteenth-century copy of the *Speculum Humanae Salvationis* (MS. 43–1950) showing Judith and Mary side by side.

13. Quoted in Herbert Musurillo, S.J., *Symbolism and the Christian Imagination* (Baltimore and Dublin, 1962), p. 70. The neoplatonist Ammonius Saccas taught Plotinus and the Christian Origen, who, reported Eusebius in *Hist. Eccles.*, VI, 8, had taken the text of Matthew 19:2 literally and castrated himself.

14. See Peter Brown, *Augustine of Hippo* (London, 1967), for the best biography of Augustine; and St. Augustine, *The Confessions,* trans. E. B. Pusey (London, 1966), for his own account of his struggle.

15. St. Athanasius, *The Life of St. Antony,* trans. Robert T. Meyer (Newman Press, 1950).

16. Alan Shestack, ed., *The Complete Engravings of Martin Schongauer* (New York, 1969), fig. 4, "The Tribulations of St. Antony"; and Gustave Flaubert, *La Tentation de Saint Antoine* (Paris, 1967), *passim.*

17. St. Jean Eudes, *The Wondrous Childhood of the Most Holy Mother of God,* anon. trans. (New York, 1915), p. 90.

18. Tertullian, *Disciplinary, Moral and Ascetical Works* (New York, 1959), trans. Rudolph Arbessman, Sister Emily Joseph Daly, and Edwin A. Quain, S.J.; quoted in France Quéré-Jaulmes, ed., *La Femme. Les Grands Textes des Peres de l'Eglise* (Paris, 1968), p. 138.

19. John Chrysostom, *To the Fallen Monk Theodore;* quoted in Musurillo, *Symbolism and the Christian Imagination,* pp. 65–6.

20. Aristotle, *Politics,* ed. H. Rackham (London, 1949), pp. 22–3.

21. St. Ignatius of Loyola, *Spiritual Exercises,* "Rules for the Discernment of Spirits," First week, Rule 12; quoted in Daly, *The Church and the Second Sex,* p. 59.

22. St. John Chrysostom; quoted in Quéré-Jaulmes, *La Femme,* p. 49.

23. St. Justin Martyr, *A Dialogue with Trypho,* 100: 5, trans. A. Lukyn Williams (London, 1930), p. 21.

24. St. Irenaeus, *Adversus Haereses* 5, 19, 1; quoted in Paul Palmer, S.J., *Mary in the Documents of the Church* (London, 1953), pp. 13–14.

25. St. Ephrem of Syria, *Hymn on the Nativity,* 17, 4. Quoted in Hilda Graef, *Mary: A History of Doctrine and Devotion* (London and New York, 1963), 1:59–60.

26. Anon., "Ave maris stella," in Brittain, ed., *Penguin Book of Latin Verse,* p. 129.

27. St. Ambrose, Hymn for Easter Eve, "Exsultet jam angelica turba caelorum," *ibid.,* pp. 93–4.

28. Helen Gardner, ed., *Oxford Book of English Verse 1250–1950* (Oxford, 1972), pp. 13–14.

29. St. Methodius, *The Symposium. A Treatise on Chastity,* trans. and annotated by Herbert A. Musurillo, S.J. (Westminster, Md., and London, 1958), p. 132.

30. See R. M. Grant, *After the New Testament* (Philadelphia, 1967).

31. Henry Chadwick, *The Early Church* (London, 1968), p. 110.

32. Origen, *Homilia 1, passim.;* Suarez, "Dignity and Virginity," p. 36.

33. Origen, *In Genesim,* Homily 17; Suarez, *ibid.,* p. 33.

34. Suarez, *ibid.,* pp. 32–6; an early litany of the Virgin, dating from the eighth century, is extant in Gaelic. The earliest litany of the Loreto type, in which she is invoked under many biblical titles and images, was composed around 1200. It was used at the popular southern Italian shrine of Loreto in the sixteenth century, and adopted its name. The learned Jesuit St. Peter Canisius (d. 1597) published the first printed copy in 1558 at Dillingen in Germany.

35. The *Akathistos* hymn, in W. Christ and M. Paranikas, *Anthologia Graeca Carminum Christianorum* (Leipzig, 1871), pp. 140–7.

36. St. Ignatius of Antioch, *Epistle to the Trallians,* ch. 9; see Maxwell Staniforth, trans., *Early Christian Writings, The Apostolic Fathers* (London, 1968), p. 97.

37. *Epistle to the Smyrnaeans,* ch. 1, *ibid.,* p. 119.

38. For the Council of Ephesus, see Chadwick, *The Early Church,* pp. 97–9; Graef, *Mary,* 1:101–11.

39. See E. O. James, *Christian Myth and Ritual* (London, 1953), p. 233.

40. See Evelyn Faye Wilson, *The Stella Maris of John of Garland* (Cambridge, Mass., 1946), pp. 184–5.

41. Quoted in Graef, *Mary,* 1:64.

## Chapter 5: Virgins and Martyrs

1. Geoffrey Chaucer, *The Canterbury Tales,* trans. into modern English by Nevill Coghill (London, 1971). The Wife of Bath's Prologue, p. 295.

2. Graef, *Mary,* 1:51.

3. See France Quéré-Jaulmes, *La Femme; Les Grands Textes des Pères de l'Eglise,* for Tertullian's writings on virginity, pp. 140–56. See St. Cyprian, *De Habitu Virginum,* a commentary, trans. and with an intro. by Sister Angela Elizabeth Keenan (Washington, D.C., 1932); and St. Ambrose, *Theological and Dogmatic Works,* trans. Roy J. Deferrari (Washington, D.C., 1963).

4. Fr. Dermot Hurley, ed., *Marian Devotions for Today. Based on the Second Vatican Council* (Dublin, 1971), p. 15.

5. Tacitus, *The Annals of Imperial Rome,* xv, 43, trans. and with an intro. by M. Grant (London, 1959), p. 354.

6. St. Ignatius of Antioch, *Epistle to the Romans,* ch. 4; quoted in *Early Christian Writings,* p. 104.

7. Quéré-Jaulmes, *La Femme,* "La Passion de Saintes Felicité et Perpétua," pp. 194–210.

8. Christopher St. John, trans., *The Plays of Hroswitha* (New York, 1923), pp. xxvi–vii.

9. See the saints' lives in Jacopus de Varagine, *Golden Legend,* trans. Granger Ryan and Helmut Ripperger (New York, 1941 and 1969). See also *Golden Legend of the Lives of the Saints as Englished by William Caxton,* 8 vols. (London, 1900).

10. Alexander Gits, S.J., *A Modern Virgin Martyr. Saint Maria Goretti* (London, 1971), *passim.*

11. Caryl Rivers, "Aphrodite at Mid-Century. Reflection on a Catholic Girlhood," excerpt from *MS Magazine,* vol. 2, no. 61 (September 1973).

12. T. E. Crane, ed., *The Exempla or Illustrative Stories from the Sermones Vulgares of Jacques de Vitry,* exemplum 247, pp. 103–4, 237–8.

13. Mary Douglas in *Purity and Danger, An Analysis of the Concepts of Pollution and Taboo* (London, 1966), pp. 186–7, suggests that when early Christians threw over the old taboos of the Old Covenant and proclaimed an egalitarian society, with freedom and equality for its female members, virginity symbolized a pure, new world. She also argues that the image of the body reflects the image of society, and that a virginal body symbolized the whole impermeable body of the Church in a hostile world.

14. St. Jerome, *Comm. in Epist. ad Ephes.* III, 5; quoted in Mary Daly, *The Church and the Second Sex,* p. 43. She also quotes St. Ambrose, from *Expos. evang. sec. Lucam,* bk. X, n. 161: "She who does not believe is a woman and should be designated by the name of her sex, whereas she who believes progresses to perfect manhood, to the measure of the adulthood of Christ. She then dispenses with the name of her sex, the seductiveness of youth, the garrulousness of old age" (*ibid.,* p. 43). Methodius of Olympus had earlier declared in the *Symposium of Ten Virgins,* ed. Herbert Musurillo, S.J.: "the enlightened spiritually receive the features and image and manliness of Christ" in their struggle to free themselves from "*feminine* passions and immorality" (p. 113). It is sobering to reflect that the root of the word "virtue" is *vir,* Latin for "man."

15. St. Ambrose, *Exhortatio Virginitatis;* quoted in Briffault, *The Mothers,* 3:373.

16. St. Jerome, Letter 22, to Eustochium, in Schaff and Wace, eds., *Post Nicene Fathers,* 6:29.

17. The preoccupation with cosmetics has a long pedigree: Jezebel's chief crime was her painted face, and wicked connotations still cling to the idea of makeup. Baudelaire, who was steeped in Christian dualism, was obsessed by the evil and the beauty in artifice, and cosmetics supplied an important image of the artificial in his poetry. Sometimes horror of cosmetics in Christian documents strikes a foolishly extreme note. St. Jean Eudes, lecturing to the order of teaching nuns that he founded, said, "Have you no horror that your hands . . . should serve as instruments of Satan, to dress these children in worldly fashion, according to worldly vanity, to adorn them gaudily after the manner of worldly girls and women? Would you not thereby render yourselves guilty as those who violate their baptismal vows?" From *The Wondrous Childhood of the Mother of God* (New York, 1915). Willi Moll, a theologian writing in the 1930s, blasts off: "What bothers us in many a woman's glamorous face is the erotic everyman programme pursued with every trick and dodge, this obtrusion upon men which is so incongruous with true womanliness." He advocates a return to the veil. From *The Christian Image of Woman,* trans. Elizabeth Reinecke and Paul C. Bailey (Notre Dame, 1967), p. 31. St. Cyprian of Carthage, trying to discipline his flock of virgins, sounds at times exactly like the principal of a modern convent school. See *De Habitu Virginum.*

18. St. Methodius, *Symposium of Ten Virgins,* p. 151.

19. St. Jerome, Letter 22, ch. 17, to Eustochium, in *Nicene and Post Nicene Fathers*, 6:**29.**

20. For information on anorexia nervosa I am grateful to Mr. J. Hevesi, with whom I discussed the illness. Also, see Jenny Richards, "When Dieting Goes Too Far," *The Sunday Times*, May 6, 1973.

21. Venantius Fortunatus, Migne, *Patrologia Latina*, vol. 72, col. 88. For the same theme expressed in even more violent terms, see *Hali Meidenhad, An alliterative homily of the thirteenth century*, MS. Bodley 34. Oxford and Cotton MSS. Titus D.18. BM, ed. O. Cockayne, revised by F. J. Furnivall (New York, 1969).

22. Joan Morris, *The Lady Was a Bishop: The Hidden History of Women with Clerical Ordination and the Jurisdiction of Bishops* (New York, 1973), pp. 105–12; for medieval prejudice, see Giovanni Battista Della Porta, *Natural Magick*, ed. Derek J. Price (New York, 1957), and Albertus Magnus (attrib.), *De Secretis Mulieribus*.

23. Sara Davidson, "Fore Mothers," *Esquire*, July 1973.

24. See Børessen, *Subordination et Equivalence*, p. 101.

25. Margery Kempe, *Memoirs of a Medieval Woman*, trans. and ed. Louise Collis (New York, 1964).

26. General note: During the first centuries of the Christian era, the figures for female vocations are startling: Pope Cornelius (d. 253) said that fifteen hundred widows had been consecrated to Christ; St. John Chrysostom (d. 404) estimated there were about three thousand virgins and widows living in Antioch in his day; the chronicler Palladius wrote that ten thousand men and twenty thousand women had retired to live in the desert. St. Syncletica (d. *c.* 400) established the first convent for women in the holy land; Paula, a Roman matron, and her daughter Eustochium, who were prominent figures in St. Jerome's circle, opened a house for pilgrims and a convent in Bethlehem. (See Morris, *The Lady Was a Bishop*, p. 7.) The numbers of women who left the world for the Church had a remarkable economic effect. Roman law permitted a woman to inherit and dispose of her own wealth independently after a certain age. In the early years of Christianity it was common for a family to bring up the sons in the old religion and the daughters in the new. As a result the Church was vastly enriched by the fortunes of Roman women who either spurned marriage for a life of virginity or, as widows, bequeathed their private revenue to the Church. The historian Charles William Previté-Orton, in the *Shorter Cambridge Medieval History*, 2 vols. (1952, 1955), 1:30, points out that, as often happens in times of decadence, many Roman families had died out in the male line altogether. The outcome was that within a century after the peace of the Church in 313, the Bishop of Rome was the greatest proprietor in Europe. Virginity was, in more ways than one, the cornerstone of the new religion. The relationship of celibacy (i.e., childlessness) to the wealth of the Church should be constantly borne in mind. Ironically, monasticism and its ideal of personal poverty is fundamental to the public riches of the institutions to which the monks or nuns belonged.

## Chapter 6: The Assumption

1. For the stories of Mary's *Transitus* see W. Wright, *Contributions to the Apocryphal Literature of the New Testament, collected and edited from Syriac MSS. in the British Museum with English translation and notes* (London, 1865); and E. Cothenet, "La Vierge Marie dans les Apocryphes," in *Maria: Études sur La Sainte Vierge*, ed. Hubert du Manoir de Juaye, S.J., 8 vols. (Paris, 1949), 6:73–156; and Jean Galot, S.J., "Le Mystère de L'Assomption," in *Maria*, 7:153–238; Martin Jugie, *La Mort et L'Assomption de la Sainte Vierge* (Rome, 1844).

2. R. L. P. Milburn, *Early Christian Interpretations of History* (New York, 1954), pp. 136 ff. and 161 ff.

3. A. Wenger, "Foi et Pieté Mariales à Byzance," in *Maria,* 5:966–7.

4. Rustem Duyuran, *Ephèse* (Ankara, 1951), *passim.*

5. Émile Mâle, *L'Art Religieux du 12e. Siècle en France. Études sur les Origines de l'Iconographie du Moyen-Age* (Paris, 1966), p. 436.

6. For Elisabeth of Schonau's vision, see J. P. Strachey, ed. *Poem on the Assumption.* Cambridge Anglo-Norman Texts (Cambridge, 1924), pp. 15–26.

7. See Shestack, *The Complete Woodcuts of Albrecht Dürer* (New York, 1963), figs. 220–1.

8. Acts of St. John, in M. R. James, ed., *The Apocryphal New Testament,* p. 270; Acts of Paul, *ibid.,* p. 296; Martyrdom of St. Matthew, *ibid.,* p. 431.

9. Pope Pius XII, "Munificentissimus Deus," the definition of the dogma that Mary, the Virgin Mother of God, was assumed body and soul into the glory of heaven (Washington, D.C., 1950).

10. Vincent Cronin, *Mary Portrayed* (London, 1968), p. 156.

11. Anon. hymn, in Brittain, ed., *Penguin Book of Latin Verse,* pp. 269–70.

12. See 3 Kings 17:17–24; 4 Kings 4:31–7; 13:21; Isaiah 26:19; Daniel 12:2; 2 Maccabees 7; 9:23; Book of Wisdom 19:1–22.

13. Jean Huizinga, *The Waning of the Middle Ages* (London, 1972), p. 159.

14. G. G. Coulton, *Life in the Middle Ages,* 4 vols. (Cambridge, 1928–30), 1:137–60.

15. T. E. Crane, ed., *The Exempla of Jacques de Vitry,* exemplum 104, pp. 48, 178.

16. Alfred Maury, *Croyances et Légendes du Moyen-Age* (Paris, 1896), p. 183.

17. Helen Waddell, ed. and trans., *The Desert Fathers* (New York, 1942), pp. 289–302.

18. St. Bernard of Clairvaux, *Life and Works of Saint Bernard Abbot of Clairvaux,* ed. Dom John Mabillon, trans. Samuel J. Eales, 4 vols. (London, 1896), Sermones 10, 12, in *Cantica Canticarum,* 4:50, 63.

19. Gautier de Coincy, *Les Chansons de la Vierge,* ed. Jacques Chailley (Paris, 1959).

20. I am indebted to le Père Valentin, the librarian of the monastery of Montserrat, for showing me the manuscript of this poem.

21. Righetti, *Manuale di Storia Liturgica,* 2:377–9; also see Ethel Urlin, *Festivals, Holy Days and Saints Days. A Study in Origins and Survivals in Church Ceremonies and Secular Customs* (London, 1915), p. 173.

22. The Venerable Bede, *A History of the English Church and People,* trans. Leo Shirley-Price (London, 1955), pp. 238–40.

23. Émile Mâle, *Religious Art from the Twelfth to the Eighteenth Century* (New York, 1970), p. 177.

### Chapter 7: Maria Regina

1. "In praise of Mary," in Helen Gardner, ed., *Oxford Book of English Verse,* pp. 1–2.

2. See Hugo Rahner, S.J., *Our Lady and the Church,* trans. Sebastian Bullough, O.P. (New York, 1961), which contains the fullest theological account of the relationship.

3. Pietro Romanelli, and Per Jonas Nordhagen, *Santa Maria Antiqua* (Rome, 1964), is the most authoritative work on this church.

4. Gertrud Schiller, *Iconography of Christian Art,* trans. Janet Seligman (New York, 1971), 1:94 ff.

5. André Grabar, *Christian Iconography. A Study of Its Origins* (London, 1969), see pl. 120.

6. For the account of the relationship of the image of Mary Queen to papal politics, I am profoundly indebted to the excellent paper by Carlo Bertelli, "Il Restauro della Madonna della Clemenza, *Bollettino dell'Istituto Centrale del Restauro* (Rome, 1964), nos. 41–4. I also wish to thank the staff of the Institute for drawing my attention to his work.

7. For the life of John VII, see L. Duschesne, ed., *Liber Pontificalis*, 2 vols. (Paris, 1886–92), 1:pp. 385–7.

8. Ernst Kitzinger, *The Cult of Images before Iconoclasm*, Dumbarton Oaks Papers 8 (Cambridge, Mass., 1954); and for Iconoclasm, see André Grabar, *L'Iconoclasme Byzantine. Dossier Archéologique* (Paris, 1957).

9. Émile Mâle, *The Early Churches of Rome*, trans. D. Buxton (London, 1960), pp. 79–81, 85–6.

10. Giuseppe Massimi, *S. Maria in Cosmedin (In Schola Graeca)* (Rome, 1953), *passim*.

11. The words of Father Elia Jarawan, the rector of S. Maria in Cosmedin, to whom I am grateful for the profound and living knowledge of his church that he shared with me.

12. John Beckwith, *Early Christian and Byzantine Art* (London, 1970), p. 86.

13. See Grabar, *Iconoclasme Byzantine.* I saw these coins at Dumbarton Oaks, in a small exhibition during the summer of 1973.

14. John Beckwith, *Early Medieval Art* (London, 1969), p. 106.

15. Mâle, *L'Art Religieux du 12e. Siècle en France*, p. 152.

16. Allan Temko, *Notre Dame de Paris. The Biography of a Cathedral* (New York, 1952), p. 98.

17. For the life of Suger, see Temko, *ibid.*, pp. 74, 87–8.

18. Mâle, *Religious Art from the Twelfth to the Eighteenth Century*, pp. 57, 81.

19. The costume historian Elisabeth Birbari in *Dress in Italian Painting 1460–1500* reveals how figures in Renaissance pictures wear contemporary dress. But she points out that in Italy, too, the Virgin's clothes "although they are never outside the fashion, are never allowed to reflect the latest innovations." P. 40.

20. For the antiphons, see an old Catholic missal in Latin; I was using the missal I had as a schoolgirl, *Missal Quotidien et Vespéral, introduction, traduction, et notes explicatives par Dom Gérard* (Paris, 1955); for their history, see Righetti, *Manuale di Storia Liturgica*, 2:789.

21. Pope Pius XII, *Ad Caeli Reginam*, Encyclical letter, October 11, 1954.

## *Chapter 8: The Song of Songs*

1. Carleton Brown, ed., *Religious Lyrics of the Fifteenth Century* (Oxford, 1939), pp. 65–7.

2. Émile Mâle, *The Early Churches of Rome*, trans. D. Buxton (London, 1960), pp. 140–1. The mosaicist made a mistake in the inscription; it should read *"ponam te in tronam meam."*

3. Roland Batey, *New Testament Nuptial Imagery* (Leiden, 1971), contains a superb analysis of the symbol of the bride in the New Testament. Herbert Musurillo, in *Symbolism and the Christian Imagination* (Baltimore and Dublin, 1962), also discusses it, pp. 18–19. See also E. O. James, *The Cult of the Mother Goddess. An Archaeological and Documentary Survey* (New York, 1959), pp. 63 ff., 74 ff., 85 ff.; S. H. Hooke, *Essays on the Myth and Ritual of the Hebrews in Relation to the Culture Pattern of the Ancient East* (Oxford, 1933), also contains material relating the Jewish symbol of the bride to other mythologies.

4. St. Ambrose, *De Historia Virginitatis*, 94, and *Expositio in Psalmium*, 118, 1, 16; quoted in Hilda Graef, *Mary: A History of Doctrine and Devotion*, 1:85, 88.

5. St. Methodius, *The Symposium*, ed. Musurillo, pp. 98, 151–7.

6. St. Cyprian, *De Habitu Virginum. A Commentary*, trans. Sister Angela Elizabeth Keenan (Washington, D.C., 1932).

7. St. Jerome, Letter 22, chs. 25, 38, to Eustochium, *Nicene and Post Nicene Fathers*, 6:32, 39.

8. Christopher St. John, trans., *The Plays of Hroswitha*, p. 125.

9. *Hali Meidenhad. An Alliterative Homily of the Thirteenth Century*, ed. O. Cockayne, rev. by F. J. Furnivall (New York, 1969), p. 57.

10. Millard Meiss, *Painting in Florence and Siena after the Black Death. The Arts, Religion and Society in the Mid-Fourteenth Century* (New York, 1964), pp. 108–9.

11. For the text of *Pearl*, see Kenneth Sisam, ed., *Fourteenth Century Verse and Prose* (Oxford, 1933), pp. 57–67.

12. E. O. James, *Christian Myth and Ritual* (London, 1953), pp. 97–8.

13. Balenciaga, Metropolitan Museum of Art, New York, 1973.

14. See St. Bernard of Clairvaux, *Life and Works of Saint Bernard, Abbot of Clairvaux*, ed. Dom John Mabillon, trans. Samuel J. Fales. Vol. 4, *Cantica Canticarum*, eighty-six sermons on the Song of Songs.

15. See Étienne Gilson, *The Mystical Theology of Saint Bernard*, trans. A. H. C. Downes (London, 1940), pp. 130–41, 150–2, for an unsurpassable analysis of Bernard's theory of mystical love and his sermons on the Song of Solomon.

16. St. Bernard, Sermon 83, in *Cantica Canticarum;* quoted in Gilson, *The Mystical Theology*, p. 137.

17. St. Bernard, *De Gemina Susceptione;* quoted in Migne, *Patrologia Latina*, 183, col. 996.

18. St. Bernard, *Homily 3 on the Missus Est;* quoted in Mabillon, *Life and Works of Saint Bernard*, 3:319.

19. St. Bernard, *In Assumptione Beatae Mariae Virginis;* quoted in Migne, *Patrologia Latina*, 183, col. 996.

20. *Ibid.*, Migne, 183, col. 1004–5.

21. Righetti, *Manuale di Storia Liturgica*, 2:353.

22. R. W. Southern, *Western Society and the Church in the Middle Ages* (London, 1970), pp. 253–60.

23. St. Alphonsus de Liguori, *The Glories of Mary*, anon. trans. (Baltimore and Dublin, 1962), pp. 95–6.

24. C. G. Jung, *The Answer to Job*, trans. R. F. C. Hull (London, 1954), p. 171.

25. Plato, *Symposium*, part 191.

26. St. Bernard, Sermon 83, *In Cantica Canticorum;* quoted in Gilson, *The Mystical Theology of Saint Bernard*, pp. 131–2.

## Chapter 9: Troubadours

1. *Abelard and Heloïse*, trans. A. S. Richardson (Boston, 1884); quoted in James Bruce Ross and Mary Martin McLaughlin, eds., *The Medieval Reader* (New York, 1950), pp. 328–9.

2. From *Reis glorious*, trans. into modern French by Alfred Jeanroy, *Les Origines de la Poésie Lyrique en France au Moyen-Age* (Paris, 1936), pp. 80–1. Raimbaut d'Orange (d. 1173) also prayed to God for success in love, and invokes his miracle-working powers to his aid: "May God if it please him, make me come to joy in that which I ask of her, as quickly as he made wine from water." Peter Dronke, *Medieval Latin and the Rise of the European Love Lyric*, 2 vols. (Oxford, 1965), 1:101.

3. C. S. Lewis, *The Allegory of Love* (Cambridge, 1936), p. 11.

4. Percy Bysshe Shelley, "One word is too often profaned"; in Guy Boas, ed., *Shelley and Keats* (London, 1948), p. 77.

5. Joseph Anglade, *Les Troubadours. Leurs vies, leurs oeuvres, leur influence* (Paris, 1908), p. 297.

6. Joseph Anglade, ed., *Anthologie des Troubadours* (Paris, 1927), p. 43.

7. *Ibid.*, p. 19.

8. *Ibid.*, p. 152.

9. *Ibid.*, p. 96.

10. *Ibid.*, pp. 83–5.

11. Andreas Capellanus, *The Art of Courtly Love*, trans. A. J. Parry (New York, 1941); quoted in Ross and McLaughlin, *The Medieval Reader*, pp. 115–17.

12. Ovid's *The Technique of Love*, which influenced Andreas Capellanus' work, also advises the use of a little force—*modica coactio*—in order to accomplish seduction, but he does not confine it to a social class of women. See Paul Turner's excellent translation of Ovid, *The Technique of Love* (London, 1968).

13. Sir Steven Runciman, *A History of the Crusades* (London, 1971), 3:174–5.

14. *Ibid.*, 2:297–300, 424, 440–2, 443; and genealogy.

15. Usama ibn Munqidh, Prince of Sharzar, *Memoirs*, quoted in Runciman, *A History of the Crusades*, 2:320.

16. *Ibid.*, 2:27.

17. Thibault IV, Comte de Champagne et de Brie, Roi de Navarre, *Chansons*, édition critique par A. Wallenskold (Paris, 1925); see intro.

18. Runciman, *A History of the Crusades*, 2:362.

19. The earliest Salic law, composed around A.D 500, declares: "Salic land is no inheritance for a woman; rather all the land goes to the male sex—the brothers"; quoted in Julia O'Faolain and Lauro Martines, eds., *Not in God's Image*, p. 98.

20. Denis de Rougemont, *Love in the Western World* (London, 1956), p. 78.

21. Sir Steven Runciman, *The Medieval Manichee. A Study of the Christian Dualist Heresy* (Cambridge, 1947), p. 131.

22. See Matthew 19:9, Mark 10:11; Luke 16:18.

23. Geoffrey Chaucer, *The Canterbury Tales*, trans. into modern English by Nevill Coghill (London, 1971), p. 276.

24. E. O. James, *Christian Myth and Ritual* (London, 1933), pp. 155 ff.; Briffault, *The Mothers*, 3:248–50.

25. M. Chibnall, ed., *John of Salisbury* (London, 1956), pp. 80 ff.; quoted in Christopher Brooke, *The Twelfth Century Renaissance* (London, 1969), pp. 73–4.

## Chapter 10: Madonna

1. Carleton Brown, ed., *Religious Lyrics of the Fourteenth Century* (Oxford, 1952), p. 65.

2. *La Chanson de la Croisade contre les Albigeois*, begun by Guillaume de Tudèle, finished by an anon. poet; ed. and trans. Paul Meyer, 2 vols. (Paris 1875–9), 1:147, lines 3320–7; 2:179.

3. *Paradiso*, Canto IX.

4. *Aube Religieuse*, from Joseph Anglade, ed., *Anthologie Des Troubadours* (Paris, 1927), pp. 142–5.

5. J. Coulet, *Le Troubadour Guilhem Montanhagol*, p. 70; quoted in Briffault, *The Mothers*, 3:489.

6. Anglade, *Anthologie*, p. 167.

7. Anglade, *Les Troubadours*, p. 215.

8. Kenneth Sisam, ed., *Fourteenth Century Verse and Prose* (Oxford, 1933); see intro.

9. Brown, *Religious Lyrics of the Fourteenth Century,* "A Song of Love to the Blessed Virgin," p. 178.

10. Sisam, *Fourteenth Century Verse and Prose,* pp. xi–xii.

11. Harley Lyric no. 77, from *Medieval English Verse,* ed. and trans. Brian Stone (London, 1964), pp. 190–1.

12. Matfré Ermengaud, *Le Breviari d'Amor,* ed. G. Azais, 2:418; quoted in Briffault, *The Mothers,* 3:490.

13. Carleton Brown, ed., *English Lyrics of the Thirteenth Century* (Oxford, 1932), p. 101; *Medieval English Verse,* ed. and trans. Brian Stone, p. 74.

14. G. M. Roschini, "La Royauté de Marie," in Hubert de Manoir de Juaye, ed., *Maria,* 1:601–18.

15. Gautier de Coincy, *Chansons de la Vierge,* ed. Chailley, no. 2, pp. 28–9.

16. *Ibid.,* no. 13.

17. *Ibid.,* no. 18.

18. Rutebeuf, "Une Chanson de Notre Dame," in *Rutebeuf's Gedichte,* ed. Adolf Krefoner(Wolfenbuttel, 1885), pp. 200–1.

19. Thibault IV, *Chansons,* ed. A. Wallenskold (Paris, 1925), song no. LVIII.

20. See *Miracles de Notre Dame par Personnages,* eds. Gaston Paris and Ulysse Robert, 8 vols. (Paris, 1898–1900).

21. Brown, *Religious Lyrics of the Fourteenth Century* (Oxford, 1932), pp. 235–7.

22. *Miracles,* vol. 3, no. 19, "Miracle de un Chanoine qui se Maria," lines 844–52.

23. *Ibid.,* line 1049.

24. *Ibid.,* lines 1153–6.

25. Gautier de Coincy, *Les Miracles de las Nostre Dame,* ed. V. Frederick Koenig, 3 vols. (Geneva, 1966); quoted in Henry Adams, *Mont St. Michel and Chartres,* p. 271.

26. Evelyn Faye Wilson, ed., *The Stella Maris of John of Garland* (Cambridge, Mass., 1946), pp. 161–5.

27. James Morris, *Oxford* (London, 1965), p. 178.

28. *Johannes Hérolt, called Discipulus, Miracles of the Blessed Virgin Mary,* trans. C. C. Swinton Bland with intro. by Eileen Power (London, 1928), p. 61.

29. *Ibid.,* p. 84.

30. Peter Brown, "A Dark Age crisis: aspects of the Iconoclastic controversy," *The English Historical Review,* no. 346 (January 1973), p. 19.

31. James Joyce, *Portrait of the Artist as a Young Man* (London, 1974), p. 145.

32. Mary Daly, *The Church and the Second Sex,* p. 118.

## Chapter 11: *Dante, Beatrice, and the Virgin Mary*

1. Dante Alighieri, *Vita Nuova* (Milan, 1952), chap. 2; English version from *La Vita Nuova* (*Poems of Youth*), trans. Barbara Reynolds (London, 1969), p. 29.

2. *Ibid.,* chap. 26; Ital., p. 65; Eng., p. 75.

3. *Ibid.,* chap. 19; Ital., p. 23; Eng., p. 40.

4. "Donne ch'avete intelletto d'amore . . .," *ibid.,* chap 19; Ital., p. 41; Eng., p. 56.

5. *Ibid.,* Ital., p. 42; Eng., p. 56.

6. "Al cor gentil sempre ripara amore . . ."; *Oxford Book of Italian Verse, Thirteenth to Nineteenth Centuries,* chosen by St. John Lucas, rev. by C. Dionisotti (Oxford, 1952), p. 28.

7. Dante Alighieri, *La Divina Commedia,* trans. and comment by John D. Sinclair (London, 1958). *Purgatorio,* p. 360.

8. *Ibid., Purgatorio,* p. 84.

9. T. S. Eliot, *Dante* (London, n.d.), p. 57.

10. Father Francis Xavier Murphy, "Petrarch and Christian Philosophers," lecture given during Petrarch Congress, Washington, D.C., April 1974.

11. *Oxford Book of Italian Verse,* pp. 112–13.

12. Petrarch, *Letter to Posterity. From Petrarch, the first modern scholar and man of letters,* trans. J. H. Robinson and H. W. Rolfe (New York and London, 1898); quoted in Ross and McLaughlin, eds., *The Medieval Reader,* p. 392.

13. Professor A. A. Parker, "Expansion and Scholarship in Spain" in *The Age of the Renaissance,* ed. Denys Hay (London, 1967), p. 242.

14. Carleton Brown, ed., *Religious Lyrics of the Fifteenth Century* (Oxford, 1939); see intro.

## Chapter 12: Let It Be

1. St. Bernard, *Sermons,* ed. J. Mabillon (London, 1896), 3:342.

2. Plato, *Timaeus and Critias,* trans. H. D. B. Lee (London, 1971), p. 58.

3. Aristotle, *Politics* I, II. 9. 11–12, ed. H. Rackman (London, 1949).

4. Mary Daly, *The Church and the Second Sex,* pp. 34–7.

5. St. Thomas Aquinas, *Summa Theologiae* 1, 93, 4 ad. 1.; quoted in Daly, *ibid.,* p. 51; see also Kari Elisabeth Børresen, *Subordination et Equivalence,* pp. 131–44, 198–202.

6. St. Bernard, Sermon, *In Missus Est,* IV, section 8, in Mabillon, 3:340.

7. Raphael Brown, *Our Lady and Saint Francis* (Chicago, 1954), p. 24.

8. *Ibid.,* p. 33.

9. Erich Auerbach, *Mimesis. The Representation of Reality in Western Literature,* trans. Willard Trask (New York, n.d.), p. 145.

10. Millard Meiss, *Painting in Florence and Siena after the Black Death,* pp. 132–45.

11. F. J. E. Raby, *A History of Christian Latin Poetry, from the beginning to the close of the middle ages* (Oxford, 1966), p. 427.

12. St. Bonaventure (attrib.), *Meditations on the Life of Christ,* ed. Rosalie Green and Isa Ragusa (Princeton, 1961), p. 69.

13. *The Revelations of Saint Birgitta,* ed. from the fifteenth-century MS. in the Garrett Collection in the library of Princeton University, ed. and trans. W. Patterson Cumming (London, 1929); see also Erwin Panofsky, *Early Netherlandish Painting. Its Origins and Character,* 2 vols. (Cambridge, Mass., 1953), and Henrik Cornell, *The Iconography of the Nativity of Christ* (Uppsala, 1924).

14. Simone de Beauvoir, *The Second Sex,* trans. H. M. Parshley (New York, 1970), p. 160.

15. G. G. Coulton, *Life in the Middle Ages* (Cambridge, 1928–30), 3:65.

16. *Hali Meidenhad,* p. 57.

17. Quoted in Janet M. Farrier, ed., *French Prose Writers of the Fourteenth and Fifteenth Centuries* (Oxford, 1966), pp. 16–17.

18. Eileen Power, *Medieval People* (London, 1925), pp. 89, 93, 96.

19. St. Bernardino da Siena, *Sermons;* quoted in Coulton, *Life in the Middle Ages,* 1:221.

20. *Le Ménagier de Paris, Traité de Morale et d'Economie Domestique Composé vers 1393 par un Bourgeois Parisien,* ed. J. Pichon (Paris, 1846), 2 vols.

21. Christine de Pisan, *L'Avision;* in Ruth Ringland Rains, *Les Septs Psaumes Allégorisés of Christine de Pisan. A Critical Edition from the Brussels and Paris Manuscripts* (Washington, D.C., 1965), p. 63.

22. Johann Nider, *Formicarius;* quoted in Coulton, *Life in the Middle Ages,* 1:210–13.

23. Abbott and Gallagher, eds., *Documents of Vatican Two* (New York, 1966), "The Life of Priests," ch. 3, para. 18, p. 570.

24. Klara Munkres, "Kitchen Prayer" (author's collection of shrine souvenirs).

25. Mary Douglas, *Natural Symbols, Explorations in Cosmology* (London, 1973), p. 18.

## Chapter 13: The Milk of Paradise

1. F. J. E. Raby, *A History of Christian-Latin Poetry* (Oxford, 1966), p. 365.

2. In a Synaxary Fragment, containing John Chrysostom's "Eulogy for the Feast of the Four Incorporeal Animals," dated 893; and in *Book of Holy Hermaniae*, dated 895 or 898. Pierpont Morgan Library.

3. From a private tomb at Giza, Old Kingdom. New York Metropolitan Museum.

4. See Andreas Feininger and Henry Miller, *The Image of Woman* (London, 1961), pls. 38–57.

5. *Book of James*, 19:2; M. R. James, *The Apocryphal New Testament*, p. 46.

6. St. Ephrem of Syria, quoted in Paul Palmer, S.J., *Mary in the Documents of the Church* (London, 1953), p. 19.

7. Henry Chadwick, *The Early Church* (London, 1968), p. 260.

8. See note on Isaiah 7:14–22 in *The Jerusalem Bible* (London, 1966).

9. William Osburn, *The Antiquities of Egypt* (London, 1847), p. 229.

10. J. Rendel Harris, *Odes and Psalms of Solomon* (Cambridge, 1909); quoted in T. D. Boslooper, *The Virgin Birth* (Philadelphia, 1962), p. 62.

11. Macrobius, *Commentary on Scipio's Dream*, chap. 12; from *Thomas Taylor the Platonist, Selected Writings*, ed. Kathleen Raine and George Mills Harper (London, 1969), pp. 309–10.

12. "Adesto, Christe, vocibus" (On Our Lady's Birthday), in Brittain, ed., *The Penguin Book of Latin Verse* (London, 1962), pp. 130–1.

13. *The Prayers and Meditations of Saint Anselm*, trans. with intro. by Sister Benedicta Ward, S.L.G. (London, 1973), pp. 141–56.

14. St. Bernard, Epistle 322; quoted in Auerbach, *Mimesis* (New York, n.d.), p. 143; Mabillon, *Life and Works of Saint Bernard*, 2:846.

15. St. Bernard, Sermon 9, *In Cantica Canticarum;* quoted in Herbert Musurillo, *Symbolism and the Christian Imagination*, p. 83; Mabillon, *ibid.*, 4:47.

16. G. G. Coulton, *Two Saints: St. Bernard and St. Francis* (Cambridge, 1932), p. 9.

17. Émile Mâle, *The Early Churches of Rome* (London, 1960), p. 136.

18. J. Huizinga, *The Waning of the Middle Ages* (London, 1972), p. 191.

19. Gautier de Coincy, *Miracles de la Nostre Dame;* quoted in U. P. J. M. Ahsmann, *Le Culte de la Sainte Vierge et la Littérature Française Profane du Moyen-Âge* (Paris and Utrecht, 1930), p. 91; see Henri Focillon, *Le Peintre des Miracles Nostre Dame* (Paris, 1950), for exquisite illuminations of the text.

20. Evelyn Faye Wilson, ed., *The Stella Maris of John of Garland* (Cambridge, Mass., 1946), p. 92.

21. Meiss, *Painting in Florence and Siena after the Black Death*, p. 152.

22. Paul Perdrizet, *La Vierge de la Miséricorde. Étude d'un Thème Iconographique* (Paris, 1908), pp. 237–52.

23. *Miracles de Notre Dame par personnages*, vol. 1, no. 1. lines 1358–9, quoted by Ahsmann, *Le Culte de la Sainte Vierge*, p. 137.

24. Meiss, *Painting in Florence and Siena after the Black Death*, p. 152.

25. Quoted in J. A. S. Collin de Plancy, *Dictionnaire Critique des Réliques et Images Miraculeuses*, 3 vols. (Paris, 1821–2), 2:160–1.

26. Odell Shepard, *The Lore of the Unicorn* (New York, 1967), *passim*. The earliest description of the unicorn occurs around 400 B.C. The Septuagint translation

of the Bible rendered the Hebrew *re'em* (wild ox in modern versions) as *monoceros* in the Greek. The translators were probably influenced by the mythological beast's popularity, but their interpretation increased it enormously. In the Old Testament the unicorn appears as an animal of strength and speed, generosity and beauty (see Psalms 22:21, 29:6, 92:10; Job 39:9–11; Numbers 23:22, 24:8; Deuteronomy 33:17.

27. Gertrud Schiller, *Iconography of Christian Art*, vol. 1, pls. 125–9; pp. 52–3.

28. R. T. Davies, ed., *Medieval English Lyrics. A Critical Anthology* (London, 1963), p. 105.

29. Huizinga, *The Waning of the Middle Ages*, pp. 62–3; Eve nursing a baby at her breast after the Fall also appears in bronze on the doors of Hildesheim Cathedral, in a relief of *c.* 1015. See Sybille Harksen, *Women in the Middle Ages* (New York, 1975), pl. 6.

30. Helen Gardner, *A Book of Religious Verse* (Oxford, 1972), pp. 36–7.

31. Molanus, *De Historia sacrorum* II, XXI (Louvain, 1570); quoted in Meiss, *Painting in Florence and Siena after the Black Death*, p. 151.

32. Denis de Godefroy in the seventeenth century first wrote down the old tradition that Etienne Chevalier, smitten by the king's mistress, had commissioned a painting of the Madonna with Agnes Sorel's features. See Huizinga, *The Waning of the Middle Ages*, p. 153.

33. Lidia Falcon, *Cartas a una Idiota Espanola* (Barcelona, 1974), pp. 107–18. I am most grateful to Christopher Hitchens for bringing this book to my attention.

## Chapter 14: Mater Dolorosa

1. Popular prayer, "Invocation to Our Lady of Sorrows."

2. N. K. Sandars, ed. and trans., *Poems of Heaven and Hell from Ancient Mesopotamia* (London, 1971), p. 163.

3. Sandars, *ibid.*, p. 118.

4. *Ibid.*, p. 149.

5. *Ibid.*, p. 156.

6. *Ibid.*, p. 163.

7. Hooke, *Middle Eastern Mythology*, pp. 39–41.

8. S. N. Kramer, *History Begins at Sumer* (London, 1958), p. 92.

9. R. Briffault, *The Mothers*, 3:97.

10. Plutarch, *Isis and Osiris* (vol. 5 of *Moralia*), trans. Frank Cole Babbitt (London, 1936), 357, paras. 16–17, p. 43.

11. Hilda Graef, *Mary*, 1:119–23, 125–7.

12. Giuseppe Cammelli, ed., *Romano il Melode: Inni* (Florence, 1930), pp. 336–61.

13. O. B. Hardison, Jr., *Christian Rite and Christian Drama in the Middle Ages, Essays in the Origins and Early History of Modern Drama* (Baltimore, 1969), p. 131; for the *improperia*, see Brittain, ed., *Penguin Book of Latin Verse* (London, 1962), pp. 293–6.

14. St. Bernard, Sermon 29, *In Cantica Canticarum;* in Mabillon, ed., 4:191.

15. F. J. E. Raby, *A History of Christian Latin Poetry* (Oxford, 1966), pp. 429–32.

16. Sir Steven Runciman, *A History of the Crusades* (Penguin, 1971), 3:160.

17. St. John Lucas, *Oxford Book of Italian Verse, Thirteenth to Nineteenth Centuries* (Oxford, 1952), pp. 20–5.

18. See Auerbach, *Mimesis*, pp. 148–50.

19. Brittain, ed., *Penguin Book of Latin Verse*, pp. 246–9.

20. Philip Ziegler, *The Black Death* (London, 1969), pp. 26–7; Fernand Braudel, *Capitalism and Material Life 1400–1800*, trans. Miriam Kochan (London, 1975), p. 16, says that the population of Europe numbered 69 million before the Black Death, 55 million after.

21. Zeigler, *The Black Death*, pp. 40 ff.

22. *Ibid.*, pp. 87–98; Millard Meiss, *Painting in Florence and Siena after the Black Death*, pp. 80–1.

23. Kathryn Henkel, *The Apocalypse. Catalogue of Exhibition at Maryland University Art Gallery, March–April 1973*, p. 72.

24. Carleton Brown, ed., *Religious Lyrics of the Fourteenth Century* (Oxford, 1952), p. 235.

25. Carleton Brown, ed., *Religious Lyrics of the Fifteenth Century* (Oxford, 1939), p. 9.

26. J. C. Broussole, *Études sur la Sainte Vierge*, 2 vols. (Paris, 1908), 2:324.

27. Maria de Agreda de Jesus, *The City of God*. Popular abridgement of the *Divine History and Life of the Mother of God*, trans. G. Blatter (Indiana, 1915), p. 502.

28. Hardison, *Christian Rite and Christian Drama*, pp. 139–67.

29. See *ibid.*, pp. 150–1.

30. Abbott and Gallagher, eds., *Documents of Vatican Two*, "The Most Sacred Mystery of the Eucharist," ch. 5, para. 103, p. 168.

31. Pope Pius X, encyclical *Ad Diem*, 1904 (Mary Mediatrix of All Graces); quoted in Paul Palmer, *Mary in the Documents of the Church* (London, 1953), pp. 94–5.

32. Joseph Pohle, *Mariology—A Dogmatic Treatise on the Blessed Virgin Mary* (London, 1953), pp. 124–5.

33. *Newsweek*, August 14, 1973.

34. Mircea Eliade, *Images and Symbols—Studies in Religious Symbolism*, trans. Philip Mairet (New York, 1969), p. 151.

35. Mons. Salvatore Giardina, *Il Pianto di Maria a Siracuca* (Syracuse, 1971), p. 62.

## Chapter 15: The Penitent Whore

1. Jacopus de Varagine, *The Golden Legend as Englished by William Caxton* (London, 1922), 4:74.

2. For legends of Mary Magdalene in the south of France, see Yves Andouard, *Camargue* (Lausanne, 1965); *Jean-Marie Lamoureux, Les Saintes Maries de Provence* (1895); A. Mazel, *Les Saintes Maries de la Mer et la Camargue* (Vaucluse, 1935).

3. Owen Chadwick, *The Reformation* (London, 1972), p. 36.

4. R. M. Grant, *After the New Testament* (Philadelphia, 1967), p. 188; for the Gnostics' treatment of Mary Magdalene see Robert Murray, *Symbols of Church and Kingdom. A Study in Early Syriac Tradition* (Cambridge, 1975), pp. 332–3.

5. *New York Times News Service*, June 30, 1973; William Phipps, *Was Jesus Married? The Distortion of Sexuality in the Christian Tradition* (New York, 1970).

6. Book of the Resurrection of Christ by Bartholomew the Apostle, in M. R. James, *The Apocryphal New Testament*, p. 183.

7. Ciro Gianelli, "Témoignages patristiques grecs en faveur d'une apparition du Christ resuscité à la Vierge Marie," in Martin Jugie, *Mélanges. Revue des Études Byzantines* (Paris, 1953), 11:106 ff.; for a discussion of the confusion between Mary Magdalene and the Virgin in the garden, see Murray, *Symbols of Church and Kingdom*, pp. 146, 329–30.

8. Maria de Agreda de Jesus, *The City of God*, p. 595.

9. Helen Waddell, *The Desert Fathers* (New York, 1942), p. 268.

10. Robert Graves, *The White Goddess* (London, 1962), pp. 394–5; Peter Brown, "A Dark Age of Crisis: Aspects of the Iconoclastic Controversy," *The English Historical Review*, no. 346 (January 1973), p. 15.

11. Émile Mâle, *Religious Art from the Twelfth to the Eighteenth Century* (New York, 1970), pp. 171–2.

12. The Oxford English Dictionary gives 1697 as the first appearance of the word "Magdalen," meaning a reformed prostitute; and 1766 for the first time the word was used to describe a home for such women.

## Chapter 16: The Immaculate Conception

1. Marbod of Rennes (d. 1123), *Stella Maris*, in Brittain, ed., *Penguin Book of Latin Verse*, pp. 189–90.

2. W. H. Auden was fond of this joke: "When the woman taken in adultery was brought to Jesus, he said 'Let he who is without sin cast the first stone.' All was silence, and the Pharisees began drifting away in shame, when suddenly a stone whizzed past Jesus' ear. Without turning, and in a tone of deep irritation, Jesus cried out: 'Mother!' " (I am most grateful to Edward Mandelson for telling me this ancedote.)

3. St. Augustine, *De Natura et Gratia*, ch. 36; Preuss, *Mariology*, p. 78.

4. Albert Dufourcq, *Comment s'éveilla La Foi à L'Immaculée Conception et à L'Assomption au Ve. et Vie. siècles* (Paris, 1946).

5. Two miniatures by Menas and Michael Micros, from the *Menologium of Emperor Basil Porphyrogenitos*, now in the Vatican. See E. Campana, "Iconografia dell'Immacolata," *Arte Cristiana* (1915), 3:354–68.

6. For a discussion of the Irish origins of the feast, now considered doubtful, see H. Thurston, S.J., "The Irish Origins of Our Lady's Conception Feast," *The Month* (1904), vol. I.

7. St. Bernard, Letter 174, to the Canons of Lyons, in Paul Palmer, *Mary in the Documents of the Church*, p. 70; see Mabillon, *Life and Works of St. Bernard*, 2:512–18, for full text.

8. R. W. Southern, "The English Origins of the 'Miracles of the Virgin,' " *Medieval and Renaissance Studies*, IV (1958), pp. 176–216, 198.

9. *Ibid.*, 191.

10. *Ibid.*, 194–5.

11. *The Prayers and Meditations of Saint Anselm*, trans. Sister Benedicta Ward, S.L.G., pp. 119–20.

12. St. Anselm, *Cur deus homo*, 2:16.

13. Mario Righetti, *Manuale di Storia Liturgica*, 2:381–4.

14. Diptych by Il Maestro Lucchese dell'Immacolata Concezione. Vatican Pinacoteca.

15. John of Verden, *Dormi Secure*, quoted in G. G. Coulton, *Life in the Middle Ages*, 1:232–4.

16. Bruno Borchert, O. Garm., "L'Immaculée dans l'Iconographie du Carmel," *Carmelus*, vol. 2 (1955).

17. Adey Horton, "The Family Life of Jesus—the Unauthorized Version," *Sunday Times Magazine*, December 16, 1973.

18. See E. Sainte-Marie-Perrine, *La Belle Vie de Colette de Corbie* (Brussels, 1921), *passim*.

19. I have seen the exquisite polyglot Bible, 1514–17 (6 vols.), on exhibition at the Pierpont Morgan Library, New York. It was instigated and directed by Cardinal Ximenes, and cost 50,000 gold ducats; 600 copies were printed at the new university Ximenes founded in 1510. The second great polyglot Bible was printed at Antwerp in 1569–72 by Christopher Plantin.

20. For a lucid exposition of the varying iconography of the Immaculate Conception, see Mirella Levi d'Ancona, *The Iconography of the Immaculate Conception in the Middle Ages and Early Renaissance* (New York, 1957).

21. St. Ephrem of Syria, in Hymn 2 on the Birth of the Lord, verse 31, wrote: "The Lord hath spoken it: Satan is cast out of heaven. And Mary has trodden on him who struck at the heel of Eve. And blessed be he who by his birth has destroyed the foe." Quoted in Hugo Rahner, S.J., *Our Lady and the Church,* trans. S. Bullough, O.P. (New York, 1971), pp. 14–15.

22. In the decree concerning original sin, made at the fifth session of the Council of Trent in 1546, the following reservation was made: "This same holy synod doth nevertheless declare that it is not its intention to include in this decree, where original sin is treated of, the blessed and Immaculate Virgin Mary, the mother of God . . ." (p. 24). In 1547 at the sixth session, on Justification, Canon 23 declared: "If anyone saith that a man once justified can sin no more, nor lose grace, and that therefore he that falls and sins was never truly justified; or, on the other hand, that he is able during his whole life, to avoid all sins, even those that are venial,—except by a special privilege from God, as the Church holds in regard of the Blessed Virgin; let him be anathema." Quoted in Rev. J. Waterworth, trans., *Canons and Decrees of the Sacred and Oecumenical Council of Trent* (London, 1948), p. 47.

23. Owen Chadwick, *The Reformation* (London, 1972), p. 277.

24. Hilda Graef, *Mary,* 2:81.

25. Émile Mâle, *Religious Art from the Twelfth to the Eighteenth Century,* pp. 50, 169.

26. St. Jean Eudes, *The Wondrous Childhood of the Most Holy Mother of God,* p. 22.

27. André Ravier, *Lourdes, Terre d'Evangile. Récit Historique des Apparitions. Présentation des principaux documents de l'epoque* (Lyon, 1965), *passim.*

28. Vincent Cronin, *Mary Portrayed* (London, 1968), p. 156.

29. Meiss, *Painting in Florence and Siena after the Black Death,* pp. 105 ff.

30. Ravier, *Lourdes,* p. 57.

31. Mâle, *Religious Art,* p. 167.

32. Jean Galot, S.J., "Le Mystère de L'Assomption," in Hubert Manoir de Juaye, ed., *Maria,* 7:191–211.

33. *Ibid.,* 7:199.

34. St. Francis de Sales, "Sermon on the Feast of the Assumption," 1602; quoted in Galot, *ibid.,* 7:208.

35. Pope Pius XII, *Munificentissimus Deus,* ch. 44 (Washington, 1950).

36. Abbott and Gallagher, eds., *Documents of Vatican Two,* "The Role of the Blessed Virgin Mary, Mother of God in the Mystery of Christ and the Church," ch. 2, para. 59. St. Augustine is the only great authority to have spoken of Mary's death, when he said, "Mary, born of Adam, died because of sin. The flesh of the Lord, born of Mary, died to destroy sin" (Enarratio in Psalmum 34,3); quoted in Galot, "Le Mystère de l'Assomption," p. 196.

37. St. Justin Martyr wrote of Jesus that he had "blood, yet not from the seed of man but of the power of God" and that "the blood of Christ would not be of human generation but of God's power." *Dialogue with Trypho,* trans. A. Lukyn Williams (London, 1930), ch. 54, pp. 108–9.

## Chapter 17: The Moon and the Stars

1. "Two Songs from a Play," *The Collected Poems of W. B. Yeats* (London, 1973), pp. 239–40. Reproduced by permission of W. B. Yeats, Miss Anne Yeats, and Macmillan of London and Basingstoke.

2. *The Works of Apuleius. Comprising the Metamorphoses, or Golden Ass, the God of Socrates,* etc. (London, 1878), pp. 224–6.

3. For the following account I am deeply indebted to Hugo Rahner, S.J., "The Christian Mystery of Sun and Moon," in *Greek Myths and Christian Mystery* (London, 1963), pp. 89–175.

4. St. Ambrose, in *Splendor paternae gloriae*, writes:

> *verusque sol, inlabere*
> *micans nitore perpeti . . .*

Quoted in F. J. E. Raby, *A History of Christian Latin Poetry* (Oxford, 1966), p. 35.

5. St. Methodius, *The Symposium*, trans. H. Musurillo, S.J. (Westminster, Md., and London, 1958), pp. 110–11.

6. Rahner, "The Christian Mystery of Sun and Moon," p. 160.

7. See Rahner, *Our Lady and the Church* (New York, 1961); René Laurentin, *Mary's Place in the Church*, trans. I. G. Ridoux (London, 1965); and Joseph C. Plumpe, *Mater Ecclesia, An enquiry into the concept of the Church as Mother in Early Christianity* (Washington, D.C., 1943).

8. In the thirteenth-century *Mirror of the Blessed Virgin Mary, and Psalter of Our Lady*, attributed to St. Bonaventure but probably written by Conrad of Saxony (d. 1279), the author writes: "Think therefore what a beautiful moon was Mary when that eternal Sun was wholly received and conceived in her. Mary therefore is that moon in whose fullness that Man returned to the Church of whom it is said: 'The days of the full moon he will return to his house'" (Proverbs 7:20). Trans. Sister Mary Emmanuel, O.S.B. (St. Louis and London, 1932), p. 127.

9. Rahner, *Greek Myths and Christian Mystery*, p. 167.

10. Quoted from Alphonsus de Liguori's *Glories of Mary*, in Briffault, *The Mothers*, 3:184.

11. Jean Daniélou, S.J., "Le Culte Marial et le Paganisme," in Hubert du Manoir de Juaye, *Maria*, 1:177.

12. Hilda Graef, *Mary: A History of Doctrine and Devotion*, 2:85–7.

13. Plutarch, *Isis and Osiris* (*Moralia*, V), trans. Frank Cole Babbitt (London, 1936), 367, para. 41, p. 101.

14. The *De Secretis Mulieribus* says that the foetus is first milky, then after nine days it turns the colour of cooked blood, and after twelve the limbs come together. The moon is "the origin of all natural virtues" and strengthens the soul. In the seventh month she "fills with her humidity all the empty spaces between the flesh." Albertus Magnus (attrib.), *Les Admirables Secrets d'Albert le Grand* (Paris, 1962), 2:25–33.

15. Meiss, *Painting in Florence and Siena after the Black Death*, pp. 42 ff.; figs. 133–7.

16. There was thought to be a physical connection between menstruation and lactation, both ultimately dependent on the moon. Even Leonardo, that supreme empiricist, partly subscribed to the same error when he drew a cord connecting the uterus to the breasts in his drawings of the different stages of a foetus' life.

17. *The Complete Woodcuts of Albrecht Dürer*, ed. Dr. Willi Kurth (New York, 1963), p. 219.

18. Mircea Eliade, *Patterns in Comparative Religion*, trans. Rosemary Sheed (New York, 1972), p. 155.

19. *Ibid.*, p. 159.

20. "The Hymns of Orpheus, To the Goddess Prothyrea, The Fumigation from Storax," in *Thomas Taylor the Platonist, Selected Writings*, eds. Kathleen Raine and George Mills Harper (London, 1969), p. 213.

21. Brian Stone, ed., *Medieval English Verse* (London, 1964), p. 24.

22. *Ave Maris Stella*, in Frederick Brittain, ed., *Penguin Book of Latin Verse*, pp. 129–30.

23. St. Anselm wrote:

*Ave perfusa lumine*
*Tuoque digna nomine*
*Nam quod Maria dicitur*
*Stella maris exprimitur.*

Quoted in R. T. Davies, ed., *Medieval English Lyrics* (London, 1963), p. 377, from Anselm's *The Psalter of Mary*.

24. St. Bernard, Homily no. 2, *In Missus Est,* in Mabillon, ed., *Life and Works of Saint Bernard,* 3:315–16.

25. *Song for Our Lady's Birthday, c.* 1300, in Stephen Gaselee, ed., *Oxford Book of Medieval Latin Verse* (Oxford, 1928), pp. 162–4.

26. Petrarch, *Hymn to the Virgin,* in St. John Lucas, ed., *Oxford Book of Italian Verse* (Oxford, 1952), pp. 109–14. Another intimate and anguished plea to the Virgin probably influenced by Petrarch, and attributed, certainly incorrectly, to Jacopone da Todi, also uses the image of the storm-tossed boat, guided by the morning star:

*Porgi soccorso, o Vergine gentile,*
*A quest'alma tapina,*
*E non guardar ch'io sia terreno e vile*
*E tu del ciel Regina;*
*O stella mattutina,*
*O tramontana del mondan viaggio,*
*Porgi il tuo santo raggio*
*Alla mia errante e debil navicella.*

From *Maria, vergine bella,* in Jacopone da Todi, *Frère Mineur de S. François,* ed. with intro. by J. Pacheu (Paris, 1914), p. 292.

27. See Briffault, *The Mothers,* 3:81.

28. R. A. B. Mynors, ed., *P. Vergili Maronis, Opera* (Oxford, 1969), p. 10; Edward J. G. Scott, trans., *The Eclogues of Virgil* (London, 1884), p. 29.

29. *Fourth Eclogue,* lines 6–7; Mynors, p. 9; author's trans.

30. *Mirabilia Urbis Romae* or *The Marvels of Rome,* ed. Francis M. Nichols (London 1889) pp. 35–8. The vision is first recorded in the *Chronographia* of Malalas, sixth century. The Limbourg Brothers, in *Les Très Riches Heures du Duc de Berry,* painted an exquisite illumination of Augustus' vision, Fol. 22, ed. Jean Longnon and Raymond Cazelles (London, 1969), pl. 19.

31. Johannes Hérolt, called Discipulus, *The Miracles of the Blessed Virgin Mary,* trans. C. C. Swinton Bland (London, 1928), miracle no. 2, pp. 16–18.

32. A. E. Perez Sanchez, The Golden Age of Spanish Painting, catalogue (London, 1976), p. 39; Michael Baxandall, *Painting and Experience in Fifteenth-Century Italy* (Oxford, 1972), p. 11.

33. Philip Hendy, *Piero della Francesca and the Early Renaissance* (London, 1968), p. 17.

34. Peter Gunn, *The Companion Guide to Southern Italy* (London, 1969), pp. 362–4.

35. Father Engelrave, *Pantheon Celeste;* quoted in E. Campana, *Arte Cristiana* (1915), 3:354–68. For symbolism of pearls, see Mircea Eliade, *Images and Symbols—Studies in Religious Symbolism,* trans. Philip Mairet (New York, 1969), pp. 144–50.

36. Kenneth Armstrong, *Hong Kong and Macao,* National Geographic Lecture (Washington, D.C., 1973).

37. For symbolism of shells, see Eliade, *Images and Symbols,* pp. 125–8.

38. Briffault, *The Mothers,* 2:641–51, 660–2; Eliade, *Patterns in Comparative Religion,* pp. 164–71.

39. Briffault, *ibid.,* pp. 645–7.

40. Briffault, *ibid.*, pp. 664–70; Eliade, *Patterns in Comparative Religion*, pp. 165–9.

41. Robert Graves, *The White Goddess* (London, 1962), pp. 248–9.

## Chapter 18: Growth in Every Thing

1. Richard Corbet (d. 1635), "Farewell, Rewards and Fairies," quoted in R. Gathorne-Hardy, *Amalfi* (London, 1968), p. 186.

2. Kenneth Lyons, trans., *What Montserrat Is*, anon. (Montserrat, 1969), *passim;* Dom Louis Montegut, *Histoire de Notre Dame de Montserrat. Avec la description de l'abbaye et de l'hermitage* (Toulouse, 1739).

3. B. Maria de Morimonte, *L'Histoire des Miracles Faicts par l'Intervention de Nostre Dame de Montserrat, depuis l'an 888, jusques l'an 1599, avec approbations authentiques d'iceux* (1601), miracle no. 83.

4. *Analecta Montserratensiana*, vol. 4, Descriptio Sylvae Montserrati (Montserrat, 1920–1), pp. 36–116.

5. St. Epiphanius, *Panarion*, ch. 78, para. 23; quoted in Jean Daniélou, S.J., "Le Culte Marial et le Paganisme," in H. Du Manoir, 1:173.

6. *Fifteenth Century Woodcuts and Metalcuts from the National Gallery of Art*, Washington, D.C. Catalogue by Richard S. Field. Figs. 153–4.

7. H. V. Morton, *A Traveller in Southern Italy*, pp. 300–6.

8. Briffault, *The Mothers*, 3:183; the museums at Agrigento and Syracuse have examples of Demeter and Kore together.

9. Thomas of Celano, *Tractatus de Miraculis;* quoted in Raphael Brown, *Our Lady and St. Francis* (Chicago, 1954), pp. 73–4.

10. See Hérolt's version in Johannes Hérolt, called Discipulus, *The Miracles of the Blessed Virgin Mary*, miracle no. 24, pp. 42–3. The miracle appears in almost every medieval collection—Latin, French, and English.

11. Dorothy Penn, *The Staging of the 'Miracles de Nostre Dame par Personnages,'* of Ms. Cangé (New York, 1932), p. 29.

12. Georgina Masson, *The Companion Guide to Rome* (London, 1972), p. 108.

13. Giuseppe Bianchini, *Notizie istoriche intorno alla sacratissima cintola di Maria Vergine, che si conserva nella città di Prato;* quoted in Anna Jameson, *Legends of the Madonna as Represented in the Fine Arts*, vol. 3 of *Sacred and Legendary Art* (London, 1864), pp. 320–2.

14. For other girdle myths, see Briffault, *The Mothers*, 3:286.

15. Robert Graves, *The Greek Myths* (London, 1966), 2:270–2; "Mythology," *New Larousse Encyclopedia* (London, 1970), p. 131.

16. *Ibid.*, p. 131.

17. *Ibid.*, p. 203.

18. Graves, *Greek Myths*, 2:124–6.

19. I am grateful to Robin Lane-Fox for pointing out this connection to me.

20. Dom F. Chamard, *Revue de L'Anjou*, vol. 5 (1896).

21. Maria Grazia Cucco, "Off to the Shrine for a Family Outing," *Observer Magazine*, May 20, 1973.

22. Righetti, *Manuale di Storia Liturgica*, 2:367.

23. Gerard Manley Hopkins, *Poems* (Oxford, 1948), pp. 81–2. Reproduced by kind permission of Oxford University Press by arrangement with the Society of Authors.

24. J. G. Frazer, *The Golden Bough* (London, 1963), pp. 157–78, 170–5; Mircea Eliade, *Patterns in Comparative Religion*, p. 311.

25. E. O. James, *The Cult of the Mother Goddess* (London, 1958), pp. 187–8. The vernal equinox coincided with the Attic spring festival of March 15–27, but

when the Julian calendar was changed the festival was fixed on May 1. In the pre-Julian calendar it would have fallen on March 25, i.e., the equinox, every other year. Folklore and the Christian calendar retained both March 25 and May 1 as feastdays.

26. See Rosemary Radford Ruether, "Can the Virgin Mary Be Saved? The Meaning of Female images in a Patriarchal Religion," a lecture lent to the author by Dr. Ruether in 1973; and the writings of Robert Briffault, Margaret Murray, Robert Graves, Elaine Morgan in *The Descent of Woman* (New York, 1972), and Elizabeth Gould Davis in *The First Sex* (Baltimore, 1972), as well as many minor works, such as Uberto Pestalozza, *l'Éternel Féminin dans la Religion Méditerranéenne*, trans. Marcel de Corte (Brussels, 1965). Mary Renault in her colourful and vivid novels about ancient Crete also perpetuates the idea of an original matriarchy in the Mediterranean, for which there is unfortunately no concrete evidence. See *Woman, Culture and Society*, Michelle Zimbalist Rosaldo and Louise Lamphere, eds. (Stanford, 1974), for a balanced and informed series of essays on the lack of authority and legal power women have in many matrifocal societies. Countries (e.g., Italy, Spain) where the mother is the center of the family, the basic social unit, are rarely countries where women are in a position to command their own destinies.

## Chapter 19: Icons and Relics

1. Quoted in Eileen Power intro. to Johannes Hérolt, called Discipulus, *Miracles of the Blessed Virgin Mary*, trans. C. C. Swinton (London, 1928), p. xiv.

2. *Akathistos* hymn, from W. Christ and M. Paranikas, *Anthologia Graeca Carminum Christianorum* (Leipzig, 1871), pp. 140–7.

3. St. Bernard, Homily 3, *In Missus Est*, Mabillon, ed., *Life and Works of Saint Bernard*, 3:321–3. *Sermo de Aquaeducto, In Nativitate Beatae Mariae Virginis*, in Migne, *Patrologia Latina*, 183, col. 1013–14.

4. A fragment of papyrus discovered in 1938 contained in Greek: "Mother of God (hear) my supplications: suffer us not (to be) in adversity, but deliver us from danger. Thou alone . . ." The date of the prayer is disputed: some scholars place the papyrus as early as the end of the third century. The prayer first appears in the west in the ninth-century *Responsorial* of Compiègne. As the Virgin is directly asked to deliver the sinner, the prayer is considered Gnostic in origin, but it is still recited today. See H. Graef, *Mary*, 1:48; Dom F. Mercenier, *Le Muséon*, 52 (1939):29–33.

5. Pope Leo XIII, Encyclical, 1891; quoted in Paul Palmer, *Mary in the Documents of the Church*, pp. 90–1.

6. *Lumen Gentium*, ch. 8, para. 60; *Documents of the Vatican Two*, eds. Abbott and Gallagher, pp. 90–1.

7. See article on the Queenship of the Blessed Virgin in the *New Catholic Encyclopaedia*, 9:386.

8. The Council of Trent's declaration on the Invocation of the Saints, formulated at its twenty-fifth session in 1563, said that ". . . Images of Christ, and of the Virgin Mother of God, and of the other Saints, are to be had and retained particularly in temples, and that due honour and veneration are to be given them; not that any divinity, or virtue, is believed to be in them; or, that trust is to be reposed in images, as was of old done by the Gentiles who placed their hope in idols; but because the honour which is shown them is referred to the prototypes which those images represent, in such wise that by the images which we kiss, and before which we uncover the head, and prostrate ourselves, we adore Christ; and we venerate the saints, whose similitude they bear. . . ." Quoted in *The Canons and Decrees of the Sacred and Oecumenical Council of Trent*, trans. Rev. J. Waterworth (London, 1848), pp. 234–5.

9. Sir Steven Runciman, *The History of the Crusades* (London, 1971), 1:40; A. Wenger, "Foi et Piété Mariales à Byzance," in Du Manoir, *Maria*, 5:966–7.

10. John Beckwith, *Early Christian and Byzantine Art* (London, 1970), p. 39.

11. Wenger, "Foi et Piété Mariales à Byzance," in Du Manoir, *Maria*, 5:963–6. The seventh-century date of many of the legends connected with Mary's relics and particularly her grave clothes indicates that they represent pious propaganda for her Assumption, which was gaining ground in the east at the time, as shown by the homilies of Andrew of Crete and John Damascene (see Chapter 6).

12. Peter Brown, "A Dark Age Crisis: Aspects of the Iconoclastic Controversy," *The English Historical Review*, 88, no. 346 (January, 1973):7.

13. Sir E. A. Wallis Budge, trans., *One Hundred and One Miracles of Our Lady Mary* (London, 1923), pp. 262–3; a western version of this miracle is told by Vincent de Beauvais in the *Speculum Historiae*, vol. 7, ch. 119.

14. Evelyn Faye Wilson, ed., *The Stella Maris of John of Garland*, p. 161.

15. Hérolt, *Miracles of the Virgin Mary*, miracle no. 14, pp. 31–2.

16. *Ibid.*, miracle no. 19, p. 29.

17. Beckwith, *Early Christian and Byzantine Art*, p. 40.

18. George Henderson, *Chartres* (London, 1968), pp. 21, 66–8.

19. Runciman, *History of the Crusades*, 1:166.

20. Jonathan Sumption, *Pilgrimage—an Image of Medieval Religion* (London, 1975), p. 49.

21. J. A. S. Collin de Plancy, *Dictionnaire Critique des Reliques et Images Miraculeuses*, 3 vols. (Paris, 1821–2), vol. 2; see under "Marie."

22. "The Pynson Ballad," printed by Pynson, *c.* 1460. From *England's Nazareth. A History of the Shrine of Our Lady of Walsingham*, anon. (1969), p. 13. H. M. Gillett, *Shrines of Our Lady in England and Wales* (London, 1957), pp. 293–325. A. and J. Gurney, *Walsingham, a Place of Pilgrimage for 700 years* (Walsingham, 1965), *passim*. During its heyday the shrine at Walsingham inspired several traditional ballads. Sir Walter Ralegh based one of his freshest and most poignant lyrics on one of the songs, ending with the memorably beautiful stanza:

> But true love is a durable fire
> In the mind ever burning;
> Never sick, never old, never dead,
> From itself never turning.

From Robert Nye, ed., *A Choice of Sir Walter Ralegh's Verse* (London, 1972), pp. 38–9. To Philip, Earl of Arundel, who was martyred under Elizabeth, is attributed the dramatic penitential poem on the shrine's destruction:

> Levell, levell with the ground
> The Towres do lye
> Which with their golden, glitt'ring tops
> Pearsed oute to the skye . . .
> Oules do scrike where the sweetest himnes
> Lately wear songe,
> Toades and serpents hold their dennes
> Where the palmers did throng . . .
> Sinne is where our Ladye sate,
> Heaven turned is to helle,
> Sathan sittes where our Lord did swaye,
> Walsingham, oh, farewell.

From Gillett, *ibid.*, pp. 313–14.

23. Geoffrey Chaucer, *The Canterbury Tales*, trans. into modern English by Nevill Coghill (London, 1971), The Prologue, p. 38.

24. Carlo Bertelli, "Il Restauro della Madonna della Clemenza," *Bollettino dell'Istituto Centrale del Restauro* (Rome, 1964) 41–4.

### Chapter 20: *Visions, the Rosary, and War*

1. Helen Gardner, ed., *A Book of Religious Verse* (Oxford: 1972), p. 232.

2. J. M. Cohen, trans., *The Life of Saint Teresa of Ávila* (London, 1957), p. 210.

3. Président des Brosses, quoted in Howard Hibbard, *Bernini* (London, 1965), pp. 241–2.

4. Parmigianino, *The Vision of Saint Jerome*, National Gallery, London. Luisa Ignacia Roldan (d. 1704), *San Diego of Alcalà Kneels Before the Virgin and Child*, Victoria and Albert Museum, London.

5. Vita Sackville-West, *The Eagle and the Dove. A Study in Contrasts* (London, 1943), pp. 93–100.

6. J. M. Cohen, trans., *Life of Saint Teresa of Ávila*, p. 247.

7. Luis Lazo de Vega's account, published in 1649; quoted in Donald Demarest and Coley Taylor, eds., *The Dark Virgin: The Book of Our Lady of Guadalupe. A Documentary Anthology* (New York, 1956), pp. 41–50. I am most grateful to Mrs. Stancioff for lending me this book.

8. Guadalupe is the name of a town in Spain, but the origins of the Mexican word of which Guadalupe is only the Spanish phonetic equivalent are interesting: in Nahuatl, the Indian language spoken by Juan Diego, the word might have been *coatalocpia* from *coatl* meaning "serpent," *tealoc* meaning "goddess" and *tlapia*, which means "watch over," i.e. the protective serpent goddess. Alternatively, a derivation from *coatl*, meaning "serpent," and *llope*, meaning "tread on," has been suggested. Both roots imply that Juan Diego, exposed to Jesuit and Franciscan missionaries' propaganda about the Immaculate Conception of the Virgin, had merged her with the native snake mother goddess of the Indians, who was worshipped locally at Tepeyac. See Demarest and Taylor, *ibid.*, pp. 30 ff.

9. Edith Hoyt, *The Silver Madonna or La Virgen de Plata. Legends of Shrines from Mexico to Guatemala* (Mexico, 1963).

10. Wilson, ed., *The Stella Maris of John of Garland*, pp. 186–7.

11. André Grabar, *L'Iconoclasme Byzantine. Dossier Archéologique* (Paris, 1957), pp. 34–5; figs. 52, 53, 54, 56.

12. Ernst Kitzinger, *The Cult of Images before Iconoclasm*, Dumbarton Oaks Papers 8 (Cambridge, Mass., 1954), pp. 111–12.

13. Joinville and Villehardouin, *Chronicles of the Crusades*, trans. M. R. B. Shaw (London, 1970), p. 314.

14. Owen Chadwick, *The Reformation* (London, 1972), pp. 317–18.

15. Georgina Masson, *The Companion Guide to Rome* (London, 1972), p. 177.

16. Eithne Wilkins, *The Rose Garden Game. The Symbolic Background to the European Prayer Beads* (London, 1969), p. 25. I am grateful to Mons. Alfred Gilben for telling me about the book.

17. Rosaries were found in the graves of the Abbess Gertrude (d. 659), daughter of King Pepin I of the Franks, and of St. Rosalia (d. 814). Wilkins, *ibid.*, p. 30, maintains there is no evidence for an eastern origin of the rosary, but other historians disagree. See S. G. F. Brandon, gen. ed., *Dictionary of Comparative Religion* (London, 1970), under "Rosary."

18. Righetti, *Manuale di Storia Liturgica*, 1:220–2; 2:363; Wilkins, *The Rose Garden Game*, p. 36.

19. Righetti, *ibid.*, 2:366; Graef, *Mary*, 2:17.

20. The Joyful Mysteries are the Annunciation, the Visitation, the Nativity, the Presentation, and the Finding in the Temple.

The Sorrowful Mysteries are the Agony in the Garden, the Scourging at the Pillar, the Crowning with Thorns, the Carrying of the Cross, the Crucifixion and Death of Our Lord.

The Glorious Mysteries are the Resurrection, the Ascension, the Descent of the Holy Spirit, the Assumption of the Virgin, and the Coronation of the Virgin in Heaven.

21. Alan Shestack, *Fifteenth-Century Woodcuts and Metalcuts from the National Gallery of Art* (Washington, D.C.), catalogue of exhibition December 3, 1967–January 7, 1968. See *Madonna in a Wreath of Roses*, Augsburg, 1490–1500, pls. 156, 157, 169–73, 208–9.

22. See, in particular, Leo X's Bull Pastor Aeternus 1516.

23. The city of Siena was dedicated to the Virgin in 1260, before the battle of Montaperti with the Florentines. The "Civitas Virginis" won the victory. The new government of burghers and merchants commissioned works of art to celebrate the city, including Duccio's masterpiece, the polyptych of *La Maestà*, which in 1311 was carried in ceremonial procession through the city as its palladium before it was set up on the high altar of the cathedral. Probably the crudest association of the Virgin with war is the colossal statue of her that dominates the town of Le Puy, still a most popular shrine. It was cast in 1860 from the cannonballs taken by the French at Sebastopol.

24. The *Ballad of Lepanto* is a classic of rollicking verse, and it contains one of the plummiest rhymes ever composed in English:

> Love-light of Spain—Hurrah!
> Death-light of Africa!
> Don John of Austria
> Is riding to the sea.

G. K. Chesterton, *Stories, Essays, Poems* (London, 1939), pp. 340–5.

25. In 1948, at Lipa in the Philippines, the Carmelite nun Teresita Cactilo saw the Virgin under the aspect "Mary, Mediatrix of All Graces"; in 1946–7 Pierini Gilli, of Montichiari, Italy, saw her as the Mystic Rose; in 1947 Bruno Cronacchiola saw the Divine Trinity with the Virgin of Revelation; in 1948 four sisters of the Gansferth family saw the Virgin at Heede in Germany; in 1950 Mrs. Van Hoof of Necedah, Wisconsin, claimed to see her. None of these visions has won any official endorsement. From 1965 to 1971, in San Sebastian de Garabandal, a tiny, remote village in the Spanish Cantabrian mountains, in the diocese of Santander, the Virgin appeared many times—with more frequency in fact than any other apparitions—to four little girls who were between eleven and twelve years old when the visions began. The visions were marked by trances, ecstatic falls, and other prodigies, all of which were photographed, recorded, and filmed. The children talked very spontaneously and at great length to the Virgin, telling her of their new haircuts, the sheep shearing, and other simple local matters. She appeared as Our Lady of Mount Carmel and gave the children, and especially their leader, called Conchita (who often saw her alone), messages of an apocalyptic nature, and many warnings about the state of the Church. For instance, on June 18, 1965, she told Conchita through the archangel Michael: ". . . Previously, the Cup was filling; now it is brimming over. Many priests are following the road to perdition, and with them they are taking many more souls. . . ." See F. Sanchez-Ventura y Pascal, *The Apparitions of Garabandal* (Detroit, 1966), p. 171. Garabandal is fascinating, not only for the extraordinary documentation of the children's ecstasies, but because it has inspired an enthusiastic and broad following, in the United States, France, and England in particular. The Bishop of Santander has refused to endorse the prodigies, and therefore the movement to recognize Garabandal is deadlocked; but there are many priests, some of them very learned men, who see the visions of Garabandal as the Virgin's rebuke for a decline in standards, following the reforms of Vatican Two.

Officially recognized visions since the Reformation include: in 1649 a fierce anti-Catholic Calvinist, Pierre Port-Courbet, was cutting down a willow tree on the feast of the Annunciation when it began to bleed profusely. The Virgin appeared and reproached him for working on her day, whereupon he was converted, and the shrine of Notre Dame de l'Osier (Our Lady of the Willow) was established on the spot, at Vinay, near Grenoble. The 1930s saw a spate of approved apparitions, including some to five children at Beauraing in Belgium, in 1932–3, during which the Virgin appeared in a hawthorn tree.

For accounts of nineteenth- and twentieth-century visions, see H. Thurston, S.J., *Beauraing and Other Apparitions* (London, 1934), *passim;* H. Graef, *Mary,* 2:90–150; John J. Delaney, ed., *A Woman Clothed with the Sun. Eight Great Appearances of Our Lady in Modern Times* (New York, 1960).

26. John S. Kennedy, "The Lady in Tears," in Delaney, *ibid.,* pp. 89–112; Graef, *Mary,* 2:99–103.

27. Graef, *ibid.,* pp. 103–6.

28. Fr. James, *The Story of Knock* (Ireland, 1950), *passim.*

29. Robert M. Maloy, "The Virgin of the Poor," in Delaney, *A Woman Clothed with the Sun,* pp. 241–67; Graef, *Mary,* 2:143–6.

30. Statistics from the tourist bureau at Lourdes, 1971; from the shrine bureau at Fatima, 1973.

31. In 1858, the year of the visions, there were six miracle cures. Between 1875 and 1911, thirty-three were confirmed. A gap of thirteen years followed, then from 1924 till 1959 there were twenty-two miracles. I am grateful to Dr. Mangiapan of the Bureau Médical de Lourdes for this information. See also M. A. H. Melvinsky, *Healing Miracles, An examination from history and experience of the place of miracle in Christian thought and medical practice* (London, 1968), pp. 162–3.

32. G. G. Coulton, *Life in the Middle Ages* (Cambridge, 1928–30), 1:1–8, for Ralph Glaber's description of *mal des ardents;* see also Wilson, ed., *The Stella Maris of John of Garland,* pp. 195–6.

33. Sackville-West, *The Eagle and the Dove,* pp. 111–12.

34. William C. McGrath, "The Lady of the Rosary," in Delaney, *A Woman Clothed with the Sun,* p. 194.

35. John Mathias Haffert, *Mary in her Scapular Promise* (New Jersey, 1940), pp. 169–72.

36. Leo XIII, *Octobri Mense,* encyclical, September 22, 1891; *Adiutricem,* encyclical, September 5, 1895; *Supremi Apostolatis Officio,* encyclical, September 1, 1883, and others, in 1884, 1887, 1891, 1892, 1893, 1896, 1897 (*"Augustissimae Virginis Mariae"*), and 1898. Popes Benedict XV, Pius XI, and Pius XII each issued an encyclical promoting the rosary.

### Chapter 21: The Hour of Our Death

1. François Villon, *Oeuvres,* ed. Auguste Longnon (Paris, 1964), Ballade from *Le Testament Villon,* p. 40.

2. *The Prayers and Meditations of Saint Anselm,* trans. Sister Benedicta Ward, p. 112.

3. *L'Ave Maria Rutebeuf* ends:

> Prie a ton fil qu'il nos apele
> Au jugement,
> Quant il fera si egrement
> Tot le monde comunement
> Trambler com feuille,
> Qu'a sa partie nos acueille!

From Adolphe Krefsner, ed., *Rutebeuf Gedichte* (Wolfenbuttel, 1885), pp. 198–9.

4. James Joyce, *Portrait of the Artist as a Young Man* (London, 1974), p. 125. After the sermon on hell, Stephen Dedalus leaves the chapel: "He could not grip the

floor with his feet and sat heavily at his desk, opening one of his books at random and poring over it. Every word for him. It was true. God was almighty. God could call him now, call him as he sat at his desk, before he had time to be conscious of the summons. God had called him. Yes? What? Yes? His flesh shrank together as it felt the approach of the ravenous tongues of flames, dried up as it felt about it the swirl of stifling air. He had died. Yes. He was judged. A wave of fire swept through his body: the first. Again a wave. His brain began to glow. Another. His brain was simmering and burst forth from his skull like a corolla, shrieking like voices: Hell! Hell! Hell! Hell! Hell!"

5. Villon, *Oeuvres*, pp. 40–1.

6. André Grabar, *Christian Iconography: A Study of Its Origins* (London, 1969), p. 44, pl. 113.

7. Émile Mâle, *Religious Art from the Twelfth to the Eighteenth Century*, p. 89.

8. *New Larousse Encyclopedia of Mythology*, pp. 41–2; Mâle, *ibid.*, pp. 54–6; George Every, *Christian Mythology* (London, 1970), p. 117; Alfred Maury, *Croyances et Légendes du Moyen-Age* (Paris, 1896), pp. 168–9.

9. M. R. James, *The Apocryphal New Testament*, The Apocalypse of the Virgin (Greek), p. 563.

10. James, *ibid.*, Apocalpyse of Paul, pp. 525–55; Dante, *Inferno*, Canto 10.

11. James, *ibid.*, Apocalypse of the Virgin (Ethiopic), pp. 563–4; see also H. Pernot, "Descente de la Vierge aux Enfers," *Revue des Études Grecs* (1900); Sir E. A. Wallis Budge, trans., *Legends of Our Lady Mary the Perpetual Virgin and Her Mother Hanna*, trans. from the Ethiopic MSS. collected by King Theodore at Makdala and now in the British Museum (London, 1922).

12. Every, *Christian Mythology*, pp. 116, 137.

13. See R. M. Grant, *Gnosticism: a Sourcebook of Heretical Writings from the Early Christian Period* (New York, 1961), p. 70; Allan Temko, *Notre Dame de Paris. The Biography of a Cathedral* (New York, 1952), pp. 256–7; M. Gonsalva Wiegand, O.S.F., ed., *The Non-Dramatic Works of Hroswitha* (St. Louis, 1936).

14. Émile Mâle, *L'art religieux du 13e. siècle* (Paris, 1902), pp. 297–300.

15. Rutebeuf, *Le Miracle de Théophile*, ed. Grace Frank (1925); quoted in Temko, *Notre Dame de Paris*, p. 263.

16. Harley MS. 2277, *c.* 1300; in Beverley Mary Boyd, *Middle English Miracles of the Virgin* (California, 1964), pp. 11–14.

17. The North English Homily Collection, MS. Ch. 5.21, fourteenth century, Royal College of Physicians, Edinburgh. Boyd, *ibid.* The miracle appears in the *Dicta Anselmi*, before 1109, told by Hugh of Cluny to Anselm the Younger. See R. W. Southern, "The English Origins of the Miracles of the Virgin," *Medieval and Renaissance Studies* (1958), pp. 188–9.

18. Henri Focillon, *Le Peintre des Miracles Nostre Dame* (Paris, 1950).

19. Caesarius of Heisterbach, quoted in G. G. Coulton, *Life in the Middle Ages*, 1:62–5.

20. Gautier de Coincy, quoted by Eileen Power in intro. to Johannes Hérolt, called Discipulus, *Miracles of the Blessed Virgin Mary*, p. xxx.

21. Mère Marie de la Visitation, "Marie et le Purgatoire," in Du Manoir, *Maria*, 5:892.

22. Sequence for the Annunciation, attributed to Peter Abelard; quoted in *Oxford Book of Medieval Latin Verse*, ed. Stephen Gaselee (Oxford, 1928), pp. 97–8.

23. Adam of St. Victor, *Hymn to the Virgin;* quoted in Henry Adams, *Mont St. Michel and Chartres* (London, 1913), p. 96.

24. Mère Marie de la Visitation, "Marie et le Purgatoire," in *Maria*, 5:892–3.

25. St. Bernardino da Siena, *Sermons;* quoted in Coulton, *Life in the Middle Ages*, 1:220–4.

26. Chronica XXIV, *Generalum Ordinum Minorum*, tome 3: quoted in Raphael Brown, *Our Lady and St. Francis* (Chicago, 1954), pp. 76–7.

27. Mâle, *Religious Art from the Twelfth to the Eighteenth Century*, pp. 150–5.

28. Paul Perdrizet, *La Vierge de la Miséricorde* (Paris, 1908), pp. 21 ff., traces the image of the Madonna sheltering singers under her mantle to a vision that Caesarius of Heisterbach, the Cistercian, describes in his *Dialogus Miraculorum*, written between 1220–30, in which a monk saw the Virgin sheltering the Cistercian order under her cloak. He points out that the gesture was "natural" because, although no antecedents warrant it in the Bible, it was common in legal custom and ritual: a legitimized or adopted child was wrapped in a cloak, and the suzerain draped his mantle over his vassal as a symbol of his protection.

29. Carleton Brown, ed., *Religious Lyrics of the Fifteenth Century*, Stabat Mater in English, pp. 22–5. Philip Hendy, *Piero della Francesca and the Early Renaissance* (London, 1968), pp. 47–8.

30. John Mathias Haffert, *Mary in her Scapular Promise* (New Jersey, 1940).

31. St. Alphonsus de Liguori, *The Glories of Mary*, anon. trans. (Baltimore and Dublin, 1962); quoted in Briffault, *The Mothers*, 3:183.

32. Maria de Agreda de Jesus, *The City of God*, p. 569.

## Epilogue

1. N. K. Sandars, ed. and trans., *The Epic of Gilgamesh*. An English version with intro. (London, 1971), p. 85.

2. Paul VI, *Devotion to the Blessed Virgin*, Apostolic Exhortation (*Marialis Cultus*), February 2, 1974, section 36; p. 26.

3. Roland Barthes, *Mythologies*, selected and trans. by Annette Lavers (New York, 1972), p. 142.

4. *Ibid.*, p. 129.

5. Canon Ten, Twenty-fourth session of the Council of Trent, in Rev. J. Waterworth, trans., *The Canons and Decrees of the Council of Trent* (London, 1848).

6. Mary Douglas, *Natural Symbols. Explorations in Cosmology* (London, 1973), pp. 87–8.

7. Paul VI, *Devotion to the Blessed Virgin*, section 37, p. 27.

8. A. R. Radcliffe-Brown, *Taboo* (1939); quoted in Claude Lévi-Strauss, *Totemism*, trans. Rodney Needham (Boston, 1963), p. 67.

9. Paul VI, *Devotion to the Blessed Virgin*, section 37, p. 27.

10. Barthes, *Mythologies*, p. 110.

### Appendix A: St. Luke's Magnificat

1. M. D. Goulder and M. L. Sanderson, "St. Luke's Genesis," *Journal of Theological Studies* (April 1957), pp. 20–2.

### Appendix B: A Muddle of Marys

1. Jacobus de Varagine, *The Golden Legend*, trans. and adapted from the Latin by Granger Ryan and Helmut Ripperger (New York, 1941), p. 520.

2. Adey Horton, "The Family Life of Jesus—the Unauthorized Version," *Sunday Times Magazine*, December 16, 1973.

3. O. B. Hardison, Jr., *Christian Rite and Christian Drama in the Middle Ages. Essays in the Origins and Early History of Modern Drama* (Baltimore, 1969), pp. 193–5.

4. André Grabar, *Christian Iconography, A Study of Its Origins*, p. 123.

5. Graves, *The White Goddess*, p. 142; Briffault, *The Mothers*, 2:608.

6. James, *The Apocryphal New Testament*, p. 87.

# Select Bibliography
## Works Consulted

Abbott, Walter M., S.J., gen. ed. *Documents of Vatican II. The Message and the Meaning of the Ecumenical Council.* Translated and edited by Rev. Joseph Gallagher. New York, 1966.

Adams, Henry. *Mont Saint Michel and Chartres.* London, 1913.

Ahsmann, U. P. J. M. *Le Culte de la Sainte Vierge et la Littérature Française Profane du Moyen-Age.* Paris and Utrecht, 1930.

Aigrain, René. *Liturgia—Encyclopédie Populaire.* Paris, 1931.

*Ante-Nicene Fathers, The. Translations of the Writings of the Fathers down to A.D. 325.* Edited by Rev. Alexander Roberts and James Donaldson. Buffalo, 1886.

Attwater, Donald. *A Dictionary of Mary.* New York, 1955.

Auden, W. H., and Pearson, Norman Holmes, eds. *Medieval and Renaissance Poets: Langland to Spenser.* New York, 1972.

Bainton, R. H. "Christianity and Sex—An Historical Survey," *Pastoral Psychology* 3,26 (1952); 4,21 (1953).

Barraclough, Geoffrey. *The Medieval Papacy.* London, 1968.

Barré, H. *Prières Anciennes de l'Occident à la Mère du Sauveur. Des Origines à Saint Anselme.* Paris, 1963.

Bernard of Clairvaux, St. *The Life and Work of Saint Bernard, Abbot of Clairvaux.* Edited by Dom Mabillon and translated with additional notes by Samuel J. Eales. 4 vols. London, 1896.

Bernen, Satia and Robert. *Myth and Religion in European Painting 1270–1700.* London, 1973.

Bérulle, Cardinal Pierre de. *Les Mystères de Marie; Vie de Jesus; Elevations; Oeuvres de Piété.* Edited by Marcel Rigal. Paris, 1961.

Bonaventure, St. (attrib.) *The Mirror of the Blessed Virgin; The Psalter of Our Lady.* Translated by Sister Mary Emmanuel, O.S.B. St. Louis and London, 1932.

————. *Meditations on the Life of Christ—An Illustrated Manuscript of the Fourteenth Century.* Translated from the Paris Bibliothèque Nationale MS. Ital. 115 by Isa Ragusa. Completed from the Latin and edited by Isa Ragusa and Rosalie B. Green. Princeton, 1961.

*Book of Saints, The. A Dictionary of the Servants of God Canonized by the Catholic Church.* Compiled by the Benedictine Monks of Saint Augustine's Abbey, Ramsgate. 5th ed. London, 1966.

Boxer, C. R. *Mary and Misogyny. Women in Iberian Expansion Overseas 1415–1815. Some Facts, Figures, and Personalities.* London, 1975.

Brandon, S. G. F., gen. ed. *Dictionary of Comparative Religion.* London, 1970.

Briffault, Robert. *The Mothers—A Study in the Origins of Sentiments and Institutions.* 3 vols. New York, 1927.

Brittain, Frederick, ed. *The Penguin Book of Latin Verse.* London, 1962.

Brooke, Christopher. *The Twelfth Century Renaissance.* London, 1969.

Broussole, J. C. *Études sur la Sainte Vierge.* 2 vols. Paris, 1908.

Brown, Carleton, ed. *English Lyrics of the Thirteenth Century.* Oxford, 1932.

————. *English Lyrics of the Fourteenth Century.* Oxford, 1952.

————. *English Lyrics of the Fifteenth Century.* Oxford, 1939.

Brown, Peter. *The World of Late Antiquity—from Marcus Aurelius to Muhammad.* London, 1971.

Budge, Sir E. A. Wallis, trans. *Legends of Our Lady the Perpetual Virgin and Her Mother Hanna.* Translated from the Ethiopic MSS., collected by King Theodore at Makdala and now in the British Museum. Liverpool and Boston, 1922.

———. *The Miracles of the Blessed Virgin Mary, and the Life of Hanna and the Magical Prayers of 'Aheta Mikael,* London, 1900.

*Canons and Decrees of the Sacred and Oecumenical Council of Trent, The.* Translated by Rev. J. Waterworth. London, 1848.

Carlen, Mary Claudia. *Dictionary of Papal Pronouncements—Leo XIII to Pius XII, 1878–1957.* New York, 1958.

Cartwright, John K. *The Catholic Shrines of Europe.* New York, 1955.

*Catholic Encyclopedia, The.* Edited by Charles G. Heilbermann, Edward A. Pace, and others. 15 vols. London and New York, 1907–14.

Chadwick, Henry. *The Early Church.* London, 1968.

Chadwick, Owen. *The Reformation.* London, 1972.

Cigala, Dr. Albin de. *The Imitation of Mary, by Saint Thomas à Kempis.* Extracts from the original works of Saint Thomas à Kempis. Newman Press, 1948.

Claudel, Paul. *La Rose et le Rosaire,* Paris, 1947.

Cole, William Graham. *Sex in Christianity and Psychoanalysis.* New York and Oxford, 1955.

Collin de Plancy, J. A. S. *Dictionnaire Critique des Reliques et Images Miraculeuses.* 3 vols. Paris, 1821–2.

Coplestone, F. C. *Aquinas.* London, 1955.

Coulton, G. G. *Two Saints: Saint Bernard and Saint Francis.* Cambridge, 1932.

———. *Life in the Middle Ages.* 4 vols. Cambridge, 1928–30.

———. *Five Centuries of Religion.* 4 vols. Cambridge, 1923–50.

———. *From Saint Francis to Dante.* London, 1906.

Cragg, Gerald R. *The Church and the Age of Reason 1648–1789.* London, 1970.

Crane, T. E., ed. *The Exempla or Illustrative Stories from the Sermones Vulgares of Jaques de Vitry.* Edited with an introduction and notes. New York, 1971.

Curtis, W. A. *A History of Creeds and Confessions of Faith in Christendom and Beyond.* Edinburgh, 1911.

Daly, Mary. *The Church and the Second Sex.* Boston, 1968.

Dante Alighieri. *Vita Nuova.* Milan, 1952.

———. *La Vita Nuova (Poems of Youth).* Translated with an introduction by Barbara Reynolds. London, 1969.

———. *La Divina Commedia.* Translated with a commentary by John D. Sinclair. 3 vols. London, 1958.

Davies, R. T., ed. *Medieval English Lyrics—A Critical Anthology.* Edited with an introduction and notes. London, 1963.

Dickens, A. G. *The Counter-Reformation.* London, 1968.

*Dictionnaire de Théologie Catholique.* Edited by A. Vacant, E. Mangenot, and E. Amann. 15 vols. Paris, 1909–50.

Doely, Sarah Bentley. *Women's Liberation and the Church—The New Demand for Freedom in the Life of the Christian Church.* New York, 1970.

Doheny, William J., and Kelly, Joseph P. *Papal Documents on Mary 1849–1953,* Milwaukee, 1954.

Douglas, Mary. *Purity and Danger—An Analysis of Concepts of Pollution and Taboo.* London, 1966.

———. *Natural Symbols—Explorations in Cosmology.* London, 1973.

*Early Christian Writings. The Apostolic Fathers.* Translated by Maxwell Staniforth. London, 1968.

Eliade, Mircea. *Images and Symbols—Studies in Religious Symbolism.* Translated by Philip Mairet. New York, 1969.

———. *Patterns in Comparative Religions.* Translated by Rosemary Sheed. New York, 1972.

Evans, Joan. *Life in Medieval France.* Oxford, 1925.

Every, George. *Christian Mythology.* London, 1970.

Feucht, O. E. *et al. Sex and the Church—A Sociological, Historical and Theological Investigation of Sex Attitudes.* St. Louis, 1961.

Feuillet, A. *Johannine Studies.* Translated by T. E. Crane. New York, 1965.

Figes, Eva. *Patriarchal Attitudes.* London, 1971.

Fliche, A. and Martin, V. *Histoire de l'Eglise depuis les Origines jusqu'a Nos Jours.* 13 vols. Paris, 1934–50.

Foster, Hazel Elora. *Jewish and Graeco-Roman Influences upon Saint Paul's Attitude Towards Women.* Chicago, 1936.

Frazer, J. G. *The Golden Bough—A Study in Magic and Religion.* Abridged ed. London, 1963.

Galot, Jean. *L'Eglise et la Femme.* Paris, 1965.

Gardner, Helen, ed. *A Book of Religious Verse.* Oxford, 1972.

Garreau, Albert. *Histoire Mariale de la France.* Paris, 1946.

Gautier de Coincy. *Les Chansons à la Vierge.* Edited by Jaques Chailley. Paris, 1959.

———. *Les Miracles de la Nostre Dame.* Edited by V. Frederick Koenig. 3 vols. Geneva, 1966.

Graef, Hilda. *Mary: A History of Doctrine and Devotion.* 2 vols. London and New York, 1963.

———. "The Devotion to Our Lady." *Twentieth Century Encyclopedia of Catholicism,* vol. 45. New York, 1963.

Greer, Germaine. *The Female Eunuch,* London, 1970.

Guitton, Jean. *The Blessed Virgin.* London, 1952.

Harding, Esther. *Woman's Mysteries. Ancient and Modern.* London, 1971.

Hastings, James. *A Dictionary of the Bible.* 5 vols. Edinburgh and New York, 1902–4.

Hay, Denys, ed. *The Medieval Centuries.* London, 1964.

Hays, H. R. *The Dangerous Sex—The Myth of Feminine Evil.* New York, 1972.

Huizinga, J. *The Waning of the Middle Ages—A Study in Forms of Life, Thought and Art in France and the Netherlands in the Fourteenth and Fifteenth Centuries.* London, 1972.

James, M. R., ed. and trans. *The Apocryphal New Testament—Being the Apocryphal Gospels, Acts, Epistles and Apocalypses.* Oxford, 1926.

James, William. *The Varieties of Religious Experience.* London, 1960.

Jameson, Anna. *Legends of the Madonna as Represented in the Fine Arts, Sacred and Legendary Art,* vol. 3. London, 1864.

*Lectionary for Mass—List of Readings and Charts for the Liturgy of the Word.* Washington, D.C., 1969.

McHugh, John. *The Mother of Jesus in the New Testament.* London, 1975.

Mâle, Émile. *Religious Art from the Twelfth to the Eighteenth Century.* New York, 1970.

———. *La Fin du Paganisme en Gaule et les plus Anciennes Basiliques Chrétiennes.* Paris, 1932.

———. *L'Art Religieux après le Concile de Trente.* Paris, 1932.

———. *L'Art Religieux du Douzième Siècle en France—Études sur les Origines de l'Iconographie du Moyen-Age.* Paris, 1966.

———. *L'Art Religieux du Treizième Siècle en France.* Paris, 1925.

————. *Notre Dame de Chartres*. Paris, 1948.

————. *The Early Churches of Rome*. Translated by D. Buxton. London, 1960.

Manoir de Juaye, Hubert du, S.J. *Maria: Études sur la Sainte Vierge*. 8 vols. Paris, 1949–71.

Mead, Margaret. *Male and Female. A Study of the Sexes in a Changing World*. New York, 1949.

Meiss, Millard. *Painting in Florence and Siena after the Black Death. The Arts, Religion and Society in the Mid-Fourteenth Century*. New York, 1964.

Miegge, Giovanni. *The Virgin Mary—The Roman Catholic Marian Doctrine*. Translated by Waldo Smith. London and Toronto, 1955.

Millett, Kate. *Sexual Politics. A Surprising Examination of Society's Most Arbitrary Folly*. London, 1970.

Mitchell, Juliet. *Woman's Estate*. New York, 1971.

Musurillo, Herbert A., S.J. *Symbolism and the Christian Imagination*. Baltimore and Dublin, 1962.

Neubert, E. *Marie dans l'Église Anté-Nicéenne*. Paris, 1908.

Neumann, Erich. *The Great Mother. An Analysis of the Archetype*. Trans. Ralph Manheim. New York, 1955.

*New Catholic Encyclopedia, The*. Prepared by the Editorial Staff at the Catholic University of America, Washington, D.C., 15 vols. New York and London, 1967.

*New Larousse Encyclopedia of Mythology, The*. Introduction by Robert Graves. London, 1970.

*Nicene and Post-Nicene Fathers of the Christian Church, A Select Library of*. Translated and annotated by Philip Schaff and Henry Wace. 14 vols. Oxford, 1890–1900.

O'Faolain, Julia, and Martines, Lauro, eds. *Not in God's Image*. London, 1973.

Palmer, Paul F., S.J., S.T.D. *Mary in the Documents of the Church*. London, 1953.

Panofsky, Erwin. *Early Netherlandish Painting—Its Origins and Character*. 2 vols. Cambridge, Mass., 1953.

Patsch, Joseph. *Our Lady in the Gospels*. London, 1958.

Pohle, Mons. Joseph, *Mariology—A Dogmatic Treatise on the Blessed Virgin Mary, Mother of God*. Adapted and edited by Arthur Preuss. London, 1953.

Rahner, Karl. *Mary, Mother of the Lord*. New York, 1963.

Righetti, Mario. *Manuale di Storia Liturgica*. 2 vols. Milan, 1959.

Rohault de Fleury, C. *La Sainte Vierge*. 2 vols. Paris, 1878.

Smart, Vivian. *The Religious Experience of Mankind*. London, 1969.

Southern, Richard. *Western Society and the Church in the Middle Ages*. London, 1970.

————. *The Making of the Middle Ages*. London, 1973.

Suarez, Francis, S.J. "The Dignity and the Virginity of the Mother of God." Disputations I, V, VI, from *The Mysteries of the Life of Christ*. Translated by Richard O'Brien, S.J. Indiana, 1954.

Taylor, Gordon Rattray. *Sex in History*. London, 1953.

Tillich, Paul. *A History of Christian Thought. From Its Judaistic and Hellenistic Origins to Existentialism*. Edited by Carl E. Braaten. New York, 1968.

Varagine, Jacobus de. *The Golden Legend*. Translated and adapted from the Latin by Granger Ryan and Helmut Ripperger. New York, 1941, 1969.

Ware, Timothy. *The Orthodox Church*. London, 1973.

Wills, Garry. *Bare Ruined Choirs—Doubt, Prophecy and Radical Religion*. New York, 1972.

Wright, W. *Contributions to the Apocryphal Literature of the New Testament*. Collected and edited from the Syriac MSS. in the British Museum, with English translation and notes. London, 1865.

## Papal Pronouncements; Pamphlets; Devotions

Anon. *The Religious Woman in Our Day.* Washington, D.C., n.d.

——. *Corona dei Sette Gaudi di Maria Santissima.* Florence, 1903.

——. *Laudi Sacre in Onore di Maria Santissima.* Florence, 1903.

——. *L'Amica dei Pargoli.* Florence, 1911.

——. *Grazie e Miracoli di S. Maria di Montenero.* Florence, 1915.

——. *Fatto Meraviglioso Avvenuto in Siena.* Florence, 1908.

——. *Storia di Nostra Signora di Lourdes.* Florence, 1906.

——. *Fatto di un Negoziante di Savona. Assalito di nette e legato ad un albero da tre Assassini e come fosse liberato per virtù di Maria Santissima della Stella.* Florence, 1892.

——. *The Message of Fatima.* Fatima, 1968.

——. *Our Lady of Fatima's Peace Plan from Heaven.* Indiana, 1971.

——. *In Festivitate B. M. V. de Monteserrato.* Montserrat, 1946.

——. *Il Devoto di Maria Santissima del Tindari.* Catania, 1964.

——. *The Way of the Cross. With the Meditations by St. Alphonsus Liguori.* New York, 1951.

——. *The Brown Scapular and Our Lady's Promise.* Dublin, n.d.

——. *The Legion of Mary.* Wisconsin, n.d.

——. *England's Nazareth. A History of the Holy Shrine of Our Lady of Walsingham.* Walsingham, 1969.

Bishops, National Conference of Catholic. *Behold Your Mother. Woman of Faith. A Pastoral Letter on the Blessed Virgin Mary.* November 21, 1973.

——. *Theological Reflections on the Ordination of Women.* Washington, D.C., n.d.

*Catechism of Christian Doctrine, A.* London Catholic Truth Society, 1971.

Chioccioni, Pietro. *La Madonna della Salute.* Rome, 1968.

Dougan, Patrick. *Refuge of Sinners.* Dublin, n.d.

——. *Gate of Heaven.* Dublin, n.d.

——. *Cause of Our Joy.* Dublin, n.d.

Garesche, Rev. Edward. *The Titles of Our Lady in the Litany of Loreto.* Dublin, 1936.

Giardina, Mons. Salvatore. *Il Pianto di Maria a Siracusa.* Syracuse, 1971.

Hubert, Father. *Knock Apparition and Purgatory.* Knock, 1962.

Hurley, Father Dermot. *Marian Devotions for Today.* Alcester and Dublin, 1971.

James, Father. *The Story of Knock.* Knock, 1950.

Jarrett, Bede, O.P. *The Catholic Mother.* London, 1964.

John XXIII, Pope. *Mater et Magistra.* Encyclical letter, May 15, 1961. Washington, D.C., 1961.

McQuaid, H. G. John Charles. *The Mother of God.* Dublin, n.d.

Paul VI, Pope. *The Rosary—during October. An Urgent Appeal for Peace.* September 15, 1966. Washington, D.C., 1966.

——. *Pilgrimage to Fatima.* Addresses, May 13, 1967. Washington, D.C., 1967.

——. *The Great Sign. Apostolic Exhortation on the Blessed Virgin Mary.* (*Signum Magnum*) May 13, 1967. Washington, D.C., 1967.

——. *On Priestly Celibacy.* Encyclical letter, June 24, 1967. Washington, D.C., 1967.

————. *Devotion to the Blessed Virgin Mary. Apostolic Exhortation.* (*Marialis Cultus.*) February 2, 1974. Washington, D.C., 1974.

Pius XII, Pope. *Munificentissimus Deus.* Washington, D.C., 1950.

————. *On Holy Virginity.* Encyclical letter, March 25, 1954.

————. *Humani Generis.* Encyclical letter, August 12, 1950.

Ripley, Rev. Francis J. *Bride of Christ.* Dublin, 1962.

Stephenson, Rev. W., S.J. *Prayers to the Blessed Virgin.* Dublin n.d.

Van de Weerd, Canon H. *Notre Dame de Tongres, Cause de Notre Joie.* Belgium, 1954.

Walsh, Michael. *The Glory of Knock.* Tuam, 1970.

Williams, Mary Kay. *Abortion: A Collision of Rights.* Washington, 1972.

Zeller, Renée. *Florilège de Notre Dame.* Paris, 1938.

# Index

## A Note About the Author

Marina Warner was born in 1946 and was educated at convents in Egypt, Belgium, and England. She studied French and Italian at Oxford and edited the university magazine *Isis*. She has worked as a journalist for the *Daily Telegraph*, *Spectator*, the *Sunday Times Magazine*, and *Vogue*. She won the *Daily Telegraph*'s Young Writer of the Year Award in 1970. She published an essay on the Virgin Mary in *Woman on Woman* (1971), and her first book, *The Dragon Empress*, appeared in 1972. She is married to the writer William Shawcross.

## A Note on the Type

The text of this book was set on the Linotype in Garamond, a modern rendering of the type first cut by Claude Garamond (1510–1561). Garamond was a pupil of Geoffroy Tory and is believed to have based his letters on the Venetian models, although he introduced a number of important differences, and it is to him we owe the letter which we know as old-style. He gave to his letters a certain elegance and a feeling of movement that won for their creator an immediate reputation and the patronage of Francis I of France.